Praise for Competition Overdose

"Stucke and Ezrachi's analysis of the nature of competition is refreshingly non-ideological and counterintuitive. Their idea that competition can be either toxic or noble—all depending on how governments structure markets—is something so clear that it's remarkable it's taken us decades to recognize the wisdom of it. This is a must-read for anyone interested in how to use public policy to harness the competitive drive for the public good." —*Chris Hughes, cofounder of Facebook*

"Entertaining and thought-provoking, *Competition Overdose* fiercely articulates the raw, hard truth behind the toxic aspects of competition."
—*Tommaso Valletti, professor of economics at Imperial College London and Chief Competition Economist (2016–2019), European Commission*

"Anything, in the wrong dosage, can be poisonous. *Competition Overdose* takes a sacred cow of contemporary western thought—that 'more competition is always good'—and reveals that while competition can be noble, it can also be toxic. An engaging and compelling read that will make you think differently about situations we all deal with every day."
—*Tim Wu, professor at Columbia Law School, contributing opinion writer for the* New York Times, *and author of* The Master Switch *and* The Attention Merchants

"A must-read for anyone concerned about the future of our economy and society, *Competition Overdose* provides a no-nonsense analysis of how toxic competition can be bad for competitors, consumers, workers, and society overall. The authors highlight the abuses of this ideology and remind us that we, as citizens and consumers, can exercise our power by choosing products, based on our values."
—*Monique Goyens, director general of BEUC, The European Consumer Organisation*

"*Competition Overdose* is probably the most important book to be published on the subject since *The Antitrust Paradox* hit bookshelves in 1978. It is destined to transform how governments across the world think about the role of competition in domestic and international policy for decades to come. Stucke and Ezrachi are the new rock stars of competition policy." —*Ali Nikpay, partner at Gibson Dunn & Crutcher*

"This beautifully written book helps us rethink economic principles from the ground up. As any good chemist knows, what can be helpful or harmless in small doses is deadly in excess. While technocrats push competition as a cure to all economic ailments, Stucke and Ezrachi deliver a dose of reality: cutthroat schemes to kneecap rivals, manipulate customers, and exploit workers harm far more than they help. Read this book for a brilliant account of the proper place of competition (and ethics) in society." —*Frank Pasquale, law professor at University of Maryland and author of* The Black Box Society

"Stucke and Ezrachi examine a multitude of perversities in today's society—colleges striving to recruit applicants they likely will reject, supermarkets stocking hundreds of varieties of jam, travel deals stuffed with hidden fees—and provide a unifying explanation: a misalignment of competition. Their book illuminates how competition can go wrong, and how individuals, businesses, and the government can set it right."
— *Jonathan Levin, dean of Stanford Graduate School of Business*

"Stucke and Ezrachi show us the important differences between destructive and noble competition and what we can do to pursue a more just and prosperous world. This book changes how you will view the role of the market in our economy and society at large." — *Spencer Weber Waller, director of the Institute for Consumer Antitrust Studies and law professor at Loyola University Chicago*

"Is more competition the solution to all our societal problems? Stucke and Ezrachi persuasively say: No, it depends; sometimes we need to rein in markets because they produce socially inferior outcomes. This book shows that the promotion of competition cannot be an end in of itself, but rather it should be used as a tool to improve overall welfare. Between too much and too little competition, the safest option is, as always, the 'aurea mediocritas'"
— *Jorge Padilla, senior managing director and head of Compass Lexecon, Europe*

"Stucke and Ezrachi ask critical questions about what types of rivalry are desirable and who benefits when all domains of society are governed by principles of unfettered competition. Countering simplistic prescriptions, *Competition Overdose* is a perceptive and timely read." — *Lina Khan, author of* Amazon's Antitrust Paradox

"*Competition Overdose* is a courageous, timely attempt by two formidable legal scholars to unpack—and in some cases demolish—the dominant shibboleth of our age: the delusion that 'more competition' is the remedy for many social or economic ills. Should be required reading for every course in public policy."
— *John Naughton, professor at University of Cambridge and technology columnist for the* London Observer

"The authors draw skilfully on a wide range of disciplines, from economics to psychology, to help us understand why more competition is not always all that it's cracked up to be. They provide support for a more humane, nobler form of competition and wider corporate purpose, debunking the myths of shareholder value and blind faith in markets. This is a must-read."
— *Simon Holmes, UK Competition Appeal Tribunal*

"Because competition has been sold for centuries as an unbridled positive, reading this book requires counterintuitive thinking and an open mind. Using a lucid, conversational style, the authors thoroughly explain each case study and anecdote. Does competition regularly result in a race to the bottom? Yes, the authors maintain, and they present ideas about how to achieve what they term 'noble competition,' in which sellers, buyers, and society at large all benefit." — *Kirkus Reviews*

Competition
Overdose

Competition Overdose

How Free Market Mythology
Transformed Us from Citizen Kings
to Market Servants

Maurice E. Stucke
and Ariel Ezrachi

HARPER
BUSINESS

An Imprint of HarperCollins*Publishers*

To Elizabeth and Miriam

HarperCollins books may be purchased for educational, business, or sales promotional use. For information, please email the Special Markets Department at SPsales@harpercollins.com.

FIRST EDITION

Designed by Bonni Leon-Berman

Library of Congress Cataloging-in-Publication Data has been applied for.

ISBN 978-0-06-289283-6

20 21 22 23 24   LSC   10 9 8 7 6 5 4 3 2 1

Contents

Preface

Politics today is divisive. But there's one subject on which just about everybody seems in agreement. Have you ever heard any American politician question the benefits of competition? Or, to put it another way, have you ever heard any lawmaker or policy maker praise *any* policy for being *anti*competitive?

Probably not.

The consensus is so absolute that it amounts to an almost religious belief in competition as the key to our prosperity: If a business behavior or law is pro-competitive, it's inherently good; if anticompetitive, it's presumptively bad.

As a result, whatever illness our society suffers, competition is often held up as the cure. Do we want better education for our children? Create competition among public schools. Better, more cost-effective, efficiently managed prisons? Same principle. Greater happiness? Same. Increase our range of choices—whether we're talking about types of cheese, possible marriage partners, or job opportunities—through competition, and we'll be happier and more prosperous. More competition promises to deliver what we want, often at a lower price.

Yet, many of us feel increasingly uneasy about the results of unbridled competition, even if we haven't identified it as the cause of our problems. Despite the promise of prosperity, we may be working harder, longer hours at our jobs, but for less money, fewer or nonexistent benefits, and no security. And those low prices we pay may also mean lower quality. Often, we're paying less, but getting *much* less. Our food has undeclared additives and dishonest labeling; our bargain airlines may be flying with dangerously low fuel loads. Or we indeed do pay less—for clothing, chocolate, and coffee, for example—but at the expense of the child slave laborers who produce these goods for us. Or we *think* we pay less—for our credit cards, for our hotels—but are actually being mercilessly exploited by companies that add hidden fees and may drive us into crippling debt. Or we pay little or nothing—in exchange for surrendering our privacy to the huge corporations that make billions off of us.

Often we are told that *more* competition is the cure for these ills, that the real problem is the bloated regulatory state. Should we continue down this path? Or is it time to wake up and notice that, beginning in the 1970s, competition has been overprescribed, the many regulations to protect us from overdosing have been stripped away, and the warning labels suggested by economists have been removed.

As consumers and citizens, we have paid a hefty price. Rather than competition serving us, we now serve it, as our laws and economic policies turn us from citizen kings to market servants.

To be clear, as our bios on the book jacket reveal, we are not two crazy Bolsheviks, seeking to bring down the capitalist machine. Quite the opposite. We have spent the past two decades promoting competition in our writings, our speeches, and the work we have done for competition agencies around the world. Both of us, of decidedly middle-class backgrounds, were instilled from childhood with the virtues of competition—whether on the athletic field, in the classroom, or at work. From early in our professional lives, we have devoted ourselves to what we both believed to be the sacred cause of competition: for Maurice, it was prosecuting anticompetitive restraints and mergers at the US Department of Justice; for Ariel, it was establishing an institute at Oxford dedicated to promoting competition law and policy. Through our studies and our work, we learned that competition is indeed often the perfect cure—an engine for modern prosperity. And we continue every year to instill in our students the lessons about the benefits of competition.

However, while we still believe that competition is often good, we also now recognize that politicians and policy makers have been pushing competition as a magical elixir, even when it is ill-suited for the task at hand. We've also noticed that the competition ideal has been misused as a cover to promote policies that may actively harm citizens, while bene-fitting the companies that are exploiting them. Sometimes unwittingly, sometimes cynically, our lawmakers have sold us out, taking away our protections and removing our safety net, all in the name of encouraging ever more competition.

So, we set out to answer the question "Is competition always good?" And if not, when not? As two competition scholars, we initially found ourselves in foreign terrain, wandering far from the path, which we ourselves as well as our colleagues have always followed. Many of our antitrust colleagues stared at us blankly. "Wait . . . are you saying that competition at times is bad?" Some were polite, others chuckled, a few were incredulous.

Our progressive colleagues thought we were turning our backs on what they see as the most significant market power problem in the United States and the European Union: *that too many markets have too little healthy competition and are therefore dominated by a powerful few.* And if you think about GAFA—Google, Apple, Facebook, and Amazon—they certainly have a point.

Our conservative friends also were deeply suspicious of our journey. *Competition isn't the problem,* they'd tell us. *What you must be describing are simply isolated instances of market failure, which are not representa-tive of any inherent problems with competition itself.* For them our inquiry threatened to provide ammunition for the government to overregulate, thereby stifling innovation and . . . competition.

But, as we continued with our journey, we found many people, from all walks of life, who welcomed our findings. They knew something had gone wrong. Some of those from whom we expected the great-est skepticism—namely the top officials of several leading competition authorities—were actually the most realistic (as well as very helpful in our research) in pointing out how competition isn't always what it's cracked up to be.

And the person we might have expected to have the least to say about this particular subject, an applied mathematics professor of complex systems from South Africa's University of Cape Town and coauthor of one of Stephen Hawking's most influential papers, had perhaps the most profound observations. He helped us understand why the competitive metrics that we employ to measure our successes often leave us hungry and unsatisfied; he inspired in us the idea that the type of competition we encourage can be about more than the simple goal of winning, can reflect some higher purpose.

And so we invite you to join us on this inquiry.

We'll see in our *First Overdose* how toxic competition is fueling a race among elite universities to woo our children, only to reject them. While you might chuckle at the *Dear Genevieve* letter in chapter 1, it will certainly change your view of the admissions process and the materials you or your children might receive from some of the leading universities. We'll see how even powerful brands like Harvard and Princeton cannot stop this race to the bottom.

From elite universities, we'll turn to the horsemeat scandal that plagued the European food industry a few years ago. What does horsemeat in our lasagna and our hamburgers have to do with competition? Welcome to our *Second Overdose*, where we'll collect the shrapnel from the explosion of the loosely regulated, unmonitored competition machine and examine the damage it does—to quality, to the environment, to workers, to safety, and, ultimately, to us.

No journey on toxic competition would be complete without a trip to Las Vegas, where you know you will be taken, but not exactly how. Here, in our *Third Overdose*, we'll see how the hotel, car rental, and airplane booking sites are all fiercely competing for our business. On the surface this competition appears to be to our advantage, but appearances are deceiving. It turns out that this is not a competition to find ever more ways to please us, the customers, the supposed sovereigns of the marketplace, in order to win our business. No, here the competition is all about funneling the companies' ingenuity into finding better ways to trick us into paying more for less, with highly sophisticated behavioral economics shaping the effort to exploit our weaknesses. After you've read that, you may find that getting picked up at the Las Vegas airport by the casino's limo isn't as wonderful as you initially thought.

But if competition does not always deliver on price, safety, or quality, at least it delivers on providing us with one of the things we most want from the marketplace: choice. Right? The belief that increasing competition can increase choices and that this is all to the good is one of the chief tenets of the competition gospel. But much as we may think we love choice, our *Fourth Overdose* explores how firms like Amazon and popular dating websites like Match.com lure us with their multitude of options, only to use the phenomenon of "choice overload" to profit at our expense.

After touring the toxic aspects of competition, we'll next explore *who is pushing this poison.* We'll meet the four main culprits, while enriching our vocabulary with the term *kudzu-ing.* Just as the invasive vine kudzu ended up smothering the US South, a reductive competition ideology has smothered any effort to limit toxic competition, and we'll explore how lobbyists, policy makers, and powerful firms have used the competition ideology to hide their corruption, exploitation, ineptitude, and ignorance. We'll learn the ominous origins of the term *privatization* (no, it wasn't Margaret Thatcher or Ronald Reagan who came up with it). Finally, we'll encounter the most sinister actors along our trip, the Gamemakers, who design the competitive process to ensure that they always profit, regardless of whoever else might seem to be winning or losing the race. Here we'll use the example of a gaming app aimed at children to see how the Gamemakers rig the competition to attract us, addict us, extract our data, and manipulate us, all in the interest of massive profits, which are concealed behind an opaque process that no one can penetrate.

By the time you've followed this investigation of each of the overdoses and learned about the forces responsible for perpetrating them, the picture should be clear enough: At times, competition can lift people out of poverty, increase well-being, and promote autonomy. But other times, when overprescribed with no safeguards, it does the opposite. And beyond the material, practical damage it does to us, which is enormous, it can also undermine the societal, ethical, and moral values that should shape our lives.

Few among us want a centrally planned economy. Nonetheless, the current path is not sustainable, especially as the healthy competition is being squeezed out by monopolies and oligopolies on one side and toxic competition on the other side.

So what's the remedy? Our inquiry concludes with a discussion of how we can promote a form of competition that actually serves us, rather than our serving it, competition that will bring out the best in us, not the worst. While you might find our definition of *noble competition* counterintuitive, we hope you will agree that competition should be more than zero-sum warfare aimed exclusively at satisfying our greed. Competition ideally should ennoble us, rather than cause our destruction or downfall.

Faced with unprecedented levels of overdosing, we offer this book as an intervention. An attempt to help all of us—society—detox.

Having been overdosed for so long, some may resist this intervention. Should we accept the possibility of competition being bad at times? And, if so, how would we recognize when that is the case?

Let's start with the famous Scottish economist Adam Smith, known as the patron saint of competition, and the hockey player Craig MacTavish.

PART I

When Is Competition Toxic?

CHAPTER 1

First Overdose

The Race to the Bottom

Two centuries after his death, the Scottish economist Adam Smith might still be the most powerful man in the world.

Although he only used the term a few times in his writing, Smith's "invisible hand" became one of social science's most well-known metaphors, and the foundational principle of a lot of complex economic systems. Everything from the price you pay for an apple at your local bodega to the machinations of multilateral international trade wars is influenced by a key assumption underlying Smith's theory.

That assumption is that society is merely the sum of individuals—from which we can conclude that if each person acts to maximize his or her own well-being, this will inevitably maximize the overall well-being of society.

With that everyone wins. Abracadabra!

When the invisible hand casts its magic wand we end up with a competitive "race to the top," a race that benefits each individual and the community as a whole. And, like any simple magic trick, it works quite well at a very basic level.

Competition can, in the right circumstances, deliver prosperity and economic growth. And since other strategies for achieving those same aims are far more complicated and far less predictable, competition has become the backbone of many countries' economic policies.

Problem is, it sometimes fails to deliver. When it does, it often leaves individuals and society worse off. The invisible hand then becomes nothing more than a sleight of hand.

So when is competition a race to the bottom rather than to the top? There are two basic circumstances in which that happens:

- **FIRST**, when the competitors' individual interests are not aligned with their collective interests, or with society's collective interests.
- **SECOND**, when either the competitors or the intended beneficiaries of competition—or both—are harmed by this race to the bottom, but no one can independently de-escalate it.

This may sound complex, but once we understand these two conditions, we'll recognize many examples of toxic competition around us.

But let's not jump into economic theory just yet. Instead, let's jump into a hockey rink.

How Do We Know When Competitors' Individual Interests Are Harmed by Competition? When They're Helmetless.

Remember Craig MacTavish? Maybe not. But as hockey trivia buffs know, he was the last person to play in the National Hockey League without a helmet.[1]

To reduce head and other injuries, all hockey players today must wear helmets, visors, and pads. It's the smart thing to do.[2] In 1980, the NHL finally instituted a policy that required all new players to wear helmets. But those who started playing the game before 1980 were exempt from that requirement, and many veterans took advantage of the exemption. When MacTavish retired in 1997, he was the last of those holdouts.

To understand why the NHL had to make helmet-wearing a rule, even though its benefits are obvious and potentially lifesaving, let's suppose that the rule didn't exist. If you were trying to break into the NHL, would you go helmetless? Probably so, if you thought that going helmetless would give you a slight competitive advantage.

Many NHL players in the 1960s and '70s did go without helmets because they believed that helmets would cut their efficiency in the game. Not wanting to be competitively disadvantaged, most of their teammates and rivals followed their lead and also went helmetless.

The result: None of the players had a competitive advantage since they were all helmetless, everyone was exposed to injuries, and collectively the team members were worse off. That, in a nutshell, is a race to the bottom—an example of toxic competition.

Now let us change the scenario. Suppose a hockey player wanting to gain a competitive advantage follows Tom Brady's diet. Like the legendary New England Patriots quarterback, this player avoids processed foods with lots of sugar, eats more fish and vegetables, and consumes less red meat. With a diet aimed at minimizing muscle inflammation, the hockey player is healthier and in better shape. Then, to maintain their competitive edge, other hockey players follow suit. Collectively the diet improves their health and prolongs their careers. That, you probably guessed, is a race to the top—an example of individual and collective interests converging in a healthy competition.

In both scenarios, it was in each hockey player's interest to gain a competitive advantage. But in one case competition produced results that were toxic to all, in the other, beneficial to all. To distinguish between good and bad competition, between races to the top and races to the bottom, we must ask whether the competitors' individual and collective interests are aligned. Basically, if all the competitors do the same thing, do they end up collectively better off—or worse?

So when you are seeking an edge over a rival, consider what will happen if others follow your lead and take similar measures. If everyone ends up worse off, with no advantage going to anyone, you're in a *race to the bottom* that benefits neither you nor society.

When Competition Harms Its Intended Beneficiary: Public School Education

In our simple scenario of helmetless hockey players, the arms race harms primarily the competitors themselves. No bystanders are injured. The hockey players don't come flying into the stands at 20 miles per hour, delivering multiple blows to the heads of their fans. If they did, most helmetless fans would simply stop attending games, and we would put an end to this toxic competition.

But there are times when it's not so much the competitors themselves who are harmed but the intended beneficiaries of their competition. Yet, instead of putting an end to the competition, we actually accelerate the race to the bottom. Sometimes this happens because we're unaware that the competition is toxic. At other times, we're aware of the toxicity but find ourselves unable to de-escalate the race.

To illustrate, we'll start with our children's education. We often hear that greater competition among schools will benefit the students. The schools will just keep getting better and better and deliver their results at ever lower costs.

One economist voiced a common point of view: Greater competition can improve public school education in several ways. First, competition can improve schools' efficiency (which means that you get "more achievement for the same dollar"); second, competition can increase innovation; and third, competition can ensure a better match between student and school so that students' individual needs are met.[3]

This seems great. Described this way, competition sounds like a race to the top, where the schools' interests are aligned with the students' individual and collective interests. The schools get better, the students get a better education.

And yet, seemingly beneficial unrestricted competition can backfire, spiraling into a race to the bottom that does the opposite of what we hope for—competition wastes resources, lessens innovation, harms students, and undermines the quality of their education.

How this happens has a lot to do with how we measure schools relative to each other—via metrics through which we create numbered rankings. The underlying assumption about such competitive rankings is simple: The higher-ranked schools do a better job educating their students. To attract prospective students, schools with lower rankings will have to improve, and everyone will end up benefiting.

Let us see how that works in the United Kingdom, where, as in the United States, rankings play a key role in spurring competition. What we (and many parents) have discovered is that in the schools' quest to improve (or maintain) their rank, the ranking itself may become the main goal, while education can become ancillary. The children's education is sacrificed to promote the school's reputation.

One way this happens is when school administration officials pressure teachers to use grade inflation to improve their schools' results and ranking.[4] As one primary school teacher and blogger noted:

> *The reality is the stakes are so high for schools now, it's just not reasonable to expect class teachers to make fair and reasonable judgments on things over which they could be hung out to dry.*[5]

The competitive pressure may lead schools and teachers to take even more extreme measures, to improve the perceived success. As chronicled in a 2017 UK documentary, this may involve orchestrated cheating.[6] One former head teacher, for example, was caught and dismissed after altering his pupils' Standard Assessment Tests. His explanation of his misdeeds is telling. Consistently bad test results may be detrimental to the school's reputation, he observed:

> *Parents will then have a choice to keep their children at the School or move them . . . If a child leaves they're taking money with them because you are funded based on the number of children you've got. Money is walking out of the School one by one . . .*
>
> *A fellow Head Teacher rang me and his exact words were "the only thing you did wrong was you got caught." I made a mistake and I paid the price.*[7]

Other teachers, with a similar motivation to cheat for the benefit of their schools' ranking, were also altering exam answers and exam results and allowing students to copy work from course books.[8] In another scandal that broke in 2017, teachers who were involved in setting the Cambridge International Pre-U exams revealed the questions to students in their respective schools. This cheating scandal implicated some of Britain's most prestigious schools. Eton College's deputy head, for example, was accused of sharing confidential information about a forthcoming economics exam. Winchester College's head of art history was accused of tipping off students about two exams. Both resigned following the revelations.[9]

Not surprisingly, we can see the same kind of toxic competition in other countries that seek to assess educational quality through competitive metrics and rankings.[10] Investigators, for example, found at least forty-four schools in Atlanta, Georgia, engaged in cheating: Nearly "180 employees, including 38 principals, were accused of wrongdoing as part of an effort to inflate test scores and misrepresent the achievement of Atlanta's students and schools."[11] That scandal, according to the Fair-Test organization, was just the tip of the test-cheating iceberg. FairTest identified widespread test-score corruption in thirty-nine states and in Washington, DC.[12] According to FairTest's public education director:

Across the country, strategies to boost scores without improving
learning—including outright cheating, narrow teaching to the test
and pushing out low-scoring students—have been widespread.
These corrupt practices are one reason for the growing movement
resisting politically mandated overuses and misuses of standard-
ized exams.[13]

Here again we see our first condition of toxic competition: If all the schools facilitate cheating, none of the schools, nor students, benefit. The schools' individual interests and our collective interests diverge.

Rather than improving quality, competition instead leads to widespread grade inflation and cheating. And when teachers are pushed to satisfy the ranking gods, students graduate from primary schools with inflated marks that do not necessarily reflect their abilities. This puts greater pressure on the secondary schools, which have to deal with students who do not have the skills and knowledge needed to succeed at this next level. Those schools, too, will then be vulnerable to ranking pressure and the manipulations it leads to. As competition for relative position among the schools intensifies, the grading bubble expands.[14] With increased competitive pressure and limited checks and balances, schools go from tolerating cheating to actually engaging in widespread fraud.[15]

Unlike the example of hockey players, who are the victims of their competition, here the competition primarily harms the intended beneficiaries—the students and their parents.

Now, let us up the stakes and move to another scenario, where it all comes together: Both the competitors and the intended beneficiaries are harmed. Such a race would seem to be avoidable. But the competition devours both the competitors (the educators) and the targets of their competition (the students and parents of some very expensive private schools). No one can afford to individually de-escalate. We are left with emotional and financial harm, victimization of the participants and—however illogically—cries for "more competition" from the government, various economists, and supposed experts in the field. Basically, the "works."

When Competition Harms Both the Competitors and Intended Beneficiaries: College Rankings

We begin with the familiar refrain: Competition is healthy, so more competition will cure the ailment. The problem, as President Barack Obama told a college audience in 2013, is that the cost of higher education is so unaffordable that many will be unable to go to college, while many of those who do go will burden themselves with loan debt so massive that it will require years for them to repay:

> . . . over the last three decades, the cost of higher education has gone up 260 percent, at a time when family incomes have gone up about 18 percent.[16]

Like so many others before and after him, President Obama prescribed competition as the cure. We have to find ways "to jump-start competition among colleges" and "think of more innovative ways to reduce costs," he said.

Increasing competition should lower college tuition, while improving quality and variety. Similarly, various members of Congress want to "increase competition and transparency among colleges and universities to help lower the burden for students and their families."[17] And this is a popular idea in the press, too. One magazine argued that "the fundamental reason for runaway costs in higher education is that the system is opaque, monopolistic, and heavily dependent on federal subsidies."[18]

Monopolistic? Hardly. Universities are one market where a lot of competition already exists. Indeed, between 1980 and 2014, the number of four-year US universities increased 55 percent, with over three thousand universities from which to choose.[19] Even if one limited oneself to "reputable" colleges, hundreds of options exist. Few other markets offer as many competitive options as higher education.

If competition is increasing in higher education, how can the escalating tuition be the result of too little competition? No one alleges that thousands of American universities are secretly colluding to hike tuition. So, what is going on?

Universities compete for students. For many universities, competition to attract students begins with their ranking. At its core, the ranking system is supposed to empower students and families by telling them how different universities perform on the same metrics. And it synthesizes all the information into one number. So we can easily see how Princeton compares to UCLA, Harvard to Yale, Hamilton to Amherst, etc. In theory, our children should benefit from the greater transparency, and so should our colleges, because it will compel them to continually compete and get better in order to attract (or keep) students.

Let's see how that works in practice.

The ranking that most universities focus on, precisely because so many parents and students rely on it, is the annual *U.S. News & World Report* college ranking.[20] The whispering among faculty begins several weeks before the results are published. Then the day of reckoning. *Did we go up or down? What, we've fallen behind . . . Heads will roll.* Then come the press releases. The winners celebrate their rise in the rankings. The losers double down on improving their relative position, hoping to return to the top 20, 50, or 100.

Whenever competition involves rankings, we can see a self-fulfilling feedback loop. Moving up in the rankings creates a positive feedback loop. If Tulane University, for example, advances its relative position, more applicants with better standardized test scores and grades will be attracted to the New Orleans university, and thereby further improve Tulane's academic reputation.[21] *U.S. News*, as part of its rankings, surveys college presidents, provosts, and deans of admissions about the quality of other universities' academic programs. Rankings affect the administrators' perceptions of the quality of peer institutions.[22]

Likewise, falling in rankings creates a negative feedback loop. If the university drops in rankings, it might attract fewer "star" students the following year, and the decline will continue.

So we can readily see how a numerical ranking spurs competition. It is the bonfire that devours resources that schools devote to winning the competition. Many universities tie their strategic goals and evaluate their administrators' performance based on these rankings.[23] As University of Virginia's former associate dean of admissions noted, "Schools are in competition, and they're after ranking rights about who's the most competitive school in the country to get into."[24]

But if universities compete fiercely to move up (or maintain) their ranking, then we should all benefit, right? A higher rank would suggest a better quality education, better student care and support, and greater affordability. So where's the overdose?

How Individual and Collective Interests Diverge in University Rankings

Beginning in their junior year, high school students can expect to find glossy college brochures in their mailboxes. But Genevieve received something more. Her credentials clearly impressed the dean of admissions at Tulane. Because of her "qualifications," the Admissions Committee identified her as an "ideal candidate." She would receive "priority consideration" for admissions and scholarships. Such an invitation by a top-40 US university is certainly an accomplishment.

Tulane University

Office of Undergraduate Admission

Dear Genevieve,

I hope your fall semester is off to a fantastic start. I wanted to check in with you to remind about some important upcoming deadlines for applying to Tulane University. If you are interested in applying Early Decision or Early Action, the deadlines are quickly approaching on November 1st and November 15th, respectively.

Whether it's your outstanding academics, countless hours of community service, portfolio of extracurricular activities, or your continued relationship with Tulane, you are an ideal candidate to apply. Because of your qualifications, the admission committee has selected you to receive priority consideration. As a priority consideration applicant you'll enjoy benefits including:

- **No application fee.**
- **Automatic consideration for partial scholarships ranging up to $32,000 per year.**
- **The opportunity to interview with an alum (if you apply Early Action or Early Decision).**

Your APPLY.TULANE.EDU Login Information
Username:
Login PIN:

Application opens: November 1
Early Action: due November 15
Complete your application at: **APPLY.TULANE.EDU or COMMONAPP.ORG**

You may submit an application through either the Tulane application or Common Application. The benefits outlined above apply to both.

Every year I get the opportunity to find exceptional students to bring them to our academically and socially vibrant community on campus. I encourage you to explore how your academic and extracurricular interests would allow you to thrive at Tulane.

I hope to review your application soon.

Best wishes,

Satyajit Dattagupta
Vice President for Enrollment Management and Dean of Undergraduate Admission

210 Gibson Hall, LA 70118-5698
tel 504-865-5731 800-873-9283
fax 504-862-8715
admission.tulane.edu

Priority consideration for Genevieve! What makes her so remarkable? While she is dear to our hearts, and of course we were very proud, Genevieve is none other than Maurice's thirteen-year-old Standard Schnauzer.

This story would seem funny, but seventeen-year-olds who received a similar letter might not laugh. And there are many seventeen-year-olds who did get such letters, as Maurice's spouse, Liz, can testify.

Liz does college admissions consulting, and she was momentarily impressed when one of her clients came into her office, bearing a crisp white letter from Tulane inviting him to apply.

"Ms. Stucke," he declared, "I decided Tulane is my top choice. Tulane not only wants me, but is considering me for numerous scholarships."

However, when Liz's dog received the exact same letter a few days later, she knew how meaningless the letter was.

So how did Tulane—and a number of other universities that also courted Genevieve with inviting letters—discover her? Liz had entered only Genevieve's name and a generic sounding public high school in the "Common App"—a platform that allows high school students to apply to hundreds of universities simultaneously. The Common Application company boasts "More than 750 colleges. Only one application."[25]

Often, applying to the more selective universities is a matter of simply clicking a box (and perhaps writing an additional personal essay). Hence Liz did not have to bother to mention Genevieve's grades, test scores, or extracurricular activities. The lack of information did not matter to the schools that replied. After all, the letter and the promise of priority considerations were only meant to convince Genevieve to apply.

Why did they want Genevieve to apply? Basically so they could then reject her (after all, dogs may have flown to outer space but are unlikely to do well at university). And why would they want to reject her? Therein lies a tale about competition and its role in rankings.

The 2018 *U.S. News* Best Colleges rankings were based on fifteen key measures,[26] one small component of which was acceptance rate. The more applicants a university rejects, the better it performs on this ranking metric. The lower its acceptance rate, the more selective the university appears (which can also boost other ranking metrics, like "undergraduate academic reputation"). Essentially, universities woo applicants in order to reject them and improve their ranking.

The result of this rankings madness is that the number of applications to many *U.S. News* top-30 universities and liberal arts colleges is increasing. As the number of applications increases so, inevitably, does the rejection rate, since class sizes are not increasing to accommodate larger numbers of students. As Harvard's applications doubled over the past two decades,[27] its rejection rate increased from 89 to 95 percent. We see this same trend with Stanford.[28] Its rejection rate increased significantly from 20 percent in the early 1950s to over 80 percent in the 1980s. With the further rise in applications in the early 2000s, Stanford's rejection rate climbed to over 95 percent. Likewise, Cornell's applications doubled over the past decade,[29] while its rejection rate increased to 87 percent. The University of Chicago's rejection rate skyrocketed[30] from 60 percent to over 90 percent. Other top-30 universities, such as Duke, Northwestern, and the University of Pennsylvania, had admission rates in 2014 that were less than half of those from a decade ago.

Although it's true that the number of international applicants to the top-ranked schools has increased, most of the increase in applications is from US high school students, and their numbers have not doubled over the past decade. So the current increase in applications did not arise from any baby boom in the late 1990s. Indeed, overall enrollment at all universities has been declining between 2014 and 2017,[31] including at four-year, nonprofit private colleges.

So if overall enrollment is declining, we see instead a shift: The top students are increasingly seeking admittance to the same small number of top-ranked universities. Imagine a theater with four doors: three are uncrowded, and most of the patrons are clawing to exit from the fourth door.

One factor is that the Common Application process makes it easier for students to apply to multiple schools. More students can easily apply to more colleges—and they have taken advantage of that benefit in droves, which further drives the competition madness.

And here is where individual and collective interests diverge. Although rankings do intensify competition, such competition will not necessarily focus on the qualities we care about, such as price, quality, or innovation. Instead, the competition will concentrate on the components of the ranking—one of which is competitiveness itself, as measured by number of applicants versus number of rejections. Competitors use rejection rates to signal quality.

And if the percentage of applicants rejected affects competitive ranking, then you can be sure that colleges will look for more ingenuous ways to attract more applicants—the better to reject them. Think of it as the *"Dear Genevieve* effect." As Christoph Guttentag, Duke's dean of undergraduate admissions, put it quite succinctly:

> *One of the ways that colleges are measured is by the number of applicants and their admit rate, and some colleges do things simply to increase their applicant pool and manipulate those numbers.*[32]

Competitors tap into the students' vulnerabilities[33] to entice them to apply. Tactics include "personalized" e-mails and letters;[34] invitations to "selective" open houses, which are intended to convey the message that the person is especially likely to gain admittance; and, in the case of Duke University, wall posters. As a former admissions officer at Duke described in her book, *Admissions Confidential*:

I travel around the country whipping kids (and their parents) into a frenzy so that they will apply. I tell them how great a school Duke is academically and how much fun they will have socially. Then, come April, we reject most of them.[35]

But does every competitor do it? Let's consider Harvard. In 2016–17, Harvard College received 39,494 applications, a "new record for the third year in a row."[36] In 2018, Harvard broke the record again, this time receiving over forty thousand applications. Its rejection rate exceeded 95 percent.[37]

Harvard has an unparalleled brand. One wouldn't think it had to play this game. But it, too, solicits applications—so actively that some have advised students to view e-mails and mailings from Harvard with a dose of skepticism. One former admissions officer at Stanford University went so far as to call Harvard's mailings "not honorable" and "misleading."[38] He argued, "The overwhelming majority of students receiving these mailings will not be admitted in the end, and Harvard knows this well."[39]

Nonetheless, every year, Harvard goes on road shows, together with Duke, Georgetown, University of Pennsylvania, Stanford, and dozens of other top-ranked schools to entice students to apply. Despite its deluge of applications,[40] Harvard assures prospective applicants a "deliberate and meticulous consideration of each applicant as a whole person. It is labor intensive, but permits extraordinary flexibility and the possibility of changing decisions virtually until the day the Admissions Committee mails them."

In any arms race, rivals will develop new weapons, often increasing the toxicity of the competition. One such toxic weapon that many selective universities now deploy is restrictive "early decision" policies. Basically, colleges use it to play "musical chairs"—to their own benefit, but at the expense of our children.

Here's how it works. For seniors seeking an early admission to a top-ranked university or liberal arts college, the frenzy starts in early

November, when early applications are due. The rules vary by college and can be quite technical. (Just look at Yale's.)[41] The lexicon and rules are bewildering, as illustrated in the chart in Appendix A.

At most top-ranked schools, the rules are designed to limit your or your child's ability to apply to other top-ranked schools early. Take University of Pennsylvania as an example. Before 2016, students could apply early to Penn and also apply to other private universities that did not have Restrictive Early Action policies. In 2016 that changed. Penn told its Early Decision applicants that they could no longer apply early to other private US universities. Students could only apply to state universities (like University of Alabama) or foreign universities. Why? To "ensure that early applicants are as committed to Penn as possible."[42]

So, why would any student apply to only one of these early decision colleges and, if accepted, be obliged to go there?

The upshot is better odds of acceptance at a top-ranked college. In 2017, for example, the Ivy League universities accepted between 14.5 and 25 percent of the early decision applicants,[43] a much higher percentage than their "regular decision" acceptance rate. The downside is that the student can only apply to one of these early decision schools. They cannot compare Penn's financial aid package with that of Williams College.

If the student is admitted, the game ends. Barring a financial aid issue, the student must commit to attending that university (except in the case of Harvard, Yale, Princeton, and Stanford, which allow students to apply to other universities).

If the early decision applicant is deferred or denied, as most are, the game of musical chairs continues. But since many selective colleges, including the Ivy League schools, fill between 40 and 54 percent of their entering class with restricted early decision applicants, they will have removed approximately half of the chairs.

The tempo now quickens as more students—namely those who did not apply early or weren't accepted—circle ever fewer chairs. To ensure that they land on at least one chair (or better yet to have a choice of chairs), students apply to more "far reach," "reach," "possible," and "likely" universities.

Yet, schools are not satisfied by even this level of applications. To gain a further competitive edge, colleges continue to entice applicants during the regular decision process with more of their *Dear Genevieve* letters, college roadshows, high school visits, and e-mails, letters, and brochures. For example, after the early admission decisions came out, the University of Chicago sent our talented Genevieve a colorful mailing. It probably predicted that she, like many high schoolers, was rejected during the early decision process. So it offered her hope, encouraging her to apply to Chicago. With "a little bit of networking at UChicago," she, too, can accomplish great things. Even students with low scores or grades (or, as in the case of Genevieve, no grades or scores) are encouraged to apply and promised a holistic review.

This two-stage competitive race helps improve ranking in two ways:[44] First, early decision improves the university's *yield*—the number of applicants who are accepted who then decide to attend that university—which is another of the factors that is weighed in the rankings. Second, by reducing the number of spots available during the regular decision period, which of course increases their rejection rate, the universities further enhance their perceived competitiveness. Thus, without having done anything to actually improve the quality of their education or career services, the colleges have now boosted their "quality" ranking.[45]

The University of Chicago, for example, once attracted fewer applicants than other top-ranked universities. No doubt the students it attracted were studious, drawn to the school's reputation. But Chicago's dean was dissatisfied. He compared his college's application total to that of Columbia University: "I believe we are a better university than they are, so I think we should have more applications than they do." (His remark was intended as a "friendly, competitive gesture.") But the message was clear: "I don't think Chicago should stand behind New York on this one. We deserve the same number of applications, if not more."[46] So, the

University of Chicago set out to entice more applicants to eventually reject. It joined the Common App, visited far more high schools, and intensified its marketing through personal appeals. To avoid being left behind, Columbia began offering invitation-only open houses.

Harm to Students and Universities

T. S. Eliot called April the cruelest month. But for high school seniors and their families, December and March are the most unkind. The same schools that wooed Genevieve and thousands of others to apply through early or regular decision will discard them in those months.

A week or two before Christmas most early decision applicants will be rejected (or deferred) from their top-ranked "dream" school. They must scramble for the remaining seats. One option is to apply to a top-ranked college that offers Early Decision II (and be prepared to commit, if accepted). Or apply regular decision. Either way, the reality is that fewer seats are now available. So the fear increases. Students must now apply to even more universities to improve the odds of admittance. They pay anywhere between $60 and $100 for each lottery ticket.

Then in late March the suspense builds. There is much reading of tea leaves. For example, parents and students ponder whether a last-minute request from a school for a financial aid form signals possible acceptance.

The university announces the date and time the decisions will be available. At the anointed time, thousands log onto the university's portal. In a matter of seconds, many hearts will drop. There are no computer-animated effects, like confetti, welcoming them. The disappointed students don't know how to react or what to do. *What will I tell my parents, my friends?*

Some express their feelings on websites like College Confidential, which has discussion boards for many universities and liberal arts colleges. Common to all the threads from those who were not accepted is disbelief. A lot of students list their outstanding grades and standardized test scores, and express shock at how they could possibly have been rejected—or, like hundreds, if not thousands of others, placed on a purgatorial waiting list, which for many, if not most, will also end up in rejection within a few months.

Here is one student, who applied to Tulane:

WAIT-LISTED

SAT: 1550-EBRW: 750, Math: 800

ACT: 35C-34W, 35M, 36R, 35S

SAT II: 800 Math 2, 800 Chemistry, 790 Physics

GPA: 4.641 W, 4.000 UW

RANK: 5/520

AP SCORES: Human Geography-5, Biology-5, World History-5, Chemistry-5, English Lang-5, US History-5, Statistics-5, Physics-5

SENIOR YEAR COURSE LOAD: AP Physics C: Mechanics/E&M, Symphony Orchestra, AP English Lit, AP US Gov, AP Macroeconomics, AP Calculus BC, AP Music Theory

Kind of ridiculous that all of these people with amazing stats are getting wait-listed. I wonder how many spots they had left after EA [Early Action] and both rounds of ED [Early Decision] for them to be THAT selective! Does anybody know why?

Next comes the anger, as the students realize how they've been played:

They wait-list an obnoxious amount of students because of the ranking game. They don't want to offer students acceptance letters if they are not coming. So, they have you apply and get wait-listed then call and write and beg to get in so they can say the kids who got accepted actually enrolled. It is all a game along with the free application! They are a joke.

Even parents weigh in, like this Tulane graduate, who seems to feel that their child just should have played the game more skillfully:

> My son is [wait-listed] RD [regular decision] round at Tulane with a 1540 SAT, 34 ACT, and a 4.0. He realizes now that he should have applied EA, ED, or ED II. His pride is pretty wounded, but I personally think that it's a good lesson for him to learn. I do not feel sorry for him because I warned him that Tulane is huge on demonstrated interest, and applying early is a no-brainer way of showing that you are gung-ho about Tulane. I do want to clarify that Tulane was never a safety school for him. The valedictorian at his high school didn't get into Tulane a couple of years ago, so we knew this was not a given by any stretch of the imagination. I seriously would LOVE to see my son at my alma mater, and we are still HUGE Tulane fans!!!

After each rejection, the students wait in dread of the next college's decision. Some prefer the college decisions that arrive unannounced in their e-mail in-box. As one student said, "I prefer not to know the day I am executed."

Meanwhile, the universities publicly, proudly recount how applications reached a record number, forcing the admissions department to accept an even-lower percentage of highly qualified applicants.

In its press release "The Class of 2022 Makes Its Mark," Tulane highlights its selectivity:

> *Receiving 38,813 applications for fall 2018—a 9 percent increase from last year—the Office of Undergraduate Admission reported that the acceptance rate was 17.5 percent as compared to 21 percent in 2017.*
>
> *"In terms of students being admitted, this is Tulane's most selective class," said [Tulane's dean of admissions], who described the*

application process as a holistic review of the students' ability to succeed at Tulane with a prime focus on academic fit.[47]

That was similar to Tulane's message to the 2021 class:

The popularity of Tulane among the best and the brightest continues to rise. As a result of that demand the competition intensifies with each passing year . . . As compared to the entering class of 2016 in which 26% of applicants were accepted, the admission process for the entering class of 2017 was more selective with 21% of applicants admitted.[48]

Invariably the admissions director attributes the strength of its applicant pool to the university's inherent quality. Tulane is a school "that is so sought after."[49] Perhaps. But it might also reflect the feverish efforts that these universities undertook to induce both high school seniors and Schnauzers to apply.

As we saw earlier, a race to the bottom may harm the competitors (e.g., hockey players) and may intensify when others bear the harm (as we saw with public school rankings). Now let's consider the toll that such toxic competition can have on *both* the competitors (the universities) *and* the supposed beneficiaries (students and their parents).

First is the emotional toll on students[50] (and consequently on their parents). As rejection rates at selective colleges soar, the collateral damage is clear: huge amounts of anxiety and painful blows to self-esteem.

Next is the financial harm. Early decision, for example, leaves students with a Hobson's choice: Either commit early to one school through its restrictive early decision program or face the prospect of even greater odds of rejection through regular decision. Once they have committed, students lose out on the opportunity to compare financial aid packages that might have been offered to them by other selective schools.

Then there's the economic waste caused by this toxic competition.

Rather than spending money on improving the product or service, competition instead causes money to be spent on the competition itself. The colleges' efforts to woo and reject applicants, for example, fuel "irrational" spending, contributing to escalating tuition.[51] The money is spent, for example, on identifying their target market. Even before the era of Big Data, many colleges bought the names of students whose standardized test scores and self-reported grade point averages fell within a particular range. In the early 1990s, the College Board sold thirty-five million names a year.[52] By 2010 it sold "80 million to approximately 1,200 colleges, at 32 cents a name." To get a jump on the competition, colleges now buy names of high school sophomores. Seizing upon Big Data, colleges will invest heavily to convert targeted, personalized invitations into applications.

Toxic competition also misallocates resources. The deluge of applications, for example, burdens an already overloaded admissions staff. With such an overwhelming number of applications to read, many of the more selective colleges have had to eliminate interviews.[53] (What university can personally interview thirty thousand applicants for fewer than three thousand slots?) Contrary to the promise of holistic review (the "deliberate and meticulous consideration of each applicant as a whole person" that Harvard, for example, claims to offer), the time that can be allotted to considering each application also inevitably suffers. At some schools, a reviewer reads only part of the application to pare down the average decision time to eight minutes.[54] Duke's dean of admissions acknowledged that 26,000 applications had swamped an evaluation process that was meant to handle half that number. But despite the insanity, he didn't anticipate much change: "The pressure for more applications isn't offset by an equal pressure for less, and no college wants to consciously put itself in a weaker competitive position."[55]

One perhaps could justify this toxic competition if it somehow improved the diversity of the incoming class. Does it? Unfortunately, the evidence, at best, is mixed. While overall enrollment of African-American and Hispanic students has increased since 1971,[56] they are, as the *New York Times* found in 2017, "more underrepresented at the nation's top [100] colleges and universities than they were thirty-five years ago." Nor has the increase in applications boosted economic diversity. Instead, the trend over the past decade at many selective colleges is *less* economic diversity.[57] "At thirty-eight colleges in America, including five in the Ivy League—Dartmouth, Princeton, Yale, Penn, and Brown," the *New York Times* found, "more students came from the top 1 percent of the income scale than from the entire bottom 60 percent."

As Dartmouth's former admissions dean observed, "It's a classic arms race—escalation for not a whole lot of gain . . . I don't think these larger applicant pools are materially improving the quality of their classes. Now what's driving it is the institutional self-interest factor, where bigger pools mean you're more popular, you're better."[58] As a former dean of admissions at Princeton and Stanford aptly concluded, "I couldn't pick a better class out of thirty thousand applicants than out of fifteen thousand. I'd just end up rejecting multiples of the same kid."[59]

A competitive game, with limited morality, has a real cost. In a twisted way, the economic and emotional burden is borne not only by the competitors, but also by all of us who are supposed to benefit from the competition.

Why Can't Powerful Competitors Independently De-escalate the Arms Race?

Ask any bored college administrator at a cocktail party about school rankings and likely a rant will follow. "I think *U.S. News* has done more damage to the higher education marketplace than any single enterprise that's out there," said Louisiana State University's president F. King Alexander.[60]

Competitors usually know when they are trapped in a race to the bottom. Each is aware that they, like the helmetless hockey players, are collectively worse off as a result of this competition. But they fear the collateral consequences of opting out.

Suppose a selective college opts out of the Common App. It does not seek to fill up seats early through binding early decision. And it stops trolling for additional applicants to reject. How is it rewarded for its ethical behavior? Its ranking will likely drop.

As its ranking drops, the negative feedback loop kicks in: The college will keep attracting fewer applicants to reject, the quality of their applicants will drop, and it will likely lose the favor of the wealthy alumni they count on to make major donations. Soon its credit ratings are dropping toward junk status.[61] Staring into the abyss, the college administrators see the financial straits of other lower-ranked colleges, most of which are struggling to fill seats and dependent on tuition to finance operations— and they are likely to decide to rejoin the race, even knowing it's a race to the bottom.

Whereas a hockey player or small organization is relatively powerless to stop this race to the bottom, one would think a leading organization would be in a position to restore sanity. Education seems like a perfect example. Few businesses have the reputation, prestige, and intellectual horsepower of Harvard or Princeton. Surely such powerful competitors, when they observe how both they and their customers are harmed, will de-escalate, and others will follow.

In 2006, Harvard, Princeton, and the University of Virginia tried exactly that. They all announced an end to early decision,[62] hoping that their competitors would follow. They didn't. Instead, applications increased 40 percent at the University of Chicago, Stanford, and Yale two years in a row.[63] Consequently, Harvard and Princeton returned to Single-Choice Early Action (where a student can apply early to its school, but not early to other private universities), and UVA allowed Early Action (which allows students to apply early to UVA, but also early to any other school that does not impose restrictions—like *early decision* schools).

As the executive director of the University of Southern California's

Center for Enrollment Research, Policy, and Practice observed, "When institutions on the order of Harvard and Princeton get whipsawed by the market we have created, you have to ask if this is the market we want."[64]

Not even Harvard, its admissions dean recognized, can afford to decelerate the race to attract and reject students:

> You've got to understand, the Ivy League is so hypercompetitive that I've heard our faculty members compare it to a loose federation of pirates.

As he conceded, "If we gave it up, other institutions inside and outside the Ivy League would carve up our class, and our faculty would carve us up."[65]

So, just as universities as renowned as Harvard, Princeton, and UVA cannot curb the arms race, big, prestigious firms in other markets are also unlikely to restore sanity unilaterally. Ultimately, all the competitors would have to agree to de-escalate.[66] But if they did agree to limit competition, as we'll later see, they could face significant civil and criminal penalties and even end up in prison.

Why Can't the Victims De-escalate the Race to the Bottom?

We now confront the penultimate missing piece of the puzzle. In situations where the competitors' individual and collective interests diverge, we can have a race to the bottom that even powerful competitors cannot stop.

But in many markets the beneficiaries of competition have a choice. They can stop this toxic competition by opting out. So why don't they?

One problem is that the intended beneficiaries of competition may be trapped in their own arms race. Rather than prevent (or at least slow down) the race to the bottom, they may actually accelerate the downward spiral.

To return to our example: Why do so many students rely on rankings to apply to the top-30 national universities and liberal arts schools, despite their college counselors' encouragement to diversify their college search? Why do they invariably gravitate to the same set of selective colleges even though they, their parents, and their high school college counselors decry the application process? The rankings competition among colleges is supposed to benefit students, not hurt them. When it doesn't, one would expect the intended beneficiaries to simply walk away.

One possible explanation is status. Status competition, the economist Thorstein Veblen observed in 1899, has long preoccupied the leisure class. Wherever prep school families congregate, one generally sees large dogs, Nantucket Reds, and European cars. Though bumper stickers are considered lowbrow in these settings and are therefore rare among such families, another kind of signifier is quite common: banners in the rear windows of their vehicles that proclaim their offspring's progression through elite educational institutions beginning with prep school through to college and graduate school.

It's true that status competition can fuel a race to the bottom, as when a neighbor's purchase of a Porsche Boxster prompts other neighbors to buy even more expensive cars, despite being unable to afford them. This has been called the "hedonic treadmill."

But are those school banners really about status? If status were driving students to apply to top-ranked colleges, the rejection rates in the 1950s and 1960s would have been higher. This would not have been a relatively recent phenomenon.

Another explanation is fear. The victims in any race to the bottom must decide if it is better to play the game or to bear the costs of opting out. The competitive pressure to enter a top-ranked university may reflect our perceived vulnerability in today's economy.

Today's economy has several troubling symptoms. Many people are working harder, yet their wages for years have stagnated. We are increasingly fearful in a precarious economy: Most Americans, in one survey, were afraid or very afraid in 2018 of not having enough money for the future[67] (57 percent compared to 50.2 percent in 2017 and 39.9 percent in 2016). More Americans fear becoming unemployed (34.4 percent in 2018 versus 30.7 percent in 2017 and 24.6 percent in 2016). In 2018, far more Americans were fearful of computers replacing them in the workforce[68] (30.7 percent) than in earlier years (25.3 percent in 2017 and 16.6 percent in 2016).

Our fear of unemployment is justified when our safety net has too many holes: 52.9 percent of Americans in 2018 were afraid or very afraid of high medical bills.[69] And our employment options are limited. The "gig" economy, like driving for Uber while renting out a bedroom on Airbnb, will not provide medical benefits and secure us financially in retirement. Avoiding corporate America is harder, as there are far fewer new businesses in the United States being created[70] (as a share of the US economy) since the late 1970s. And even corporate America is getting smaller: Fewer public firms exist today in the United States than in the 1970s.

So as the balance of power has shifted away from individuals, our very economic survival seems to be at stake. The desperation felt by many can fuel an arms race. The economist Irving Fisher compared it to patrons competing to exit a burning theater; it is in each individual's interest to get ahead of others, but "the very intensity of such efforts in the aggregate defeat their own ends."[71]

Frightened by our own precarious position in today's economy, we will want to do all what we can to improve our children's odds of success. Interestingly, right about the time when workers' share of profits in the United States began to sharply decline was also when college applications to top-60 colleges began skyrocketing. This could, of course, be a mere coincidence. But there's no denying that for many, college seems to represent the best route to upward social mobility, the place where students can network to find superior mates, friends—and jobs.

Thus, the *U.S. News* rankings don't simply represent quality. The higher the ranking of our child's school, the better, we think, are the child's odds for prevailing in an increasingly inequitable, precarious economy. So parents, too, become complicit in the race to the bottom. Why disadvantage our child by having her apply to only two or three universities, based on some ethical principle? And why settle for the local state university? Of course, we know our child can do quite well there. But won't she have a better chance of withstanding the blows of automation and uncertainty in this winner-take-all economy if she goes to a top-ranked school?

In any race to the bottom, we might expect those at the forefront of this frenzy to be the people with the most to fear. So, in the college rankings frenzy, is it the parents in the Appalachian trailer homes who are seeking to push their children up the economic ladder by sending them to Harvard? Or is it the people with the most to lose, the wealthy and upper-middle class, who fear their children will slide down the economic ladder? Here we see it is the wealthy and upper-middle class who help drive the race to the bottom.

This phenomenon was evident when the US Department of Justice brought criminal charges against California college admissions consultant William "Rick" Singer and the thirty-three wealthy parents he helped. Rather than induce Yale, Georgetown, USC, and other selective schools indirectly (through large donations), he gave parents the "sure thing" by bribing the colleges' coaches.[72] After all, these universities designate a significant number of admissions slots for recruited athletes. In exchange for $25 million in bribes, the college coaches would designate the wealthy children as recruited athletes. What's amazing was the lack of oversight by the university, as these students, given their lack of athletic ability, would never actually play on the team once admitted. One "recruited" student, who gained acceptance through one of Georgetown's approximately 158 admissions slots for recruited athletes, claimed in her college essay how she was among the top-50 ranked junior girls tennis players, even though US Tennis Association records never showed her playing any USTA tournaments in high school, and the highest level she achieved in the under-12 girls division was when she was ranked 207th in Northern California with a 2–8 record.

One would expect affluent parents, given their wealth and connections, to be less beholden to university rankings. Some made their wealth without an Ivy League education. Some may even have skipped college altogether. Well-to-do parents are also likely to be well-informed enough to know about the empirical studies that cast considerable doubt on the economic advantage of attending some of these aspirational schools—as we'll discuss at the end of this chapter.

But the primordial need to ensure their children's survival in a winner-take-all economy triumphs. For the upper-middle class and wealthy, the race begins not in senior year, but much earlier. To increase the odds of admittance to a top college, parents now compete for entry into elite private and magnet public high schools with the understanding that attendance at these schools gives students a competitive edge at securing placement at the top-ranked national universities and liberal arts colleges.

The recent private school matriculation data we obtained from fifteen selective private boarding and day schools across the United States bear this out.[73] First let us explain our methodology. *U.S. News* has separate rankings for national universities and liberal arts colleges. We selected the top-30 national universities and top-30 liberal arts colleges from the 2018 *U.S. News* rankings. Then for each prep school, using its most recent matriculation data, we calculated what percentage of its graduating class went to these top-ranked schools. (For example, of all the Exeter graduates in the past few years, we inquired what percentage of these Exeter students went to one of these sixty national universities and liberal arts colleges.) While the years for which we have data do not exactly overlap, what we generally found was that each of these prep schools sends most of their students to these same sixty schools. As Appendix B reflects, on average, over 70 percent of these students matriculate at schools that are among *U.S. News*'s top-30 rankings for national universities and liberal arts colleges:

- 25 percent go to the Ivy League schools,
- 25 percent go to the remaining top-30 ranked national private universities,
- 11 percent go to the top-ranked "Little Ivy" liberal arts colleges,
- 10 percent go to *U.S. News*'s other top-30 liberal arts colleges, and
- 5 percent attend the "Public Ivies" (University of Michigan, UC Berkeley, UCLA, University of Virginia, and University of North Carolina).

Even private schools on the West Coast, such as Harvard-Westlake in Los Angeles, send most of their students to these same colleges, which are primarily on the East Coast and in the Midwest.

With private schools and magnet public schools competing to get their students admitted into one of these top-ranked colleges, the arms race becomes all the more fierce. And in the admissions game, no market is as fiercely hypercompetitive as the New York City day school market.

This is why the headmaster at New York's Trinity School made the national news in 2017 with an astonishing letter he wrote to parents.[74] He noted how "consumerist families . . . treat teachers and the school in entirely instrumental ways, seeking to use us exclusively to advance their child's narrow self-interests." The headmaster proposed how his school could transform its approach to community service, integrating what students would do outside the classroom with what they were learning inside. Otherwise they would continue to suffer from this soulless competition:

[F]or an increasing number of our older students, with increasing intensity, as they leave our Lower School, our students' default understanding of the purpose of their schoolwork becomes to make good grades, gain admissions to a highly selective college, set themselves

on a path of lifelong superior achievement. And this default setting—one of narrowly individualistic self-advancement—has been locked into place by a frenetic pace of life and expectations of perfection that devour the energy and time students need to reflect on the meaning of their schoolwork. To deconstruct this default understanding of Trinity as a credentialing factory, we need to actively develop in our students compelling alternative understandings of the socially redeeming purposes their knowledge and skills could and should serve. If we do not, our well-intentioned work to develop their powers of critical thinking and creative self-expression will serve to secure for our students a comfortable perch atop a cognitive elite that is self-serving, callous, and spiritually barren.

Our data from several New York City day schools reflect this competitive channeling. Over 80 percent of the students at Brearley, Collegiate, Dalton, and Spence attend the *U.S. News* top-30 national and liberal arts colleges. Moreover, about 40 percent of the Brearley and Collegiate graduates, 37 percent of the Dalton graduates, and 34 percent of the Spence graduates—a much higher percentage than many other elite boarding schools and day schools elsewhere in the United States—enroll in the Ivy League schools.

Of course, in particularly competitive places—like New York City—the educational race to the bottom doesn't start in high school. Children are groomed from a very young age with the goal of obtaining a place at an Ivy League school or at least one of the other top-ranked colleges over a decade later. Beginning not just in grade school or even in kindergarten but in pre-kindergarten, wealthy parents will send their children to elite programs designed to give their children an edge at getting into the right day (or boarding) school—which will then funnel their child into one of the desired colleges.

Ultimately, the intended beneficiaries of competition will not necessarily walk away, even when the toxic competition harms them and their children. As Trinity, and no doubt other schools, found, this rankings competition can take a toll on the students' well-being long before their junior year, causing many students, as Trinity's headmaster said in his letter, "regardless of class or race or privilege, [to] feel disconnected, isolated, alienated from their peers."[75] And while entering college freshmen are healthier on many metrics—less smoking, for example—they score themselves much lower on mental well-being than preceding generations.[76]

Yale, for example, has a reputation as the "happy Ivy." Yet over half of its students in 2013 sought mental health care while they were there.[77] And that percentage is increasing.[78] The grind needed to get into Yale (and these other top-ranked universities) doesn't end at Freshman Orientation. As a Yale report on mental health notes, many qualities that made the students compelling to admissions officers, like the excellent high school grades "pursued at the cost of stress and anxiety," are the same things that make them vulnerable to mental health issues.[79] The students continue to grind away at college. So what Yale course has the largest enrollment, by far, in its 317-year history? A Happiness 101 class.[80] Laurie Santos, a psychology professor, offered the class after seeing students grinding away, stressed and unhappy: "They feel they're in this crazy rat race, they're working so hard they can't take a single hour off—that's awful." Needless to say, Yale is not alone in this story.

Is Competition Always Rational?

No. Despite what we know about the toxicity of competition, we may find the perceived benefits too great or seductive to ignore. We fear that regret may hound us if we opt out. So we join the fray, aware that in doing so we are only accelerating the race to the bottom. And the faster we run, the harder we find it to get off the treadmill.

In the context of higher education, this means that once we commit our kids to a path of success, we cannot look back. To understand why, let's consider the following experiment that Professors Max Bazerman and Don Moore did to demonstrate their "Competitive Escalation Paradigm," which involved auctioning off a $20 bill to their students at Harvard.[81] The first bid is low, and from there the bidding escalates, in increments of a dollar. If there were no penalty for a losing bid, no one of course would bid over $20.

But here, as with many bidding wars, there is a penalty. The highest bidder wins the $20; but the second highest bidder, as the loser, must pay the auctioneer his or her bid. (So, if the highest bid is $4, the winner makes $16; if the second highest bid is $3, the loser pays the auctioneer $3.)

Suppose we are invited to play this game. Bidding over $20 for a $20 bill is illogical. Given the cost of losing, it is also illogical to enter a bidding war. But if we all believe this, no one plays so no one gets the chance to bid $1 for $20—this, too, is illogical.

So there's always someone who will bid, and then others will join in. Once multiple bidders emerge, no one wants to be the second highest bidder. Which means that people just keep bidding.[82] As a result, the bidding, not just in experiments with undergraduate students and graduate students but with executives, too, "typically ends between $20 and $70, but hits $100 with some regularity." Which is, of course, a ridiculous outcome.

Ideally, no one would start an arms race—whether by sending a *Dear Genevieve* letter or bidding for $20. But the immediate gain for some is too tempting. If everyone else is ignoring the $20 bill, someone would whisper a bid of $1. Others hear it, and, quickly, as the fear of losing increases, the commitment to the irrational competition intensifies. In the case of the $20 bill, people begin by playing to win, but end by playing not to lose.

One possible antidote to irrational competition is learning by doing. Eventually, after losing a number of times, we will stop bidding for the $20 bill. But, in other markets, we lack opportunities to learn from our mistakes. For some momentous decisions, we lack a ready counter-factual.

We don't know how we would fare if we opt out—so out of fear, we don't. Essentially fear and anxiety help fuel the race to the bottom.

Returning to our higher education example, whether it is fear or some other motivation, wealthy and upper-middle class parents are spending a lot of time, energy, and money to get their children into these top-ranked universities. With higher education, the benefit isn't necessarily the education itself, but the signaling effect of the university's reputation, as well as its alumni network. Parents feel they cannot avoid this competition if they at the very least want to maintain their children's precarious social and economic position, if not to improve it.

Is it rational? As Appendix C reflects, there are some schools that parents, focused on their children's future earning potential, may never have considered—or even heard of. But Babson College's $91,400 median earnings certainly compares well to Harvard's $90,900, and the Stevens Institute of Technology's $87,300 outdoes Yale's $83,200. And how about that Rose-Hulman Institute of Technology, which at $79,300 is very close to Princeton's $80,500 and comes in ahead of Columbia's $78,200 and Cornell's $73,600? There are many other surprising comparisons to be made in a granular examination of Appendix C.

But even this is deceiving. Ivy League students generally do well in terms of earnings. But the output (high earnings) may simply reflect the input (smart, driven students). Students with higher standardized test scores tend to go on to earn higher incomes.[83] So the real issue is how much would the Yale student have earned if he or she went instead to a "moderately selective" college? Would she end up in a trailer park in the Ozarks rather than a Brooklyn Heights brownstone?

Here we can't directly test the counterfactual. After all, the student went to Yale. However, in lieu of a good counterfactual for higher education, Stacy Dale, a senior researcher at Mathematica, and Alan B. Krueger, an economics professor at Princeton, came up with an interesting alternative.[84] They looked at students who applied to a highly selective university but instead attended a less selective school. How did these students fare—in terms of earnings—compared to those who attended the highly selective universities?

African-American and Hispanic students and students who came from families with less formal education did benefit financially from attending a highly selective university. But for everyone else, there was no meaningful difference in their later earnings. What Dale and Krueger discovered was that a stronger predictor of subsequent income than the school that one attended was the schools to which one applied. They dubbed this the "Steven Spielberg effect."[85] Rejected by both USC and UCLA film schools, the famous filmmaker attended Cal State Long Beach. As the study observed, "[e]vidently, students' motivation, ambition, and desire to learn have a much stronger effect on their subsequent success than the average academic ability of their classmates."

One would expect Yale graduates, given their higher SAT/ACT scores, family background, etc., to earn more on average than students from Long Island University. But are Yale students making as much as one would predict, based on their characteristics? One study sought to show the value a college added (in the form of lifting students above the earnings that would have been predicted based on their GPA and SAT/ACT scores).[86] As we see from the table in Appendix D, many of the *U.S. News* top-ranked colleges significantly underperform on this metric. Oberlin, Colorado College, Vassar, and Swarthmore, for example, were near the bottom. As seen in Appendix E, of all the Ivy League schools, only Harvard and Columbia were at the top of this list. Many universities that add the greatest value are ones you have likely never heard of, including Long Island University, Kettering College, and, once again, Babson College and Rose-Hulman Institute of Technology.

One 2018 economic study shows how competition backfires.[87] Parents and students focus on rankings and absolute levels of student achievement (such as the admitted students' average SAT or ACT scores). They undervalue what is critical, namely the amount of value that the college will actually deliver in improving a student's skills.

But even with this data, the siren song of competition for a place at one of those high-ranked *U.S. News* schools woos us. Fear and regret still motivate us. Yes, our children can succeed at many schools, but *it can't hurt if they got into Yale.* So, even when we know that the competition is toxic and irrational, we still compete.

Reflections

In September 2018, *U.S. News & World Report* reconfigured the way it would rank national universities and liberal arts colleges.[88] Rejection rate, which was a small component to begin with, was dropped from its metrics.

Will this end the arms race, or simply redirect it to other factors in the rankings? That remains unclear. But the 2019 *U.S. News* rankings is how 20 percent of academics and high school counselors perceive a college's academic quality. If rejection rates influence their perception of quality, we should expect more *Dear Genevieve* letters. And the letters indeed are arriving. In late September 2018, Tulane again told Genevieve that as a "priority consideration applicant" she will be considered "for partial merit scholarships ranging between $5,000 and $32,000 per year." (They must be cranking out so many *Dear Genevieve* letters that they never bother to wonder why, a year later, she is still a high school senior.) Wake Forest University's dean of admissions told Genevieve, "You're an interesting person, so we want to know more about you." As time was running out for early decision, Dean Martha Blevins Allman added, "Apply today because you could potentially do well at Wake Forest, and now's the time to show us." Likewise, in late October 2018, Genevieve was told, "Because of your impressive accomplishments, you've been chosen by University of Portland to apply with Priority Status." Of course, Genevieve never applied. She was busy chasing her tail. But that did not deter Portland's dean of admissions, who, unsolicited, extended Genevieve's application deadline so that she could receive her "Priority Status advantages" including immediate scholarship consideration. Plus, Dean Jason McDonald added, "we've waived your application fee!"

To return to our central theme: Competition, while often increasing our welfare and prosperity, can, at times, backfire. In those instances, the common cure—that is, more competition—may worsen the problem.

The economist Robert Frank predicted that in a hundred years, most economists will identify Charles Darwin, and not Adam Smith, as their discipline's intellectual father:

> As Darwin saw clearly, the fact that unfettered competition in nature often fails to promote the common good has nothing to do with monopoly exploitation. Rather, it's a simple consequence of an often sharp divergence between individual and group interests.[89]

Frank used the bull elk as an example. It is in each elk's interest to have relatively larger antlers to defeat other bull elks. But the larger antlers compromise the elks' mobility, handicapping the group overall.

At times in our daily life, it may be hard to say whether we are locked in a race to the top or bottom. Are we the lone losers in good competition? Or are many others also losing and harmed from this toxic competition? At other times, we suffer competition blindness, where we're told, notwithstanding the economic and emotional harm, more competition will cure our problems.

The problem is the belief by policy makers of competition as a magical cure-all. So whether it is school rankings, standardized tests, or vouchers, they have this faith in this one-stop solution. Policy makers "do not claim to know how exactly the market will achieve the promised miracle, but it will do it (indeed, for them this unpredictability is part of its appeal)."[90]

Once we stop assuming that competition is always beneficial, we will start seeing toxic competition all around us, and we'll have a better understanding of why companies seek to improve their relative competitive position by behaving unethically or misleading consumers[91]—why competition can sometimes encourage companies to invest less in legal compliance, pay kickbacks to secure business, underreport profits to avoid taxes, and manipulate the ordering protocols on liver transplants.[92]

So, we should not blindly accept policy makers' rhetoric for more competition. *Competition is good,* they tell us. *Not always,* we must learn to reply.

To distinguish between good and bad competition, policy makers must first ask whether individual and collective interests are aligned. If each market participant engages in the same behavior, are they and society better off overall? If yes, then competition might improve our overall welfare. But, if the answer is no, we next must ask whether the competitors or intended beneficiaries can de-escalate the race to the bottom.

Here skepticism is in order. If wealthy parents and three prestigious universities with over $68 billion in endowments cannot stop the race to the bottom in the rankings competition, why should we expect something different to happen in other markets? Powerful players may be powerless in preventing bad competition.

If de-escalation is not possible, then these markets will not correct themselves. Increasing competition will only spread the toxicity. But, as we'll later explore, this toxic competition is preventable. Policy makers can realign the competitive process and competitors' incentives, to promote a race to the top.

Until policy makers ask these questions, this toxic competition will continue. Our children or grandchildren will continue receiving *Dear Genevieve* letters. And policy makers, to fix the spiraling costs and deteriorating quality, will continue arguing for more competition.

CHAPTER 2

Second Overdose

"Excuse Me, Sir, I Did Not Order Horsemeat"

Like many, we enjoy our food. A hamburger made from high-quality beef tastes good; a high-quality hamburger that costs less, thanks to healthy competition, tastes even better. And for a while it seemed as though Europeans were getting exactly that because of the way market forces work to lower prices while maintaining (or even increasing) quality. Yet, a few years ago, Ariel, along with many Europeans, awoke to an alarming headline. We were consuming horsemeat in our hamburgers.

Little did we know that our beef burgers included meat from the Irish hunter horse Carnesella Lady, the Polish horses Trak and Wiktor, and countless other horses. How did we learn the horses' names? From the ID chips, roughly the size of a grain of rice, that were found in the meat.[1] Unbeknownst to their original owners, the horses, which were sold for slaughter, were relabeled as beef and found their way into the food supply chain.[2] As the horsegate scandal swept Europe, meat from horses as well as from pigs was discovered in what were alleged to be fresh beef, frozen beef burgers, and frozen meat-based ready-made meals.[3] Inspections of producers' warehouses found blocks of supposed beef that was made up of over 80 percent horsemeat.

Soon the finger-pointing began. Supermarkets blamed their suppliers, who blamed the meat traders. The shock from the unprecedented scale of fraud sent prosecutors and policy makers hunting for culprits. Some characterized horsegate as the work of a few seasoned criminals, intent on deceiving consumers for financial gain.

But nobody blamed competition. Indeed, the intense competition among Costco, Walmart, Tesco, Aldi, and other supermarkets is celebrated, credited with delivering tasty meat and meat-based meals at affordable prices. What could horsegate have to do with competition?

Competition, as we'll see, cannot magically produce high-quality, nutritious, healthy food at ever lower prices even as costs are increasing. Something must give. And that something is likely to be the weakest link—which is often quality.

Think of competition as a steam engine. When regulated and properly oiled, steam powers the pistons and the machine churns out products reliably and efficiently. Now imagine an unregulated, unmonitored competition machine in which, to accelerate the pistons, more coal is added to feed the hungry flames and the resulting pressure on the boiler's weaker bolts causes them to loosen and ultimately to give way.

From afar we do not hear the threads of the bolts being stripped and the rifle-like explosions of the loosened bolts ricocheting within the machine. To us it seems as though the competition machine is effortlessly accelerating the pistons of our economy. Policy makers marvel at the sight. But few care to inspect the internal workings of the competition machine. It is, after all, self-regulating. No monitoring is required because the invisible hand will ensure that the machine continues to work well. Competition in the marketplace will keep delivering affordable, tasty meals at ever lower costs, and all of us will benefit. Or so we think—until the internal pressure increases to the point that we end up with stories of horse and pig meat splattered across the front pages of our newspapers.

Welcome to our Second Overdose, where we consider the shrapnel resulting from the explosion of the loosely regulated, unmonitored competition machine and the damage it does—to quality, to the environment, to workers, to safety, and, ultimately, to us.

This toxic competition not only delivers Carnesella Lady to our grills.

Under certain conditions, competition can also pressure sellers to skimp on safety, to pollute, to grind away at wages and health benefits, and to turn places of work into sweatshops. As the pressure mounts, additional bolts snap, and rural economies disintegrate, resulting in bankruptcies, foreclosures, and even suicides.

Yet, because of our unquestioning assumption that competition is an unqualified good, we rarely put the blame where it belongs. Instead, policy makers find other reasons for the shrapnel. Indeed, in trying to give full sway to the benefits of competition, they often argue for further deregulation, thus unwittingly inviting even more degradation of quality. Their trust in the efficacy of the self-regulating competition machine is so profound that they consider safeguards to be the problem, inhibiting the workings of the machine. This means that any attempt at monitoring will be, at best, imperfect, and, at worst, nonexistent.

Horsemeat Anyone?

Leading up to the horsemeat scandal, the competition machine was overheating. In 2012, the UK retailer Tesco was aggressively discounting to lure back customers. Its weekly basket of thirty-three standard everyday items, which included fresh meat, bread, milk, fruit, vegetables, and other staples, was beating the price of the weekly baskets of its rivals Asda, Morrisons, Sainsbury's, and Waitrose. Sainsbury's countered with its Brand Match promotion scheme, which rang up the shopper's basket of groceries at the cash register and instantly calculated whether Asda and Tesco offered the branded goods at a lower price. If so, Sainsbury's gave the customer a coupon for an amount of money equivalent to the difference in price.[4]

We welcomed the competitive discounting, precisely because so many of us, in the fallout from the economic crisis, were already strapped for cash. Chart 2.1 reflects the disappearing banknotes in many UK households.

Chart 2.1

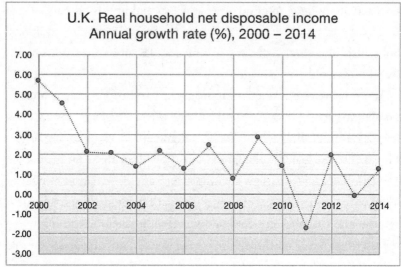

Source: OECD[5]

Even when eating out, most Britons in 2010–2012 were switching from the independent pubs and restaurants to the cheap meals at fast-food chains.[6] Another clear winner during this economic slump were the meat-based, ready-made meals offered by the supermarkets, which were increasingly popular, especially among lower-income households.[7]

The pressure within the competition machine to deliver tasty, affordable meals that could be easily popped into the oven or microwave kept intensifying. Italian ready-made meal sales alone were approaching £407 million in 2012, with pizza, lasagna, and spaghetti Bolognese topping the list.[8]

But as consumer demand for cheap, ready-made meals and inexpensive beef was increasing, ranchers' costs and therefore global beef prices were also escalating.[9]

Normally, with higher costs come higher prices. But because of the competitive pressure to hold the line on prices, supermarkets in turn pressured the meal preparers and beef suppliers. *We need to keep the price of the beef burgers and ready-made meal prices low*, the UK retailers reasoned, *otherwise our customers will turn to our rivals.* Over a three-year period the retail prices for ready-made meals in the United Kingdom remained roughly the same—£2.31, increasing by only a modest 4 percent.[10] To do this the supermarkets had to, in turn, pressure their suppliers to keep prices down. Given this pressure, by 2012 some meat processing plants had begun going out of business.[11]

With diminishing profits and mounting losses on the horizon, the options for some of the meat suppliers appeared dire: "cheat or die." Inevitably, some opted to cheat, which seemed the only way to relieve the competitive pressure. Looking around for the weakest bolts in the machine, they chose to compromise on quality. And that's how we ended up with horsemeat in our meals.

At the time horsemeat was roughly one-fifth the price of beef.[12] Pork was also cheaper. So the decision was made by some beef suppliers to add a little Carnesella Lady and a little pork to the mix. It was assumed that nobody would notice, and for a while that assumption proved correct and the pressure temporarily eased. But as cattle supplies got tighter, and ranchers' costs continued to escalate, beef prices reached new records.[13] Another bolt in the competition machine popped. So a little more pork and horsemeat were added to the supply chain and found their way to beef burgers, lasagna, spaghetti Bolognese, and meatballs. And a little more.

The cheating extravaganza continued until November 2012, when the Irish Food Safety Authority tested a range of cheap frozen beef burgers and supermarket ready-made meals. To its astonishment, it found horse DNA in over one-third of the beef burger samples and pig DNA in 85 percent of them.[14] As more foods were tested, it was revealed that the "beef" in some meals was actually 80 percent horse.[15]

In the United Kingdom, the horsegate scandal led to prosecutions (though it wasn't until 2017 that the first UK convictions resulting in prison sentences were handed down, with one man sentenced to four and a half years, another to three and a half, and a suspended sentence given to a third man). During the proceedings the court heard how "when processing to meet the low prices set by the supermarkets, manufacturers generally put out a call to traders to supply blocks of frozen meat at the cheapest price possible. By substituting much cheaper horsemeat, the traders on trial were able to increase their profits by 30 to 40 percent."[16]

To better understand how mainstream food producers found themselves selling horsemeat, let's start in Ireland. Some of the horsemeat came from Silvercrest, an Irish factory that was part of the ABP Food Group, which was one of Europe's leading beef processors. On its website, ABP promotes its "Grass Advantage" and stress-free cattle.[17] ABP says its goal is to ensure that its cattle "are relaxed and stress-free prior to slaughter." Apparently, stress-free cows have lower premortem glycogen levels and pH balance, which makes the meat tenderer.[18] We imagine happy cattle grazing contentedly off Ireland's green coasts, delivering, according to the company, "natural, sustainable" grass-fed beef that is "low in saturated fat, high in vitamins and minerals and always Ultra-Tender.®"

So how did this organization get mixed up with horsemeat? ABP publicly blamed "rogue Silvercrest managers [who] had strayed from specifications in buying some meat from an Irish trader." ABP claimed that they, too, "were victims of the fraud and had no idea they had ever handled horse."[19]

But why would rogue managers jeopardize their careers by buying worn-out old farm horses instead of happy cows? We turned to a key figure in unraveling the horsemeat fraud, Chris Elliott, OBE, of the Queen's University Belfast. The soft-spoken professor recounted how the competitive pressure in the industry caught up to ABP, which, in order to deal with these outside pressures, brought the competition steam engine into its own company. To stimulate competition, efficiency, and lower prices, ABP was pitting its meat processing subsidiaries against each other—until one of them became so desperate that it did what it felt it had to do to survive:

This was an unintended consequence of driving competition inside the ABP group. Each of the companies owned by ABP was pressurized to reduce costs and increase efficiency, in competition with each other. Working toward competitive targets, and in an attempt to keep up with the competition within the ABP group, "Silvercrest" began buying meat outside the specifications as set by the supermarkets. The pressure on price and the departure from technical specification has exposed the supply chain to fraud, with devastating results.[20]

Intense competition, greed, opportunity, and lack of sufficient monitoring all contributed to the horsemeat scandal. But we don't often hear about scandals of such magnitude. So, we may think the horsemeat scandal is an anomaly, a once-in-a-lifetime event. However, once we begin to question some of the underlying assumptions about the self-regulating competition machine, we'll start seeing the shrapnel all around us.

Alas, there's nothing unique about horsegate. Maybe it's uniquely horrifying because our stomachs churn at the thought, but it's only too typical of what happens under the pressure of competition when there are no safeguards in place to prevent the whole machine from blowing up. Yet, we persist in thinking that such disasters are the exception. One reason is that we have an overblown faith in our own ability to detect fraud. We are sure we recognize quality when we see it—or taste it.

Do We Get What We Pay For?

We often trust that we know how to identify a bargain, to get more for less. As smart shoppers, we compare prices, collect coupons, and sometimes read the nutrition facts label on the food package. Our aim: to get a quality product that satisfies our needs at a reasonable and, if possible, low price.

Our expectation is that competition will deliver exactly that. We believe that market forces, besides lowering prices, should result in improvements in product quality, the level of services, the number of choices, and, ultimately, our welfare, while eliminating the slackers and the cheaters. Walking into Costco, Walmart, or Kroger, we feel confident that we'll enjoy both higher quality and lower prices because of the miraculous power of competition.

Our trust in the formidable competition machine is based on two assumptions. Suppliers lack the incentive to lower quality for a given price, because:

- consumers can accurately assess any quality difference; and
- any changes to quality will be quickly communicated to us by competitive producers and sellers or other customers.

We can readily see how these assumptions can be woven together into the strong, coherent, logical story line we tell ourselves. If the retailer or its supplier cannot degrade quality, then no worries. We'll get what we ordered. But if retailers do try to sneak us horsemeat, we'll taste the difference. And because we'll quickly detect the difference in quality, competition will pressure retailers to ensure that we'll get beef, not horsemeat. And even if our own taste buds (or quality control mechanisms) don't detect the horsemeat, somebody else's will. A leading supermarket chain will gleefully tell shoppers what's in its competitor's lasagna. Given this risk, supermarkets will have a stake in ensuring the quality of their beef lasagna.

These two assumptions seem so intuitively correct that the competition machine appears fraud-proof. Even if we increase the competitive pressure, competition will continue to deliver high-quality beef burgers, at a low price.[21] Weak bolts should not concern us.

While intuitively appealing, these assumptions are not airtight. If they were, we wouldn't end up with horsemeat.

In some markets, the competition machine, under intense pressure, will exert its greatest stress on quality—often the weakest component in the supply chain. Competition turns toxic under the following conditions:

- **FIRST**, suppliers face increasing costs at the same time that there is intense competitive pressure to lower price.
- **SECOND**, with diminishing profits and mounting losses, some suppliers will choose the path of least resistance to survive, looking for any and all weak bolts in the machine. One such path (though only one of many) is to reduce costs. But having bought cheaper materials to lower their costs, they maintain a façade—selling the lower-quality product under the same brand name as before. This requires evading whatever quality controls exist and lying to the consumer.
- **THIRD**, consumers, contrary to their expectations, do not in fact notice this degradation. They continue to assume that the competition machine works. In fact, since their own wages are squeezed and their work benefits have been pared, they are delighted when the retailer lowers the price for the beef lasagna. Similarly, the retailers themselves often remain unaware of the degradation as they lack appropriate monitoring tools and quality controls.
- **FINALLY**, it is difficult and costly for others to convey to consumers the quality differences in goods and services that might prompt consumers to switch. Supermarkets do not regularly test their beef lasagna, much less that of their rivals. They, too, assume that the competition machine is working. Just as consumers have expectations about retailers, the retailers have expectations about their suppliers. Surely no meat seller would jeopardize its relationship with a buyer by adding horsemeat to its beef products.

Under these four conditions, we can see how intense competition, loose quality controls, and limited consumer ability to detect the quality erosion create a toxic mix. It may take a surprisingly long time before we see the competition machine explode. Or we might never see it. The horsemeat may not be discovered. In other industries, suppliers looking for cheaper prices—in a faster and faster race to the bottom—search abroad for locales where the environmental and labor regulations are laxer, the factories dingier and more dangerous, the workers younger, and the wages lower. Now let us explore, in greater detail, each of these conditions.

The Four Conditions

First, intense competitive pressure

Price wars are hailed as a boon to consumers. Indeed, often they are. But at times, intense competition may backfire. As we illustrated above, supermarkets pressure suppliers to keep costs down, so that we get everyday low prices. The name of the game is for consumers to *perceive* the retailer as having the lowest price.[22] Whoever sells the cheapest beef (or whatever) wins the competition. In response to competitive pressure, companies can lower price, by lowering costs. The UK retailers followed this cost-cutting, price-lowering strategy for their ready-made meals. Enough said.

Second, with diminishing profitability, suppliers keep looking for whatever weak bolts they can find, in order to survive

So which bolt will pop first in the competition machine? The weakest is usually the first to go. Often, the weakest bolt is quality, as we saw with horsemeat, and a few dishonest traders can find ways to cheat on quality in order to maintain their competitive edge. But quality degradation may go beyond the work of a few fraudsters. It can be much more widespread, may even be company policy, and may actually be legal—albeit enacted in a very quiet, borderline dishonest way.

At times, for example, the degradation of our food supply is selectively applied to particular territories and consumers. The Europeans labeled this practice "food apartheid." If you recently traveled to some eastern European countries, your strawberry yogurt likely had 40 percent less strawberries than in the same brand of yogurt in Austria, and your child's fish fingers likely had less fish, as was revealed in 2017, when Europe awoke to another food scandal. This time it was discovered that many producers were discriminating against eastern European shoppers by using the same packaging to peddle inferior versions of their well-known products.[23]

In one study, up to half of the foods examined were shown to have less meat, more fats, more artificial sweeteners, and more preservatives in the versions available to eastern Europeans.[24] Headlines of "food racism" and "Europe food apartheid" revealed the fury of shoppers when they found out.[25]

Defending their quality degradation practice, the producers claimed that they had adjusted their products to meet national tastes. And yet, whatever their justification, they chose to bury detailed information about what exactly was in these products in the fine print on the labels—while using the same branding and packaging as the superior versions of the products. The European Commissioner in charge called this practice "manifest cheating."[26] The Czech secretary of state for EU affairs, Aleš Chmelař, refuted the argument that national tastes drove the degradation: "A luncheon meat was tested as part of our study . . . It contains normal pork in Germany and contains mechanically extracted poultry, a general mixture, in the Czech Republic. In this case, I don't think you can really argue about taste or preferences."[27]

So if you live on the other side of the tracks, you can expect that many of the products available to you will be inferior. Even if you are aware of the degradation, your choices nonetheless remain limited.

But the competition machine has more work to do. Under ever-increasing cost pressures, it will find ways to lower quality for those of us in well-to-do countries and neighborhoods, too. Now we'll experience other forms of degradation that are not illegal.

An economy beef burger in the United Kingdom, for example, can legally include as little as 47 percent beef. Beef and chicken can be enhanced with additives—categorized as "seasoning"—including fat, water, and concentrated proteins (often made from pork rind).[28] In the United States, hydrated textured soy flour is added to beef patties to reduce raw material costs by 18 percent.[29]

So we shouldn't be surprised when water is injected into our pork, chicken, and fish;[30] when cheap beef waste and water are injected into our chicken nuggets;[31] or when water is the main ingredient in our sauces.[32]

As the competitive pressure mounts, firms, as in the horsemeat scandal, will be increasingly tempted to engage not just in legal (if ethically dubious) degradation but in outright fraud. This happens with a wide variety of products in many different places.

In Sweden, a conspiracy to repackage out-of-date meat was exposed and led to a criminal investigation into four stores in the Swedish ICA supermarket chain.[33] In Asia, McDonald's sales dropped after the discovery that its supplier repackaged old meat as new.[34] In Italy, leading olive oil producers sold their lower-grade olive oil as expensive extra-virgin olive oil.[35] After the revelation of the Italian olive oil fraud, a University of California study that tested 186 samples of olive oil estimated that 69 percent of all store-bought extra-virgin olive oils in the United States probably were fake.[36]

Spices are another product susceptible to fraud. To gain a competitive edge, some suppliers sell lower-priced "look-alikes," thereby undercutting the providers of spices that are genuine. In the United States, tests carried on dried oregano sold in outlets revealed 25 percent of the samples were adulterated.[37] In Australia, similar tests revealed an "oregano fraud" as dried oregano jars included olive leaves and other undisclosed ingredients.[38] Astonishingly, one jar of oregano contained less than 10 percent of actual oregano leaves.

But the competitive pressure will not only undermine the quality of our food. Increasing pressure will find other weak bolts all along the supply chain.

The increasing demand for inexpensive meat, for example, has led to industrial farming. To increase their growth, cattle today are injected with natural and synthetic versions of estrogen, progesterone, and testosterone.[39] (One concern is the potential risks to human health from hormone residues in meat and meat products treated with six hormones used for growth promotion.)[40] The cattle ranchers aren't greedy. Nor is there a sinister design. But when competitive pressures get down to their level, squeezing their already thin profit margins, the ranchers also have to do something to stay in business. So, they pump cattle with growth-promoting hormones and antibiotics to improve efficiency and ultimately survive.

Chicken and fish farmers come under similar pressures. The competition machine can encourage farmers and slaughterhouses to skimp on safety and sanitary conditions. According to one Spanish news report, in order to lower prices, Vietnamese fish farmers were raising pangasius (also known as shark catfish) "in unclean cages and fed with nonindustrialized feed like dead fish and other food waste."[41]

The pressure for inexpensive chicken raises many environmental concerns. Arsenic, along with other metals, for many years, was added in the United States to the chicken feed "to prevent disease, improve weight gain and feed conversion, and increase egg production."[42] About 70 percent of broiler chickens in the United States were fed arsenic. But chickens can absorb only a small percentage of the arsenic they ingest. Most of the arsenic ends up in waste, which is used as fertilizer. The arsenic-laced manure is absorbed in the soil, seeps into the groundwater, and with runoff after rainfalls, enters our water supply. (The US Food and Drug Administration, during the Obama administration, withdrew marketing approvals for arsenic-based feed additives.)[43] But arsenic-based feed additives, noted one 2017 study, "are still legally and widely used in food animal production in many countries."[44] The study found that the "incremental lifetime cancer risk (bladder and lung cancer) from dietary exposure to arsenic contained in chicken meat products on local markets was above the serious or priority level for 70 percent of the adult populations in Guangzhou, China."

Moving further along the supply chain we find another weak bolt in the competition machine—the laborers. Faced with increasing competitive pressure to keep prices low, producers will look for places that provide cheaper labor, and looser controls over working and environmental conditions. We have only to consider the factories where our mobile phones, laptops, and tablets are produced to find a multitude of examples of this kind of exploitation. Be it inhumanly long hours, dangerous workplaces, or starvation-level wages, the working conditions of those who produce our gadgets are likely to be in violation of any reasonable interpretation of employees' rights.[45] We tend to close our eyes to the conditions that make it possible for us to enjoy our electronic toys at such low prices, especially because many of the factories that produce them are in faraway countries like China and Vietnam.[46] But there is no denying that our pleasure comes at the expense of other people's suffering.

The clothing and garment industry does no better.[47] And the abuses are not confined to countries somewhere far across the globe. According to an official in the US Department of Labor, the garment industry is marked by widespread minimum wage, overtime, and record-keeping violations, which deprive thousands of workers of money they are owed. Some of these domestic factories are the modern-day equivalent of sweatshops.

As companies go on the chase for cheaper labor, competitive pressure may eventually tempt them to take ever more radical steps until they sink to employing slave and child labor. In one example, children were taken from Mali and forced to work in appalling conditions on the cocoa plantations in Ivory Coast.[48] With guns pointed at them, the twelve- to fourteen-year-olds worked inhumanly long days—sometimes as long as fourteen hours—with no pay.

As the appellate court judges, in one US case, noted:

The use of child slave labor in the Ivory Coast is a humanitarian tragedy. Studies by International Labour Organization, UNICEF, the Department of State, and numerous other organizations have confirmed that thousands of children are forced to work without pay in the Ivorian economy. Besides the obvious moral implications, this widespread use of child slavery contributes to poverty in the Ivory Coast, degrades its victims by treating them as commodities, and causes long-term mental and physical trauma.[49]

Some of the child slaves escaped and sued the largest buyers of cocoa beans in the world, namely Nestlé USA, Inc., Archer Daniels Midland Company, Cargill Incorporated Company, and Cargill Cocoa. They claimed that these companies knew of Ivory Coast's child slavery problem.[50] And, in fact, Nestlé acknowledged its awareness of child and slave labor in its Ivorian supply chain for cocoa, but in a court of law made the remarkable argument "that it has no duty to disclose labor conditions in its supply chain because the information at issue does not relate to product safety."[51] The court agreed, albeit on broader grounds: Companies are not legally required to disclose on the packaging of their products child slavery or labor abuses in their supply chain.[52]

No doubt the child labor and slavery problem has complex political, social, and economic causes. But intense competition, with limited safeguards, surely plays a large role. The demand for chocolate is increasing, and rising demand usually results in larger profits for those who supply a product. Not here, however. The average cocoa farmer in Ivory Coast and Ghana still lives well below the international poverty line.[53] With companies looking to find the cheapest sources of cocoa, the cocoa farmers find themselves in a cutthroat competition that means they can't raise their prices.[54] Why? Many cocoa farms are small and have no power to resist these competitive pressures; even the cocoa cooperatives often lack bargaining power. So competition causes the cocoa farmers to seek out ever cheaper sources of labor.

And it is not just cocoa. In 2016, Nestlé and Jacobs Douwe Egberts admitted that their coffee might have come from Brazilian plantations that use slave labor.[55] Nestlé also admitted that the seafood it purchased in Thailand for its Fancy Feast cat food brand came from slave labor.[56]

Common to all of the above examples is the single-minded focus on price—which begins at the consumer level and affects every other level of the supply chain. The consumers, trusting in the magic of the competition machine and enjoying the low prices that result, would seem to be the beneficiaries of all this fierce competition, and therefore it is perhaps not surprising that they don't want to peer into the inner workings of the machine to see what makes their cheap hamburgers, candy bars, coffee, and clothing possible. Nor do they insist on a tightening of the regulations that would protect them from inferior quality and prevent the abuse of those who labor to supply their products. After all, "if it's not broke, don't fix it."

But consumers and customers might be more concerned if they understood that in some instances they themselves may suffer the consequences of this laxness—consequences that have the potential to be far worse than a meal of horsemeat.

Airlines provide a useful illustration. In another example of "legal degradation," the airlines' constant drive for greater efficiency and higher savings has led some operators to carry less fuel per flight than many pilots think advisable. Pilots in the United Kingdom and elsewhere have complained about being under pressure from the airlines to minimize costs by carrying the lowest fuel reserves permitted by EU regulations.[57] According to the EU regulatory framework, planes must carry enough fuel to reach their destination as well as alternative airports contained in their flight plan plus an additional thirty minutes flying time and a final approach before landing.[58]

Lighter planes are cheaper to fly, but are they safe? Usually, low fuel incidents take place in the event of bad weather, when planes tend to have to remain in the air longer than originally planned.[59] As one pilot reported: "I'm constantly under pressure to carry less fuel than I'm comfortable with . . . Sometimes if you carry just enough fuel and you hit thunderstorms or delays, then suddenly you're running out of gas and you have to go to an alternate airport."[60]

Figures published by the UK Civil Aviation Authority reveal increasing numbers of instances in which pilots had to make emergency landings at British airports because of fuel shortages.[61] The "legality" of the practice should not mask the risk of these Mayday landings.[62] The pilots' union, BALPA, raised concerns about the dangers, which are not limited to the plane issuing the Mayday call:

Aircraft flying on low fuel not only put that aircraft potentially at risk, but also impact on the wider operation. Handling an aircraft on low-fuel means that other aircraft may have to hold longer to give appropriate priority to the emergency aircraft resulting in a possible "avalanche effect." It is natural, in such a competitive industry, for airlines to look to carry as little fuel as they can in order to save weight and save money. But that commercial pressure must never be at the expense of ensuring a safe flight.[63]

Fuel shortage incidents that result in emergency landings don't just occur in the United Kingdom, of course. On a single day on July 2012, no fewer than three Ryanair flights prevented from arriving at their destination in Madrid because of bad weather had to make emergency landings 300 kilometers away in Valencia when they ran short of fuel. This prompted the Spanish transport ministry to launch an investigation and led the Spanish consumers' association to issue a strong condemnation,

accusing Ryanair of putting passengers' safety at risk and calling for a
€4.5 million fine together with a three-year suspension of its operating
license should the investigation confirm any wrongdoing. Ryanair was
eventually ordered to "review" the amount of fuel it carries. Strictly
speaking, however, it did not violate the rules, and the watchdogs ultimately accepted that all three Ryanair planes had left for Madrid "with
fuel in excess of flight plan requirements" and also with fuel "in excess of
the minimum diversion" as required.

Thus, a Ryanair spokesman was able to honestly state that "All three
aircraft landed with reserve fuel of at least 30 minutes (300 miles) additional flying—in full compliance with published Boeing and European
Aviation Safety Agency safety requirements." Thirty minutes may not
seem like a generous margin to passengers, however, who may well wonder why this state of affairs is allowed to continue, especially when pilots
themselves (some of whom have been rebuked by Ryanair for taking on
more fuel than company policy allows) are concerned. One may also
wonder how competition between manufacturers of airplanes affects
their fuel recommendations.

So, when the competitive pressure intensifies, and there are few safeguards against the results, what we see is that weaker bolts all along
the supply chain start popping. Horsemeat gets into our beef. Slime is
dumped into our waterways. Pilots nervously check their fuel gauges.
Children work inhuman hours in the factories that produce our clothing, and slaves harvest cocoa, coffee beans, and other commodities.

Third, consumers do not notice the quality degradation

So, why don't we see the competition machine's shrapnel flying across
the sky? There are many reasons inferior quality and other problems can
be hard to detect, starting with our fallible taste buds—think horsemeat.
Think also about the tomato sauce you buy. Companies may unethically
(yet legally) lower the quality through small incremental changes, like
adding water and cheaper tomatoes to the sauce. In acclimating to the

slow erosion of quality over the years, we forget what the sauce tasted like when our grandmother made it, and we simply trust the brand (or are too busy to read the labels, where the amount of water and additives is revealed in the fine print).[64]

For many products and services, assessments of quality are so individual that they are hard to measure objectively.[65] Even when some attributes are measurable, the overall perception of quality is often based on a combination of multiple factors and a complex, subjective, and imprecise assessment.[66]

Marketers are well aware of our inability to assess quality with any precision. And given how price-conscious we generally are, the method some have devised for exploiting that inability is oddly counterintuitive, in that it rests on our sense that higher price signals higher quality.

Suppose, for example, that you are tasting two different wines—a cheap one and an expensive one. Will knowledge of the price affect your perception of the taste? Of course not. You are sure you can taste the difference. But researchers at the Stanford Graduate School of Business and the California Institute of Technology tested this proposition.[67] They hooked subjects to a brain imaging machine to gauge their brain activity. Then they gave the subjects glasses of wine and told them they were tasting two different wines, one that cost $5, the other $45—when, in fact, they were tasting the same wine. But the part of the brain that experiences pleasure became more active when the drinkers thought they were drinking the more expensive vintage.

So not only do we expect the higher-priced wine to taste better, we actually experience measurably greater pleasure in drinking it—even if it is in fact the same as the cheaper wine. Other behavioral experiments have confirmed the signaling power of higher prices.[68]

Some companies don't just price their products higher to signal quality; they actually highlight the price as part of their marketing strategy. In the 1980s, for example, a leading Belgian beer producer launched an advertising campaign that stated that its beer was "Reassuringly Expensive."

This ingenious campaign, which ran over two decades, encapsulated the notion that high quality is worth paying for. As the brewery advertised, "Perfection has a Price." The campaign successfully shifted customers' focus from comparing beer prices to comparing quality, the tacit assumption being that lower-priced beers were not as good. Based on what the Stanford researchers found in their wine test, we can probably assume that the high price of the beer also enhanced the enjoyment of those privileged enough to consume it.

Such marketing is not deception per se; it's just taking advantage of what is known about the way our brains work. Understanding this natural limitation to our rationality is one of many steps we must take to understand why the competition machine may sometimes deliver less than expected.

Other kinds of products besides beer and wine may also use price as a proxy for superior quality—which the product may or may not possess. In one experiment, nearly all the participants reported less pain after taking a placebo priced at $2.50 per dose; when the same placebo was discounted to $0.10 per dose, only half of the participants experienced less pain.[69]

Similarly, a study of MIT students who paid full price for the SoBe Adrenaline Rush beverage showed that they reported less fatigue than the students who paid one-third of the regular price for the same drink.[70] And when SoBe Adrenaline Rush was promoted as energy for the mind, students who paid the regular price for the drink got on average nine correct responses to a word puzzle in the thirty minutes allotted to them compared to students who paid a discounted price for the same drink, who got on average six and a half questions right.

Indeed, our minds work in mysterious ways. Which is why a drug manufacturer may not want to price its drug lower than other comparable pills even if it could still make a decent profit. If consumers perceive the lower price as a signal of inferior quality, companies are actually incentivized to keep their prices high, regardless of whether the price is warranted by any attributes of the drug itself.

Price can serve as a marker of quality in products much more mundane than fine wines, beer, or even drugs or energy drinks. Why on earth do we pay 33 percent more for Clorox liquid bleach than for others?[71] Again, presumably because we think we get what we pay for, in this case a more powerful whitening and cleaning agent. But, as the US Supreme Court noted in the 1960s, "all liquid bleach is chemically identical."[72] Even back then Clorox had invested millions of dollars in advertising and promotions to imprint in our grandparents' and parents' minds its superior value.[73]

Yet, all of these examples are just the beginning of why we so often fail to understand problems with the products and services sold to us. We don't have enough knowledge to think to ask how much fuel is in the planes we fly, nor are we aware that the regional airlines, which now account for more than half of all domestic flights in the United States, for example, operate under safety standards that are different from those of the major airlines.[74] Environmental pollution is often invisible. The sweatshop workers who make our clothes and the factory workers who produce our electronics often labor in places that are far away from us. And it may seem simply inconceivable that the cocoa beans that made the chocolate in our candy were harvested by slaves. Few people are even aware that slavery still exists in the modern world. And then there's the simple fact that we don't want to see the shrapnel, because we are so happy with the low prices.

But even if we want to see it, we may simply be unable to trace the cause of any problems we experience. If we get sick, for example, even if we suspect it was from something we ate, we may not know which meal was contaminated. Was it the pork or the soup we ate at dinner? Or the sandwich we had for lunch? And even if we are certain which meal caused it, we may not know the particular ingredient that was contaminated.

As several researchers noted, "If the place of purchase/consumption is known, the producer of the specific food may be unknown because the store may have bought meat or poultry products from many suppliers, obscuring the producer's identity."[75]

Or think about your recent travel. Did you get a cold or flu right after you were on a plane? You may not be aware of the degradation of air quality in airplanes, but your recent illness may be linked to poor air circulation, and the latter linked to savings achieved in the face of extreme competition.[76] Or it may not—and you may never know which is true.

In the end, despite our innocent faith that the invisible hand will do right by us, that competition will always benefit the consumer, our faith is not warranted. We don't always get what we pay for, and, worse still, we often don't know that we didn't. But surely we can count on competitors to the companies that sold us the substandard goods to tell us we've been had. Right?

Fourth, it is difficult or costly for other sellers to convey to consumers the degradation and prompt them to switch

What all of the above examples make clear is this: The competition machine does not necessarily reward quality. When faced with a choice between surviving competitive pressures or going under, individuals and companies at all levels of the supply chain may compromise on everything from the quality of the product they supply to the morality of their employment practices—the hope always being that their practices can escape detection.

And for all the reasons discussed, sometimes their strategy works. But why, one has to wonder, don't their rivals call them on it? Isn't it in the interest of the sellers of genuine beef products to point out to consumers that those meals that bear the cheaper prices have horsemeat, not beef, in them? That our clothes sell for higher prices because we pay our employees fairly, unlike Company X? That our plane fares are higher because we have a greater concern for safety than Company Y? That our chickens cost more because they were raised humanely and in ways that don't pollute the environment?

At times, sellers can't convey to consumers the quality degradation, as they, too, are unaware of it. British Airways doesn't know how much fuel is in Ryanair's jets.

Also, when customers lack the knowledge and expertise to assess product quality accurately, firms recognize that they may not be rewarded for improving quality. More competition may not yield greater quality when (i) firms have difficulty explaining the quality improvement to the consumer, (ii) rivals can confuse consumers with similar claims, (iii) consumers cannot readily identify the better quality products, and (iv) as a result, the honest sellers' sales do not increase. In those instances, the cost in improving quality outweighs the likely gain. Competition instead favors the more crooked dealers.

In many markets, one side knows more than the other. We know more about our health, diet, etc. than our life insurers. Used car salespeople know more about their cars' condition than we do. This imbalance in information, as the Nobel laureate economist George Akerlof described, can create a "market for lemons."[77] It explains why competition in markets with imperfect information flow can actually be a disincentive to sellers to invest in quality.

Akerlof showed how a lemon problem may affect the used car market. Suppose driving to and from work you pass the used car lot. Then you see the British racing-green Jaguar that captured your imagination over a decade ago. You have no credible information about the true condition and value of the Jaguar. Sure, you can get a mechanic to inspect it. You might also check the service records for that Jag on Carfax. But you, like many buyers, cannot distinguish the lemon from the higher-quality Jag. You face the risk of overpaying for a defective used car (a lemon).

So what do you, like many buyers, do? All the used Jaguar dealers tout their cars as high quality. Some dealers might disparage other dealers. You don't know which one to trust. So you offer less money for the used car. Competition in these markets favors the crooked sellers with lemons. Even if you, like many other buyers, pay the average Blue Book price, the crooked sellers still profit, as they obtain a premium above the defective car's real value.

On the other hand, the honest sellers of high-quality used cars are poorly rewarded. They told you they were honest. But unless they can effectively tell you why you should believe them, you can't tell whether they are telling the truth or exaggerating like the other dealers. So unless they can develop a reputation for honesty, which customers reward, the honest sellers eventually will exit the market. In this environment, sellers have less incentive to improve the quality of the cars they sell. No one will invest in turning a lemon into lemonade.

Moreover, firms won't tell consumers when they can profit more by also degrading quality. Companies, under competitive pressure to trim costs, may simply degrade the healthiness of their foods with cheaper ingredients and fillers.

The irony of the horsemeat scandal was that the filler was actually healthier than other additives. Competition can pressure companies to engineer foods with fats, sugar, and salt that appeal to our desires, but that contribute to the obesity crisis.

Sometimes companies degrade quality (in terms of its healthiness) precisely because the additives make it addictive. We hear of late how sugar might be as addictive as cocaine.[78] Suppose your rival starts adding more sugar to its yogurt. Consumers crave the taste. Are you really going to gain sales by telling customers about what rivals are doing? Or will you simply join the fray? As the CEO of General Mills said, "Bottom line being, though, that we need to ensure that our products taste good, because our accountability is also to our shareholders. And there's no way we could start down-formulating the usage of salt, sugar, fat if the end result is going to be something that people do not want to eat."[79]

Kellogg's, for example, prepared for a reporter special versions of some of its most iconic products without any salt. The purpose was to show why the company was having trouble cutting back on salt:

And, I have to say, it was a god-awful experience . . . starting with Cheez-Its, which normally I could eat all day long. The Cheez-Its without salt stuck to the roof of my mouth and I could barely swallow. Then we moved onto frozen waffles, which tasted like straw. The real moment came in tasting a cereal—I think it was Corn Flakes— which tasted hugely, awfully metallic. It was almost like a filling had come out of my mouth and it was sloshing around.[80]

Imagine a rival offered the Corn Flakes that tasted like our dental fillings. Would you buy it?

Thus the competition machine can pressure producers to add sweeteners and flavors to their processed meals to optimize taste. We crave it. No competitor can afford to spoil the party with a blander, unsweetened, salt-free version. The intense competition can induce companies to not only exploit our taste buds, but our weaknesses. So, don't expect these sellers to convey to consumers the quality degradation.

Reflections

Although an unregulated competition machine will sometimes deliver lower prices and higher quality, all too often when the pressure becomes too great those who drive the overheated machine will seek out the weaker bolts—whether food quality, safety, the environment, or labor conditions—and compromise them. Regulators and policy makers, for reasons that we will explore more fully in Part II, may respond to such abuses not by tightening up on controls, but loosening them even further. This may be the result of ideology, poor judgment, or lobbying.

The solution, however, is not simply more regulation, but rather regulatory awareness. Call it smart regulation—regulatory policy that takes into account not just the benefits but also the drawbacks of the competitive process.

Industry itself has a role to play in devising procedures that will ensure the safety and integrity of its products. Better internal safeguards and closer inspections and monitoring may be needed to check for hairline cracks in all those vulnerable bolts and can do wonders to limit degradation. Our final chapter will consider how, for example, the UK food industry reacted to the horsemeat scandal and established the Food Industry Intelligence Network to control quality. We'll also discuss how it is within our power, as consumers, to promote competition that actually benefits us. But before delving into solutions, we need to fully understand the scope of the toxic competition, and where better to explore this than Las Vegas.

CHAPTER 3

Third Overdose

Exploiting Human Weakness

Imagine a bargain-hunting antitrust professor, excited about an upcoming trip, going online to book his hotel. After spending an hour or two searching various sites for the best hotel offer, he finds what he thinks is a great value. Triumphantly, he proceeds with the booking. Vegas, baby!

As he clicks through on the website, getting ever deeper into the complicated reservation process, other pressing needs, like picking the kids up from school, loom. With only fifteen minutes until he has to leave to get them, he realizes he has to finish this reservation fast.

Wait . . . little fees keep being tacked onto that offer he thought was so great.

Does he ignore the additional credit card fee and city tax? Yes, he does. Time's a-wasting, there are now only ten minutes until he has to leave, and besides, there's nothing to be done about these fees. Ready to hit confirm, he sees yet another fee—something called a "resort fee," which is quite hefty—being added into his total. Does he finish the reservation or decide to start over later with another website—which is likely to be doing the same thing?

As though sensing his hesitation, the hotel website now starts its own countdown. It informs him that ten other customers are also looking at the exact same room. If he waits until after school pickup, the deal on the room might vanish.

Wait . . . suddenly it's twenty-three people who are now looking at this room. How did that happen? A red signal flashes: "In high demand!" The pressure is mounting, and it's now only seven minutes until he has to leave for school pickup—and another kind of countdown starts, because if he's late, the school will charge for aftercare.

The digital clock on the screen now provides an apocalyptic countdown—the discount is seemingly on life support. He's seen this happen before and knows that if the clock winds down, he'll get a message like this: "You just missed it! Our last room sold out a few seconds ago. Your dates are popular—we've run out of rooms at this property! Check out more below."

With a sense of resignation, rather than his initial triumph, he hits the purchase button. A pop-up window congratulates him for grabbing the discount over his tardy rivals. It reassures him that he saved 45 percent in comparison to the list price. Great—it seems that all turned out well in the end.

Until the day he reaches the hotel on the Vegas Strip and reality begins to set in. Smiles greet him at the reception desk where he's told about some minor issues that need to be addressed. No, sir, the resort fee does not include fast Wi-Fi connection or access to the spa. Nor does the resort fee cover parking—by valet or by himself. Actually, he has no idea what the resort fee is supposed to cover because it's not spelled out anywhere. But he's here to have a good time, he reminds himself, as part of his stress-reducing program, so he goes with the flow and hands over his new credit card.

The card offer came with a very low annual interest rate. It was surprisingly low, in fact—far better than what the other card companies seemed to be offering. Sure, it was a temporary teaser rate. Probably somewhere way down there in the fine print there's something about when that rate expires and also something about overdraft fees. But he was too busy to take the time to read it. And besides, those charges are irrelevant to him. He intends to pay in full and on time. He'll never carry a balance.

Five days later his vacation is over. He enjoyed himself in Vegas and liked his hotel, but as he is checking out, he sees a few other unanticipated charges on the bill. Twenty bucks for extra towels? That $100-a-night room has ended up costing double what he'd expected. But there's no time to argue. His plane is leaving soon, and the rescheduling fee is more than the airfare. Later that month, another surprise awaits him. His new credit card apparently has a higher interest rate than he expected and sky-high late fees, too, which he discovered after he overlooked his bill because so much work had piled up on his desk while he was on vacation. His assumption that he would always pay on time has already been proved wrong.

Astonishingly, all of this takes place in two intensely competitive markets—hotels and credit cards—where, in theory, the power of competition will mean that we consumers can expect to get great deals, where our interests will reign supreme as the merchants fight tooth and nail for our business. And yet, even in an environment where competition is so rich, we can still receive less than we bargained for—a lot less.

We've already seen toxic competition among helmetless hockey players. We've seen toxic competition as a steam engine spewing horsemeat. Now, imagine competition as a turquoise sea. Its waves, cooling our toes and inviting us to take the plunge, call us seaward. We accept the invitation. We go with the flow and with every stroke we glide farther from the security of our beach towels.

As we frolic in these waters, enjoying ourselves, something tells us we should turn around. But our strokes are slackening and we are carried farther into the sea. Swimming harder to try to return, we are caught up in rip currents we hadn't seen, which pull us seaward at eight feet per second, and the beach keeps receding. We're in over our heads and can't seem to get ourselves back to shore. We're drowning!

Welcome to our Third Overdose—where on the surface competition appears to be to our advantage. But appearances are deceiving, and it's easy to end up struggling to come up for air. The hotel, car rental, and airplane booking sites are all in a fierce competition for our business. But this is not a competition that operates by finding more and more ways to please its customers, as we might expect; instead it funnels the companies' ingenuity into finding ways to drag us ever farther out to sea. The rivals offer promotions that drain our wealth. They outmaneuver each other to find our weaknesses, and they draw us unsuspectingly into debt.

We swim against a rip current of late fees, of automatic enrollment in programs we don't want that charge us even more fees, of misleading and deceptive information about terms, prices, or payments. If we slacken even briefly, we are carried deeper into debt. Some of us make it to shore. Yet, embarrassed by our failure to do due diligence, by our gullibility, we don't speak up.

How does this overdose differ from the other two? Unlike our First Overdose, with the helmetless hockey players and entice-and-reject universities, the competitors' collective and individual interests are aligned—against us. They achieve their profits by exploiting us.

Unlike our Second Overdose of horsemeat scandals, quality isn't degraded. We actually got a nice suite at Caesars Palace. It just ended up costing about double what we expected because we didn't know about all the fees that were going to be added to the base price—and didn't protest them once we became aware of them. And our credit card works perfectly well—that is, it allows us to buy what we want when we want it without much concern about how we're going to pay for it, which we enjoy a lot—until we come face-to-face with the high interest rate and late fees that were hidden in the fine print. But since we can keep making just minimum payments, we can keep closing our eyes to the real cost.

As a measure of how topsy-turvy these competitive markets are, the credit card industry has turned the definition of *deadbeat* upside down. Credit card deadbeats are customers who successfully avoid the hidden fees because they pay in full and on time, and live within their means. This deprives the industry of the fees, where they make most of their profit. "Star" customers, by contrast, are those who can't avoid the exploitation.

Are You Calling Me Irrational?

On paper, competition works well. Assuming that we generally know what serves our own interest, and that we have the time, judgment, mental energy, and willpower to ensure that we get it, competition can indeed deliver what we want at a fair price. In their full-throated defense of competition, most economists, for decades, did make these assumptions. The term *homo economicus* has been used (often mockingly, sometimes earnestly) to refer to these specimens of supreme rationality, who are believed to be always capable of acting in their own self-interest. Objective and deliberative, they seek out the optimal amount of information, readily and continually update their beliefs with relevant and reliable data, and choose the best action according to stable preferences. As *homo economicus* obtains new facts, it revises its beliefs and modifies its behavior. With its admirable rationality and willpower, the *homo economicus* can shop, save, exercise, eat, and drink appropriately, resisting temptations that undermine its well-being and always following practices that maximize it.

However, in the real world, few if any of us are perfectly rational. As Fyodor Dostoyevsky remarked in *Notes from the Underground*, "[t]he trouble with man is that he's stupid. Phenomenally stupid."

Maybe "phenomenally stupid" is too harsh. But our intelligence and rationality are constantly being tested in the marketplace, and we often fail the test there.

Suppose Lavazza and illy coffee are both on sale at your local supermarket. For both, the standard price per pound is $9.00. However, right now illy is offering a discount of 33 percent on its one-pound bag, bringing the price down to $6.00. Lavazza hasn't lowered its price, but is offering 1.33 pounds for $9.00. Assuming you like both brands equally, which option is better—a 33 percent reduction in price, or a 33 percent increase in quantity? Or are they the same?

Suppose Bloomingdale's has a sale—slashing 40 percent off a $1,000 Ralph Lauren jacket. The Ralph Lauren outlet shop has that same jacket, but has marked it down twice: first by 20 percent and then by an additional 25 percent. Which one offers the better deal?

When we each asked our children, they began crunching the numbers on their calculators. *Who shops with a calculator?* we responded. Few of us take the time to compute these math problems, and even fewer of us can do the math in our heads. We rely on intuition.

So, for the first problem, most shoppers generally opt for the 33 percent extra, the *Wall Street Journal* reported, even though the discount is the better option. For the two deals to break even, the price discount of 33 percent would have to be matched by an offer of 50 percent more quantity, not 33 percent.[1]

Likewise, the double discount (20 percent and then an additional 25 percent off) seems like the better deal, but it is the same as the 40 percent off offer.

Now put yourself in the seller's position. Why offer the better bargain (33 percent off) when many would choose the inferior option (33 percent more coffee)? Why offer a steep discount, when you can entice more consumers by discounting the items twice?

Here's another example—in this case one that doesn't turn on our math abilities but our basic psychological makeup.

Suppose you are offered $100 today or $120 next week. Which would you choose?

Many choose the $100, despite the fact that the better choice is, of course, to delay gratification in order to net an additional $20.[2]

Now suppose you are offered $100 in fifty-two weeks from now or $120 in fifty-three weeks from now. Many now choose the $120.

Neurological research has examined why this is the case. The discrepancy between our short-run and long-run preferences could reflect which part of our brain's neural system is activated.[3] The research suggests that choices that involve an immediate reward (such as $100 today versus $120 next week) can disproportionately activate the impulsive part of our brain (the limbic system), which goes for the short-term benefit. Like

Veruca Salt in *Willy Wonka and the Chocolate Factory*, we want it, and we want it now. But when the rewards are in the relatively distant future, they activate the brain's more deliberative part (the lateral prefrontal cortex), which engages in long-term cost-benefit analyses and encourages us to make the better choice to wait the additional week.

These examples give us just a glimpse of when and why our own fallibility encourages competition to turn toxic. To understand this better, we can look at this and the three other conditions that characterize markets in which our Third Overdose is likely to flourish.

FIRST, as we've been discussing, in all these markets consumers are not the rational superhero *homo economicus*. They are human and have human weaknesses that get in the way of their deliberative reasoning and willpower.

Many consumers rely on intuition rather than deliberative reasoning. They succumb to the temptations of instant gratification, misjudge the strength of their willpower, and overestimate their ability to detect manipulation and exploitation. As anyone who has ever overeaten, overspent, or otherwise succumbed to temptation (despite having the best intentions to the contrary) can confirm, few of us have the willpower or the rationality we think we do.[4]

SECOND, firms know how to *identify* and *exploit* these customers' weaknesses. Competitors tap into these "irrational moments" and exploit them to their benefit.

THIRD, although some consumers are savvier than others and know how to avoid the traps set for them, these consumers do not protect the weaker ones. This happens, as we'll see, in part because savvier consumers benefit, to some extent, from the exploitation.

FOURTH, firms profit more from exploiting their customers' weaknesses than from helping them. In these markets, there may be few, if any, "angelic" companies that come to our aid because there is no advantage to their doing so. It may be too costly to educate the naive customers, and even if they succeed, there is no assurance that these customers, once educated, will stick with them and use their products. Eventually competition encourages even once-angelic companies to exploit.[5] Companies or managers who resist will lose business to those without moral qualms.[6] Rather than a race to the top, companies compete in devising ever cleverer ways to exploit consumers' shortcomings—the result being that increasing competition delivers ever worse products and services to us.[7]

The Good, the Bad, and the Ugly

Using these four factors, let us consider how the same companies might compete to help us in some markets, while competing to exploit us in other markets. This will help us to understand what the circumstances are that encourage exploitation. We'll start with the banks, institutions that are highly knowledgeable about how to identify and exploit their customers' weaknesses when it is to their advantage to do so. Banks operate in many different markets—lending, savings, mortgages, and credit cards. The competition in some, like credit cards, can be toxic to consumers, while in others, like savings, it is healthy. It is not the consumers who are the chameleons, switching between ignorant, incompetent "Homer Simpson" mode and hyperrational *homo economicus* mode. Rather, it is the companies who change, in response to the imperatives of the marketplace. In the case of banks, this will depend on whether they will profit more from helping us or from exploiting our human weaknesses.

With respect to savings accounts and retirement funds, financial institutions profit more by helping us—that is, by encouraging us to save. As competition has increased with the rise of online banks, banks have not only improved their interest rates and terms, they have designed tools that appeal to our deliberative sides and help us overcome our weak willpower.[8] Automatic savings plans, for example, take the decision-making out of savings. When we get our weekly paycheck, we don't have to fight between our temptation to blow part of it on a new pair of shoes or to put money aside for some long-term goal. Instead, the bank automatically deducts money from our paycheck and puts it into our retirement fund or our children's college fund, or toward other long-term objectives. As one bank noted, consumers "often find they do not even notice the smaller amount they have to spend each month."[9]

Now let us turn to credit cards. Here banks make more money the more often we use their credit card—from the transaction fees they charge merchants to the often very hefty interest and fees they charge us. Thus, compulsive shopping, from the banks' perspective, is a gold mine. Credit cards feed into the impulsive I-want-it-now part of our brain.[10] We get the immediate reward, whether it's one of those $5 lattes or a $500 pair of shoes, while delaying the payment for it. Unlike taking cash out of our wallet, swiping a card is abstract. And because we can delay payment not just until our bill comes but for months and even years thereafter, the cost can continue to seem abstract, even as the interest and penalties build up and drain our pocketbooks.

Moreover, credit card companies often encourage us to live beyond our means. As the *Harvard Business Review* noted, "Many credit card issuers, for example, choose not to deny a transaction that would put the cardholder over his or her credit limit; it's more profitable to let the customer overspend and then impose penalties."[11] When the credit card bill arrives, there is no Calvinist reproach to our extravagance, no need to repent by promptly paying down these debts. Instead, we are comforted— only a minimum payment is needed. We are lulled into becoming less conscious of what we are spending and more likely to overspend and incur huge penalties in the form of high interest rates on the balances we carry. The consequences became so damaging that Congress passed a law in 2009 requiring credit card issuers to tell us the consequences of making only the minimum payments each month.[12]

While the froth from the toxic competition has subsided, it nonetheless remains. Unlike the savings market, banks in the credit market continue to compete to exploit our weak willpower (rather than help us overcome it) and appeal to our impulsive nature (rather than the deliberative sides of our brain). Thus they are still offering us a never-ending stream of products that look superficially appealing (low teaser rate, 1 percent back in rebates, etc.), but where the costs of borrowing—including overdraft charges, late fees, and interest rates—are unconscionably high. Ultimately, their goal seems to be to put us into a debtors' "sweatbox" in order to turn a profit.[13]

But as we've seen, the banks also profit when they encourage us to save. So, why don't banks put their focus on helping us instead of sabotaging us? Let's look again at those four conditions we discussed above.

FIRST, because we are not in fact *homo economicus*, we ourselves allow this to happen. Toxic competition intensifies when naive consumers do not demand or use better products.

SECOND, because the banks know this, they exploit us. One former CEO, for example, explained how his credit card company targeted low-income customers "by offering 'free' credit cards that carried heavy hidden fees."[14] The former CEO explained how these ads targeted consumers' optimism: "When people make the buying decision, they don't look at the penalty fees because they never believe they'll be late. They never believe they'll be over limit, right?"

THIRD, because the consumers who know how to game the system don't protect the victims of it, competition delivers the benefits unequally: The money flows from the pockets of the exploitable to the exploiters, and also to those sophisticates savvy enough to be able to avoid the pitfalls of debt and high interest rates. So the savvy consumers do not call for reform. Rather, they are focused on preserving the current competition, as they want to hold on to whatever perks they can extract from the credit card company, like the 1 percent rebates, the refundable membership fees, the extended warranties, the mileage awards, and the zero fees on foreign transactions—perks the exploitive credit card issuers can afford to offer because of the fees they charge the more naive consumers.

And finally because, per the **FOURTH** condition, although it's true that banks can profit from both helping and hurting their customers, exploitation turns out to be much more profitable. Banks typically earn considerably higher returns from credit cards than from their other commercial banking activities. Earnings patterns for 2016 were consistent with historical experience: In that year, the average return on all assets, before taxes and extraordinary items, was 1.32 percent for all commercial banks, compared with 4.04 percent for the large credit card banks.[15]

But let us suppose that an angelic bank does take the time and effort to help naive credit card users get out of debt and start saving. Where does this now solvent consumer turn? Well, probably to one of those exploitive credit card companies, the ones that offer such tempting perks as rebates, airplane miles, etc. *So what is the point in helping these customers, if they won't bank with me in the future?*

In short, banks have little financial incentive to help consumers choose better products (e.g., credit cards with higher annual fees, but significantly lower late fees and interest rates). Market forces will instead skew toward products and services that exploit or reinforce consumers' weaknesses.

Even those of us who don't succumb to these temptations may get swept out to sea if an emergency of some kind—a catastrophic medical bill, a fire, flood, or hurricane—lands us in the debtors' sweatbox. And even the most fastidious of Calvinists, looking disapprovingly at the other swimmers struggling in the distance, may find themselves being billed for monthly services, such as credit monitoring, without their knowledge. Many older Americans complained to one federal agency of being billed for these subscriptions that they did not want or need, and discovered only "when a family member or other trusted third party reviewed their accounts."[16] According to a government report, people who are not vigilant may end up making payments for unwanted services that continue for months (if not years).[17] Ultimately, as one UK study found, many of us, when it comes to banks, are "paying above-average prices for below-average service quality."[18]

Having seen how competition can turn toxic under these four conditions, let us travel to where the rip current is the strongest, where there
are the perfect conditions of human weaknesses and of competitors who
know how to sense and exploit these weaknesses for profit. Let us go,
in short, to Las Vegas. The brief summary we gave you earlier of what
happens when you try to get a good deal on a hotel room doesn't really
do justice to the seductive insidiousness of the process.

Exploitation, Las Vegas Style

The casinos, most of which are located in hotels, need to attract visitors
in order to make money, and those visitors need a place to stay. So, one
might expect that this would result in a very healthy competition with
multiple casinos wooing you to stay in their hotels. You'll end up with
a great deal on a hotel and presumably they'll make money off of your
gambling. But somehow it doesn't work out that way.

In booking a hotel room along the Strip, as in many places across
America, you'll find that online reservation sites typically quote a very
low "total price" or "estimated price." The price includes "only the room
rate and applicable taxes." On other websites, the quoted price has an
asterisk next to it. To find out what the asterisk means, you would have
to go to another page on the website, where, if you read the fine print,
you will find the resort fee, though you may or may not find out what
this mysterious but mandatory fee covers. A few online sites don't even
identify any additional fees. You are simply told that "other undefined
fees may apply."[19]

Welcome to the world of "partition" pricing and "drip" pricing—two
strategies that do a great job of exploiting our weaknesses. Partition pricing works by separating the room price into two or more components.
To see partition pricing, try booking a room at the Luxor Hotel and
Casino in Las Vegas. You'll see the room rate in large type ($79 when we

last checked), highlighted in a blue panel; in smaller print, which isn't highlighted, you might notice "Plus $35 daily resort fee plus applicable taxes."

With drip pricing the hotel offers a room price that keeps increasing as the customer goes through the buying process.[20] Here's an example for Circus Circus on one booking site, where it appears that you are only going to have to pay $26 a night.[21] Wow, that's quite a deal! Once you click through to book the room, however, the price increases 150 percent to $66.65, once the mandatory resort fees and taxes are added.

How is it possible that these practices have become standard in the hotel industry? In competitive markets, we, the consumers, should reign as sovereign. And, as a survey of three thousand consumers conducted by the UK's competition agency revealed, we hate drip pricing—with 75 percent of those surveyed objecting to it, and 70 percent stating that they believed all compulsory charges should be revealed up front.[22] Consumer advocates also decry drip pricing. As the person who writes the Travel Troubleshooter blog says, "Quite simply, it's lying."[23]

So is competition eliminating this exploitation? To the contrary: We see drip pricing spreading across many seemingly competitive markets, including online booking sites like Airbnb and eDreams,[24] airline tickets,[25] car rentals,[26] and prepaid telephone calling cards.[27]

If the marketplace is getting more competitive, yet more firms are resorting to the unpopular practice of drip pricing, something would seem to be wrong with this picture. To diagnose it, let's start with our first factor: consumers' weaknesses.

Our superhuman *homo economicus* would not fall prey to drip pricing.[28] It would continue searching all the online sites, while calculating the different hotel rooms' costs—until, in economics jargon, the marginal cost exceeded the marginal benefit—and ultimately it would end up with the cheapest rate.

But many consumers fail to anticipate the existence of additional fees or the high prices of add-ons. To see why, let us consider how drip pricing taps into several human weaknesses. Try this thought experiment on yourself or friends.

First, think of a number, such as the last two digits of your social security number. Next, convert that number into dollars. Now, would you pay that amount—let's say it's $14—for a 1998 Côtes du Rhône? Finally, what is the maximum amount that you are willing to pay for that bottle of wine? Should thinking about the last two digits of your social security number affect how much you are willing to bid?

Before you answer, consider a second experiment, in which forty-two experienced judges and prosecutors were given a legal file about a rape case and asked to consider what kind of sentence they would hand down if they were the judge on the case. They were further asked to imagine that during a recess in the court, a journalist called them to ask what kind of sentence they intended to impose. Half of the judges and prosecutors were told that the journalist would ask: "Do you think the sentence for the defendant in this case will be higher or lower than *one year?*" The other half were told that the journalist would ask: "Do you think the sentence for the defendant in this case will be higher or lower than *three years?*" They were all told not to answer the journalist. After the supposed recess, these legal professionals were to render their verdicts. Do you think that the question asked by the journalist affected the duration of the sentences they imposed?

When we give these examples to our students, the overwhelming response to both questions is *No.* Nonetheless, in both examples, what economists call "the anchor value"—in these cases the social security number and the suggested sentencing times—did indeed influence the participants.

In the first set of experiments, participants with the highest-ending social security numbers (80 to 99) bid, on average, the highest for the bottle of wine; those with the lowest-ending SSNs (1 to 20) bid, on average, the lowest. Those with the higher SSNs bid, on average, 216 percent to 346 percent more than those with the lower SSNs.[29]

Similarly, whether the journalist asked about a one-year sentence or a three-year sentence did influence the judgment of those experienced judges and prosecutors. Participants who heard the higher sentencing anchor gave considerably higher sentences (mean of 33.38 months) than those given the low anchor (25.43 months).[30] As the authors of this study concluded, from this and other similar experiments they conducted, "God may not play dice with the universe—as Albert Einstein reassured us. But judges may unintentionally play dice with criminal sentences." And these "anchoring effects" may result in rolls of the dice in many other areas of judgment, too, including prices set by hotel reservation sites and real estate agents.[31]

We may reject the idea that an arbitrary number could have an impact on our own decisions. But drip pricing is a way of anchoring us to a low headline price (say $26 for the Circus Circus hotel room). Once we've got that price of $26 in our head, we fail to adjust our "perception of the 'value of the offer' sufficiently as more costs are revealed."[32]

Drip pricing also taps into a second weakness. Although as we shop for a hotel room we haven't actually purchased that reservation for $26, some part of us feels like we have and we now feel attached to it. With drip pricing, a former chief economist of the UK competition authority noted, "Consumers feel they've already made the decision to purchase [which] creates loss aversion—consumers have committed time and effort to the search before being hit with extra charges."[33]

A third weakness is something we often perceive as a strength, namely commitment and consistency. Here, after having invested a lot of time and effort into this purchase, we want to see the purchase through to its end.[34] Economists call this the *sunk cost fallacy*.

Finally, drip pricing taps into brain fatigue. Each Las Vegas hotel on the Strip offers many different types of rooms, with varying square footage, number of beds and bathrooms, and views. Each type of room has a different room rate, with different promotions for rewards club members. If you want to bring your parrot, check in early, or check out late, additional fees apply. And different hotels impose different resort fees—plus tax. Now, to decide which kind of room you want and where you want to stay, run calculations for two types of rooms at five different casinos on the Strip. That requires a lot of mental processing. That is what the consumer protection agency, the Federal Trade Commission (FTC), concluded in its 2017 report, *Economic Issues: Economic Analysis of Hotel Resort Fees*. Drip pricing increases the "cognitive costs of making purchase decisions."[35] Consumers not only expend the time and cost of searching for the best deal, they must also expend mental energy to calculate and evaluate each option to determine how it fares against the other options.

This takes us to our second factor for toxic competition. Firms can *identify* and *exploit* the customers' weaknesses. Drip pricing is a shiny lure. The UK's competition agency, for example, experimented with five common price schemes to see which would most appeal to consumers:

- *drip pricing*;
- *sales*, where the "sale" price is based on an inflated regular price (e.g., was $2, now $1);
- *complex pricing* (e.g., three-for-two offers), where the unit price requires some computation;
- *baiting*, where sellers promote special deals with only a limited number of goods available at the discounted price; and
- *time-limited offers*, where the special price is available for a short period.[36]

As the experiment found, firms can use any and all of these pricing schemes to manipulate our purchasing behavior to our disadvantage. But guess which pricing practices were the most harmful to consumers, in terms of making errors and overpaying? Drip pricing and time-limited offers. And not surprisingly, online hotel reservation sites make widespread use of both tactics.

Now let us return to the example of the Luxor Hotel and Casino, where the hotel posts a base price and a surcharge, and puts both on the same page.

That shouldn't trick us. But even here, according to the FTC report, many consumers "tend to underestimate the total price."[37] For a night at the Luxor, the total comes out to $129.25, once we add up $79 a night plus a $35 daily resort fee plus $15.25 in "applicable" taxes—which we have to go to another page to find. We react quite differently to "$129.25" than to "**$79** (plus a $35 daily resort fee plus applicable taxes)." According to the FTC, putting the surcharge in smaller font increases our tendency to underestimate the total price or to ignore the surcharge. Requiring us to click through to another page to find the "applicable taxes" no doubt further increases that tendency. Drip and partition pricing cause us, as the FTC found, "to behave as if the price is lower than it is."[38]

This brings us to the third condition for toxic competition. Savvy consumers, if they actually do spend the time and mental effort required to quantify the total price for the different rooms, might find the cheapest one. But their mathematical gymnastics will not protect the rest of us (unless they call you up and tell you which hotel offers the lowest or best value). In fact, their efforts won't even help *them* the next time they research hotel room prices. Prices for hotel rooms, in Vegas and elsewhere, change regularly. The price that savvy customers pay today might differ from tomorrow's price. So, unless they are prepared to put in the exact same amount of work they put in today to find the best price tomorrow, they won't.

Moreover, as we'll see, some casinos are engaged in sophisticated price discrimination, so the VIP price you receive might be higher or lower than the VIP price your grandmother or neighbor received.[39] So, like credit card companies, the hotels can offer sophisticated buyers better deals, which are subsidized by the resort fees that the rest of us pay. Competition in these circumstances can indeed make things worse.[40]

Won't people eventually recognize the scam and start adding up the fees? Potentially. According to the FTC, behavioral experiments showed that people who went through the drip pricing scenario multiple times made fewer buying mistakes. But they still made more mistakes than those people in the "transparent price setting"—where the total price was revealed much more quickly and easily.[41]

Before we even step on the casino floor, the casinos have begun exploiting our weaknesses—especially if we are among the many naive consumers who book rooms infrequently and are unaware of the way add-ons increase the overall purchase price.

In the effort to deceive consumers, drip pricing is spreading. Hotels across the United States are now imposing—and concealing—mandatory resort fees "for amenities such as newspapers, use of onsite exercise or pool facilities, or Internet access."[42] As one New York University report found, these mandatory fees and surcharges emerged as an industry practice around 1997 and have increased every year since except for periods following 2001 and 2008 when demand for hotel rooms declined.[43]

That takes us to the final factor for toxic competition: when firms have a greater incentive to exploit us than to help us. The casinos and their hotels certainly exemplify this motivation. Given that so much of their profit derives from these deceptive practices, why would they choose to do otherwise?

And yet, there are occasional instances in which companies do try to do the right thing by their customers. And one might expect that when they do, they can stop the toxic competition. After all, if, for example, consumers hate drip pricing as much as they say they do, then one powerful casino, in doing the right thing, should certainly be able to triumph over its rivals. Right?

The Case of Caesars

In 2011, about fifty showgirls from Caesars Entertainment took to the Las Vegas streets.

The showgirls—with their signs, "Just Say No to Resort Fees!" and "Our Money, Our Choice!"—were exposing the injustice of hidden resort fees.[44] Other Vegas celebrities, including Marie Osmond and Penn &

Teller, joined the protest. Caesars wrapped its casinos with ads proclaiming that unlike its rivals, Caesars did not exploit customers with resort fees. Caesars estimated it saved Las Vegas visitors $37 million a year by not engaging in this drip pricing.[45] Caesars also launched a Facebook page inviting consumers to "join the fight against Las Vegas resort fees."[46]

Here we have a powerful company, which owns several popular casinos on the Las Vegas Strip, taking a powerful stand against an unpopular, and abusive, pricing scheme. Caesars' "no resort fees" Facebook page drew tens of thousands of followers.[47] Under these circumstances we might expect the toxic competition to end.

But in fact the unpopular, exploitive practice did not stop. Resort fees on the Strip, and throughout the United States, continued to increase, and more competitors kept adding them. A trend analysis report written by a professor at NYU concluded that such "fees and surcharges are highly profitable; many have incremental profitability of 80 to 90 percent or more of the amounts collected, so they represent significant contributors to industry profits."[48]

Source of data: 2017 NYU School of Professional Studies: Trend Analysis Report[49]

So a powerful casino chain takes a stand against an unpopular, exploitive practice. And not only does it fail, but by 2013, Caesars gives up on its quest to warn consumers of these resort fees and joins the race to exploit.

Why did Caesars cave? The answer is very simple. Showing us the true price led to a fall in sales. On the other hand, drip pricing paid off. Initially Caesars charged resort fees primarily for its Las Vegas properties. In 2015, Caesars began charging resort fees for all its properties, which drove most of the increase in its rooms revenue.[50] Caesars' net revenue in 2016 increased $41 million, or 1.9 percent, compared with 2015.[51] As the FTC report concluded:

> *The experience of Caesars Entertainment may suggest that it is difficult for a hotel not to charge a separately-disclosed resort fee when competing hotels charge such fees. The prices of hotels that charge separate, mandatory resort fees will appear lower than the prices of hotels that do not charge the fees, even if the total prices are the same. Consumers are attracted to resort fee hotels because they advertise the lowest upfront price. If search and cognitive costs did not exist, consumers would ultimately find the hotel of the quality they wanted at the lowest price. However, if separately-disclosed resort fees increase search and cognitive costs, it would be harder for consumers to discover a hotel with no resort fee that offers a better deal. This situation suggests a "Prisoner's Dilemma" style game where the efficient outcome cannot be achieved because any hotel offering a better deal without a resort fee will lose business to competitors charging separate resort fees and lower advertised room rates.[52]*

Ultimately, deceptive drip pricing proved to be a shinier lure than Caesars' truthful all-inclusive price. We, the customers, did not back Caesars' efforts. We may think we don't like drip pricing, but nevertheless we fall prey to it and don't do the work to find out which is the cheapest rate.

You could say, shame on us. Maybe we deserve to be exploited. But it has to be acknowledged that with hotels, airlines, and rental car agencies all now engaging in drip pricing, it takes more and more work to try to figure out the actual cost of booking a vacation. If we are really determined to find the best deals, planning our Vegas trip becomes a full day spreadsheet exercise.

Since few of us have this spare time, this puts the honest seller—and us—at a disadvantage.[53] The competitors who make it easier for consumers to see the overall price ultimately lose business, as tourists flock to the manipulative hotels. Eventually, as more hotels engage in drip pricing, the few remaining decent competitors buckle under the competitive pressure, until they, too, exploit us.

And there we have it—a seemingly competitive market in which the rivals compete on how best to exploit us, rather than benefit us.

The Power of Behavioral Analytics

By the 2020s, as companies develop tools to monitor and profile us, exploitation via drip pricing will likely appear downright quaint. Big data and analytics are the next stage in consumer manipulation. And the future is here.

To catch a glimpse of this next wave of toxic competition, let us return to Las Vegas. It's no longer true that what happens in Vegas stays in Vegas. Instead, what we do there will go into a data dump that enables us to be exploited with ever greater efficiency—as we'll see when we examine one recent experiment involving about 1.5 million consumers who frequented MGM's Las Vegas casinos.[54] A team of experts in data-driven marketing analytics developed a computer program that allowed

MGM to determine the profitability of various kinds of promotional offers—and it worked very well indeed.

Like all the larger casinos, MGM uses loyalty cards and other sources to amass this data. Advertisements for MGM's loyalty card, for example, promise "amazing rewards and benefits" for every dollar one spends at its resorts.

So, when you exchange your cash for a casino's play-card, the card is linked to your unique loyalty-card ID. As you use the casino's play-card, you can earn more perks, like priority hotel check-in lines. The casino's database now can easily capture "where, when, how long, and how much" you played, as well as your activities ("rooms stayed at, shows watched").[55] The data helps the casino to "price optimize"—that is, to offer you the cheapest mix of perks that will work to entice you to spend the most amount of money at their casino—not just once, but over your lifetime.

To arrive at this conclusion the casino first considers whether you are a low-value, high-value, or loyal customer.

You would be a "low-value" customer if you're either: *too good* (highly skilled "experts" who win back from the house more than they wager), a *freeloader* (consumers "who utilize comps but do not play at the resort"), or *too strategic* (consumers "who wager nothing more than their Free-play dollars, thereby gaining the upside from the promotion, with little downside for themselves and no gain for the 'house'").[56]

If you're too good, too cheap, or too strategic, MGM doesn't want you and won't compete with the other casinos to attract you. So don't expect any attractive promotions—from MGM or any of the other Vegas casinos.

On the other hand, if you're a "loyal" customer, you might expect your loyalty to be rewarded. And relative to the low-value customers, it will be. But because MGM knows you are likely to stick with MGM with or without a promotion, MGM does not want to condition you to expect promotions. You'll get them sometimes, other times you won't.

So the real competition is in identifying and wooing the "high-value" customers, namely those whom the casino can hook and keep profiting from over the gamblers' lifetimes. The "high-value" consumers are those with the highest marginal propensity to respond to a promotion, basically those who would spend the greatest amount in response to the smallest inducement needed to woo and hook them.

Suppose you're a high-value customer. MGM, like the other casinos, has multiple promotions to woo you. These include:

- room offers (like the room type, room discount, number of comp nights, whether the comp is midweek or weekend);
- entertainment, sports, and facility offers;
- retail and spa offers;
- air and limo offers;
- free-play and promo-chip offers;
- resort credits; and
- food and beverage offers.

But the challenge is not simply snagging the high-value customer once. Rather, it is assessing the dynamic effects of promotions on each such customer "to get an accurate picture of the ROI [return on investment] profile from the promotions, and to allocate them appropriately based on their expected long-run benefits to the firm." Basically, what is the cheapest inducement they can offer to get you to come to MGM on your next trip—and trips thereafter—and spend money not just on the slots and tables but at the restaurants, shows, and shops? Would a limousine at the airport do the trick? Or would a free drink suffice? Or does MGM need to offer you a limo as well as a free dinner and show?

To answer these questions with a higher level of precision and sophistication than MGM had been able to do in the past, the casino turned to a computer model designed by its marketing analytics experts. The computer first compiled all the available data on each consumer's observed behavior "at all past visits (and not just the most recent visits)." That would include not only their time at MGM Grand, but the other MGM-owned casinos: ARIA, Bellagio, Circus Circus, Excalibur, Luxor, Mandalay Bay, Mirage, New York–New York, and Park MGM. The model also used "information across the entire range of activities by the consumer to measure how promotions affect behavior."[57] For those consumers on whom very little data existed, the computer model pooled information from the behavior of similar consumers.

In processing all this data, MGM's computer program then identified for each consumer how that person would likely respond to myriad combinations of promotions, and the likely profits from that consumer over the long run under the different inducements. This information shaped the marketing strategies it then used.

Ultimately, the behavioral discrimination was highly effective and profitable. When MGM ran its new data-driven personalized promotions, the profits, the study found, were about $1 million to $5 million higher per campaign than under MGM's existing marketing strategy. In other words, every dollar MGM spent on promotions that used the data-driven computer model generated about 20¢ more in incremental profits than the earlier promotional campaign.

In short, the data helped MGM identify with greater accuracy whom to target, and how, in order to maximize the profit it got from each person. As the study documenting these changes noted, "The source of the improvement arises from shifting marketing dollars away from average consumers who would have played even in the absence of the promotion toward marginal consumers for whom the promotion has an incremental impact; and from the improved matching of promotion types to consumer types."

Now it's clear that the other casinos on the Strip are going to want in on this data-driven success, and soon everyone will be competing to collect even more (and better) data on us in order to exploit us with maximum efficiency. The casinos will all crunch their own data and they'll also increasingly work with data assembled by data brokers. If Google, Facebook, Amazon, and other super-platforms acquire a casino, they'll add this rich data to their extensive profiles of us, which will only get richer with the data available through our digital assistants like Alexa and Google Home.

Going forward, the toxic competition will become highly stratified. If you resemble the *homo economicus* or are a skilled gambler, few, if any, of the casinos will compete to attract you. No perks for you.

If you are loyal to a casino (that is, if you are one of those "average consumers who would have played even in the absence of the promotion"), you won't get much in the way of perks either, because the casino already knows that you don't require a limo at the airport to convince you to spend money at its hotel and its restaurants and slots.

The rest of you, however, can expect some perks—whatever the casino's computer models have determined are necessary to hook you. You might get a free show or limo, if the data indicate that the cost of offering these perks will be worth it. But don't expect this competition to benefit you in the end. The casinos will be competing, but only in finding your weaknesses. So when that limousine driver greets you at the airport, keep in mind that he's really just another cog in the machine that is designed to extract your money with maximum efficiency.

Reflections

The tactics used today are like rip currents—calm and inviting on the surface while seducing us into taking the plunge and inevitably dragging us out to sea. Assuming we stay the current course, the future will likely require a new analogy: gazelle sprinting across the savanna. In the online world, the gazelle all have trackers. The lions can determine when the gazelle are thirsty or tired. They know where each gazelle is, and where, based on its routines, it is likely to go. With all the data, the gazelles' instincts and nerves appear as patterns on a screen. Pinch a bundle of fibers here, see the sensation produced in the brain neuron there, get the desired behavioral response now. Even if there is an honest pride of lions, which seeks to give the gazelles a sporting chance, their pride will thin out, as other prides increase in size because they are hunting their prey with ever-greater efficiency.

What's most alarming about this overdose is that unlike what happened with the two overdoses described in the previous chapters, businesses in this overdose all profit handsomely from the competition, so they have little incentive to halt the competition. Indeed, the very nature of competition has now been changed—from sellers trying to figure out how best to attract us by improving service and quality and reducing price to trying to figure out how best to exploit us.

Since the rivals don't want this toxic competition to end, they want to be sure no one intervenes to protect us. So they'll decry regulation as paternalistic and appeal to our rugged individualism. As we'll see later, they will prescribe competition as the cure.

If we continue to accept this explanation, then we will indeed become prey—stalked with ever increasing skill and sophistication. Firms will track our behavior, collect data about us, and use this information to better exploit our weaknesses. Occasionally, we might escape our trackers, with their personalized advertisements, promotions, and pricing. But, over the long term, as we limp across the savanna, most of us are going to get savaged.

Or we can demand change. But before we do, let us see our final competition overdose.

CHAPTER 4

Fourth Overdose

Choice Overload

In the satirical film *Borat*, Sacha Baron Cohen, posing as the TV journalist Borat from Kazakhstan, claims to be doing a documentary about what makes America great. As he walks down a US supermarket aisle lined with packages of cheese, accompanied by Dean McCool, the manager of the supermarket, Borat queries him about the products.

"What is this?" he asks McCool, picking up a package of cheese.

"Cheese," responds McCool.

"And this?" picking up another.

"Cheese."

"And this?"

"Cheese."

"And this?"

"Cheese . . ."

"Is this rice?"

"That's cheese also . . ."

After three agonizing minutes of asking about each package of cheese, Borat asks McCool why Americans eat only cheese, which the preternaturally patient store manager explains is not the case—they eat many other things, too. Whereupon Borat proceeds to the vast assortment of butter, then milk. . . . [1] And on it goes.

Whatever other message this scene delivers, it makes the point that supermarkets in developed countries provide a wealth of choices. Competitive pressure could trigger several market failures—e.g., *Dear Genevieve* letters from colleges, horsemeat in our burgers, drip pricing, and other exploitive tactics. But one clear benefit of competition is choice. Right?

We are fortunate to be able to exercise choice, we truly are. If you don't believe this, ask yourself where you would rather shop: a Soviet-era store or a modern Western supermarket?

Few, if any, would yearn for the paltry options and long lines of Soviet-era stores. To walk down an American or European supermarket aisle is to behold the wonders of competition—a veritable cornucopia of products catering to different tastes, desires, and needs; different pocketbooks; and different ethnicities. And if we can't find what we're looking for at our local retailer, we can shop online. On one website, for example, we can peruse 1,831 varieties of cheese, either alphabetically by name or by country of origin, kind of milk used to produce it, color, or even texture.[2] (Do you prefer brittle or buttery, chalky or chewy, flaky or fluffy, stringy or supple, etc.?)

This might seem overwhelming, but apparently there are times when we just can't get enough choices. In a study of customers at several wine stores where between 1,200 and 1,800 wines were on offer, nearly 80 percent of those surveyed either wanted more choices or were satisfied with the number of choices available.[3] If we spent 15 seconds looking at each wine, we would spend between 5 and 7.5 hours in the liquor store.

In fact, we are born with a highly developed desire for choice. Choice is part of what defines us as human. As John Stuart Mill observed, "The human faculties of perception, judgment, discriminative feeling, mental activity, and even moral preference, are exercised only in making a choice."[4]

Choice is good in all kinds of ways. It can increase our intrinsic motivation and sense of control. It can empower our autonomy and free-dom.[5] It allows us to find professions, employers, products, and services aligned with our moral and ethical values,[6] lifestyle,[7] and culture.[8] We value having the choice to take our business elsewhere.[9] Studies have found that people given choices "experience increased life satisfaction and health status, whereas the absence or removal of choice makes them helpless and hopeless."[10] An ideal position in an affluent Western world.

Competition, Markets, and Choice

Let us consider how competition presents a seemingly win-win situation: We are wired to value and exercise choice, and competition delivers exactly that.

One website, for example, rates over 1,700 kinds of shampoo.[11] You can search the site to find the right one based on your price range, hair characteristics, and health, environmental, and societal concerns. You care deeply about a specific product attribute—vegan, organic, fragrance-free, PETA-approved, gluten-free? Competition will likely deliver.

Same goes for so many of the other products we consume. If you're sipping a gin and tonic by the pool while reading this chapter, you might be surprised to learn that your tonic choices go far beyond the few you've probably encountered at your local supermarket, like Schweppes and the supermarket's private brand. If you were to include those two plus Bramley & Gage's 6 O'clock, 1724, Fentimans, Fever-Tree Indian, and Fever-Tree Mediterranean, and to experiment with mixing them with twenty-five brands of gin, you would come up with 175 possible combinations of gin and tonic, which, depending on your capacity for alcohol, would likely preoccupy you for some time.

That might seem sufficient, but it's possible to experiment far beyond that. If we increase our sample to five hundred types of gin (including London Dry, Genever, Old Tom, and flavored gins) and ten types of tonic, we end up with five thousand possible variations, more than all but the most dedicated of tipplers might consume in a lifetime. The fact is, we don't want this many options. Eventually the pleasure we experience from choice will be exceeded by the cost of the mental effort it takes to make the choice.

But we believe that we can count on market forces to save the day. The invisible hand will naturally set the right mix and level of variety. So, we need not worry about having too many choices.

How so? Retailers, for example, have limited shelf space. They won't add more gin varieties unless doing so will increase their profits, and their profits will only increase if we, the consumers, want to buy the additional varieties of gin. So, retailers will keep adding gins until the returns have diminished to the point where they can earn greater profits from using that shelf space for another product, like bourbon. Though online retailers can carry more brands, they, too, face a diminishing return to increasing variety.

To illustrate diminishing returns, imagine taking two of those pool noodles you've been floating on as you drink your gin and tonic and forming an X with them.

Marginal cost

Marginal benefit

The downward sloping noodle represents the marginal benefit—the increasing profit—a retailer gets from adding another option.

The upward sloping noodle represents the marginal cost of adding another option instead of some other products. Where they intersect is the point where the marginal benefit of gin options equals the marginal cost.

Going beyond this point (to the right) by adding one more variety, Elderflower Gin Liqueur, for example, means that the additional cost to the retailer will exceed the resulting benefit. A canny, competitive retailer knows when the line has been crossed and doesn't go there. So, in competitive markets we can expect the invisible hand to deliver the optimal level of choices—whether for gin, tonic, retirement plans, or jams. Not too few, not too many.

So far so good. We crave choice, competition delivers the right amount of variety, and we pick what best suits our needs. So, where's the overdose? Well, here it comes . . .

Turns out that the invisible hand—and the retailers it presumably guides in their decisions—*doesn't* always know when the line has been crossed.

Choice Overload—
Too Much of a Good Thing . . .

In the television show *Frasier*, Niles questions his brother on whether he needs so many musicians for his concert. Frasier smugly replies yes, for the sound he wants.

"Whatever happened to the concept of 'less is more'?" asks Niles.

"Ah, but if less is more, then just think of how much more 'more' will be!"

Less is more, but more is seemingly better. Some policy makers, economic theorists, and merchants assume that, as far as consumers are concerned, the more choices the better. But is it? Let us consider jam.

Imagine your supermarket is going to set up a tasting booth of Wilkin & Sons jams. It asks your advice. To increase jam sales, should the tasting booth have six or twenty-four different flavors of jam? Would it make a difference? If so, why?

We like choice. Smucker's alone offers over forty varieties of jam. So the tasting booth should definitely offer twenty-four jam flavors.

But, in fact, when we have too many choices, we get confused and overwhelmed (cognitive costs) and we may then become inhibited about making choices. Professors Sheena Iyengar and Mark Lepper found this in their iconic study.[12] From the point of view of merchants wanting our dollars, this means many of us don't purchase any product, which, of course, the merchants don't like.

Professors Iyengar and Lepper set up a tasting booth on two consecutive Saturdays in an upscale supermarket in Menlo Park, California. The booths offered six or twenty-four different flavors of Wilkin & Sons jam. They monitored the amount of traffic at the tasting booth and the number of sales of Wilkin & Sons jam. To test for choice overload, they wanted to make sure that the customers didn't simply try the familiar flavors, like strawberry and raspberry. Instead, consumers had a choice of more exotic flavors.

What they found was that when the tasting booth had twenty-four flavors, more customers (60 percent of the 242 customers) stopped to sample the displayed jams. In contrast, when the booth had only six flavors, only 40 percent of the 260 customers stopped. Customers clearly were attracted to the greater choices. But in the end, far fewer customers who tasted the twenty-four flavors actually purchased a jar of jam relative to the customers tasting only six flavors of jam. In other words, although customers thought they preferred more choices, which is why more people stopped by the twenty-four-flavor booth, in the end thirty-one people bought when there were few choices, versus four people when there were many more choices.

What is perhaps most interesting about the jam story is that the store's shelves routinely stock over three hundred varieties of jam. So, argu-ably consumers who tasted only six flavors of jam could conceivably face choice overload when they had to pick the jar off the shelf. Rather, the culprit was the twenty-four-flavor booth. When it was in the store, over-all sales of jam plummeted by roughly 87 percent. It was as though the presence of the twenty-four-flavor booth had somehow highlighted the mental effort of making a choice—even a choice about a relatively low-cost item with relatively few variables beyond flavor. This is even more astonishing when one realizes that all customers were given a coupon of $1. Nonetheless, when shoppers were reminded of the work involved in choosing, this discouraged them from buying the jam, even at a dis-count.

One reason this happens is that as the number of options and product attributes increases, we have to think more. Deliberative, rational think-ing is tiring. So we are likelier to suffer brain fatigue.[13] More choices may also present more trade-offs, which creates mental conflict and can make all the choices look unappealing.[14] And finally, as options increase, the pressure increases to pick the right one and defend it to ourselves and others.[15] The result of all these factors is that we experience choice overload.

Sometimes choice overload leads us to avoid choosing, even when any choice would be preferable to not choosing at all.[16] One example is when people have to choose where to put money in their 401(k) retirement funds. As the number and variety of investment options increase, mak-ing a decision becomes more complex, and people become *less* likely to participate. Making any choice would be more advantageous than not making one, as often employers offer matching contributions, while the employees lower their income (and potential tax rate) and defer paying tax on the savings until they withdraw from their account.

Or if we do choose, the mental toll involved in considering too many options and product attributes can reduce the likelihood of our pursuing other, better options.[17] Returning to our 401(k) example, when confronted with many options, employees who do invest are more likely to opt for less risky bond and money market accounts, which yield less over the long run than investments in stocks. Perhaps with many more equity options, some people cannot process all the trade-offs between risk and reward, and retreat to less risky, but suboptimal, investments.

So, if you want to discourage your employees from investing in the company's 401(k) plan—thereby lowering the company's cost in matching contributions—the lesson is offer many, many options. One study found that for every additional ten options, the participation rate dropped by 2 percent.[18]

Furthermore, once we finally purchase after calculating the many trade-offs posed by the many options, we may experience buyer's regret because we now have to consider more counterfactuals ("what ifs") about the options not chosen.[19] After all, with so many options, we had no excuse for not choosing the "right one."[20]

The consequences of choice overload have been documented for many other products, including crackers, gift boxes, prizes, coffee, consumer electronics, and chocolates.[21] Take travel services as another example. Few vacationers would be thrilled if their travel agent offered only one option. When considering their next holiday, one study found, participants enjoyed increasing satisfaction when offered multiple holiday options—up to twenty-two choices. But being offered more than twenty-two choices resulted in choice overload, with more customers making no choice.[22]

However, the study of the effects of choice overload is not by any means an exact science. For example, several attempts to replicate Iyengar and Lepper's jam study did not find evidence of choice overload.[23] One meta-analysis of fifty experiments found mixed results.[24] Another meta-analysis identified four factors that can influence choice overload: *first*, the complexity of the choices; *second*, the difficulty in deciding (such as decisions under time pressure versus choices with no time constraints); *third*, whether we have clear preferences (such as organic food); and *fourth*, our ultimate goal (are we browsing or seeking to find the best choice).[25]

Because choice overload can depend on so many situational and individual factors, there is no magic number of options that will prove to be the trigger. Some of us will be overwhelmed by being offered 1,200 different wines or 1,700 different cheeses. For others, such large numbers of options are exactly what we want. It's hard to draw any absolute conclusions. But one thing we do know is that we cannot count on competition to automatically correct for choice overload and always deliver the right variety of products and services.

Of course, if too many choices of cheese results in no cheese purchases, that's too bad for the seller of cheese but not so serious for the consumer. If, on the other hand, there are so many investment options that employees do not fund their retirement accounts, that's an example of competition hurting us. But it gets grimmer. What if rather than giving us fewer choices, which might seem like the logical thing to do, merchants actively exploit our confusion by (i) offering too many choices and then (ii) helping us narrow them down in ways that are ultimately to their own benefit, not ours? Now competition's toxicity increases.

How Does the Market React to Choice Overload?

Humans are a study in contradictions. We crave choices, the forces of competition deliver abundantly, but the abundance itself can leave us feeling anxious, frustrated, regretful, even paralyzed. When merchants see their consumers reacting to choice overload, they can respond with one of four strategies.

FIRST, sellers can help us by reducing the mental burden and counterfactuals. One way is through decision aids. For example, sellers can organize the options available to us in ways that match our intuitive habit of organizing things into categories.

We see this on our in-flight entertainment guides, which display the offerings under headings like Films, Television, and Music, and then under subcategories within each, like Comedy, Drama, Thriller, and Children's. The offerings are free. The airlines have no incentive to confuse or overwhelm us. When the seller's external ordering matches our internal ordering, we expend less mental energy, and our satisfaction in our choice can increase. (We can grumble instead over the poor food selection in economy, relative to business and first class.)

SECOND, sellers can offer fewer options per product category. This can increase the likelihood of our purchasing an item and the satisfaction we feel over our purchase.

But limiting choice can present challenges to merchants, since they know their customers crave choice and may be disappointed when confronted with fewer offerings. Consumers often perceive stores with greater variety to be of higher quality.[26] And because they do, the sellers try to give them what they want.

Think, for example, about the market for televisions. One US retailer, Best Buy, offers 260 varieties of television sets online and hundreds in some of its stores. They do this even though television manufacturers and retailers recognize that offering so many types of television sets, while attracting consumers to their websites and stores, can also increase the risk of choice overload and regret.[27] It is therefore at least theoretically in their interest to offer fewer televisions, as sales and profits would likely increase.[28]

This puts retailers in a quandary. Each retailer might want to limit the number of TV sets. But no one will do so unilaterally because of the risk that it would devalue the retailer's image relative to its competitors, thus reducing foot traffic and sales of other products. So, they all continue to offer more choices than is optimal, to avoid losing customers to rivals.

Some retailers have escaped this conundrum by offering an entirely different shopping experience. Club stores, like Costco, offer fewer choices (in terms of brand, the size of product, and quantity), but promise much lower prices. Some, like Aldi and Trader Joe's, offer primarily their own labels.

Traditional retailers who feel they can't escape and must continue to offer the variety that consumers expect will bear the burden of higher costs in inventorying and selling, and lower profits. Ultimately, however, it will be the consumers who bear the burden, as the sellers will pass on their costs in the form of higher prices.

You may wonder why the competitors, to reduce the risk of acting unilaterally, don't simply agree among themselves to put limits on the selection of TV sets. They can't, as we'll see in the next chapter, because if they did they would likely face stiff fines and damages (or even end up in prison) for violating the antitrust laws.[29]

A **THIRD** approach is simply to go with the competitive flow. Sellers cannot unilaterally limit choice without losing profits, so they offer us the variety that we crave. After all, the customer is always right. Though some smaller retailers may survive by focusing on service and uniqueness, generally speaking the trend is toward bigger. Think, for example, of the rise of big-box retailers, which attract us with greater choices of hardware, books, toys, clothing, furniture, stationery, etc. But now some of these big-box retailers are losing sales to online merchants that offer even greater variety. By 2017, Amazon offered over four hundred million products on its website, which was six times the sixty million products Walmart offered on its website.[30] As one drives past the shuttered Toys "R" Us and Babies "R" Us stores, one wonders whether even the bigger brick-and-mortar stores will be able to survive.

The Fourth Overdose takes a page from our Third Overdose: competitors use choice overload to exploit us. Here rivals intentionally increase the complexity of their products and terms of contract and shower us with *excessive choices* to profit at our expense. This seems counterintuitive. But it is actually quite logical. And just about any product we buy can present us with a mind-boggling set of alternatives—if a seller wants to boggle our minds.

For example, do you think buying a pen is a complex decision? Probably not. But one experiment showed how complexity can be introduced into the process, and how that affected choice.[31] Participants were divided into two groups and people in both groups were asked to choose the pen that they liked the most—first from an assortment of six pens, then fifteen, then thirty. For one group, the pens varied only along one attribute, namely color. For a second group, the pens varied along six attributes (not just color but pen design, ink color, ink's fade resistance, pen point width, and projected duration of use). Both groups reported it more complex to make a choice as the number of possibilities increased from six to fifteen to thirty. But the second group found the decision far more complex, as they had to choose among six, fifteen, or thirty pens, and also among pens that varied along six different attributes. *Do I go with the white ergonomic pen with aquamarine ink that is fade resistant for two years and has enough ink for twenty hours' worth of writing? Or should I get the trendy red pen with cobalt blue ink that won't fade for eight years and has enough ink for ten hours' worth of writing?* Not surprisingly, the second group, unlike the first group, became less satisfied with their choice as the number of alternatives increased. Thus, it isn't strictly the number of choices; it is also the complexity of the choice that overwhelms consumers.

Given that the conclusion seems to be that this kind of complexity doesn't make consumers happy, why would sellers want to expose us to it? Why do they want to boggle our minds?

First, of course, there's the fact that the seller knows what the jam experiment found, namely increasing the variety of choices will attract us. But the seller also knows that the complexity will soon mentally drain us. And when it does, we will likely blame ourselves, because we feel that buying a pen shouldn't be such a hard job, and we wonder what's wrong with us. And that's when the seller can send its helpful online assistant to our aid, taking us by the hand and quickly identifying the right option for us. It might choose the "top-rated" pen, the pen other similar customers purchased (similar based on the massive quantities of personal data it has accumulated about us), or the pen that appears on the top of the search results.

Think of Amazon. If offering too many choices causes us to cease buying, Amazon would have been bankrupt ages ago. Amazon attracts us with its many choices within each of its many product categories.

But Amazon then tailors which products it recommends for us, based on our profile. Once we've decided what we want, we can then choose among the many sellers on Amazon's platform. Wading through all the seller options—which may involve having to click through several times in order to find not just the price, delivery time, and customer satisfaction ratings but also the shipping charges—can itself be taxing. So we often opt for the choice we see in Amazon's buy box—another way Amazon simplifies our task for us.

Having mastered the ability to attract us with choice, personalize the shopping experience, and streamline it, Amazon is, of course, a huge success story, and its customers are happy with it. Fifty-six percent of consumers in one 2015 survey said Amazon demonstrated "an understanding of their individual preferences and needs on a regular basis"— which they considered to be far greater than that shown by traditional retailers.[32]

But Amazon's helpfulness in guiding us to products we want when we are faced with choice overload is also aimed at steering us to those options on which it earns greater profits. ProPublica, an independent, nonprofit investigative news outlet, surveyed 250 products that are frequently purchased on Amazon. About three-quarters of the time, Amazon placed its own products and those of companies that pay for its services in the "buy box" even when other sellers on Amazon had substantially cheaper offers.[33] And because it's so easy just to click the "add to cart" button for the offer highlighted in the buy box, that's what many consumers do, without spending the time to compare offers more carefully. "It's the most valuable small button on the Internet today," according to Shmuli

Goldberg, an Israeli technologist who is quoted in the ProPublica article. The result of hitting that Amazon buy button instead of taking advantage of the cheapest offers for the 250 products ProPublica surveyed? Paying an extra $1,400.

Likewise, Amazon's free digital personal assistant, Alexa, may not always recommend the best product for our needs. Rather, she may offer the product that gives Amazon a little more in profit.

One booming business for Amazon is its own products. In having access to data on what customers look at, their price sensitivity, and what they buy, Amazon can swoop in and displace third-party sellers with its own private-label brand. As the *New York Times* reported:

> *Amazon is utilizing its knowledge of its powerful marketplace machine—from optimizing word-search algorithms to analyzing competitors' sales data to using its customer-review networks—to steer shoppers toward its in-house brands and away from its competitors, say analysts. And as consumers increasingly shop using voice technology, the playing field becomes even more tilted. For instance, consumers asking Amazon's Alexa to "buy batteries" get only one option: AmazonBasics.*[34]

Put simply, if we request something for which Amazon offers a private-label version, then Alexa will likely recommend its own product.[35] As Amazon sells its own products under many private-label brands (over one hundred), we won't always know that it's Amazon's product. Alexa may also push "sponsored" products, without disclosing the seller's payment to Amazon to promote its product.[36]

So we may rely on Alexa to wade through the panoply of options and offer us the one that best suits our needs. After all, Alexa is meant to serve us, right? But ultimately she works for Amazon, whose interests at times diverge from ours, and the largest Internet retailer can use choice overload to profit at our expense.

Forget Alexa, you say. You'll read what other consumers say, especially the "honest and unbiased feedback from some of Amazon's most trusted reviewers."[37] One problem is that Amazon actively recruits popular reviewers, which it calls Vine Voices, to review its private-label brands. "In exchange for free products, which they disclose receiving," the *New York Times* reports, "the reviewers agree to write evaluations on Amazon's site."[38] The *Times* found that for over 1,600 products across ten of Amazon's private-label brands, about half had Vine reviews. Of those 835 products, more than half of the first 30 reviews were from Amazon's Vine program. "While, for the most part, the Vine and non-Vine reviews were similarly rated, in a handful of cases, the Vine reviews were significantly better. For instance, Vine reviews for Amazon's Mama Bear diapers and baby products averaged 4.36 stars; non-Vine reviews averaged 3.82 stars."

Now we begin to see why sellers might want to offer us so many choices that we start to buckle under choice overload. They lure us with variety and increase the complexity of our choices to the point that, like rabbits frozen before the headlights of an oncoming locomotive, we are paralyzed. We simply seize up when confronted with the myriad choices and plans. But then the sellers gently nudge us with "personalized" recommendations, guiding us to products where the profit margins work in their favor.[39] All of this in what is seemingly a competitive environment.

Sellers can also use product complexity to lock us in. In some markets, like mobile phones, the challenge isn't simply attracting new users. It is also keeping current users. As Professor Adi Ayal observed in his study of the cell phone market, when a consumer's cell phone contract is up, sellers use choice overload to increase the perceived (and actual) cost of switching.[40] Rather than wade through the many competing choices, we choose the default—sticking with what we've got or going for an automatic upgrade.

There's nothing accidental about this use of product complexity to confuse consumers. One study found that as competition in the US tele-communication markets increased, cell phone providers offered more complicated, bad-value price plans.[41] As Professor Ayal observed, the increased competition caused "cell phone providers to focus on raising profitability through creating confusion and gaining from consumer mistakes," rather than through charging monopoly prices. In short, the mobile phone industry deliberately makes our choices more complex in order to exploit us.[42]

You may have noticed this combination of choice overload and default setting when it comes to relatively simple services that have somehow be-come needlessly complex—not just your mobile provider but your utility and energy contracts, insurance policies, and health plans.

In sum, competitors increase complexity and use it as a tool to get us to pay more—often for attributes or services that we don't need.

Dating and Mating:
When Is More More, and When Is It Less?

Now let us consider a higher stakes competition, namely dating. Thanks to the multitude of options offered on online dating platforms, like Match, Tinder, POF (formerly Plenty of Fish), and OkCupid, dating today has become a much more competitive enterprise.[43]

The market offers a multitude of services, catering to a range of desires. For example, OkCupid's website promotes how its "algorithm looks at your preferences, and how you answer match questions, to find the people perfect for you."[44]

Tinder . . . well, it celebrates "single culture," which is "committed to standing up for singles on and off the app, and supporting their single experience, however they choose to live it."[45]

Match.com, however, defines success simply: "More relationships & more marriages than any other site." It offers to "take the lottery out of love."[46] Match.com touts how it fosters marriages and long-term relationships: "Every month, we hear from hundreds of successful couples from all over the world—sharing love stories, sending invitations to weddings and announcing the births of new babies."[47]

Look at the success page of POF and you'll also find a lot of wedding photos.[48]

While each of these dating platforms offers something different, all of them are owned by the same company, InterActiveCorp (IAC).

Competition exists on two levels. On one level, singles (although not always) compete against others, and the competition is fierce. Log onto Match.com in any major city, and it is likely you will immediately have thousands of potential matches. Let's say we elected to meet one of the thousands of matches for dinner. If that doesn't instantly appeal, we know the person across the restaurant table can be replaced by thousands of others who match our desired traits. And in sizing us up, she knows that she has thousands of alternatives, too.

On a second level, IAC's online dating platforms compete against the old, inefficient dating world. As IAC tells investors, one competitive risk is if "a meaningful number of users" return to offline dating, which includes everything from "social networks to bars, churches, nosey aunts, prying neighbors and concerned parents."[49] Thus, to remain successful, IAC's leading online dating platforms must "continue to provide dating products that users find more efficient, effective, comfortable and convenient relative to traditional means of meeting people."[50]

From a potential dater's perspective, this sounds like heaven.

FIRST, the dating platform reduces one's *search costs*. Rather than go to spin classes, bars, and funerals (or dinner at your aunt's) where we will meet a few potential matches, if that, we can, in a matter of hours, scan hundreds of potential candidates to find good prospects.

SECOND, unlike the lemon markets, online dating increases *transparency*. We can quickly gain access to a lot of information on people in the dating market. Granted we still go on dates, but when we do, we already know if the person believes in astrology, how many times a week they exercise, their interests and sports, their bucket list of personal goals and adventures, what they do for fun, their pets, and their criteria for a match. OkCupid even asks, "Would you ever sleep with a serial killer?"—a question that might not have occurred to you but might indeed help winnow down the field of potential dates.

THIRD, online dating makes it easier to find people who share our interests, hobbies, and values. Online dating thus reduces our *transaction costs*. Rather than spend money on multiple dates to see if the person is right, we can quickly scan all the essential details.

FOURTH, online dating platforms eliminate *traditional barriers*. As the *Economist* noted, "For most of human history, the choice of life partner was limited by class, location and parental diktat."[51] Now, the magazine notes, "There are services for Jews, Christians, Muslims, Trump supporters, people who self-select as intelligent and vegans. There's BikerKiss ('Two Wheels, Two Hearts, One Road'), FarmersOnly ('Single in the Country') and Ugly Bug Ball ('Dating for the Aesthetically Average')."

FIFTH, online dating platforms reduce our *switching costs*. In the old inefficient dating world, we often lost a lot of time, emotion, and money with the wrong person until we were able to find someone with similar hobbies, such as extreme ironing or competitive dog grooming. With online dating platforms these "sunk costs"—which, according to the behavioral economics literature, can cause us to commit to a project even if it is not satisfactory—are minimized. Our choices are more easily reversible. If we don't like Ann or Andrew after one week, we can switch to Beth or Ben the next week. We, like many others, can join multiple dating platforms. We can review profiles without signaling to others what we're doing.

So competition among those who use these online dating sites is intensifying, as more people are joining the platform, giving us still more options.[52] Among younger Americans, the share of eighteen- to twenty-four-year-olds who report using online dating has nearly tripled in just a couple of years.[53] And the competition keeps increasing, as Figure 4.1 reflects, with hundreds of thousands of people joining IAC's various online dating platforms each month.

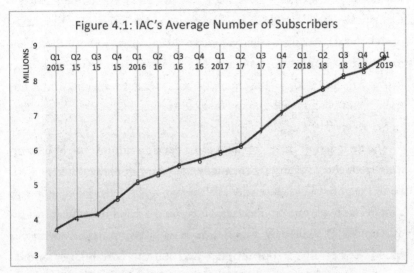

Figure 4.1: IAC's Average Number of Subscribers

Source: IAC Q1 2018 Earnings Supplemental Financial Information and Operating Metrics[54]

The additional choice that comes with this increase in numbers is staggering. As more people turn to these online platforms, each person can consider more dating options at the same time. According to one 2017 survey, over half were communicating with four or more people at the same time on a dating platform, with 19 percent juggling over ten people at the same time. Imagine trying that in a spin class.

Here we also see the power of network effects, where the benefits increase as other people join the platform. Not everyone uses the dating platform for true love or long-term relationships. But as the platforms differentiate themselves, one can visit certain platforms for one-night hookups.[55] If we are seeking entertainment, then we can try other platforms. If marriage or long-term relationships is our aim, then some platforms, like Match.com, seem a better bet. As more people look for relationships and marriages on a particular online platform, others, who initially view the platform with suspicion, will eventually relent. (After all, we have to go where everyone else is searching for romance.) But the increasing competition, in reducing our costs and improving efficiency (perhaps we can communicate with twenty potential partners simultaneously), should increase the likelihood for marriage, as some of these platforms promise. With so many good alternatives from which to choose, it improves the odds of finding not only love, but someone whom our friends and parents will support (or at least tolerate).

So, where is the catch?

The designers of these popular online dating platforms might be profiting from choice overload. The many options with many different attributes (height, weight, education, profession, looks, religion, etc.) present a lot of trade-offs and counterfactuals (what if I dated Beth/Walt instead of Ann/Will?). Moreover, we often have to justify our choice with our friends and family, so our ultimate decision can have high emotional (and potential financial) stakes. And being lured back to the dating site with its many options can increase the dating platform's bottom line.

Some of the early behavioral experiments, however, did not find anxiety or regret when the participants compared four or sixty-four dating profiles.[56] As choices increase, participants in those experiments simply became lazier and used less mentally strenuous strategies. They also made fewer trade-offs.[57] Speed-dating studies tell a similar story.[58]

But Professors Jonathan D'Angelo and Catalina Toma tried a different approach.[59] Rather than test for choice overload while participants were swiping potential candidates, they tested what happened one week after participants selected a potential date. They created an online dating service modeled after Match.com, with potential mates of similar attractiveness, and offered a larger dating pool of twenty-four candidates and a smaller one consisting of six candidates (who were drawn from the larger dating pool).

Participants were divided into one of four groups: (i) the *low competi-*

tion group/low freedom group—where they chose from the small dating pool and were told that they could *not* switch to other online dates the following week; (ii) the *low competition group/greater freedom* group— where they also chose from the small dating pool but could select someone else the following week; (iii) the *high competition group/low freedom* group—where they chose from twenty-four dating options but could *not* switch to other online dates the following week; and (iv) the *high competition group/greater freedom* group—where they chose from twenty-four dating options and could switch to other online dates the following week.

As in earlier studies, there was no evidence of choice overload when people initially made their choice. But one week later, things changed. Of the two groups that could switch, one would think that those with fewer options would more likely switch the following week. Instead, online daters who chose from the larger pool were more likely to switch than those choosing from a small pool.

Who had the greatest drop in satisfaction in the one-week period? One would think the group where competition was the weakest, namely those with fewer options and no ability to switch the following week. Instead, the group that benefitted from the greatest competition had the greatest drop in satisfaction and were generally the least satisfied with their choice, relative to the other groups.

The choice that attracted us to the platform seems to affect our satisfaction and subsequently pulls us back into the dating pool.

These findings need to be replicated across a broader cross-section of singles. But switching does seem to be a feature of online dating. In one 2016 Pew Research survey, 31 percent of online dating users agreed "that online dating keeps people from settling down, because they always have options for people to date."[60] Similarly, one complaint of Match.com is that because everyone "has so many choices, you may experience people dropping out of touch—sometimes in the middle of an e-mail conversation."[61] Others complain of ending up "on an assembly-line of dates."[62]

One dating historian noted that the stress of the popular online dating platforms is different from what is experienced in traditional forms of dating: "There is something new about the intensity with which these apps wear people out."[63]

Helen Fisher, biological anthropologist and chief scientific officer at Match.com, acknowledged the biggest problem with dating apps is "cognitive overload," as "the brain is not well built to choose between hundreds or thousands of alternatives."[64] She recommends that people stop when they've hit nine matches and consider those. Likewise, eharmony's relationship psychologist commented, "You could say online dating allows people to get into relationships, learn things, and ultimately make a better selection. But you could also easily see a world in which online dating leads to people leaving relationships the moment they're not working—an overall weakening of commitment."[65]

Granted, but some of the larger dating platforms, like Match.com, promote their success in fostering marriage. So is online dating delivering on this metric?

Although some of the leading dating platforms provide anecdotal success stories of marriage, none compare the marriage rate arising from their platform versus other venues. On a macro level, the data does not suggest that the increase in competition, brought by online dating platforms, has actually increased the marriage rate. Instead, the overall trends suggest the contrary. The percentage of American men and women over twenty-five who have never married more than doubled between 1960 and 2012.[66]

Many more of today's young adults will likely never marry. Pew Research projects, based on US census data, found that "when today's young adults reach their mid-40s to mid-50s, a record-high share (25%) is likely to have never been married."[67] That, according to Pew Research, would be the highest share of unmarried Americans in modern history. Evidently, the reasons for this social trend go beyond simple competition, but choice overload in an ultracompetitive environment may play a role here.

That said, according to one study, among those who did meet online and married, their marriages are associated with a slightly higher rate of satisfaction and slightly lower rate of breakup than the surveyed couples who met offline.[68]

All we can really say for sure right now is that online dating platforms have increased competition, as more people go online to look for relationships. While it may be true that Match.com fostered "more marriages than any other site," that does not mean it increases one's likelihood of finding a spouse compared to other means. Fewer people are getting married (as a percentage of their age group), and those who do marry are likely to have found their partner in the less efficient, choice-poor world. While there is no conclusive evidence that online dating is *causing* this decline in marriages,[69] one can safely conclude that online dating, despite lowering search, transaction, and switching costs, isn't significantly *increasing* marriages.

So, does our happiness increase or decrease as the dating competition increases? The answer, alas, is that as of now we don't know. About all we can say is that the multitude of choices appears to undermine our willingness to commit, but for those who do commit, the satisfaction seems to be slightly higher.

Another thing we can say for sure is that many online dating platforms are profiting. Of the $2.9 billion dating industry, mobile dating services is the fastest growing segment.[70] IAC is clobbering the old, inefficient ways of dating. Its revenue from the dating platforms increased 23 percent between 2015 and 2016, and increased another 19 percent for 2017 to $1.33 billion, thanks largely to Tinder.[71]

Although all of IAC's dating products are free, in that you can establish a profile and review the profiles of other users without charge,[72] you actually need to subscribe to communicate with potential matches. Thus IAC's Match Group makes its money primarily from users "in the form of recurring subscriptions."[73] And if the dating platform makes its money from subscriptions, it follows that the longer the platform fascinates us with new potential matches, the longer we subscribe, and the more money it collects. Imagine if online platforms that promised marriages actually delivered on this promise very quickly. We would likely meet our ideal match in a month or so, and continue dating off-line. Thus, we would cancel our subscription after a few months. The platform's user turnover would be very high, as couples quickly meet and go offline. While the platform's success rate would attract others, the bad news is that the high turnover rate would likely reduce subscription fees (as people cancel their subscriptions and no longer pay extra fees for additional services). Thus, the platform's bottom line would likely suffer.

If, however, the dating site can entice us to stay on its platform longer, then its revenue will likely increase—whether by targeting us with ads, using us to attract others to the dating platform, or extending our six-month subscription services. So the dating platform continually gives us new options (which we crave), in exchange for automatically recurring subscription fees. If we are reluctant to commit, because next week's (or month's) singles might prove even better, all the better.

Thus, the competition among dating platforms can easily turn toxic as they use choice overload to profit. Each week, for example, Match.com sends users profiles of sixteen new potential matches. It tells users of the tens of thousands of new single women or men who joined the platform in the past week. And as users communicate with these new potential matches, their subscription continues. Its enticements raise the interesting question of whether an industry that feeds from our ongoing quest for choices has the incentive to fuel our desire for a little more?

Reflections

We like choice. We think it's great to have many choices. But, at times, we can overdose from too many choices brought about by too much competition. Competition becomes our blind spot.

What happens when we have too many choices is that we get confused and overwhelmed (cognitive costs) and we may then become inhibited about making choices. Or we experience buyer's remorse. We can't complain about this abundance from competition. It is hard to justify to others and ourselves the emotional and economic toll from competition overdose. And the frustration and nagging regret we experience—well, that is our own peculiar shortcoming. After all, if you or I mess up, we have only ourselves to blame.

Rather than giving us fewer choices, sellers can actively exploit our confusion by offering too many choices and then helping us narrow them down in ways that are ultimately to their own benefit, not ours. But we can't blame retailers or manufacturers for increasing variety or complexity of the product's features—that's competition.

Thus, we should be grateful when Alexa makes recommendations. She cannot be blamed when she steers us to higher-margin products—because we could always choose something else. We have the freedom to choose.

Nor should we complain when the online dating platform tells us of the potential matches it selected especially for us from the tens of thousands of new singles or of messages waiting for us (right before we're about to cancel our subscription). We can always choose to ignore these entreaties.

So, it is not surprising that a relationship trend in 2018 was something *anti*competitive, namely "slow dating" where niche dating services are intentionally offering far fewer options to subscribers each day.[74] As researchers have argued, our commitment to foster a relationship may depend on our perception of supply. If we perceive many competing alternatives to the person sitting across the table, then why not fake the emergency phone call? But if we perceive few competing alternatives, then we might look beyond slight flaws.

So don't expect competition to magically deliver the right level of choice, especially when companies are profiting from our choice overload. You can expect, at times, entreaties like this one from Tinder:

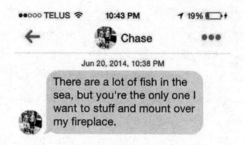

Source: *Ranker*[75]

But competition will deliver more options, as you swipe past this one, and be assured, that with so many options, you must be better off.

PART II

Who Is Pushing the Toxic Competition?

CHAPTER 5

The Ideologues

The Defenders of Competition Ideology

Robert T. Alexander spent his entire thirty-four-year professional career with the US Coast Guard. He began in 1928 as a cadet at the Coast Guard Academy. After graduating second in his class, he went on to become a successful officer, rising to the rank of captain. He and his wife had no children, and after she died, he bequeathed over $1 million to the Coast Guard Academy. The money was to be used to fund a prize for the graduating cadet who attained the highest grade point average in chemistry and physics.

The Coast Guard, however, declined to accept money to be used for those purposes. Why? In one word: competition.

The academy's superintendent warned that the generous prize would spur "unhealthy competition," which would jeopardize the service academy's mission.[1] According to the superintendent, the sizable award, estimated to amount to between $65,000 and $130,000 per year for the winner, would

(i) engender intense, unhealthy competition among cadets, (ii) spawn honor code offenses, (iii) distort the competition to major in the sciences at the expense of other majors, (iv) erode, if not destroy, the class and interpersonal relationships and esprit de corps so vital to the Academy's goal of instilling in cadets the value of teamwork and (v) serve to teach cadets, wrongly, that the reward for a job well done in a life

of public service in the Coast Guard is cash rather than the personal
satisfaction that comes from doing well one's duty as an officer.

When the academy mounted a legal challenge to the terms of the bequest, the federal judge agreed with the academy's assessment of the dangers. "No student of human nature can seriously doubt the validity of
Admiral's views in this regard," the judge stated in his decision. "Attempts
at literal enforcement of the trust would fundamentally change the academy in ways neither contemplated nor desired by Captain Alexander."

To spread the benefits of Alexander's bequest more broadly and thereby
offset the disadvantages that the Admiral had identified, the court modi-
fied the terms of the trust, so that more cadets would receive smaller cash
awards in the form of not just prizes for achievement, but also research
grants and fellowships to fund graduate studies.

Why do we mention this 1993 case? Because it is one of the few modern cases where a US court agreed that under some circumstances competition could indeed be unhealthy.

Economists have long known this. And at some level we all intuitively
recognize it. While we see the benefit of competition in many circumstances, we also see its toxic effects in others, which is why, for example,
we don't encourage our children to compete for our affection (unlike King
Lear, who paid a high price for that mistake). Nor do the mainstream religions endorse a deity who wants people to compete for His (or Her) love.

Despite acknowledging the potential for toxic competition, there is
little societal consensus on whether, or how, to restrain it.

As we saw in our First Overdose, even institutions as powerful and
prestigious as Harvard and Princeton could not unilaterally de-escalate
(or withdraw from) the competition that they knew was harming both
themselves and their prospective students. There was simply no regulatory policy that might have helped them to do so. Our economic and
legal institutions are primed to foster, not put the brakes on, the competitive race to the bottom.

In the Second Overdose, we saw how competitive price pressure caused rivals to secretly degrade quality and undermine safety, just in order to survive. Yet again, there were no effective legal or regulatory mechanisms in place to ensure that these abuses did not occur.

In our Third Overdose, we saw how businesses like hotels and credit card companies compete to exploit our weaknesses. Even the "good" companies, like Caesars, for example, were eventually forced to recognize that toxic competition would require them to exploit if they were not to lose business. Consumers resent these practices, but rarely do consumer protection agencies in the US come to the rescue.

Finally, in our Fourth Overdose, consumers are presented with a mind-boggling multitude of choices, geared to attract them and, once overwhelmed, to profit at their expense, whether it's Amazon steering users to products with higher margins or Match.com, while promising marriage, undercutting commitment by enticing users back to its dating platform with even more attractive options. Businesses are using choice overload to get us to pay more—for less. Yet again, this toxic competition is encouraged.

For each overdose, we can identify multiple scenarios in which competition hurts consumers and society at large—and sometimes even the competitors themselves. So why does this toxic competition ideology spread?

Here we identify the first of four culprits: our oversimplified competition ideology, which holds that competition is necessary and always good. This ideology has prevented us, as a society, from making the changes that are needed to curb competition when it becomes harmful.

"Competition Is Not All It Is Cracked Up to Be"

On several occasions, we presented our ideas about competition to antitrust officials and economists. How would these promoters of competition

respond to our thesis that competition, at times, is toxic, and might therefore require some remedies? Would security escort us to the door?

Quite the opposite. As a top economist remarked in one of our meetings: "Competition is not all it is cracked up to be." Economists, he
noted, have outlined numerous instances when markets—despite being
competitive—might not deliver a positive social outcome. "Promoting
competition, for the sake of competition," he added, "does not guarantee
the optimal or fair outcome. It is for the state to balance between efficiency, competition, and other social values." No one disagreed.

Indeed, economists over the years have identified circumstances when
competition can be suboptimal, if not downright toxic, and have examined possible antidotes.[2]

One example of suboptimal competition, which we saw in chapter 2,
is "lemon markets," where dealers know more about the problems of
their products than their customers do (think of the used Jaguar sales-
person), and the dishonest dealers drive out the honest ones.

Another example involves "negative externalities"—meaning situations in which the producers don't bear the cost of the damage caused by
their activities. Such markets may exist when there are no regulations to
force them to assume those costs. Think, for example, of the air pollution that is a by-product of using coal to blast the furnaces used to make
steel.[3] Without any environmental laws to require the steel producers to
invest in cleaner technology, their mills will continue to pollute, and the
polluted air they throw off will make people sick—a cost borne by the
public, not the polluters.

A third example concerns "public goods," where no one can be excluded from enjoying the benefit. Think of a fireworks show, where
regardless of whether members of the public have paid the price of
admission for it, anyone can look up to the sky and see it. So, without
an ability to charge for the benefit, market forces may not necessarily
provide this public good. Often for critical public goods, like national
defense, we rely on the government to offer it, and it protects all of us,

regardless of how little or how much our tax dollars have contributed to it.

The list of imperfections and market failures goes on.[4] But despite this, there is often a public misunderstanding of what competition does. Competition can often lead to the most economically efficient outcome. But an economically efficient outcome does not necessarily mean an outcome that is good, fair, or just—for consumers, society, or even for other competitors. As a society, we don't simply want competition per se; we want *fair* methods of competition that benefit all (even when some rivals may lose a particular customer or bid).

Policy makers, however, rarely voice such a balanced or detached assessment of competition. Nor do the enforcement agencies. Instead, they tend to evangelize an all-out, go-go form of competition ideology, along these lines, as noted by a well-known antitrust lawyer:

> *Americans love competition. In sports. In politics. In ideas. In business. In everything. They demand it. They fight for it. In the marketplace, they know that competition guarantees the best possible product or service at the lowest possible price, and that everyone has the chance to make a better mousetrap. It is obvious to them that the more competitors there are, the more competition there is. And the more competition there is, the better the services and products and the lower the prices.[5]*

In their rulings, the courts have largely echoed the evangelism of the true believers. Thus, the US Supreme Court has reiterated over the years its continuing support for the proposition that the competition philosophy on which we have staked our economy is inherently good: "The heart of our national economic policy long has been faith in the value of competition."[6] Competition cannot lead to higher prices, poorer quality, or greater safety risks. The assumption is that competition will lower prices and improve quality and safety.

Judges, antitrust enforcers, and policy makers might privately recognize that competition isn't always what it's cracked up to be. But in their day-to-day work they typically enforce the competition ideology. They have to, because that ideology is now, for the most part, enshrined in the law. Thus, courts and governmental agencies are not allowed to entertain complex inquiries into the nature or problems of different kinds of competition. The law is the law, and they are required to apply it.

As one such decision by the Supreme Court said very clearly: "Even assuming occasional exceptions to the presumed consequences of competition, the statutory policy precludes inquiry into the question whether competition is good or bad."[7] And from being required to comply with the law to mounting a passionate defense of its underlying assumption— the belief that competition "is the best method of allocating resources in a free market"[8]—is only too short a step.

From Subtlety to Slogan, Idea to Ideology— More Competition and Less Regulation

How did we, as a society, arrive at this reductivist consensus?

To begin with, we often are attracted to simplified narratives. They are easy to understand, govern, and follow. When they are often correct, society is willing to turn a blind eye to their limitations.

What also may be surprising to some is that the competition ideology frequently comes from a counterintuitive source: powerful companies. For them, the competition ideology, when carefully deployed, can serve as an excellent shield against state intervention and as a sword to control the market, dictate the rules of the game, and eliminate threats to their profits.

And so, as we'll see in the next few chapters, big business uses its money and power to promote the reductive competition ideology. Its lobbying has captured many of our elected officials. It is therefore of little surprise that our policies and legislation are shaped by this distorted competition ideology: If competition is strong enough, we can get rid of regulations; and the self-correcting markets will promote prosperity and consumers' welfare. Key governmental policies blindly rely on market forces to fix it all, willingly remove any state regulation (as the market will offer a better alternative), and set aside any consideration of other societal values. So, in 1991 we saw President George H. W. Bush asking his Council on Competitiveness "to put an end to what he has called 'regulatory creep' in the federal government."[9]

Sounds doubtful? Well, let's consider the financial sector.

The US Supreme Court in 1963 characterized the banking regulations as one of the most, if not the most, successful systems of economic regulation.[10] Commercial banking, as a result of federal laws, like the Glass-Steagall Act of 1933 and Bank Holding Company Act of 1956, as well as state laws, was diffused through many independent, local banks, rather than concentrated in a few nationwide banks, as in England and Germany. With this federal and state regulatory framework for commercial banking, the Court noted the "virtual disappearance of bank failures from the American economic scene."

But the financial industry in the 1980s began pushing for deregulation. Pushing the reductivist narrative, the industry argued that if competition is viewed as inherently organic and good, then regulation must be seen as inherently artificial, intrusive, and bad—something that interferes with natural market forces. Interest groups, businesses, lobbyists, and politicians repeated the magical formula.

One victim in the late 1990s was the Glass-Steagall Act, which was meant to prevent banks from becoming too-big-and-integrated-to-fail, by hampering affiliations between the commercial banking and securities industries. The financial industry was calling the law "an anticompetitive anachronism."[11]

The act was hobbled, and then eventually cut down to pave the way for the $70 billion merger of Travelers Group Inc. and Citicorp, which created the largest commercial banking organization in the world, with total consolidated assets of approximately $751 billion. During its merger review, the US Department of Justice (DOJ) Antitrust Division "heard numerous complaints that Citigroup would have an undue aggregation of resources—that the deal would create a firm too big to be allowed to fail."[12] But the DOJ "essentially viewed this as primarily a regulatory issue" for the Federal Reserve Board.

The Federal Reserve Board, however, dismissed this and other concerns, which presaged the financial crisis a decade later, like how consumers were harmed by "Travelers's marketing and sales practices for its subprime mortgage loans, personal loans and insurance products" and how the merger "would provide incentives for Citigroup to 'steer' [low to moderate income] and minority consumers to its subprime lenders."[13]

The chairman of the Fed, Alan Greenspan, urged Congress that removing the regulatory barriers "would permit banking organizations to compete more effectively in their natural markets. The result would be a more efficient financial system providing better services to the public."[14] Greenspan in 2000 pressed for more deregulation, including federal legislation that eliminated virtually all federal government regulation of the over-the-counter derivatives market and also preempted certain state laws relating to it.

As an editor of the *Financial Times* noted, "All the ingredients—including, crucially, a laissez-faire Federal Reserve under Alan Greenspan—were now in place for high-octane financial capitalism."[15] Not only did the government deregulate, but Greenspan, among others, under the guise of promoting competition, resisted recommendations to crack down on subprime mortgages or impose regulations on the complex financial instruments that include credit default swaps, which figured prominently in the financial crisis.[16]

As the economist Paul Krugman chronicled in a column written during the George W. Bush administration:

Consider the press conference held on June 3, 2003—just about the time subprime lending was starting to go wild—to announce a new initiative aimed at reducing the regulatory burden on banks. Representatives of four of the five government agencies responsible for financial supervision used tree shears to attack a stack of paper representing bank regulations. The fifth representative, James Gilleran of the Office of Thrift Supervision, wielded a chainsaw.[7]

Just to make sure that the deregulation was effective, the federal government intervened and prevented the states from protecting their citizens. As Krugman noted at the end of 2007:

Two months after that event [the 2003 press conference with the chainsaw-wielding regulator] the US Office of the Comptroller of the Currency, one of the tree-shears-wielding agencies, moved to exempt national banks from state regulations that protect consumers against predatory lending. If, say, New York State wanted to protect its own residents—well, sorry, that wasn't allowed.[8]

In short, back in the years that preceded the global economic crisis precipitated by the United States, the regulators disappeared—perhaps hiding behind the chainsaw wielders—as "liar" or NINJA ("no income, no job, no assets") mortgages and other shady practices spread. The NINJA mortgages were simply repackaged into investments that Wall Street peddled on supposedly more sophisticated, but also unsuspecting, clients. Competition was fierce—to offer more innovative (and risky) financial instruments. Wall Street wanted the party to continue, and most, if not all, of the regulators acceded. Competition in the financial industry became a race to recklessness.

With their mindless belief in the curative powers of competition, Greenspan and the other public stewards of our financial system ignored the red flags. As the Financial Crisis Inquiry Commission, which was created in 2009 to examine the causes of the economic crisis, reported, Greenspan and the other regulators "ignored warnings and failed to question, understand, and manage evolving risks within a system essential to the well-being of the American public."[19] Among the red flags they failed to see were "risky subprime lending and securitization, an unsustainable rise in housing prices, widespread reports of egregious and predatory lending practices, dramatic increases in household mortgage debt, and exponential growth in financial firms' trading activities, unregulated derivatives, and short-term 'repo' lending markets." In paraphrasing Shakespeare, the Commission noted that "the fault lies not in the stars, but in us"—namely our policy makers.

When it all came crashing down, the former Fed Chair Greenspan admitted making a "mistake" in believing that banks, operating in their own self-interest, would do what was necessary to protect their shareholders and institutions.[20] "A critical pillar to market competition and free markets did break down," Greenspan said. "I still do not fully understand why it happened."

Winning Rhetoric

If there is any doubt that competition is the ideology that rules our lives, ask yourself: Do you remember any policy maker within your lifetime issuing a warning about competition's potential for toxicity? Almost certainly not.

Instead you hear policy makers from both parties invoking the verities of the competition ideology. As President Obama noted in his weekly address, "Competition is good for consumers, workers, businesses, and our economy," and the "most essential ingredient in a healthy free market . . ."[21] Likewise, his predecessor George W. Bush opined that competition is good and "brings out the best in everybody."[22]

While competition can often produce an efficient outcome, policy makers rarely, if ever, add the qualifiers—competition does not always yield the good, fair, or just outcome, and can be at times downright toxic. Among the ideologues, any such nuance is heretical.

One measure of how deeply the competition ideology has taken root in our society is its dominance in the public discourse—something we can observe with Google Books Ngram Viewer, an online tool that charts the frequency of use of a given word or phrase. The results appear in a graph showing how often such words have appeared in the vast number of books Google has scanned for use in its search engine.

Graph 5.1 shows a rise in the use of the words *competition* (upper line) and *markets* (lower line) beginning in the early 1900s.

Graph 5.1

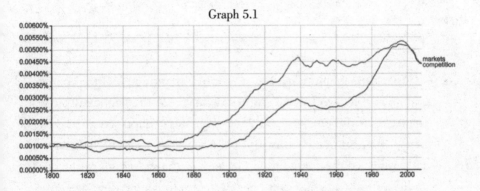

This in itself is unsurprising. The value of competition has powered our modern economy. But beginnning in the 1960s and flourishing in recent years is also the term *anticompetitive regulation.*

Graph 5.2

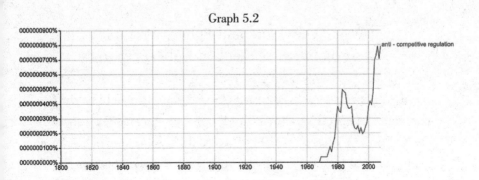

Its frequency probably reflects the increased ferver in dismantling the role of the state in safeguarding its citizens. We also see the rise of *deregulation* compared to *more regulations* or *tougher regulations*—both of which have flatlined.

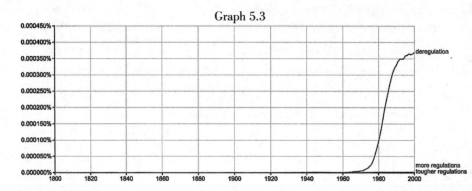

Graph 5.3

What these graphs illustrate so vividly is the triumph of the competition ideology—and the defeat of any nuance in the public discourse. To be clear, this book (and our professional experience) recognizes that competition is often healthy. But because we, as a society, have so totally embraced the competition ideology, we have overlooked the possibility of providing antidotes and remedies to competition overdoses when they occur—which they often do. Actually, such remedies are not only overlooked; they tend to be explicitly forbidden. Let us illustrate.

When Our Laws and Polices Prohibit De-escalation: A Look at College Sports

It would seem that the easiest kind of overdose to fix would be the first one, where competition can hurt nearly everyone—competitors, consumers, and society—and presumably there would be some kind of consensus about the need to find a way to de-escalate the toxic competition.

But as we saw with the universities, for example, it wasn't easy at all. Although few, if any, of the nonprofit universities we cited in our first chapter are competition ideologues (just ask their faculty), they did not take the obvious step, which would have been to come to a collective agreement to de-escalate a practice that most of them surely viewed as harmful.

The reason? Very simply, it's because the law forbids them to take collective anticompetitive action. Since the competition ideology has become enshrined in law, if the universities were to have agreed to collectively end the early admissions process and all the abuses it engenders, they would have opened themselves to significant civil (and possibly criminal) liability.

If you're skeptical about whether that is a real danger, let's look at what happened when a number of universities did try to take collaborative action in another arena where the competition ideology was proving harmful—the sports arena, specifically college football and basketball.

Many decry the vast sums of money sloshing around college sports. This is a classic arms race in which each university competes to outspend its rivals in order to gain a relative advantage—and most end up worse off as a result. Yet rarely does anyone do anything to try to stop the race.

To see why, let's go on the tour that, a few years (and coaches) ago, the head football coach at the University of Tennessee (UT) gave to the press so that they could view the new $45 million football practice facility being built on campus. He was very eager to show off this building because it increased the "wow" factor that would help him in the fierce competition to recruit the best football players. Other parts of the university were in need of repair, and many departments were facing severe constraints on their resources. But the 145,000-square-foot football practice facility under construction, which was to contain a grand team meeting room, custom-designed chairs, hydrotherapy room, restaurant, nutrition bar, and lockers equipped to charge iPads and cell phones, was intended to be the finest of its kind. However, as he concluded the tour, the coach observed that several rival universities, upon seeing the plans for UT's facility, were constructing even more expensive training facilities.

With the rivals spending tens of millions on ever more elaborate facilities, it was surely inevitable that none of the universities would be able to sustain a competitive advantage for long. Meanwhile, the enormous sums of money that went into these arms races would mean that other student needs would go unmet. Yet this competition was ultimately subsidized by all the students (through higher student fees and tuition) and, in the case of public universities, by taxpayers.[23]

There was nothing new about this story, really. Over a decade before that UT coach conducted his press tour, the Knight Commission on Intercollegiate Athletics had made an extensive study of the arms race problem in college sports. To curb the athletics arms race, they concluded in their 2001 report that no "single college or university can afford to act unilaterally, nor can one conference act alone."[24] Basically, the colleges would have to come to a collective agreement:

As long as there is an athletics arms race, unilateral disarmament on the part of one institution would most assuredly be punished swiftly by loss of position and increased vulnerability. Change will come, sanity will be restored, only when the higher education community comes together to meet collectively the challenges its members face.[25]

One obvious way of limiting the pernicious financial damage done by the arms race would be for schools to collectively agree to cap the amount spent on their football and basketball programs. This would stem the flood of money allocated to sports and allow more money to be spent on educational objectives—presumably the core mission of the university.

Well, that had actually been tried already. Back in the 1980s, the National Collegiate Athletic Association (NCAA) and its member universities were troubled by spiraling athletic budgets. Between 1978 and 1985, athletic expenses at Division I institutions (the highest echelon of college sports) had increased over 100 percent.[26] By 1985, 42 percent of Division I universities were reporting deficits averaging $824,000 per school in their overall athletic program budgets. Though those were boon years for college basketball, 51 percent of the surveyed Division I schools' basketball programs lost money—on average $145,000. One significant contributing factor, the NCAA found, was the escalating costs associated with salaries for part-time assistant basketball coaches, so they decided to do something about it.

To de-escalate the arms race, the NCAA suggested coming to an agreement to put caps on the salaries to be paid to those part-time assistant coaches, and also to restrict the overall number of basketball coaches. Division I basketball teams were to be limited to three full-time coaches and two part-time coaches. The part-time coach positions were to be filled by part-time assistants, graduate assistants, or volunteer coaches, and their salaries were to be restricted, with no one paid more than an amount in the value of graduate student Grants-in-Aid.[27] However, many athletic departments found creative ways to circumvent the NCAA restrictions, and paid some of these part-time coaches salaries as high as $60,000 to $70,000 per year.[28]

So, in 1989, the NCAA assembled a committee to find new ways to curb the escalating costs of intercollegiate athletics, "without disturbing the competitive balance" among NCAA members.[29] Charged with the mission of attempting "to save intercollegiate athletics from itself," the Cost Reduction Committee, which consisted of financial aid personnel, intercollegiate athletic administrators, college presidents, university faculty members, and one university chancellor, recommended limiting Division I basketball coaching staffs to four members: one head coach, two assistant coaches, and one entry-level, so-called restricted-earnings coach. The restricted-earnings coaches were to be drawn from the ranks of graduate assistants and paid a salary capped at $16,000 (which represented the cost of out-of-state tuition for graduate schools at public institutions at that time and the average graduate school tuition at private institutions). This seemed an entirely common-sense approach for academic institutions.

However, the NCAA agreement was soon attacked in court. The restricted-earnings coaches brought a class action lawsuit against the NCAA. Universities normally compete with each other in the labor market for their coaching services, and coaching salaries reflect that competition. Thus, the coaches argued that the NCAA's collective action to restrict salaries was *anti*competitive and illegal under the federal antitrust laws.

Yes, the NCAA responded, but this competition is toxic. It diverts resources from the core function of colleges—namely education. Thus, collective action is the only way to curb this arms race. The NCAA had ample evidence of the harmful effects of the competition. (It could provide even more evidence today.)

So, who won? The case never even went to trial. Finding the NCAA's reasoning unpersuasive, in 1996 the court ruled for the coaches on what's called a summary judgment motion.

The NCAA appealed, but the appellate court was equally unpersuaded. Neither the NCAA nor anyone else could defend themselves in an antitrust lawsuit by arguing that competition can be damaging at times (even under narrow circumstances, when it harms the core mission of the university). As the federal appellate court wrote in its 1998 decision, quoting the Supreme Court's words we cited earlier, "the Sherman Act precludes inquiry into the question whether competition is good or bad."[30]

The Arms Race Redux

With the competition ideology hindering the universities' ability to collectively limit the amount spent on football and basketball, and absent any kind of government regulation, the arms race accelerated. By 2010, the Knight Commission painted a bleaker picture:

> *The costs of competing in big-time intercollegiate sports have soared. Rates of spending growth are breathtaking. This financial arms race threatens the continued viability of athletics programs and the integrity of our universities. It cannot be maintained.*[31]

As its 2010 report notes, "The intensely competitive environment at the top levels of college sports has prompted four rounds of realignment among athletic conferences since 1994; a bidding war for prominent coaches; and accelerating expenses across the board."[32]

The Commission's findings are stunning and shocking:

- At many universities, institutional spending on high-profile sports was growing at double or triple the pace of spending on academics, with only seven college athletic programs actually making money between 2005 and 2010.
- Spending by the top ten public universities on athletics was projected to climb from $69 million per school in 2005 to $250 million by 2020—to serve an average of six hundred student-athletes per school.
- In each major athletic conference, spending per athlete was outpacing academic spending per student by four to eleven times. For example, in 2008, the colleges in the Southeastern Conference (SEC) spent on academics the equivalent of $13,410 per student; in contrast they spent on coaching and other athletic-related activities the equivalent of $144,592 per athlete.

Escalating coaches' salaries was deemed the single largest contributing factor to the unsustainable growth of athletic expenditures. But the report acknowledges that the federal antitrust laws prevent the NCAA and the universities to place reasonable caps on coaches' salaries.[33]

So basically what the Commission recommends by way of remedying all these abuses is transparency—in the belief that if we knew the truth about what these programs cost and how they undermine the educational goals of the university, reform would come about.

But it hasn't. By 2018, the head college football coaches at twenty universities were making on average $5,727,689 per year.[34] To put it another way, each coach's salary could fund over sixty college department chairs (who annually make on average $84,747).[35]

Still in doubt as to the toxicity? Let's continue . . .

The Cost of the Competition Ideology

Who offers more varsity sports: the SEC universities, like Alabama and Vanderbilt, or the Division III Little Ivies, like Williams, Hamilton, and Amherst, who compete in the New England Small College Athletic Conference (NESCAC)? One initially might expect the SEC universities. After all, their athletic conference captures most of the hundreds of millions of dollars in television revenue.[36] Plus, the SEC state universities have nearly ten times more undergraduate students than the Little Ivies. Texas A&M's 44,975 undergraduate enrollment, by itself, is double the size of all eleven Little Ivies combined.

But the answer is the Little Ivies. Since they don't funnel most of their money into men's football and basketball, these small liberal arts colleges can offer more varsity sports than their SEC counterparts.[37] With more opportunities to participate, more students at the Little Ivies (on average, 30 percent of the student body) participate in a varsity sport compared to the SEC schools (2 percent of the student body). (If interested in the data, see Appendix F.) Even in absolute numbers, the results are striking:

Fewer women play varsity sports at nine SEC schools than at any Little Ivy. Only 311 of the nearly 23,000 male undergraduates at Texas A&M play varsity sports, which is less than at any Little Ivy (except Connecticut College).

While approximately 30 percent of surveyed freshmen at private and public universities identified the opportunity to play sports as a factor in their college decisions,[38] the opportunities to play college sports, on a varsity level, are dwindling at many Division I schools, as more money is being funneled into the football and basketball programs. Other programs will have to be cut—including other athletic programs. Of course, many big-time football universities, like Alabama, have already made such cuts.

Once varsity sports are pared, the only thing left to cut is academics. Among the others who don't benefit from this expensive arms race are the students who pay for it, not just in the form of higher tuition and fees but also reduced educational offerings. By 2001, the Knight Commission was warning that the "considerable financial pressures and ever-increasing spending in today's college sports system could lead to permanent and untenable competition between academics and athletics." By 2010, that was already happening. The high cost of athletic programs had caused some institutions to have to choose between funding sections of freshman English and funding the football team.[39] Since so few of these hugely expensive sports programs generate enough revenue to pay for themselves, the universities subsidize them, which, of course, comes at the expense of academic excellence and education.[40]

And as with other forms of toxic competition, even those who presumably are the beneficiaries—among them the college athletes themselves—are not necessarily better off. Depending on where they are enrolled, college football and basketball players may lose their athletic scholarships (and often their ability to remain in school) should they be unable for any reason, including injury, to play.

The football and basketball players may also ultimately lose out on getting an education—and a degree. Given the number of hours they have to devote to training and preparing for games, their academic performance often suffers. For those college athletes who go on to hugely lucrative careers in the pros, that may seem like an acceptable trade-off. But the fact is that fewer than 2 percent of college basketball or football players make it to the pros. A college degree might provide another route to a good future for those who don't. But at the sixty-five institutions in the five wealthiest leagues, only 69 percent of athletes graduate within six years, compared to 76 percent of undergraduates overall. The percentage is even worse for African-American male athletes—just over half of whom graduate within six years.[41]

It doesn't have to be this way. The Little Ivies created their athletic conference "out of a concern for the direction of intercollegiate athletic programs."[42] So they, unlike the SEC schools, pay their athletic coaches far less and more in line with the faculty (on average $78,591 for coaches on the women's teams and $88,616 on the men's teams in 2016).[43]

But many NCAA Division I colleges remain in a quandary. Their football and basketball programs are losing a lot of money. Should individual schools make the unilateral decision to spend less on these sports and bear the consequences? Or should they keep trying to compete with their rivals, paying higher salaries, recruiting better athletes, building flashier facilities, etc.?

De-escalation Now—or Never?

Concerned about the drain on its resources, one university, University of Alabama at Birmingham (UAB), did something in 2014 that no other Division I school had tried in over twenty years: After commissioning a study of the cost of its sports programs, which calculated the university's escalating losses in this arms race (an estimated $25.3 million over five years alone),[44] UAB opted to shut down its football team. While fiscally prudent, the decision prompted hate mail, threats, a vote of "no confidence" by the faculty for the college president—and ultimately a reversal. Football not only returned, but at a greater expense than before, with the university spending money on new practice fields and state-of-the-art facilities. The new football coach, in one local news story, proclaimed that his college now "has the best facility in Conference USA."[45]

So no matter what the cost, universities seem unable to unilaterally de-escalate. Some do the reverse. After the University of Massachusetts Amherst made the decision (an expensive one) to move its football team into the top echelon of college football—the Football Bowl Subdivision (FBS)—the additional revenues they expected from ticket sales, etc. failed to materialize; the team had to rely on even more financial support from the university than it had received before the move. So an ad hoc faculty committee was formed to look into the financial impact of being in the FBS. As a professor who co-chaired the committee said, "I see nothing changing in terms of the financial viability [of the move to the FBS]. It's going to continue to drain money from the core mission of the university. And there's no end in sight. How many years do we do this?"[46]

By now, you should know the answers:

As long as the schools remain in thrall to the lure of big-ticket athletics and engage in the high-stakes competition that goes along with it. (Witness what happened at the University of Massachusetts: It discontinued the committee that questioned the high costs of being in the FBS—while voting in favor of keeping the team there rather than moving it down to a less expensive division.)

And, of course, as long as the reductive competition ideology remains entrenched in the law.

Reflections

Clearly, universities are in a catch-22. In his satirical novel *Catch-22*, Joseph Heller described an Air Force rule that captures the essential irrationality of bureaucracy:

> *There was only one catch and that was Catch-22, which specified that a concern for one's safety in the face of dangers that were real and immediate was the process of a rational mind. Orr was crazy and could be grounded. All he had to do was ask; and as soon as he did, he would no longer be crazy and would have to fly more missions. Orr would be crazy to fly more missions and sane if he didn't, but if he were sane he had to fly them. If he flew them he was crazy and didn't have to, but if he didn't want to he was sane and had to.*[47]

To curb the arms race, the universities must come to some kind of collective agreement because no one wants to act unilaterally. Even arriving at such an agreement would be a challenge because some universities don't want to de-escalate, as they are among the few who are prospering, while others believe they *can* prosper if only they hire the right coach or build an even grander athletic facility. Some fear the kind of public outcry that met UAB's decision, while others may simply need to continue filling the seats of the colossal football stadiums and arenas they've built.

But if they were to collectively agree, they are likely to be challenged in court, as happened to the NCAA—and to lose, as the NCAA did. And to lose big time—to the tune of nearly $55 million, which is the sum the NCAA paid the part-time coaches to settle the antitrust lawsuit over twenty years ago.[48]

Thus, competitors who are mired in toxic competition are also the prisoners of a catch-22. They can't unilaterally stop this arms race, nor can they join forces to stop it because if they do, they risk significant antitrust liability, including automatic treble damages plus attorneys' fees, and potentially criminal liability. They could also face civil antitrust liability in Europe, Asia, and elsewhere.

So what about changing the law that keeps them entangled in a catch 22—or getting exemptions from it in certain circumstances? Some colleges have succeeded in getting an exemption from the antitrust laws, so that they can collectively agree on the ground rules for awarding financial aid.[49] One would think that with their extensive network of alumni, which includes members of Congress, and the increasing evidence of the damage done by the arms race—most recently the college basketball recruiting scandals that involved large payoffs (essentially bribes) to players and their families—Congress would have intervened with legislation carefully targeted to set limits on competition in specific areas.

For example, legislation can provide guardrails marking areas that are open for competition (such as universities competing for athletes through their educational opportunities and financial aid) and areas closed to competition (such as the amount each school can spend on their athletic programs generally, or football and basketball in particular).

But Congress hasn't acted. And the arms race continues, as do the antitrust lawsuits that protect it—and the money drains and the scandals.

One reason for the inaction is that some legislators are competition ideologues who reject the notion that competition can ever be bad. One senator, for example, noted in 2017, "You see, when you have competition, good things happen. When you have competition, it inevitably brings down prices, and it inevitably results in higher quality."[50] Another senator argued that "college football, like most other industries in this country, must conduct business in a manner that does not intentionally stifle competition or systemically favor speci-fied competitors."[51]

Most elected officials would agree publicly. Privately, many are probably realists, well aware that competition can at times be harmful to consumers (aka their constituency, the voters), society at large, and even, as in the case of the universities with their hugely expensive athletic programs, many or most of the competitors themselves. But even those who understand that there are circumstances in which the competition ideology needs to be moderated are aware that support-ing any kind of antitrust exemption or immunity, or trying to pass any kind of regulation, will be difficult, because of the degree to which the ideology is embedded within our legal system. It may be unpopular, too, because of how deeply we, as a society, have drunk of the compe-tition Kool-Aid.

Legislators are also aware that requests for anticompetitive re-straints are frequently cynical moves in the interest of benefitting a few at the expense of many. So when they hear companies or institu-tions expressing concerns about "ruinous" competition, what they of-ten hear is that those competitors are simply reaching for our wallets. Not surprisingly, some have learned to be jaded about such requests, and to turn a deaf ear to them, when they don't help their reelection efforts. In environments like that there is opposition not only to spe-cial interest regulations specifically, but to just about all forms of reg-ulation.

If competition is viewed as inherently organic and good, then for the ideologue, regulation must be seen as inherently artificial, intru-sive, and bad—something that interferes with natural market forces. Even seemingly benign regulations will spread and smother competi-tion. Thus, regulation is to be avoided whenever possible.

But just because some regulations are bad (because they stifle economic growth) does not mean all regulations should be viewed as bad. Once the regulations that put limits on toxic competition are eliminated, then the inspections, minimum safety requirements, and requirements for transparency and truth in advertising required by those regulations also disappear. And when the competition ideology reigns supreme, many of the services that unrestrained competition does not always provide—like universal health care or mail service—may also disappear.

As long as our laws and polices assume that competition is inherently good, and as long as our policy makers rely on dogma in deregulating industries for the sake of promoting competition, then toxic competition will continue to spread.

CHAPTER 6

The Lobbyists

How to Kudzu the Competition Ideology Like a Pro

If you've ever been in America's South, you've seen kudzu—a climbing plant that systematically overtakes everything in its path. It's an invasive vine that carpets forests, trees, and bushes as well as telephone poles, garages, and abandoned homes and cars. Years ago, during the Depression, Southerners were told that kudzu "would make barren Southern farms 'live again.' There were hundreds of thousands of acres in the South 'waiting for the healing touch of the miracle vine.'"[1] But what was introduced in the South to prevent the damage caused by soil erosion is today an uncontrolled plant that strangles everything in its path and enables other invasive plants and pests to flourish.

Just as kudzu ended up smothering the South, climbing all over its vegetation rather than helping it to live again, the reductive competition ideology smothers efforts to limit toxic competition. Like kudzu, society's uncontrolled drive toward liberalization and intense competition threatens everything in its path, including the values that it initially set out to protect.

But like kudzu, the *real* danger of the competition ideology is in what it hides. Just as kudzu "veils more serious threats to the countryside, like suburban sprawl, or more destructive invasive plants,"[2] the competition ideology can hide corruption, exploitation, ineptitude, and ignorance.

So, let us create a new verb: *to kudzu*—meaning to veil exploitation by evangelizing the virtues of the competition ideology (and arguing in favor of minimal state regulation). To keep regulators at bay, powerful companies and their lobbyists *kudzu*—namely they use the reductive competition ideology to profit at our expense. Government officials also *kudzu* by promoting privatization and competition to cover their political contributions and payoffs or, less sinisterly, their incompetence.

We saw in two of our overdoses—exploitation of our human weaknesses and choice overload—how competitors can profit from toxic competition. To see how these companies and their lobbyists fuel the reductive competition ideology and use it to cover their tracks, let us return to Las Vegas and the drip pricing that has taken over the hotel booking industry.

To Kudzu, Las Vegas–Style

Drip pricing, as we saw in chapter 3, is profitable. So it spreads. We compared this Third Overdose to rip currents. When competition turns toxic and consumers are being swept out to sea, one would expect the government lifeguards to intervene. The government could simply pass legislation to bring industry practice in line with consumer interests. Such regulatory legislation could bring a rapid end to this abusive practice. How are we so confident?

Suppose you and a friend from Australia want to vacation together in a hotel with dignified, understated elegance. Both of you naturally turn to Trump International Hotel Las Vegas. If you are booking in the United States, you'll see the room rate in large bold print (which at the time of writing this chapter was **$120.00**) and the disclaimer in smaller print ("Excluding Taxes & Resort Fees"). When you are ready to make the booking, your total jumps 46 percent—to $175.74. How did that happen? If you want to know, you have to click another button "View Price Breakdown," where you'll then see the $39.68 in resort fees. Drip pricing at its glory.

Now what happens when your Australian friend books the same room at Trump International Hotel Las Vegas? We asked our colleague Dr. Rob Nicholls, who teaches at Australia's UNSW Business School, to book a room through the Australian version of Hotels.com. In contrast to what an American consumer sees when trying to book a room, he was presented with an all-inclusive price (in Australian dollars).

No drip pricing. Just an all-inclusive price. This isn't because competition is stronger in Australia. No, it's because Australian law bans the use of drip pricing, and an Australian lifeguard is on duty.[3]

There's nothing unique about Australia, either. We see lifeguards on duty around the globe prohibiting drip pricing. In 2017, Canada fined car rental companies $1.25 million for engaging in marketing practices like drip pricing.[4] That same year, the Dutch fined online tour operators for drip pricing[5] and agreed with online ticket agencies that extra costs should be listed in the "base price" of the ticket.[6] In 2017, the United Kingdom opened an investigation into drip pricing, hidden charges, and pressure selling on hotel booking sites. By 2019, the United Kingdom has secured a victory for UK holidaymakers as online hotel booking sites agreed to stop their exploitation.[7]

But for Americans, there is no lifeguard in sight, even though resort fees are spreading and increasing. (Most of the ninety-two Las Vegas hotels, for example, now charge them.)[8] For US customers—and also for anyone who books on a US website, no matter what the prevailing laws are in their own country—that's the reality.

So if the British, Canadian, Dutch, and Australian lifeguards, among others, are on duty, you might wonder what happened to the US lifeguards. How come Americans are not protected?

Here is where it gets interesting. In years prior, the US lifeguards were on duty and they blew the whistle! In 2012, the chairman of the Federal Trade Commission (FTC) said drip pricing was "a huge disservice to American consumers."[9] The FTC's condemnation of drip pricing reflected the sentiment of many customers. Poised to stop this abusive practice, the FTC warned twenty-two hotel operators that their drip pricing "may violate the law by misrepresenting the price consumers can expect to pay for their hotel rooms."[10]

The FTC put the hotels on notice that in order to avoid legal repercussions, they were required to "include in the *quoted total price* any unavoidable and mandatory fees, such as resort fees, that consumers will be charged to stay at the hotel."[11] Just like the Australians. Nor could the hotel play around with fonts on their booking sites, by highlighting the low hotel room rate while putting the inclusive price in a smaller font. Instead, the FTC instructed, "the most prominent figure for consumers should be the total inclusive estimate."[12]

Among the hotels investigated by the FTC was—you guessed it—the Trump International Hotel Las Vegas. If the hotel continued with its drip pricing, the FTC warned in a 2013 letter, it would face legal action:

> We reviewed your website at TrumpHotelCollection.com/las-vegas and found that in at least some instances mandatory resort fees are not included in the reservation rate quoted to consumers. We strongly encourage you to review your company's website to ensure you are not misrepresenting the total price consumers can expect to pay when making a reservation to stay in your hotel. Please be advised that the FTC may take action to enforce and seek redress for any violation of the FTC Act as the public interest may require.[13]

Meanwhile, the FTC was collecting consumer complaints about drip pricing, including this one from 2014 regarding Trump International Sonesta Beach Resort:

> When my party arrived to check into the resort we were told about a $465.00 additional fee to be paid and held for incidentals, a $24 per day resort fee for use of the resort facilities, and $30 per day to park my rental car since they don't have personal parking, only valet parking.

We booked this trip through a travel agency who was only aware of one of the hidden fees at this resort, the daily usage fee of $24. There were too many fees involved to not have been informed prior to booking and traveling. The room cost us (for 2 people), $1,033 for 3 nights. Why weren't the other fees disclosed then? . . . I have made reservations for many years and I have never seen anything like this before in my life. Never have I heard of so many hidden fees. Everything should have been included in the price of the room except the parking which is ridiculous. This was a situation that did not have to be if we were told these things prior to coming, there was plenty of time. The travel agency didn't know.[14]

With consumer complaints mounting, Congress was also threatening action. Senator Claire McCaskill of Missouri introduced a bill—the Truth in Hotel Advertising Act of 2016—that would specifically prohibit drip pricing by hotels.[15] "It's clear there's a bait-and-switch going on when it comes to these hidden hotel fees, and consumers are paying the price," said McCaskill, the former chair of the consumer protection subcommittee. "What I heard from Missourians was clear—families who've saved for a well-deserved vacation are too often facing sticker shock when they're slapped with their final bill. This legislation provides a common sense solution, requiring hotels to be upfront about mandatory costs by including them in room rates."[16]

So if the FTC was poised to stop this abusive practice, what stopped them and the proposed legislation? The casinos' lobbyists. They went to Washington, DC, and . . . they won big time!

Recall that the Vegas casinos were profiting from this toxic competition. They wanted it to continue. The casinos' trade association estimated "that resort fees account for approximately $500 million in annual revenue in Las Vegas alone."[17]

So, to ward off the FTC and potential legislation, the casinos enlisted their industry trade group, the American Gaming Association. Their trade association works to "shape a positive and compelling image of the casino gaming industry." When it came to drip pricing, the trade group, according to the internal minutes of its board of directors, "worked diligently to combat the Federal Trade Commission's (FTC's) efforts to significantly alter the collection of resort fees."[18]

Their campaign to beat back the FTC is a classic. We often hear of the revolving door between government regulatory agencies and the industries they're supposed to monitor. Well, the trade group began its efforts by hiring Julie Brill, a former FTC commissioner, as counsel "to support [their] engagement on this emerging issue."[19] Next they kudzu-ed the Capitol. Efforts included targeted political pressure, mobilization of congressional allies, and a white paper they submitted to the FTC to explain:

- current industry resort fee disclosure practices;
- reasons these disclosures are neither unfair nor deceptive; and
- reasons the proposed new FTC guidance will result in unintended consequences that will hurt consumers, competition, and marketplace transparency.[20]

Yes, you read that correctly. Although as the Gaming Association's annual board meeting report noted, "FTC Chairwoman Edith Ramirez, in particular, strongly believes mandatory resort fees must be factored into a total price advertisement and displayed as such on the first page," the casinos' trade group disagreed. "[B]ased on extensive conversations, her opinion does not appear to be based on consumer complaints or data suggesting a problem in the current marketplace."

Other than extensive conversations with one another, it's hard to imagine to whom the members of the Gaming Association might have been talking.

To continue the spread of toxic competition, the lobbyists used the competition ideology. Competition is good, intervention is bad. Resort fees are good for consumers. The lifeguards just don't understand right from wrong. But consumers do. So trust competition.

Politicians picked up the lobbyists' message. In a 2016 Senate oversight hearing of the FTC, we can see the kudzu-ing in action. Dean Heller, the then senator from Nevada, first lectured the FTC chair on the importance of the hotel and gaming industry to the economy of his state, citing the "nearly $60 billion of travel spending . . . injected into Nevada's economy every year, accounting for about 13 percent of the State's annual GDP. The Las Vegas Convention and Visitor Authorities has estimated that our tourism economy generates more than $50 billion annually and supports over 366,000 jobs in southern Nevada alone, which is about 40 percent of the total jobs in that area of the state."[21]

Code for "hands off." We don't want any kind of regulatory intervention that would undermine the profits of a business responsible for a big chunk of our economy.

Heller also explained that consumers "expect to be treated like kings and queens and pampered with the latest and the greatest amenities. It's all part of the Las Vegas and Nevada experience."[22] Presumably this was his way of saying that if consumers expect all that, that's because competition has delivered these wonderful amenities to them.

When FTC chair Edith Ramirez offered to clarify the agency's initiative against mandatory resort fees that were not being properly disclosed to consumers, the senator immediately cut her off: "Don't take up too much of my time."

Interrupting the FTC chair again, Senator Heller surmised that the FTC received only eight to ten complaints on these fees. Where the senator got that number is unclear. (One FTC spreadsheet, mentioned in the hearing, lists over four hundred complaints over a three-and-a-half year period.)[23] "You get eight or ten [complaints] on this," Heller continued. "And now you want to enact new regulations."

This is textbook kudzu-ing—the implication that any regulatory action would threaten the economy, the minimizing of the problem that regulation would address ("eight to ten" complaints), and the expression of dismay over would-be enforcers who fail to appreciate that what they perceive as harmful is in fact competition at its very best. It's all about markets, free enterprise, and smart consumers being treated like kings and queens. It's about autonomy, freedom, and the American dream.

Surely any rational policy maker would see through this kudzu-ing. And yet. . . .

"Welcome to the Party"

By 2017, the casinos' lobbyists had trounced the lifeguards. In his key-note address before the industry stakeholders, a veritable drumroll of victories on the anti-regulatory front, the American Gaming Association president cited as a key win its "thwarting an effort to crack down on resort fees charged to hotel customers in Las Vegas."[24] "Federal mur-murings about banning resort fees [were] 'beaten back,'" the AGA president noted[25]—referring to the $500 million collected on the Vegas Strip alone.

And with casino owner Donald Trump the newly elected president of the United States, the AGA was looking forward to success on new battlefronts—for example, getting Congress "to see legalization of sports betting as a consumer protection issue. . . . It's about understanding how Washington works," the AGA president said. "[Congress] is reactive: It responds to problems. It fixes things when there is no other choice."[26] The Justice Department, under the Trump administration, delivered on that front, when it reversed its legal position on online gambling, mirroring the arguments made by lobbyists for the Las Vegas casino magnate and top Republican donor Sheldon Adelson.[27]

Speaking of "consumer protection" and Congress fixing things—what about the Truth in Hotel Advertising Act of 2016, the purpose of which was to "prohibit certain entities that are subject to the enforcement authority of the Federal Trade Commission (FTC) from advertising a rate for a hotel room that does not include all required fees . . ."? The bill was referred to the Senate Committee on Commerce, Science, and Transportation, where it has since languished. With the bill's sponsor, Senator McCaskill, having lost her seat in the 2018 elections, it is not likely to be brought up for a vote in the foreseeable future.

To celebrate their win, the casinos took the opportunity to further exploit us. After Caesars' futile attempt to resist resort fees, it not only adopted them but increased them in 2018, with MGM soon following. As MGM's CEO told Wall Street analysts in early 2018, by way of explaining the increase: "We are lagging the market—Caesars properties have higher resort fees, which is a great change since they started with no resort fees not long ago, but welcome to the party."[28] Between 2016 and 2017, the average resort fee increased 7 percent to $24.38 per hotel.[29] In 2018, the casinos increased their resort fees on average 8.6 percent to $26.48 per hotel.[30] In some hotels, the resort fees now surpass the advertised price of the room.[31]

Welcome to the American dream. And do Americans love it? Well, in the same article that detailed all these increases, it was noted that "The legality of imposing resort fees is currently being investigated by attorney generals in 46 states as well as the District of Columbia . . . Nevada is among the four states not investigating the fees. That hasn't stopped disgruntled Las Vegas visitors from taking their case to court. A class action lawsuit relating to internet fees at several Strip properties was filed in November."[32]

Nevada's representatives in Congress may not be interested in doing anything to disrupt the money flowing into their state's coffers, but apparently some visitors to Nevada don't like seeing hidden fees flowing out of their own bank accounts. And even if Congress is not disposed to act, the states may come to the rescue of consumers. Time will tell how effective the actions of those attorney generals are.

A Short "How-To" Guide on Using the Competition Ideology to Deregulate

Today, corporations and trade groups spend billions of dollars lobbying the US government. Lobbying makes economic sense since it can affect outcomes. The Supreme Court worsened the situation when its ruling in the Citizens United case deemed corporate spending on election contributions to be a form of protected speech under the First Amendment, which guarantees freedom of speech.[33] So under the guise of another cherished freedom, the Supreme Court substantially weakened the limitations on corporate political spending—and thereby vastly increased the importance of pleasing large donors in order to win elections.

Regulators may not require much persuasion if they can promote the industry's needs under the reductive competition ideology. So lobbyists kudzu using the competition ideology. The rhetoric used to advance their anti-regulatory policies is based on a steroid-infused competition rationale, which is promoted regardless of facts, employing buzz words such as *freedom*, *prosperity*, and *efficiency*. At its core, it is based on four simple arguments. Let us explore this winning formula and apply it to drip pricing as practiced by the Las Vegas hotel and gaming industry:

- **FIRST, TRUST IN THE FULL FORCE OF FREE MARKET COMPETITION.** In the long run, free market competition will deliver optimal results. Competition will increase our sovereignty, fatten our wallets, and increase our overall well-being, all the while guaranteeing that sleazy sellers will be forced out of the marketplace. If things appear suboptimal, markets will self-correct. If consumers feel that hotels are trying to cheat them with drip pricing, they'll go elsewhere. If demand exists for hotels without resort fees, new entrants will provide it.

- **SECOND, BECAUSE THE MARKETPLACE OFFERS A SUPERIOR INSTRUMENT TO DELIVER SERVICES, THE STATE'S ROLE IN REGULATING THESE MARKETS SHOULD BE LIMITED.** Competition, after all, is a natural curative force, whereas regulation is artificial and can have unintended and unfortunate consequences. Competition will self-correct abuses more quickly and efficiently than regulators.

- **THIRD, DECRY REGULATION AS PATERNALISTIC AND APPEAL TO OUR RUGGED INDIVIDUALISM AND PRIDE.** Consumers are not dumb. Through trial and error, they're capable of learning and behaving like the superhuman *homo economicus*. Transactions are presumably mutually beneficial. Consumers contract to further their interests. They don't need government bureaucrats to protect them because they know what they're doing and the government will only mess things up.

- **FOURTH, FRAME THE EXPLOITIVE PRACTICE AS A PRO-COMPETITIVE INNOVATION.** Competition is good. So is innovation. Now take these two propositions, put them on steroids, and use circular reasoning to prove your point: If the hotel industry is competitive, and the industry uses drip pricing, then by definition drip pricing must be a pro-competitive innovation, and something that will make markets even more competitive. Las Vegas, as its US senator will tell us, is under tremendous competitive pressure. That's why it treats consumers like kings and queens. So drip pricing (skillfully rebranded as "a la carte" pricing to suggest that it's offering us a choice of items as opposed to a set menu that we're locked into) must actually be an innovation in providing consumers with more options that serve their personal interest.

In arguing these four points, one must casually ignore key facts: Drip pricing undermines consumers' ability to compare prices. The opacity of the market is also reflected in most online comparison sites that do not factor the resort fees when they rank results; ownership of the hotels on the Vegas Strip is concentrated, with four companies now accounting for more than 80 percent of the rooms, which leaves consumers with very limited options. So, the idea that you can simply choose to go elsewhere is not true;[34] resort fees are not a form of a la carte pricing because they're not optional—a hotel guest can't decide that parking or Internet access or whatever those fees supposedly cover is something he doesn't need and doesn't want to pay for. Even in more competitive markets, the alignment of interests among most hotels to impose these mandatory fees has led the practice to spread to the point that consumers have no choice in paying them.

And finally, notwithstanding Senator Heller's contention that consumers are being treated like kings and queens, we're actually being treated more like suckers, and many of us are not happy about it—but we can't fight back since there is no regulation to protect us. And, of course, we are paying more—because we have to.

But don't expect the FTC to stop drip pricing during the Trump administration, especially when the Trump hotels profit from this exploitation. According to the attorney general of the District of Columbia who, along with the attorneys general of forty-six states, was helping to lead an investigation into the hidden resort fees charged by a dozen major hotel chains, the FTC backed away from such attempts after Trump's election.[35]

So next time you're going to Vegas, maybe ask someone in Australia to book your hotel room.

The Global Meltdown

In chapter 5 we discussed how the competition ideology and deregulation contributed to the financial crisis. Revolving doors and lots of kudzuing helped the large corporations advance their agenda. Taxpayers, as a

result, bailed out the major financial institutions, automobile manufacturers, the insurer AIG, and other large corporations. One lesson from
the financial crisis is how the economically powerful have every desire
to use the government to protect their economic interests. When it all
came crashing down, some members of Congress—though not nearly
enough—did question how big business and their lobbyists peddled the
competition ideology. This quote is telling:

> It is bizarre that (President) Obama and (Secretary) Geithner are chan-
> neling President Reagan and claiming the government can't do any-
> thing and the market is all knowing.
>
> We have learned that the market is not all knowing, especially when
> it is distorted by greed and avarice and government complicity. We have
> learned the hard way the costs of "too big to fail." We have learned not
> to trust the right-wing ideologues who peddled a devil's brew of deregu-
> lated and free market fundamentalism.
>
> We have learned a hard lesson about free market fundamentalism.
> Just as we have learned a hard lesson about free trade fundamentalism.
> This snake oil was peddled by the big banks and the big corporations.
> You can see the effects by walking down the main street of almost any
> city or town in any state, surely in the State of Ohio.
>
> We need to learn the lessons of history and apply them. We need to use
> the proper government instrumentalities. The proper use of the market to
> resolve this economic crisis. Otherwise we will make the same mistakes.
> And again the American people will be left holding the bag of bad debts
> for generations to come, throttling economic growth and compromising
> our future.
>
> In the end, we must do what is right, not what might be politically
> expedient.[36]

Congresswoman Marcy Kaptur of Ohio gave this speech in 2009,
after the financial crisis. But what actually have we learned?

Eight years later, the *L.A. Times* reported, the Trump administration "has been single-mindedly focused on getting rid of rules and regulations that businesses say hindered competition, innovation and free markets."[37] The Brookings Institute is tracking deregulation in the Trump administration, which encompasses financial safeguards, consumer protection, environmental protections, labor, train safety, and health (such as requirements governing the manufacture of uninspected inedible meat products used for pets).[38] Some of these regulations may indeed hinder healthy competition. But how many beneficial laws will evaporate due to kudzu-ing?

Reflections

With ever increasing lobbying expenditures, targeted campaigns, and super PACs, the appetite for profits paves the way to intellectual and regulatory capture of policy makers. Money talks. Mick Mulvaney (who in 2018 was serving in President Donald Trump's cabinet as director of the office of management and budget, as well as acting White House chief of staff), commented in an address to the American Bankers Association, that during his time as a South Carolina congressman:

> We had a hierarchy in my office in Congress... If you were a lobbyist who never gave us [campaign] money, I didn't talk to you. If you were a lobbyist who gave us money, I might talk to you.[39]

His comments drew significant backlash. Congressman Adam Schiff remarked, "Nothing says drain the swamp like telling a room full of bankers to give more money to politicians who put the interests of banks ahead of people."[40]

Lobbying and money can suffocate democratic values. Add the competition ideology and it becomes invasive. After all, that is the effect of kudzu.

And there you have it. Lobbyists utilize the competition ideology to support crony capitalism, militate against important regulation and safeguards, and ensure that power and money are allowed to subvert democracy. And most of our legislators go along with it, either out of genuine belief in unbridled competition or for more craven political purposes.

The result, in our case, is a distorted ideology that is often used as a smoke screen to benefit the few. To put it simply—the people and companies with the most money and power want to keep themselves at the top. They use their money to hire the lobbyists who influence Congress and to make the campaign contributions that further influence Congress. Their goal is to derail any attempts at regulation that would protect the rest of us, and they have largely succeeded.

With money powering policy making, under the guise of promoting competition, kudzu-ing becomes child's play, revealing the darker sides of competition, society, and power.

To see how subversive this kudzu-ing has become, let us return to first principles. Competition, at its core, is supposed to erode concentrated economic power, not increase it. So, with the rise of the competition ideology over the past few decades, why has the wealth of so many Americans been lagging or declining, while the wealth of the very few has increased so dramatically? The numbers are revealing. In the United States, between 2000 and 2011, the poorest 20 percent of households became even poorer.[41] Their net worth declined 566 percent. And that net worth was negative to begin with. It went from $-905 to $-6,029.

The lower-middle class (20th to 40th percentile) saw their net worth decline 49 percent, to $7,263. So, if they liquefied all their assets and paid off all their debts, they might be able to buy an eight-year-old used Dodge Grand Caravan minivan (without any options).

The middle class (40th to 60th percentile) saw their net worth decline 7 percent, to $68,839.

The upper class and wealthy, on the other hand, saw their net worth increase. But most of them are not exactly flush with cash. The net worth of the upper-middle class (60th to 80th percentile) was $205,985. That may appear to be a lot, but if they liquefied everything, they probably couldn't purchase their own houses.

For the wealthiest 20th percentile, their net worth increased 11 percent, to $630,754. That seems like a lot also, but college tuition for two children would likely deplete this bundle.

Most of the money in the United States is going to the top 1 percent. Their net worth in 2016 was over $10 million.[42] Many of them are far, far beyond this threshold.

Imagine a hundred people at a town hall meeting splitting up the $1,000 in surplus revenue collected over the year. The first person grabs $386 (you guessed it—the top 1 percent). The next nine people together grab $386. And the ninety other people (bottom 90 percent)—well, they're left dividing the remaining $228 in wealth.[43]

How could this kind of inequality, which is getting worse, not better, have resulted from our competition ideology? Part of the answer lies in toxic competition—in markets where companies compete to better exploit us, not to better serve us, and get away with it because we have no protections against it. The exploiters and their lobbyists are anti-regulation because they know that their profits will diminish if the rest of us get the protection we deserve.

And as more regulators take chainsaws to their regulations, and as policy makers increasingly rely on markets to self-regulate, the toxic competition will continue to spread.

CHAPTER 7

The Privatizers

When in Doubt, Privatize!

Who preaches the privatization gospel? Those who want to switch from services paid for and controlled by the government to services obtained through the private marketplace. The idea is that privatization allows competition—and all the benefits that come with competition—to flourish. We'll enjoy better quality, more choices, and lower costs when private markets displace the government.

No wonder privatization seems so alluring: It appeals to competition, choice, and autonomy—the touchstones of a free market and, if a number of its supporters are to be believed, of a free society. With these three tenets in their arsenal, supporters of privatization can dismiss the arguments of their opponents as *against* competition, *against* choice, and *pro*-enslavement to the government monopoly.

There have been many instances in which privatization successfully delivered what the state could not. Indeed, competitive markets can often deliver more efficient outcomes. In the past few decades, many countries have increasingly privatized certain core public services, such as electricity, water, telecommunications, transport, education, and health care, and the results have sometimes been good. At other times, however, privatization has not delivered the promised benefits.

But this chapter is not about the successes or failures of privatization. That's a whole different book (or better yet, series of books). Rather, here we are looking at policy makers who use the competition ideology to push for privatization. They do so, even though they know, or should know, that outsourcing government services to private companies in these particular cases will mean that citizens and consumers end up paying higher costs, in the form of taxes and budget deficits, for inferior services, and that we end up worse off as a result. At times, policy makers kudzu to shrug fiscal responsibility—better to blame private firms for poor quality and high prices than the government. Other times, the support for privatization is driven by crony capitalism, where big government is in bed with big business.

To be clear, the support for privatization isn't always suspect. Many of its supporters, among them libertarians who want to reduce government's footprint and competition ideologues who believe competition always works, are genuine in their conviction that privatization is for the benefit of society. Often they are right. But we want to show that these supposed benefits do not always materialize and explain why not.

Private Prisons, Profit Centers, and Pixie Dust

To see an example of the problems that can be caused by privatization, and the motivations of those who are nonetheless pushing for it, there is no better place to look than the American prison system.

Here is how a typical public policy study pushing for privatization of the prisons invokes the competition ideology:

> When governments contract with the private sector, efficiency and innovation do not come about because private firms have some magic pixie dust, unobtainable by the public sector, to sprinkle about. It is competition that creates efficiency and innovation, because competition punishes inefficiency and inertia. That means two things: first, that the contracting process needs to be competitive in the long run for efficiency to remain, and second, that

competition from the private sector makes the public sector more efficient as well.

This is the great uncounted benefit of private-sector provision of correctional services. Contracts usually save money not only directly, but also indirectly, by forcing the government corrections departments to tighten up their ships.[1]

By unleashing the competitive powers of the marketplace, private prisons will save the government and taxpayers money. So the argument goes. To ensure that the private prisons deliver on their promises, the government will draft contracts that make them accountable for their results. Such contracts can also incentivize the for-profit prisons to advance desirable societal goals and limit recidivism.

One thing that the public policy paper gets right is that there is indeed no magic pixie dust in the private sector. It suggests by implication that the pixie dust is in competition, the results of which will be money-saving and ship-tightening. But there's a dark side to those results that the paper does not acknowledge. As economist and 2016 Nobel laureate Oliver Hart explored in his writing, the pitfalls of prison privatization often mean that the private contractor faces an either/or situation—reduce costs or maintain quality. Typically, the incentive to engage in cost reduction will be so strong that it will adversely affect quality.[2] Although contracts are supposed to prevent any decrease in quality, because of the unquantifiable nature of many of the determinants of quality, it will be hard for the government to draft contracts that ensure that this doesn't occur.

Privatization and Prisons: Making Crime Pay

It is easy, and appropriate, to be critical of the American prison system as it has operated under federal and state auspices. Privatization of the prison system is actually just the latest iteration of a view of the prison system as a potential profit center.[3] During the 1980s, the prison system was faced with severe overcrowding as tough-on-crime legislation and mandatory minimum-sentencing guidelines sent far more offenders to prison, and kept them there for longer, than the system could handle. The result was a prison system in crisis.

Thus, the siren song of the privatizers—*Whatever the government can do, we can do better*—proved very alluring. And in 1983, Corrections Corporation of America came on the scene to offer the country its first private prison—a motel in Texas that was remodeled to hold immigration detainees. Privatizing US prisons was supposed to offer a cheaper, more efficient, and better-managed alternative to the overcrowded government prisons. It would allow federal and state governments to lock up the burgeoning inflow of inmates without taking on additional debt or having to go to the voters to approve bonds for new prisons (which voters were often reluctant to do). The power of market incentives would result not just in lower costs and higher quality but reduced recidivism, too. So society would benefit in every way, as would the prisoners themselves, ultimately.

Sounds good, right? So here is a pop quiz. Which of these statements are true:

1. Private prisons provide the same (or better) level of correctional services, programs, security, and resources as federal prisons, at substantially lower costs.
2. Private prisons provide better rehabilitative services, such as educational programs and job training, than what the federal government can provide.
3. Private prisons have the same interests as society does: to reduce crime, to promote leniency in parole for older nonviolent criminals, to release criminals early for good behavior, and to find alternatives to locking people up, like work release programs.

The answer is none of them.

The boon in private prisons has resulted in spending more tax dollars for poorer quality services. One mismanaged US prison—run by Corrections Corporation of America, the first of America's private prison companies and one of the largest in the country—fostered such an extreme culture of violence among both guards and prisoners that it was nicknamed *Gladiator School* (by the inmates themselves).

But this decrease in quality has not deterred the expansion of privatization. Between 2000 and 2016, the total number of people—about 128,000—incarcerated in private prisons increased 47 percent (compared to an overall rise in the prison population of 9 percent). The number of people the federal government housed in private prisons—over 34,000—represented an increase of 120 percent.[4]

There are at least four major factors that help to explain how this expansion of privatization has occurred, what the private contractors do to ensure profitability, and why this has worked out so badly for all concerned—except the private prison corporations themselves.

At times, privatization skews the incentives

Competition does not always ensure that the private sector's incentives will align with societal goals. Sometimes, as with for-profit prisons, marketplace incentives may be intrinsically contrary to society's. Consider the following text from the 2017 annual report filed by CoreCivic (formerly Corrections Corporation of America, until it was "rebranded" in 2016, at a time when its operation was under investigation). Under the heading "Risks to Our Business and Industry," CoreCivic cautioned investors about a number of potential downsides to its revenue, including:

> . . . *the relaxation of enforcement efforts, the expansion of alternatives to incarceration and detention, leniency in conviction or parole standards and sentencing practices or through the decriminalization of certain activities that are currently proscribed by criminal laws . . .*

Legislation has also been proposed in numerous jurisdictions that could lower minimum sentences for some non-violent crimes and make more inmates eligible for early release based on good behavior. Also, the expansion of alternatives to incarceration and detention, such as electronic monitoring, may reduce the number of offenders who would otherwise be incarcerated or detained. Similarly, reductions in crime rates or resources dedicated to prevent and enforce crime could lead to reductions in arrests, convictions and sentences requiring incarceration at correctional facilities.[5]

From society's perspective, many of these possibilities—finding alternatives to locking people up, leniency in conviction, improving sentencing practices and parole for nonviolent crimes, releasing criminals early for good behavior, and reduced crime—are highly desirable. Yet, from the perspective of a private contractor, even though it is supposed to operate on our behalf, such outcomes must be seen as "risks" to its bottom line.

To understand why a positive becomes a negative in the distorted world of the private prison corporation, we need to consider its business model, which is similar to that of a hotel chain. The government pays for-profit prisons on a per diem basis. Basically, the prison's occupancy rate is key to the corporation's earnings. The more prisoners locked up each day, the longer they stay, the higher the prison's occupancy rate, and the lower the per-person fixed costs, the more revenue the prison earns, and the greater the profit.

This is all succinctly explained in the 2017 annual report issued by the GEO Group, another large prison operator: ". . . [A] material decrease in occupancy levels at one or more of our facilities could have a material adverse effect on our revenues and profitability, and consequently, on our financial condition and results of operations."[6]

Since private prisons profit when they can detain people for longer periods, they are incentivized to do so. One study, for example, found that in comparison to public prisons, private prisons in Mississippi prolonged the stay of inmates by as much as ninety additional days, which equaled 7 percent of the average time served and was estimated to cost an additional $10,000 to $15,000 per inmate.[7] Why were the inmates locked up longer in private prisons? Because in order to make more money, private prisons found ways to discipline prisoners that resulted in these longer prison terms. For example, at one of its prisons CoreCivic added thirty days to an inmate's sentence for taking a broom out of the closet at the wrong time.[8] Those extra thirty days increased the for-profit prison's revenue by over $1,000. But, despite the additional time served, there isn't any evidence that these tougher measures reduce the recidivism rate. Instead, the longer detention reflects the perverse incentives arising from the free market.

Because private prisons are a for-profit business, they all share a fundamental goal: to increase occupancy rate. Lowering the occupancy rate, whether it's through reductions in crime, decreases in sentencing duration, or alternatives to incarceration, is not in their interest.

But lowering the occupancy rate *is* good for society, and there is a growing consensus that mass incarceration has become too mass. Voters have begun questioning the diminishing returns of locking more and more people up for longer time periods. One 2012 report noted how a "growing body of research suggests—and government officials acknowledge—that beyond a certain point, further increases in incarceration have significantly diminishing returns as a means of making communities safer."[9]

Optimal deterrence occurs when the cost of reducing crime equals the social benefit. Going beyond that point, such as by locking up nonviolent criminals for even longer periods, sometimes on shaky ground, will not reduce their potential threat to society, nor will it deter other criminals.[10] But it will mean that society loses out in several ways: Taxpayers lose the money they must pay to keep the nonviolent criminals behind bars; the prisoners' relatives lose the presence of a family member and the wages that person might be earning; and society at large loses the productive contributions that person might make and the taxes he or she might be paying.

The First Step Act, the 2018 legislation passed by Congress and signed by President Trump, is the outcome of a bipartisan effort to take some of these ideas into account in reforming the federal criminal justice system. The act expands early-release programs and modifies sentencing laws, including mandatory minimum sentences for nonviolent drug offenders. It also expands job training and other programming aimed at reducing recidivism rates.

Nonetheless, CoreCivic's total revenue for its prisons is increasing—by 2.8 percent in its third quarter of 2018 (compared to the third quarter of 2017)—from existing and new contracts, including the US Immigration and Customs Enforcement, where locking up nonviolent undocumented immigrants is a profitable growth segment.[11] Its rival GEO in 2018 likewise was "marketing approximately 4,700 vacant beds . . . to potential customers."[12]

Privatization takes the low-cost "profitable" inmates and offloads more expensive inmates to the state

The good news for private prisons is that the United States has both the highest reported rate of incarceration, by far, in the world—655 inmates per 100,000 people, versus 142 for every 100,000 in England and Wales, 102 per 100,000 in France, and 77 per 100,000 in Germany[13]—and the longest average length of detention—63 months versus 4 months in Canada, 12 months in Germany, and 36 months in Australia.[14]

To continue growing revenues, for-profit prisons need even more people locked up for longer periods—including undocumented immigrants, low-level drug offenders, deadbeat parents who don't pay child support, and other nonviolent criminals.

But not necessarily *all* prisoners. Just those that make them money. If the private prison has to cover the inmates' medical costs, then they will build into their contracts provisions that allow them to avoid these high-cost prisoners. For example, "at the out-of-state prisons where California ships some of its inmates," CoreCivic will not accept any prisoners who are "over sixty-five years old, have mental health issues, or serious conditions like HIV."[15] Such prisoners must remain in state facilities.

We'll revisit the concept of cream skimming later in the chapter, in the context of the UK's National Health Service. But in both contexts the outcome is the same: Private providers benefit at the cost of the state.

Privatization saves money at the expense of quality— and human misery

As we saw with our Second Overdose involving horsemeat, the pressure to keep costs down can cause firms to skimp on quality and safety. Because they must answer to their shareholders, private prison corporations face similar pressure to reduce costs—and respond to that pressure in similar ways. The results can be much worse than horsemeat in your hamburger.

Journalist Shane Bauer went undercover in 2014 as an entry-level correctional officer (CO) for Corrections Corporation of America (CCA; now CoreCivic), which employed him at Winn Correctional Center in Winnfield, Louisiana. His sobering account of his experience, which appears in his book *American Prison: A Reporter's Undercover Journey into the Business of Punishment*, describes firsthand how CCA, in order to eke out profits and pay its shareholders, degraded quality to such extremes that both the guards and the inmates were put at risk.

The company's obligation to its shareholders was invoked during orientation for new correctional officers, who were lectured about CCA's commitment to cost-effective practices that "deliver value to our shareholders. . . . When the company is hurt, we all hurt."

These cost-effective practices enabled the company to charge only about $34 per day for each inmate at Winn—versus the $52 per day that was the average daily cost at Louisiana's state-run facilities. Looking only at those numbers it would appear that competition was delivering.

But Bauer witnessed how such price reductions were achieved. Guards were poorly vetted—Bauer was hired even though on his job application he had given his real name and his real employer, the publisher of *Mother Jones*, which might have been an indicator that he was a journalist who may conceivably have taken such a job in order to do some investigative work. But it seemed as though no one was interested in the details of his resume. Once hired, the guards were poorly trained. Given the high attrition rate, Bauer himself was already training recruits within just months of being employed at the prison. They were poorly paid—$9 per hour for regular guards, including those who had worked there for more than twenty years, versus $12.50 per hour for entry-level guards at the state facility. The benefits were meager. (As Bauer was told, "Try not to get sick, because we don't get paid sick time.") And they were understaffed.

The deliberate understaffing was the biggest complaint—among the guards as well as the inmates, both of whom were put at risk because of it. Typically there was one guard per 176 inmates at Winn. Mealtimes were even worse. One instructor warned the guards, "At chow time there are eight hundred inmates and just two COs." The result, predictably, was a very high level of violence. As one Winn inmate told a new correctional officer, "You see this chaos. If you'd been to other camps, you'd see the order they got. Ain't no order here. Inmates run this bitch, son."

The understaffing meant that guard towers were unmanned, and the prison had only one correctional officer to watch the thirty video feeds. Security checks were a mere paperwork exercise. During Bauer's time at Winn, one prisoner easily escaped. Only when another inmate brought it to their attention did the guards even realize he was gone.

CCA also cut costs by providing cut-rate meals—so substandard that aside from any measure of quality, they were 250 calories below the USDA's daily recommendation. CCA severely limited the inmates' access to medical care, work programs, and many vocational programs. The hobby shops became storage units. The big recreation yard was usually vacant, as there were not enough personnel to watch over it and guard the gates. One day when an inmate asked why they were on lockdown—lockdowns usually occur only after major disturbances, but that day there was no apparent reason—the correctional officer was brutally honest: "You know half of the fucking people don't want to work here. We so short-staffed and shit, so most of the gates ain't got officers."[16] During his four months at Winn, Bauer witnessed a preventable suicide, knife fights, and mental and physical illnesses that were deliberately left untreated.

CCA brought in its SWAT-like tactical unit to deal with the violence and chaos that were endemic in the facility. Over a four-month period, Winn, which is a medium-security prison, used pepper spray and other chemical agents about eighty times, a rate seven times higher than at Louisiana State Penitentiary, Angola, which is a maximum-security prison. During a ten-month period in 2015, Winn reported twice as many "immediate" uses of force as the eight other Louisiana prisons combined.

Not surprisingly, given the terrible working conditions and low wages, the prison had high employee turnover. Why, after all, work at fast-food wages at a place deliberately understaffed, where the inmates have little to do, and the cost-cutting results in constant abuse, threats, and fear of physical violence? While Bauer was there, the Winn prison had forty-two vacancies for regular guards and nine vacancies for ranking officers.

And there's nothing unique about this one Louisiana private prison. Private prisons generally pay guards far less. Private prison guards in Mississippi, for example, earned $35,000, compared to $50,000 for public prison guards.[17] Violence and abuse are endemic at privately operated correctional facilities. In a class action lawsuit brought against the state of Mississippi because of abuses that occurred at a youth detention center run by a company under contract to the GEO Group, the US Department of Justice (DOJ) found the "brazen" staff sexual misconduct and brutal youth-on-youth rapes to be "among the worst that we have seen in any facility anywhere in the nation."[18] Given that the private prison was hiring correctional officers affiliated with gangs (to help save costs), the court found this situation inevitable.[19]

Private prisons, another DOJ investigation found, had far greater safety and security shortcomings compared to federal prisons. Private prisons, for example, "had higher rates of assaults, both by inmates on other inmates and by inmates on staff."[20] CoreCivic's prisons, in particular, had the highest rates of inmate fights and inmate assaults on other inmates.[21] Private prisons had nearly twice as many weapons confiscated as federal prisons—3.2 compared to 1.8 per month. But, if prisoners at these mismanaged institutions disobey, assault the poorly compensated and trained guards, or assault one another, the prisons only stand to benefit. Now they can justify detaining the inmates even longer, thereby increasing their occupancy rate and their profits.

Private prison corporations lobby and sometimes even subvert and corrupt the legislative and legal system

Private prisons have strong incentives to lobby governments for harsher sentences. After all, longer sentences for nonviolent offenders mean higher profits for them. According to the Justice Policy Institute, the private prison industry employs a three-pronged approach to achieving political influence in order to increase profits: lobbying, direct campaign contributions, and building relationships and networks.[22]

On its website, however, CoreCivic disavows any lobbying on policies that affect "the basis for or duration of an individual's incarceration or detention."[23]

But that does not mean they are passive onlookers. Private prison corporations spend millions of dollars lobbying.[24] As the *Washington Post* reported in 2015, "The two largest for-profit prison companies in the United States—GEO and Corrections Corporation of America [now CoreCivic]—and their associates have funneled more than $10 million to candidates since 1989 and have spent nearly $25 million on lobbying efforts."[25]

Sometimes private prisons simply go directly to the sentencing source and bribe judges. Two Pennsylvania judges were convicted for taking millions of dollars in kickbacks to send teenagers to privately run youth detention centers.[26] "I've never encountered, and I don't think that we will in our lifetimes, a case where literally thousands of kids' lives were just tossed aside in order for a couple of judges to make some money," said one attorney who represented the victims.[27]

Given scandals like the Pennsylvania "pay for kids" bribery case, multiplying lawsuits against the abuses that occur in private prisons, and spiraling prison costs, one might expect change to happen—as seemed to be the case under the Obama administration. In 2016, the DOJ announced the phasing out of the use of private prisons in the federal system.[28] As the deputy attorney general noted:

> Private prisons served an important role during a difficult period, but time has shown that they compare poorly to our own Bureau facilities. They simply do not provide the same level of correctional services, programs, and resources; they do not save substantially on costs; and as noted in a recent report by the Department's Office of Inspector General, they do not maintain the same level of safety and security. The rehabilitative services that the Bureau provides, such as educational programs and job training, have proved difficult to replicate and outsource—and these services are essential to reducing recidivism and improving public safety.[29]

With the Obama administration poised to end the use of private prisons at the federal level, the private prison corporations looked to presidential candidate Donald Trump. Calling the nation's prison system "a disaster," Trump said before the election, "I do think we can do a lot of privatizations and private prisons. It seems to work a lot better."[30] So, during the 2016 election cycle the industry invested in lobbying and also supported Trump's election campaign.[31] The GEO Group, for example, stepped up its contributions, with its employee-financed political action committee giving federal candidates, PACs, and parties about $732,000—more than four times as much as in the previous presidential cycle, according to federal filings, and most of it to Republicans.

The day after the 2016 presidential elections, the GEO Group saw its stock increase 30 percent. CoreCivic's stock jumped 40 percent.[32] By February 2017, stocks in those companies were up more than 100 percent.[33]

And Trump delivered on expectations quite promptly. In February 2017, the then Attorney General Jeff Sessions rescinded the 2016 federal policy to phase out the use of private prisons.[34] This set in motion the start of new bidding processes for additional facilities in private immigrant detention centers.[35] A memorandum sent by the Federal Bureau of Prisons followed. It noted that to alleviate overcrowding "and to maximize the effectiveness of the private contracts," federal prisons should send low-security (and the higher-profit margin) nonviolent inmates to private prisons.[36]

Commenting on the reversal, Senator Bernie Sanders said, "Private prison companies invested hundreds of thousands of dollars in Donald Trump's presidential campaign and today they got their reward."[37] Other senators were similarly dismayed.[38]

Part of the change may be attributed to successful lobbying from the leading for-profit operators who, naturally, were not willing to give up on a multibillion dollar sector without a fight. The incoming administration's change in policy led to marked increase in profitability.[39] GEO Group and CoreCivic, which are publicly traded, had revenues last year of $2.3 billion and $1.8 billion, respectively.

By 2018, private prisons were brimming with optimism when talking with investors. CoreCivic said it has an "almost daily conversation" with US Immigration and Customs Enforcement officials about the agency's needs.[40] Detaining undocumented immigrants is profitable: "Among the immigrant detention population, 26,249 people—73 percent of the detained population—were confined in privately run facilities in 2017."[41] Many immigrants are enrolled in "Voluntary Work Programs," where they work for a dollar a day and are punished if they refuse.[42] The prison recoups, charging them as much as $12.75 for a fifteen-minute phone call or $11 for a four-ounce tube of toothpaste.[43]

Under the Trump administration, privatization is again fashionable.[44] And just as Trump has delivered for the prison corporations, they continue to deliver for him. Thus, in 2017, the GEO Group held its annual leadership conference at the Florida golf resort that is the largest single source of revenue to the Trump Organization.[45]

A Kudzu Gem

With the election of Donald Trump, the reductive competition ideologues would seem to have triumphed. But here's the ironic truth: There is very little competition in today's private prison market. All that is currently left are a few bidders dominating a heavily concentrated market, which is further consolidating. According to a 2016 Brookings Institution study, "Based on available prison facility information, we calculate that the two largest private prison companies account for around 55 and 30 percent of all private prison beds, respectively, and the three largest firms provide over 96 percent of the total number of private prison beds."[46] Some states rely on a single for-profit prison provider to operate a number of their prisons.[47]

The for-profit prison story is a kudzu gem—reflecting how powerful firms and their lobbyists can use the competition ideology to promote privatization, even in the absence of any real competition. With privatization (fueled by significant political contributions), we get more people spending longer sentences without serving any greater purpose, like reducing recidivism. With their executives focused on occupancy rates and profits, private prison companies will continue to kudzu—funneling money to policy makers who support even tougher state and federal criminal laws, and incarcerating even more immigrants. Cost pressures will cause degradation of quality and will result in decreases in spending, including on salaries for guards and other prison personnel. Therefore, the high turnover and low morale among employees will continue.

Meanwhile, the executives who run these companies will earn ever greater amounts of money. As the *New York Times* reported, George Zoley, chief executive of the GEO Group, made $9.6 million in 2017—almost double his 2016 earnings, while Damon T. Hininger, CoreCivic's chief executive, earned $2.3 million in total compensation in 2017.[48]

While the for-profit prison executives and their shareholders profit, and millions of dollars find their way into campaign coffers and other forms of lobbying, society pays the price for the gladiator training camps.

UK Forensic Science

Our for-profit prison story focuses on how private prison companies deploy lobbying, campaign contributions, and other forms of political pressure to promote privatization. Let us now tell a different story, in which it was the government itself that led the drive to privatize. Here the government (with the help of lobbyists from the private sector, of course) kudzu-ed the public in order to justify the sale of another state asset.

This happened in the United Kingdom, where in late 2010 a decision was made to close the UK Forensic Science Service (FSS) and transfer it to private hands—a decision that not only undermined the credibility of the successful media franchise *CSI: Crime Scene Investigation* to the UK audience, but also, more significantly, it might be argued, the credibility (and integrity) of forensic services in the United Kingdom.

The United Kingdom was one of the pioneers in forensic science. Under the auspices of the FSS, investing in research for ever new and improved means to analyze evidence led to great strides in the science. But, citing increased debt and inefficiencies at the FSS, the government announced in late 2010 that it had had enough. It was going to privatize the service. The vision was that in a competitive environment, the duties of the FSS (which amounted to 60 percent of forensic work in the United Kingdom) would be taken over by private sector operators, and everyone would benefit. The Home Office minister, at the time, assured the public that the use of private providers would allow crimes to be solved more quickly and more efficiently, as these companies would compete to provide "innovative services at the lowest cost."[49] Sound familiar?

Forensic experts, however, questioned the competitive promise. Quality would suffer, they warned. Overall, 92.3 percent of UK forensic scientists predicted that closing the FSS and turning over forensic work to private companies—and in-house police labs—would have a mostly negative impact on criminal justice, and 76.4 percent predicted it would lead to an increase in miscarriages of justice.[50]

Why weren't the pessimistic forensic scientists blinded by the competition ideology?

FIRST, they were aware that crime had declined in the United Kingdom, which meant that private sector forensic companies would be operating in an industry that was shrinking. Profit-maximizing firms would therefore have much less incentive to make significant investments in research and development, which would add to their costs but not, given the decrease in crime, to their bottom line. Innovation and progress would suffer, and a field in which the United Kingdom had long been a global leader in making groundbreaking discoveries would fall into decline.[51]

SECOND, they were concerned that private firms, under the pressure of toxic competition, might compromise the integrity of their analysis.

This concern was well-based on events from recent history, which show how intense competition can cause an intermediary to shade its findings to the buyer's liking, but society's overall detriment. One example is the investment ratings industry, where the entry of a third player, Fitch, caused the other two main ratings agencies—Moody's and S&P—to become fiercely competitive with each other during the run-up to the financial crisis of 2008 to 2009. This changed the culture of the ratings agencies and put pressure on them to deliver the highest ratings (AAA) on questionable investments. In order to retain or capture business from the issuers, namely the big investment banks, the ratings agencies relaxed their standards.[52] One former Moody's executive testified how the bankers "would threaten you all of the time. . . . It's like, 'Well, next time, we're just going to go with Fitch and S&P.'"[53]

Similarly, in a completely different industry, home appraisers, when under the threat of losing business to competitors, inflated their valuations to the benefit of real estate brokers (who would earn higher commissions) and lenders (who would make bigger loans and earn greater returns when selling them to investors).[54]

Likewise, more competition among New York's vehicle emissions testing centers led to a compromised outcome, namely testing centers that improperly gave passing grades to vehicles regardless of actual emissions in order "to garner more consumer loyalty by delivering to consumers what they want: a passing Smog Check result."[55]

These are all instances of toxic competition. And the forensic scientists were rightly concerned that competitive pressures in the marketplace would do something similar to private sector forensic labs—incentivizing them to cut corners or issue biased results.

THIRD, they were concerned about how using police in-house forensic laboratories would affect impartiality. There was bound to be pressure on the in-house labs to deliver results that would help police build a case.[56] While employees of a government forensic agency may feel pressure from police to produce certain results, the future of that agency does not depend on pleasing the police. The same could not be said for employees at an in-house lab. In an earlier review of the downsizing of the FSS and the outsourcing of much of its work to police labs, one expert noted that "One has to question whether it is right that the police are the sole arbiters of what scene of crime samples are sent for analysis and what are discarded . . ." He also expressed concern over whether police lab analysts, who owe their paychecks and careers to the police, could maintain their independence in an adversarial court system in which the police are seeking a conviction.[57]

Given all these concerns, when asked about the effect of switching forensic work to private and in-house police labs, 70.3 percent of forensic scientists "agreed or strongly agreed that this would reduce impartiality in the interpretation of evidence, while 64.7 percent said it would make it harder for scientists to accurately interpret evidence."[58]

But these reservations notwithstanding, the competition ideology and perceived benefits from privatization were too alluring. So, in 2012, the state-run FSS, which had been winding down for years, finally closed its doors and transferred most of its activities to the private sector. The United Kingdom was left with some state capacity for forensic work in the police in-house laboratories, but the private sector was supposed to deliver the bulk of the analysis—*faster, cheaper, and better*—because of the salutary effects of competition. Imagine a world of competing CSI units, each discovering even better technology to nab the criminals.

Too Good to Be True? Indeed So.

The new market-driven forensic service companies needed a constant flow of business to operate effectively. If the closing down of the FSS was not to damage UK forensic science, the market "had to be of a sufficient size to enable competition between dedicated market participants, as well as to support investments in efficiency and innovation."[59] Yet, with the decline in the crime rate, the UK government cut police department budgets, which in turn led police forces to limit the number of tests sent to private laboratories and to rely increasingly on their in-house capacity.

In essence, the government budget cuts undermined the transfer of forensic services from the state-run FSS to the private sector. After opening up the market for forensic services, the government suffocated it, even while continuing to expect miraculous efficiencies and lower prices for quality work. A classic case of the kudzu-ers believing their own gospel.

With business in short supply, quality soon began to suffer.[60] In 2012, one private lab, run by Trimega Laboratories, which did forensic testing used in family court and child protection cases, was criticized for its inaccurate results. Among other mistakes, the lab had wrongly informed a court that a mother of two young children had been using increasing amounts of cocaine. Had another lab not retested her blood samples, her children would have been taken away from her.

The full extent of the damage done by privatization to the criminal justice system began to be revealed in 2017. With increasing concerns over the integrity of forensic evidence, and evidence of possible manipulation by Randox Testing Services (which had taken over the lab formerly run by Trimega), the police had to recall lab work samples that had been used in over ten thousand criminal cases—including violent crimes, sex cases, and unexplained deaths across England and Wales. The inquiry revealed that thousands of Randox Testing Services' lab results had been compromised.[61]

As a result, according to a statement issued by a government minister at the end of 2017, "Results from all tests carried out by Trimega between 2010 and 2014 are currently being treated as potentially unreliable . . . [and] Most drug tests from [Randox Testing Services] between 2013 and 2017 are being treated as potentially unreliable." Since some of the tests may have been relied upon in court proceedings, the same government minister said that they would be reviewing any impact such tests had had on court decisions and trying to arrange for retesting where necessary—while also acknowledging that some samples had degraded to a point where they could not be retested. He noted that "The Government recognises the seriousness of this issue and the potential impact on public confidence in the use of forensic science within the justice system."[62]

And yet, public confidence in forensics was soon to take another hit when another private forensic company, Key Forensic Services, closed its doors in 2018. The collapse of this company jeopardized evidence used in thousands of cases, including rape and murder. After the UK Home Office reportedly refused to save the failing private firm, the police were left with no option but to divert part of their budget into a multimillion-pound bailout that would allow the company to continue functioning long enough to process the evidence involved in the open cases.[63]

These worrying developments were not left unnoticed. In its annual report, released in 2019, the UK Forensic Science Regulator warned that "profound changes to funding and governance are required to ensure that forensic science survives and begins to flourish rather than lurching from crisis to crisis."[64] A House of Lords Select Committee (Science and Technology), which conducted an inquiry into the impact of the forensic sciences on the UK criminal justice system, shared these concerns.[65]

With the UK forensic science market now dominated by three private providers, one can only wonder why the government was so determined to detach itself from forensic services in the first place. Its justification—that the state service was operating at a loss and that the private sector would operate much more efficiently—was nothing but a smoke screen. So what actually drove the privatization frenzy?

Besides ideology, the other driver may have been the desire to cut state expenditures. According to the UK opposition party, the privatization frenzy was the government's attempt to raise funds and balance its books by simply "selling off anything [it] can lay [its] hands on to massage the figures."[66] Such a strategy is, of course, unsustainable in the long run. The International Monetary Fund (IMF) warned against the "fiscal illusion that arises when governments on face value improve the fiscal position by lowering the immediate debt and deficits but reduce net worth over time."[67] As the IMF noted:

Privatizations increase revenue and lower deficits but also reduce the government's asset holdings. Similarly, cutting back maintenance expenditure reduces the deficit and lowers debt, but also reduces the value of infrastructure assets, which could cost more in the long term.[68]

Be it ideology or fiscal strategy, whichever explanation you believe, we hope you can appreciate the limits of privatization and competition. Sometimes they deliver. But sometimes the reliance on market dynamics backfires. And as we've seen with the UK forensics disaster, when a new market is created in circumstances where there is dwindling demand and cash available for the service, and serious incentives to compromise quality and integrity in the interest of profits, the results can be devastating.

Cream Skimming—UK National Health Service

One way companies in privatized markets create a mirage of competitive efficiency is by dumping costs and risks on the state. This ploy, known as "cream skimming," leaves responsibility for high-cost services and customers to the government while providing the private sector the "high-value" (in other words, low-cost) customers. In essence, the practice allows the private sector to look far more efficient than the government— because the for-profit services are free-riding on government infrastructure and services. Consider it photoshopping the kudzu to appear as an attractive ornamental.

We saw this in our story of the US prison system, where private prison companies accepted only the younger, healthier inmates, while refusing to accept older, sicker inmates with higher medical costs, who had to remain in the government prison system.

To explore how cream skimming makes privatization look so good, let's see how this has worked with the UK National Health Service (NHS). Launched in 1948 to provide equal access to medical services, regardless of wealth or ability to pay, the NHS is free at the point of delivery for all UK residents. Over the years, the NHS has had to cope with changes in demographics, a rise in chronic disease, an overall increased demand for its services, and therefore higher costs.

With funding that has not sufficiently risen to meet the increased demand, the ability of the NHS to deliver on its promise has suffered accordingly. The dream of free treatment for all has become, at times, something of a nightmare as patients face long delays and must meet an increasingly high threshold for treatment (that is, how sick you need to be in order to be treated). General practitioner clinics have reached a breaking point as the doctors struggle to cope with rising patient demands. Non-emergency services have been cut back and outsourced. Mental health, drug and alcohol services, and the availability of family liaison officers and of nurses for children are only some examples of areas in which the availability of care has steadily deteriorated.

The rise in costs and shortfalls in funding put a strain on the organization and on a government that has been struggling to balance its budget in recent years. So the United Kingdom has explored possible alternatives to the status quo, including modernizing the NHS, opening the market for health services to greater competition, or even outright privatization of the NHS.

The topic is vast and complex, not least because of a number of features that arguably make health services incompatible with a competition dynamic.[69] For our purpose, we will refrain from delving into the moral and social debate surrounding health services, and focus on a narrow aspect of competition and privatization. We will first consider the use of the competition ideology to justify cuts in government spending and, subsequently, how cream skimming makes the story so convincing.

How budget cuts prove the point: a self-fulfilling prophecy
While repeatedly stating its commitment to continuing to provide free treatment for all, the UK government has pushed for greater involvement

of the private sector.[70] As with our forensic services story, the government kudzu-ed: It assured citizens of free market efficiencies, which would result from competition and offer superior health care. With more private sector providers moving into the marketplace in response to the demand for better services, people who could afford to pay for these private insurers and providers began using them, rather than the NHS.

One may call this a "crawling privatization." As the UK government keeps underfunding the NHS, the resulting deterioration of its services keeps driving more patients into the hands of the private sector, which in turn allows the government to question the viability of the NHS and restrict funding even further. As more and more functions of the NHS are outsourced,[71] the free market option appears increasingly attractive.[72] In short, the government is slowly suffocating selective parts of the NHS, as it did the FSS in the forensic sciences story. The difference lies in the ability of some patients to opt out and pay (directly or through insurance policies) for private health care. Which leads us to the next part of the story.

How cream skimming provides the "proof" for kudzu-ing

In a health system with a mixture of private and state providers, the private providers can increase their profits by free-riding off the services that the government must continue to offer. The private health providers accept only the high-value profitable patients, and then spend only on essential immediate services, not on the infrastructure that supports them. Specialist doctor needed? If you're a private provider, you don't want or need to incur the costs to train doctors. Instead you hire away doctors trained at the state hospital. Need medicine or blood during a shortage? Private providers stock only the amount of medicine and blood to supply immediate needs, relying on the government to provide during the kinds of emergencies that result in shortages. Need ambulance and emergency room services? Why incur these costs when you can free-ride on the state services. Need to refer a patient to a doctor over the weekend? No need to pay private doctors overtime, when you can instead send patients to the state hospital.

Meanwhile, because the NHS is tasked with ensuring every citizen's well-being and is subject to regulatory constraints, it must act in a socially responsible way, which translates into "inefficiency." Examples of this inefficiency: The NHS trains doctors and nurses, and it keeps employing them even over seasonal periods with reduced demand for health services (rather than relying on temporary workers), so as to ensure the availability of trained staff and continuity of standards of treatment. Similarly, it maintains "empty" hospital beds over the summer to ensure enough capacity during the winter months. Further "inefficiencies": It treats the weak and the poor, and provides them with transport services, consulting, and social support; stocks a wide range of medicines, some rarely required, but essential; and maintains a large blood supply for possible surges in demand. It provides emergency rooms and intensive care services, including for those who received treatment in a private setting but were then transferred back to the NHS after suffering complications. It accepts all cases, including those patients with complex medical conditions who were rejected by private health providers.

So, cream skimming enables the private health care provider to increase profits—at the taxpayers' expense. The private sector appears very efficient. Cash-rich, often relatively healthy patients are treated rapidly and with high success. The market delivers in wonderful ways. In reality, the private sector's efficiency depends on the "inefficiency" of the non-selective state system, which is left with an increased portion of costly, complex cases; a poorer, sicker caseload; and the responsibility for maintaining staff, supplies, and infrastructure through all seasons. In short, the NHS does the heavy lifting and incurs the heavy costs, which are passed on to the taxpayers.

Cream skimming provides the screen for kudzu-ing. Even though a review of health systems indicates the likely superiority of the public system,[73] expect the kudzu-ing to continue. Driven by short-term planning goals and the political need for "fiscal illusion," policy makers will rally us with the competition ideology, as they deliver other basic necessities, like water, to the private sector.

Show Me the Money!

Perhaps some markets, like prisons, forensic services, and health care, cannot be entirely, or even largely, privatized. But what about commodities like water supply? Surely in such markets privatization can provide us with greater efficiencies, better services, and lower prices.

Let's see how that worked out in England. In 1989, the UK government privatized all ten water and sewage companies as part of the wider privatization plan driven by the then Prime Minister Margaret Thatcher. Privatization was meant to enable the sector, which was starved of cash, to gain better access to the financing it needed to invest in infrastructure and services. In a speech to the Conservative Central Council, Thatcher celebrated the privatization of water services in the usual language of the competition ideology:

> . . . Nationalisation seldom spares the people's pockets. It's too inefficient. Hence, the reason for privatising water . . . Under Public ownership, water investment had to take its place in the queue behind schools and hospitals . . . Once water is in the private sector, and free from treasury control, companies will have the resources to invest in the latest technology and give the customer a far better deal . . . Indeed under privatisation the consumer will have much better protection . . .[74]

In the years that followed, the price of water supplied by the private companies in England steadily increased, in contrast to Scotland, where services remain publicly held.

Why those price increases occurred under privatization is the subject of a study by Karol Yearwood. In what the study refers to as "an ATM for investors," the private water companies in England opted to accumulate massive amounts of debt for the purpose of paying dividends that were so high they exceeded, at times, the companies' cash balances:

> . . . despite this cash depletion, the industry proceeded to pay out nearly £2bn in dividends per year, which directly implies that to finance them, the companies had to borrow around £1.9bn per year in Debt . . . As a result, total dividends paid since privatisation, till 2017 amounted to around £53bn, which led to an aggregate £51.7bn shortfall in cash. Today, the industry's debt level stands at around £51bn and the similarity of those numbers doesn't look to be coincidental . . .
>
> . . . Our econometric analysis suggests that the 40% increase in real household bills since privatisation was mainly driven by continuously growing interest payments on debt, contrary to the regulator attributing them to growing costs and investments.[75]

The 2018 study concludes that the "companies could have afforded to finance all their operations and investments without taking on any debt at all. Instead, evidence suggests their debt taking was driven by overly high dividends."

An article published a few years earlier noted that one company's price for water was so high that the government had to step in with a £50 subsidy for each household—and that this was not the only time the private sector has had to appeal to the government for help. In addition to the problem of high dividends and high prices that Yearwood's study explored, this article cited "allegations that the water companies are using debt to lower their tax obligation."[76] Because of rising prices, the UK regulator of the water sector has estimated that 1.8 million people will need financial assistance to pay their water bills by 2020.[77]

For once the public seems to be immune to the claims of the kudzu-ers. Reacting with fury to the water companies' extortionate prices and continuing calls for additional tax breaks, UK citizens are increasingly demanding a return to a nationalized water service. One poll showed 83 percent of respondents favoring renationalization.[78]

A Short History of a Word

Given privatization's star role in the competition ideology, we began wondering about the origins of the term. Who coined the word *privatization* (or, to be more precise, *reprivatization*—the opposite of *renationalization*)?

Not Margaret Thatcher or Ronald Reagan. Rather, the Nazis.

During the early 1930s, the word *Reprivatisierung* began to appear in press and journal articles in Germany to describe the shift of state-controlled functions, like urban transport, banking, and steel production, to the private sector under the Nazis. What "may well be the first recorded use of the term 'reprivatization'" in the English language then occurred in a 1936 economics journal article reporting on the sale of three banks under the Reich.[79]

According to a 1941 book written by an American scholar who was an expert on the structure of the German economy, "In return for business assistance, the Nazis hastened to give evidence of their good will by restoring to private capitalism a number of monopolies held or controlled by the state."[80] She went on to say, "The practical significance of the transference of government enterprises into private hands was thus that the capitalist class continued to serve as a vessel for the accumulation of income. Profit-making and the return of property to private hands, moreover, have assisted the consolidation of Nazi party power."[81]

Another economist, writing in 1943, explained that the Nazi party "facilitate[d] the accumulation of private fortunes and industrial empires by its foremost members and collaborators through 'privatization' and other measures, thereby intensifying centralization of economic affairs and government in an increasingly narrow group that may for all practical purposes be termed the national socialist elite."[82]

In short, privatization was explicitly for the purpose of benefiting "the wealthiest sectors" in order to gain the political support of the elite.[83]

And it worked as planned. The German industrialists were eager to support Adolf Hitler's economic policies and rise to power. For example, in 1933, twenty days after seizing control of the German state, the Nazis convened a meeting at which twenty leading German industrialists were enlisted in a secret rearmament program. At the meeting Hitler and Hermann Göring explained their program to the industrialists—among them Krupp von Bohlen of the Krupp Armament Works and representatives of I.G. Farbenindustrie and other Ruhr heavy industries—who "became so enthusiastic that they set about to raise 3 million Reichsmark to strengthen and confirm the Nazi Party in power. Two months later Krupp was working to bring a reorganized association of German industry into agreement with the political aims of the Nazi Government."[84]

Thus, *privatization* was a tool the Nazis used to centralize power and benefit the few, at the expense of the many. Fast forward to the present. From its ignoble origins, the term *privatize* has been reframed so that it is now used to convey a process that is supposed to result in a *decentralization* of power for the benefit of all.

Reflections

As anyone who has experienced some of China's better private restaurants or hotels can attest, society—or at least some parts of society—can often benefit from privatization. Liberalization of many markets can indeed yield efficiencies and prosperity.

But privatization, like competition, is not necessarily a panacea. When we hear lobbyists and policy makers call for privatization and invoke competition as pixie dust, with no explanation of how competition under a given market structure operating with a particular set of incentives will actually deliver, then we should reach for our wallets. They are likely angling for another opportunity to sell public assets for a quick profit, while offloading significant costs onto taxpayers' hands.

Yet, lobbyists and powerful private firms will continue to use the competition ideology to hide their redistribution of public assets because it enables them to extract greater profits at public expense. For them, kudzu-ing is a tool to achieve privatization, old style.

CHAPTER 8

The Gamemakers

In the previous chapters we saw how toxic competition can flourish as a result of the competition ideology, psychological manipulation, lobbying, and privatization. Now imagine if someone could create at the very outset a toxic competitive dynamic that exploits the participants, while primarily benefiting the creator. The privileged architects of these competitive environments—who create the toxicity and benefit from it—are what we will call the *Gamemakers*, after the characters who go by that name in *The Hunger Games* book and film trilogy.

Think of the twenty or so purple-robed Gamemakers who create and control all the rules governing the televised games in those books (and their film adaptations)—from the death traps planted around the arena where the games are fought, down to the clothes worn by the competitors and even the height of the campfires. In these annual games, the contenders, known as "tributes," two each from the nation's twelve districts, fight to the death until only one of them survives. The real winner, however, isn't the last living tribute, but the architects of the game. The Gamemakers design the game to ensure that the Capitol elite always benefit, regardless of which contestant ultimately prevails. Everyone else is essentially a loser.

We see a version of the Hunger Games played out (less violently) on reality shows like the *The Amazing Race* and *Survivor*. By creating and controlling the competitive process for maximum entertainment value, the shows' producers ensure that whoever wins the million dollar bounty, they themselves will be the prime beneficiaries, thanks to the millions of viewers these shows attract and the hundreds of millions they earn in advertising and ancillary revenues.

So where can we find these Gamemakers in our own lives? You need look no further than your mobile phone—and to Google and Facebook, the main protagonists of this chapter. No doubt, we benefit immensely from their services and innovations. Besides Google's own apps for searching, navigating, shopping, socializing, and communicating, Google offers over two million apps in its Android app store. Many of the apps are free (or inexpensive), and the company promises to carefully screen and police them to ensure that we get what is promised. Likewise, Facebook and its three messaging platforms, Instagram, Messenger, and WhatsApp, allow us to connect with friends and family in ways that have transformed our lives.

But Google and Facebook are not just providers of helpful and enjoyable products. Their vast wealth, power, and sophistication elevate them to the level of Gamemakers—architects of their own competitive environment.

To tell the story of what the Gamemakers do, we'll begin with the Fun Kid Racing app on the Google platform. Its creator, a small Lithuanian start-up company called Tiny Lab Productions, speaks directly to our children:

> *Hey kid! Would you like to have a fun ride? Jump in a car and join other fast racers! Explore different race tracks, meet cartoonish characters and make some funny car flips! Collect coins to unlock new cars and new worlds!*[1]

Tiny Lab assures parents:

> *Parents can leave 2 year old or 3 year old alone and do not worry for any distractions* [sic]. . . . *Fun Kid Racing will help your kid to develop*

hand-eye coordination, self-preservation and self-control, stimulate reaction and improve problem solving, quick decision making and flexible thinking skills.[2]

Google classified Tiny Lab's gaming app as age-appropriate with an "Everyone" rating and distributed it in the family section of its Google Play store. Google also awarded Tiny Lab with its "Top Developer badge, which confirms high quality and innovativeness of the games."[3] As this app is clearly directed to children under the age of thirteen, neither Tiny Lab nor Google, under the terms of the US privacy statute, the Children's Online Privacy Protection Act, could collect the children's data without first obtaining the parents' consent.[4]

The Fun Kid Racing app promises to "keep your kids entertained for months."[5] No wonder it's been downloaded over seventy-five million times, suggesting that a lot of kids were indeed entertained for long periods of time.

So where is the catch?

Well, *If You're Not Paying for the Product*, the Internet saying goes, *You Become the Product*.[6] Here the product is the children playing the Fun Kid Racing app. While they were playing, Tiny Lab was surreptitiously harvesting the children's personal data and sharing it with Google, Twitter, and several advertising companies.[7]

The way this game is designed and played—not Fun Kid Racing but the online advertising game—is that once an app or website user's personal data has been harvested, the Gamemaker hosts an auction among the advertisers, who bid to see which one will get to target that person with an ad and promotion. In the advertising world, this is known as "behavioral advertising"—in which personal and behavioral data mined from online activities are used to match ads to the interests of the target audience.

The Fun Kid Racing app's marketing of its users' data through the Google ecosystem is one small instance of the phenomenon Harvard

Business School Professor Emerita Shoshana Zuboff has defined as "surveillance capitalism." Surveillance capitalism "operates through unprecedented asymmetries in knowledge and the power that accrues to knowledge. Surveillance capitalists know everything *about us*, whereas their operations are designed to be unknowable *to us*. They accumulate vast domains of new knowledge *from us*, but not *for us* . . . for the sake of others' gain, not ours."[8]

By piecing together information gleaned from multiple sources, including the 2018 lawsuit brought by New Mexico's attorney general against Tiny Lab, Google, and others,[9] and recent reports from the United Kingdom,[10] French,[11] Australian,[12] and German[13] antitrust agencies, we can get a few glimpses of how this environment is designed by the likes of Google and Facebook. As the Gamemakers, they have the skills to orchestrate a competitive environment that is toxic for all the participants—consumers, app and website developers, and online advertisers—while they themselves reap the vast majority of the profits. We can also learn some of the Gamemakers' tricks of the trade:

- How Gamemakers use their Tom Sawyer–esque ingenuity to attract us into working for them.
- How Gamemakers make the competitive contest opaque and complex, so that we fail to appreciate its toll.
- How Gamemakers, in control of the key levers, design the game so that none of the competitors have the clout to challenge the Gamemakers' rules of competition or to compete (or subsist) outside of the Gamemakers' arena.
- How Gamemakers promote the illusion of choice and control, while, behind the scenes, they control multiple levers, all designed to channel power and profits in one direction—theirs.

To illustrate the insidious spread of toxic competition, we will focus on three of the levers that the Gamemakers Facebook and Google control. This will allow us to appreciate how the Gamemakers use toxic competition to attract and addict us, extract our personal data, and exploit that data for profit.

Lever 1—How the Gamemakers Hook Us

To attract competitors among the advertising firms from which they glean most of their revenues, the Gamemakers must offer some bounty. For Google and Facebook, we and our personal data are the bounty.

We spend a lot of time on Facebook's platforms. In 2016, the *New York Times* noted, we spent on average more time on Facebook, Instagram, and Messenger (fifty minutes per day) than on any other leisure activity except watching television programs and movies (on average 2.8 hours per day).[14] That was more time than we spent reading (nineteen minutes), participating in sports or exercise (seventeen minutes), or attending social events (four minutes). Add it all up and users spend about 950 million hours on Facebook each day.[15]

We also spend a lot of time on Google's platform.[16] As Google noted in 2017, "people around the world are now watching a billion hours of YouTube's incredible content every single day!"[17] To put that in perspective, Google calculated that if you were to sit and watch a billion hours of YouTube, it would take you back over 100,000 years, to the time when "our ancestors were crafting stone tools and migrating out of Africa while mammoths and mastodons roamed the Earth."[18]

Google's core products, such as Android, Chrome, Gmail, Google Drive, Google Maps, Google Play, Search, and YouTube, each have over one billion active users per month.[19] YouTube, on mobile phones alone, reaches more eighteen- to thirty-four-year-olds in the United States than any TV network.[20] According to one 2017 study, 80 percent of US children between six and twelve years old used YouTube daily.[21]

Increasingly we are mesmerized by our mobile phone apps—well over four hours per day, on average, in 2017.[22] So much so that psychologists have coined a word for the fear of being without one's phone, *nomophobia* (no mobile phone phobia), and some have called for it to be included in the American Psychiatric Association's taxonomic and diagnostic tool, the *DSM-5*.[23] Symptoms include "regular and time-consuming use, feelings of anxiety when the phone is not available, 'ringxiety' (i.e., repeatedly checking one's phone for messages, sometimes leading to phantom ring tones), constant availability, preference for mobile communication over face to face communication, and financial problems as a consequence of use."[24] Psychologists have defined as disorders "social network site addiction" and "Facebook addiction,"[25] in which users are "overly concerned about social media, driven by an uncontrollable motivation to log on to or use social media, and devoting so much time and effort to [social network sites] that it impairs other important life areas."[26]

Whether we are addicted or not in the medical sense of that word, the time we spend on social media clearly eats into other activities—like sleeping, studying, and actually doing things with other people.[27] The situation has gotten so bad that in January 2018, a hedge fund joined a California pension fund to demand that Apple do more to address the effects of its devices on children. As the *Economist* noted, "You know you are in trouble if a Wall Street firm is lecturing you about morality."[28]

But how did so many of us get hooked on our phones?

"Your kid is not weak-willed because he can't get off his phone," one neuroscientist noted. "Your kid's brain is being engineered to get him to stay on his phone."[29] The same could be said of all of us. Developers are fiercely competing against each other to make their apps and games as addictive as possible, thereby eroding our capacity for free choice.[30] The Holy Grail are the so-called diaper apps—apps "so addictive" we "don't even want to get up to pee."[31]

Why so addictive?

Many app developers compete so hard to addict us, because the longer we spend on their apps—the more "eyeball time" we put in—the more personal data they can extract from us and the more money they can make by selling access to that data to advertisers.

This is the new business reality, and game developers like Tiny Lab cannot afford to opt out, especially when their target audience is children.[32] So to get kids to jump in a car and race for hours, Tiny Lab must incorporate many of the design tricks that the designers of the advertising ecosystem—in this case Google—have developed to encourage addiction.

Google, like many of the other Gamemakers, stands ready to help the app developers on its advertising platform create ever more addictive products. Among its offerings are "rewarded ads." Suppose you are engrossed in a survival game like *The Hunger Games* on your phone. Your mobile game player "dies" upon reaching a critical point. Having spent the past hour getting this far, you are clearly disappointed. You would prefer continuing to play instead of having to start over from the beginning. Knowing this, the Gamemaker gives you the option to watch an ad in exchange for a reward, namely an extra "life," which enables you to continue competing in *The Hunger Games* exactly where you left off. You associate the ad with the reward, and click away.

As Google explains on AdMob, its advertising service designed for these app developers, these "rewarded ads" can help app developers in two key ways. The point of these "rewarded ads" is that "[w]ith increasing competition in the mobile gaming market, developers need to be more focused on engagement and retention."[33] These rewarded ads have been proven to increase the session length and retention of game app users. Plus, because users want to keep playing, they'll—in the jargon of the industry—"often convert throughout the whole funnel," which means potentially far more ad revenue for the app developer. For the app developer, the combination of addiction and extra ad revenue is very alluring. Thus, it is not surprising that the number of apps using AdMob's rewarded ads quadrupled in 2017 alone. And, for any developer with an app that has over 100,000 downloads, Google will provide them with a "free consultation" on the use of these "rewarded ads."

Facebook's business model is similar to Google's: "Both are reliant on consumer attention and consumer data in order to sell advertising opportunities," according to the antitrust authority of the Australian government.[34] And both are highly aware of the addictive qualities of their products, which they have designed for that very purpose, according to a group of former employees and early investors in Google, Facebook, and other giant tech companies, who have formed an alliance to sound the alarm about the dangers of technology and social media.[35]

The complaint (the document that generally starts a lawsuit) lodged by the attorney general of New Mexico against Tiny Lab and its enablers, among them Google, speaks directly to these dangers. It alleges that Google helps the app developers within its advertising network exploit our weaknesses in order to attract and addict us and our children.[36] According to the complaint, the defendants used the children's personal data "to analyze their demographics and behavior, and trigger events—both within the [Fun Kid Racing] app and across the Internet—that will encourage them to play the app more often and for longer periods."[37] Basically, Google used its vast data trove to help Tiny Lab "'hook' children and to keep them playing the app."[38] Indeed, Google markets its "ability to help app developers such as Tiny Lab increase user retention, and thereby their profits. Children are specifically targeted as part of this goal."[39] Moreover, by representing that Tiny Lab's apps were "suitable and safe for children, complying with all applicable privacy laws,"[40] Google is alleged to have engaged in "unfair or deceptive acts or practices" in violation of New Mexico's laws and to the detriment of consumers.

Google's efforts to addict us and our children are surely matched in their effectiveness—if not their precise methods—by Facebook's. As explained by Roger McNamee, author of *Zucked: Waking Up to the Facebook Catastrophe*, who was an early investor in Facebook and a longtime mentor to Mark Zuckerberg but has since become one of Facebook's fiercest (and most knowledgeable) critics: The company's business model "depends on advertising, which in turn depends on manipulating the attention of users so they see more ads. One of the best ways to manipulate attention is to appeal to outrage and fear, emotions that increase engagement."[41] Evoking outrage and fear is only part of the strategy. Between late 2012 and 2017, Facebook "experimented constantly with algorithms, new data types and small changes in design, measuring everything."[42] The goal was to use the company's best minds to figure out ever better ways to exploit our psychological weaknesses.[43] "Instead of technology being a tool in service to humanity," McNamee noted, "it is humans who are in service to technology."[44]

Take, for example, our "fear of missing out." This phenomenon is so widespread that it has its own widely recognized acronym: FOMO. The fear that others—our friends, family, classmates, coworkers, and acquaintances—are seemingly enjoying pleasurable experiences from which we have been excluded can be a powerful motivator.[45] This fear, which is grounded in our need to belong, drives us back repeatedly to the social network in order to keep up with what others are doing. It's easy to get hooked when every 60 seconds, another 510,000 new comments on average are posted on Facebook, 293,000 statuses are updated, and 136,000 new photos are uploaded.[46] On Instagram, over four hundred million new Stories are posted every day.[47] So we return reflexively to see what we're missing—spending about fifty-three minutes each day in 2018, on average, on Instagram and fifty-eight minutes on Facebook.[48] This is how we end up working for the Gamemakers—for free: by posting content and commenting on other people's posts, which in turn supports Facebook's advertisers. As Facebook tells investors, "With more than 2 billion people using at least one of our services every day, we're the best place for these advertisers to show people ads that work."[49]

The Gamemaker can also rope us into competition—whether for the number of "likes" for our online post, the number of times our message has been sent to others, or the number of favorable comments we received. Since we enjoy it when others "like" our posts, some of us compete for "likes" and the presumed social status that accrues to "likes."[50] One experiment, in looking at the effect of "likes" on Facebook users, found that, when users were told about the number of hypothetical "likes" they received after writing a status update (none, two, or thirty) and from whom (close friends or acquaintance), "likes" became the "currency for self-esteem and belonging."[51] The more "likes" (regardless of whom they came from), the greater the temporary boost to self-esteem and sense of belongingness. As Facebook's early investor McNamee added, "Millions of users reciprocate one another's "likes" and friend requests all day long, not aware that platforms orchestrate all of this behavior upstream, like a puppet master."[52]

And the more often we toil away on Facebook and Instagram, returning obsessively to the social networking sites in order to read and comment on each other's posts, the more free content we provide via our posts, which the Gamemakers exploit to attract yet more users. If we were to tire of this labor, the quality and frequency of postings would likely decrease, as would Facebook's profits.[53] Thus, for Facebook, it is "'vital' . . . to encourage a broad range of users to contribute content."[54] It has many strategies to nudge us to "contribute."[55]

For example, to spur more conversations, since May 2015, Facebook has drawn on users' "likes" and location to place "prompts related to ongoing events at the top of some users' news feeds."[56] According to its spokesperson, the response rate to these "timely reminders about things people might want to post about" was "excellent."[57] To further encourage even more content sharing and user interaction, in December 2016, Facebook announced that it would be using the real estate above its news feed to:

- give people ways to connect and share with friends during holidays and events,
- help people discover fun and interesting cultural moments, and
- celebrate moments in history that continue to make the world more open and connected.[58]

And so, the social network we use ends up using us. In reality, we work for Facebook, posting content to attract others, becoming endorsers for its advertisers, and allowing it to extract our data. If one takes the reported hours we collectively spend on Facebook (950 million hours each day), think about how much that amounts to at the federal minimum wage scale of $7.25 per hour: $6.8875 trillion. Even after one deducts likely benefits from using the social network, the value of "unpaid labor" is staggering.

While we benefit from some of the apps and services, this competition to attract and addict us comes at a significant cost, especially, as the New Mexico attorney general outlined in its complaint against Tiny Lab, Google, et al., as it affects our children:

> *Defendants' "retention" efforts take place in a context where mobile device usage among children is widespread and growing . . . The consequences of mobile device overuse, particularly among children, is well-known in the tech industry, with many industry leaders refusing to allow their own children to own or use devices, or attend schools where such devices are prevalent . . .*
>
> *Parents are increasingly concerned about their children's mobile device usage, and for good reason: research has associated increasing usage with negative consequences for children, such as increasing rates of ADHD, depression, anxiety, and reduced focus in the classroom. One recent study showed that children between the ages of 12 and 18 who spent more time playing games had lower than average social-emotional well-being . . . The World Health Organization ("WHO") recently added "gaming disorder" to its globally-recognized compendium of medical conditions and diagnoses. In the 11th International Classification of Diseases, the WHO describes the condition as "impaired control over gaming, increasing priority given to gaming over other activities to the extent that gaming takes precedence over other interests and daily activities, and continuation or escalation of gaming despite the occurrence of negative consequences."*[59]

We don't know the full toll from this toxic competition. A recently launched NIH study of 11,000 nine- and ten-year-olds hopes to provide some answers over the course of the next decade, but one thing is already clear: Kids who spent more than two hours a day on screens got lower scores on thinking and language tests.[60] Other studies have found that the risks of spending large amounts of time on games, Instagram, and Facebook include, among other things, higher rates of depression and less satisfaction with nearly every aspect of their lives.[61] Such findings do not deter the Gamemakers and their app developers from their determination to make money at our expense.

Lever 2—How the Gamemakers Extract Our Personal Data

Skillful Gamemakers, as we saw, have the Tom Sawyer–esque ingenuity of getting us to paint the fence—i.e., create content and spend time on their platforms—so that the personal data, which is the source of their profits, can be extracted. Their next challenge is to get their hands on that data. So, with millions of app developers and websites competing to attract and addict us, the skilled Gamemakers design the game so that once all of these competitors have extracted our personal data, they will deliver this valuable resource to the Gamemakers.

To understand how this second lever works, put yourself in Tiny Lab's position. As Tiny Lab's CEO lamented, the competition in the gaming industry is cutthroat: "There are a lot of competitors who can plagiarize your game, steal game ideas or even game graphics by trying to create as successful game as yours—especially if your game is small simple title for kids."[62] To make matters worse, they are operating in an environment in which consumers have become accustomed to free apps and online services. For a developer like Tiny Lab, the problem is even more acute because their target audience is children: "Another difficulty—there is a low buying power of our players who are mainly under thirteen years old. It's hard to convince them to spend their money on additional game items or levels as most of them have to ask their parents for the purchase."[63]

So Tiny Lab cannot pitch *Hey kid! Would you like to go on a fun ride? Go get Mom or Dad's credit card.* It has to offer its app for free. To make money, then, it must rely on advertising dollars.[64] But to get the ad revenue, Tiny Lab must now compete against the Gamemaker's own popular free apps and services, and the millions of other free apps, blogs, and websites within the Gamemaker's ecosystem, all of which are also trying to maximize their advertising revenue.

Since the Gamemaker has skillfully designed the competitive environment in such a way as to maximize its own revenue, it offers the app developers a helping hand, which they find hard to refuse—the opportunity to join the Gamemaker's sprawling advertising network in order to gain access to potential advertisers. But to join this network, the app developer must agree to extract a lot of personal data about its users and deliver that information to the Gamemaker.[65] To find out how we and our children spend most of our time, the Gamemaker installs tracking software on the websites and apps.[66] Once embedded, the Gamemaker's software automatically sends our highly detailed personal information to the Gamemaker, who analyzes it, and uses it to build its profile on each of us.

The longer and more often a child plays Fun Kid Racing, for example, the more personal data about that child becomes available to both Tiny Lab and Google, the more behavioral ads they can test on the child, and the more skillfully they can target the child (and the child's parents) with ads. This is how both the app developer and the Gamemaker can make a profit even from free apps.

All that personal data enables highly sophisticated targeting—of advertising, sales pitches, products, and pricing. As Facebook's chief operating officer Sheryl Sandberg explained in a January 2018 earnings call with investors, its "dynamic ads" are another way to target. Suppose, for example, people searched the Holiday Inn website looking for a room in a given city on a given date, but did not book a room. Using the data it had collected about those people from their browsing history, Facebook helped Holiday Inn Express target them with videos that showed them "a personalized selection" of Holiday Inn hotels for that very city and those exact dates. This personalized targeting was a success, according to Sandberg, resulting in three times the return on what the hotel chain spent on its previous campaigns.[67] This is just one of numerous examples of how the Gamemakers use their machine-learning algorithms to track and profile us; identify our shopping habits and willingness to pay; and even pinpoint when we or our children feel "worthless," "insecure," or "anxious."[68] According to a leaked internal document, Facebook promoted advertising campaigns that monitored and exploited its users' emotional states, including users as young as fourteen years old:

> [T]he selling point of this 2017 document is that Facebook's algorithms can determine, and allow advertisers to pinpoint, "moments when young people need a confidence boost." If that phrase isn't clear enough, Facebook's document offers a litany of teen emotional states that the company claims it can estimate based on how teens use the service, including "worthless," "insecure," "defeated," "anxious," "silly," "useless," "stupid," "overwhelmed," "stressed," and "a failure." . . . [T]he documents also reveal a particular interest in helping advertisers target moments in which young users are interested in "looking good and body confidence" or "working out and losing weight."[69]

Facebook denied offering tools to target vulnerable teenagers.[70] Even if it is telling the truth, the document illustrates how companies are seeking ways to profile us in order to manipulate our behavior. When the *New York Times* reviewed hundreds of Facebook's patent applications, its review revealed how "the company has considered tracking almost every aspect of its users' lives: where you are, who you spend time with, whether you're in a romantic relationship, which brands and politicians you're talking about. The company has even attempted to patent a method for predicting when your friends will die."[71] As a media analyst quoted in the article said: "I've seen no indication that Facebook has changed its commitment to watch everything we do, record everything we do and exploit everything we do." Marketers who collect these massive amounts of data on us can then use behavioral economics to refine their strategies.[72] The ultimate aim is to induce us to buy things we otherwise wouldn't have purchased at the highest price we are willing to pay.[73]

Even seemingly benign data, such as what we "like," can give the Gamemaker a lot of useful information about us. Using a dataset compiled from over fifty-eight thousand volunteers who provided their Facebook "likes," computer scientists at one university did a study and found that they could make predictions about eleven different variables, including the Facebook user's age, gender, sexual orientation, ethnicity, religious and political views, and use of addictive substances—with degrees of accuracy ranging between 60 and 95 percent depending on the variable.[74]

But the Gamemakers do not simply decree that the personal data should flow to it. The Gamemakers want their app developers and other publishers to compete at finding ever more ingenious ways of extracting personal data from us. This is an effort in which everyone's interests— Gamemakers', creators', and advertisers'—are aligned (everyone's except ours, that is). The more data that are extracted, the more carefully the advertising can be targeted, the more money the advertisers will be willing to pay, and the greater the Gamemakers' cut.[75]

With all these incentives, the toxic competition keeps spawning new data-extraction technologies to degrade our privacy, our autonomy, and our very well-being. If you, like most people, use Google's Chrome browser, you are being tracked, even in incognito mode.[76] Ditto for Android phone users.[77] Think you can avoid Google or Facebook if you use a privacy-friendly browser on your Apple device? Think again. Whenever you visit a website that uses Google's advertising services (of which Google claims there are more than two million sites, reaching 90 percent of users worldwide), you are being tracked.[78]

Even if you install ad blockers, the Gamemakers can co-opt or circumvent many of them.[79] If you have a Facebook account, Facebook is tracking you even when you are not logged into its social network. As Germany's competition authority found in its investigation, whenever you visit any of the millions of websites with a Facebook "like" or "share" button, Facebook is collecting data about you as soon as the webpage opens.[80] Even if you could avoid the webpages with "like" buttons, your data is almost certainly still flowing to Facebook, via third-party sources that include not just Facebook-owned services like Instagram and WhatsApp, but the huge number of websites and apps that link to Facebook via embedded, hidden interfaces.[81] This automatically provides the Gamemaker even more socio-demographic and behavioral data about you.[82] So if you've ever wondered why you can log onto so many third-party websites using your Google or Facebook account, that's why.

Another data-extraction method, this one is anything but hidden: If you're between ages thirteen and thirty-five, Facebook might just pay you up to $20 per month to suck up all of your personal data by installing on your phone a Facebook Research app.[83] Facebook will even ask for screenshots of your Amazon order history page.

Lever 3—How the Gamemakers
Use Our Data to Attract Bidders

The game is almost complete. After driving competition to mine your data ever more successfully, the Gamemaker will next dangle that resource— your highly detailed, continually updated personal profile, as well as your eyeballs—before the advertisers who are clamoring to reach you. And then the Gamemaker commences the bidding process.

On the surface, the advertising market looks robustly competitive. Between the advertisers and the apps and websites that publish the ads (for our purposes, the *publishers*) are several layers of intermediaries, each layer containing multiple competitors.[84] But in reality Google and Facebook are the key gateways for advertisers looking to place online ads[85] and publishers seeking ad revenue.[86] No one else has the same reach and control.

Advertisers go where we go, and most often that will be to Google's and Facebook's services and the many websites and apps within their advertising networks. Only Google and Facebook can provide online advertisers with access to (i) their own websites, applications, and other services, which have the largest audiences; (ii) the largest two advertising networks, composed of third-party websites and applications; and (iii) the refined data profiles they've assembled on billions of users.[87]

The Gamemaker becomes the auctioneer. To target us with behavioral ads, the advertisers bid against each other on the Gamemaker's advanced real-time automated bidding platform.[88]

For an example of how this works, let's focus on display ads auctioned through Google's Display Network, which, according to the company, "reaches 90% of Internet users worldwide, across millions of websites, news pages, blogs, and Google sites like Gmail and YouTube."[89]

Suppose you want to make an Adirondack chair. In googling for free woodworking plans, you choose, from among the links, the website BuildEazy.[90] As your web browser, say Safari or Google Chrome, opens the BuildEazy website, for an infinitesimal fraction of a second the opening page has an empty space marked for a display ad. Your browser sends a request to BuildEazy's ad server to see if the ad space is already committed. Probably not—if BuildEazy's New Zealand owner is like many small and mid-sized publishers. Within one hundred milliseconds, behind the scenes, without your ever noticing this is happening, one or more auctions will then occur.[91]

How heated the bidding becomes will depend on how attractive—

meaning lucrative—the potential target of the ad appears to be. That, in turn, will depend in part on the richness of the data about the potential target, and what that data tells the advertisers. For example, a six-year-old playing Fun Kid Racing might command a higher bid if the data extracted about her indicate that she can significantly influence her parents' spending.[92] In general, the more data there is, the more attractive the target, which will translate into a higher number of advertisers participating in the auction and higher bids.[93]

How the Gamemakers Profit from This Competition

The competition continues every waking hour of every day, as advertisers compete to determine which personalized ad (and stealth influencer) we will see next on our mobile phone, laptop, or tablet. In this competition, the Gamemakers themselves always win, regardless of which advertiser places the highest bid. But what do the app developers and websites who extract our data get out of the deal? Like any skilled Gamemaker, Google and Facebook purposefully made their competitive system so complex and opaque that neither the publishers nor the advertisers actually know how much money is coming in or how it is split.[94]

No outsider—including the antitrust agencies who spent months studying the Gamemakers' advertising ecosystem, not to mention the advertisers and the app developers and other creators who participate in that ecosystem—really knows how much of the advertising dollar actually reaches the publisher, versus the pockets of the Gamemakers and other intermediaries. The French antitrust agency, relying on one estimate, said publishers get on average 40 cents of every advertising dollar. The remaining 60 cents goes to the Gamemakers and other intermediaries.[95] Google says its publishers get significantly more (about 71 cents per dollar), while others say significantly less.[96] In an interesting experiment, the *Guardian* placed ads on its own website. Acting as both advertiser and publisher, the UK newspaper observed how much money flowing in for each ad actually reached its pocket. At times, the newspaper received only 30 percent of the amount spent on that ad, with the remainder going to the Gamemakers and other intermediaries.[97]

As is now obvious, this competition primarily benefits the Gamemakers, not the publishers,[98] and certainly not us. Nearly all of their revenues come from advertising.[99] And their revenue and profits continue to grow.[100] By 2018, Google and Facebook extracted 58 percent of the $111 billion in revenues from the digital ad market—more than all of their online competitors combined.[101] The closest competitor is Amazon, which is still expanding its advertising network. According to *Bloomberg*, "In the first half of 2018, Google and Facebook accounted for 75 percent of all digital ad growth; Amazon was responsible for much of the rest."[102]

Even the revenues from locally targeted advertising flow to the Gamemakers. Google and Facebook gobbled up 48 percent of local ad revenues in 2018. The revenue for Google alone ($19 billion) already exceeds the ad revenues for 11,044 commercial radio stations in the United States in 2018.[103] So how did that happen? As the former chair of the Federal Communications Commission (FCC) observed, "This is not because they are a part of the local community, but because their ubiquitous collection allows them to know more about the members of the local community than even the neighbors."[104]

The Gamemakers have also had a profound effect on our local and national media. Numerous news agencies, for example, rely on traffic from Google, Apple, and Facebook for their readers. According to a report from the Australian competition agency, approximately 50 percent of traffic to Australian news media websites comes from Google or Facebook.[105] In the United States, Facebook outstripped "all other social media sites as a source of news," with over 40 percent of Americans receiving news on Facebook.[106] YouTube is also a popular social media site for news. While dependent on the Gamemakers for readers, newspapers for the last decade have watched these same Gamemakers siphon away their advertising revenue, which has damaged their ability to pay for high-quality journalism.[107] But the Gamemakers are not concerned if the quality of the journalism deteriorates, even to the level of "fake news" (which tends to appeal to the fear and anger that keep us engaged), so long as it attracts users.

The Gamemakers are not just siphoning away newspapers' ad revenues but also their subscription revenues. As one newspaper executive told us, for the privilege of being accessed through the Android smartphone, publishers must hand over between 15 and 30 percent of their in-app subscription revenues and payments to Google.

The Illusion of Choice and Control

The brilliance of the Gamemakers in designing this competitive landscape is that it seems that everyone has options.

No one forces us to use the Gamemakers' services or free apps. Even if they are potentially addictive, so too are many other substances and activities, like caffeine, nicotine, alcohol, prescription drugs, cannabis, gambling, pornography, sex, working, exercising, pain seeking, and shopping.[108]

And we can take relatively easy steps to reduce the apps' allure, like changing the phone's screen to grayscale,[109] turning off notifications and sounds, abandoning Snapchat streaks, deleting addictive apps, keeping our phone in our pocket or the other room instead of checking it obsessively, and turning off our phone's location tracker. Google even allows you to choose "the privacy settings that are right for you with your Privacy Checkup."[110] Facebook states, "You're In Charge" and "in control of your Facebook experience."[111]

Nor are advertisers forced to advertise with Google's and Facebook's networks. Other options remain.

And publishers can always wean themselves off the Gamemakers' advertising networks and charge for their products.

But how real are any of these options?

First, are we, the users, really in control? By one count, Mark Zuckerberg, Facebook's CEO, said, "You are in control of your data" forty-five times during the two congressional hearings, where he was called to testify after the fallout from the Cambridge Analytica/Facebook scandal.[112] The scandal, contrary to this illusion—or delusion—of control, exposed how Cambridge Analytica accessed the Facebook data of up to eighty-seven million people, entirely unbeknownst to them, in order to develop techniques designed to help Donald Trump win the 2016 presidential election.[113]

We typically view the Gamemaker as the servant that keeps providing us with services at no cost, rather than as the master that it really is. Enjoying this illusion of autonomy and control, we downplay the power and the dangers of information harvesting.

But this is intentional. Behind the scenes, the Gamemakers cultivate that illusion by making it harder for us to see the full picture. As the Australian antitrust authority noted, the Gamemakers "tend to understate to consumers the extent of their data collection practices while overstating the level of consumer control over their personal user data."[114]

Google, for example, tells us, "You can turn off Location History at any time. With Location History off, the places you go are no longer stored." But a 2018 Associated Press investigation found otherwise: "Many Google services on Android devices and iPhones store your location data even if you've used a privacy setting that says it will prevent Google from doing so."[115] Search online for something completely unrelated to your location, like "chocolate chip cookies" or "kids science kits," and Google will still "pinpoint your precise latitude and longitude—accurate to the square foot—and save it to your Google account."

Google's "do not track" feature also gives us the illusion of control. But most websites, including Google and Facebook, ignore our "do not track" request.[116] "Do not track," one report found, is "like spray-on sun-screen, a product that makes you feel safe while doing little to actually protect you."[117]

Though Zuckerberg tells us we're in control of our data, one 2018 study found that at least 61 percent of the thirty-four apps it tested, which included language-learning tool Duolingo, travel and restaurant website TripAdvisor, and flight search engine Skyscanner, automatically transferred data to Facebook the moment a user opened the app.[118] "This happens whether people have a Facebook account or not, or whether they are logged into Facebook or not," the report said. A 2019 study found many popular apps are delivering even more sensitive health and finan-cial information to Facebook, without affording users any way to stop it. So, if you are among the twenty-five million active users of the Flo Period & Ovulation Tracker, then Facebook (and its advertisers) would likely know when you are menstruating or wanting to get pregnant.[119]

In theory, we have the power to ignore the behavioral ads, and indeed, most of us think we do. Like most of the Internet users in one study, we probably believe that the targeted behavioral ads are "almost completely ineffective" or have "no effect whatsoever."[120] In reality, experiments re-veal that these ads have "substantial persuasive and subtle distracting effects."[121] Moreover, with celebrities as well as friends, coworkers, and other people who have no discernible connections to a commercial en-terprise now engaged in promoting products, sometimes we don't even recognize that an ad is an ad, or know which photos or videos the "insta celebs" are being paid or rewarded for posting.[122] Facebook, for example, is actively helping advertisers to enlist these "influencers" on Instagram and elsewhere to convince us to buy.[123]

No matter how disgusted we are with the rapacious data harvesting, opting out remains difficult. "Where am I supposed to go?" lamented one user who had quit Facebook (but migrated to Facebook-owned In-stagram). "I wish there was something else."[124] Unless we can convince our schools, clubs, friends, and family to switch en masse to another social network, we remain stuck with Instagram and Facebook. Unless we primarily post videos on other domains, we are stuck with Google. And we are stuck with covering our computer camera with masking tape (as laptop manufacturers can't even offer a lens cap as an option), never quite sure when we're being observed.

Just as it's hard for us to opt out, the same goes for the publishers and advertisers in the Gamemakers' world. With over two million independent websites and one million apps participating in Google's advertising network,[125] and with two hundred of the top five hundred apps integrated with Facebook's "Audience Network,"[126] any single publisher will find it extremely challenging to compete outside this ecosystem.[127] Publishers rely on the Gamemakers' algorithms for traffic to their websites and apps.[128] They also need the Gamemakers' data to attract the advertisers.[129]

Any show of defiance on the publishers' part is likely to be met with swift retribution. Exile is one possibility. Google, for example, can kick the defiant app developer out of its Google Play store. It can also demote a defiant website in its search results, while favoring those who play along.[130]

As the UK House of Commons found, Facebook can cut off access to its users' data, as it did to Twitter's now-defunct Vine video app (which Facebook perceived as a competitive threat).[131] Conversely it can give special access to our data to those apps that reciprocate. To access the Facebook user data, companies every year had to spend substantial sums with Facebook.[132] To "gain as much information as possible," Facebook also imposed "reciprocity" agreements with certain apps. Facebook would encourage these developers to build their apps, using Facebook data. In exchange, the apps had to allow their users to share "their data back to Facebook (with scant regard to users' privacy)."[133] By logging into an app such as Tinder, for instance, "the user would not have realised they were giving away all their information on Facebook."[134]

Nor can advertisers opt out. Without Google and Facebook and their vast networks, advertisers would find it very difficult to identify and target individuals who at that very moment are looking for products or services like theirs.[135] Yet often the advertisers are reluctant participants. Many of them complain of the Gamemakers' lack of transparency,[136] which leaves them unable to verify whether their advertisements actually reached their intended audience,[137] and which deceives them into thinking "their advertisements perform better than they actually do."[138] Arguably, that opacity has facilitated fraud and billions of dollars of losses in digital advertising.[139] Advertisers dependent on the Gamemakers' algorithms for ad placement may also find that their ads appear in juxtaposition to content utterly repugnant to their values, like YouTube channels promoting white supremacy, North Korean propaganda, and pedophilia.[140] Yet, what can they do about their complaints? As Australia's antitrust authority noted, "Google and Facebook are critical and, in many cases, unavoidable business partners."[141]

Even if advertisers and publishers were to rise up and revolt by organizing a boycott against the Gamemakers, or agreeing among themselves to hold out for better terms, the all-powerful Gamemakers can, paradoxically, use the antitrust laws against them. Like the socialists and union leaders who were the very first people to serve jail sentences resulting from violating the Sherman Antitrust Act of 1890,[142] they, too, would be subject to legal penalties. The competition ideology, as we saw in chapter 5, helps shield the Gamemakers from attack.

Because of the tremendous power Gamemakers wield over who can and can't participate in their ecosystem, millions of websites and app developers remain mired in the competition to attract and addict us, extract valuable data about us, and deliver it to the Gamemakers. And millions of advertisers will continue accessing the Gamemakers' advanced audience optimization and measurement tools in order to target us across the Gamemakers' sprawling savanna. As for us—with shopping, media, communications, and social networks all migrating online, we'll remain glued to our phones.

How Much Do We Really Pay for Free Services?

Many of us are vaguely aware of being tracked. But we don't know the extent to which we are being tracked and manipulated. Under the Gamemakers' opaque system, there's no way of knowing whether we're getting a fair deal. We have little idea how much personal data we have provided, how it is used and by whom, and what it's worth.[143] While Google's and Facebook's services are ostensibly "free," in essence we are working hard for those services by providing the Gamemakers with valuable data and content, for which we receive no compensation. As several European antitrust officials observed, if a website "would start requiring more personal data from users or supplying such data to third parties as a condition for delivering its 'free' product," then this "could be seen as either increasing its price or as degrading the quality of its product."[144] So, consider this: Over the past few years, Facebook and Google have harvested even more data from you. Their profits have swelled accordingly. Have you gotten more as a result?

But there are more hidden charges. As the ad-blocker browser Brave notes on its website, the "average mobile browser user pays as much as $23 a month in data charges to download ads and trackers—that's $276 a year."[145] Of course those costs are dwarfed by the money we spend because we have been so skillfully targeted by advertisers and by the psychological toll exacted by Facebook and Google addiction, which in turn are dwarfed by the cost to our democracy when the Gamemakers' products are weaponized against us, as happened in the 2016 US presidential election. Over time we learn more how Russia used Facebook, Google, and Twitter to "sow discord in the US political system." According to an internal Russian document, the operatives were instructed to "use any opportunity to criticize Hillary [Clinton] and the rest (except [Democratic Primary Candidate Bernie] Sanders and [Republican candidate Donald] Trump—we support them)."[146] Russia's campaign likely reached 126 million people on Facebook, 20 million more on Instagram, and countless more on YouTube.[147]

Yet, we cannot negotiate better terms, because the Gamemakers are so powerful.[148] What can we do? Tell Google and Facebook to stop tracking us across our devices and Internet? Not likely. So, we live in a world of "Orwellian doublespeak," as the former FCC chair observed, where "the 'privacy policies' that are made to sound as though they protect privacy are actually about permission to violate your privacy."[149] In any case, few among us actually read the lengthy, jargon-ridden privacy notices on the apps we use and the websites we visit—which would take on average four months according to one estimate.[150] And even if we did, how much could we rely on what they say, given what we know about the false claims made by the Gamemakers in their privacy policies?

What about the lifeguards? In Europe, some enforcers are taking action. In 2019, the French data protection watchdog found that Google had infringed upon the European privacy laws and fined it for failing to provide users with a clear and accessible account of data tracking and processing.[151] But that fine—$57 million (US)—won't stop the Gamemaker. It's peanuts to them, just the cost of doing business. Indeed, in 2018, Google paid more in fines to European enforcers than it did in taxes.[152] The German antitrust authority weighed in against Facebook in the same year, demanding changes in Facebook's data collection and sharing policies. It has ruled that "Facebook must explicitly undertake not to process data or not to process them without consent. This must be enforceable by the users. Under data protection law Facebook is obliged to make transparent which data processing activities the company is actually carrying out."[153] But in 2019, a German appellate court disagreed with the competition agency, and while the litigation drags on, Facebook has little incentive to change the rules of its game.

Meanwhile, in the United States, the FTC, despite multiple complaints and privacy scandals, for many years made no moves to stop the

Gamemakers. In 2019, the FTC imposed a $5 billion fine on Facebook, which looks significant, but represents a small percentage of Facebook's 2018 revenue ($55.8 billion) and an even smaller percentage of its expected 2019 revenue. Two FTC commissioners dissented, believing the settlement was too lax. As one observed,

> *The proposed settlement does little to change the business model or practices that led to the recidivism. The settlement imposes no meaningful changes to the company's structure or financial incentives, which led to these violations. Nor does it include any restrictions on the company's mass surveillance or advertising tactics. Instead, the order allows Facebook to decide for itself how much information it can harvest from users and what it can do with that information, as long as it creates a paper trail.[154]*

Future Control

And so the abuses continue. In a particularly egregious one, in 2014, Facebook did something it called an "emotional contagion" study in which it manipulated 689,003 users' News Feeds, to see if they could influence the users' emotions.[155] People who post on Facebook frequently express positive or negative emotions, which their friends later see via Facebook's News Feed product. By intervening in the News Feed ranking algorithm that they usually use to determine, for their users, "the content they will find most relevant and engaging,"[156] Facebook controlled the number of positive and negative posts their users received over the course of a week. Some received fewer positive posts; others received fewer negative posts. And then the study tracked them to see whether this would have any effect on the users' moods. It did. Those receiving fewer positive posts were, in turn, less positive themselves.[157] Those who received less negative content were less negative.

The conclusion: "[E]motions expressed by others on Facebook influence our own emotions, constituting experimental evidence for massive-scale contagion via social networks."

Had any of the 689,003 users been asked their permission to be included in this study? "Informed consent" would be required of participants in any respectable academic or medical study. But Facebook felt no such obligation. The potential dangers of this kind of manipulation can hardly be overstated. Even the title of the study—"Massive-Scale Emotional Contagion"—should set off the alarm.

This study offers just a glimpse into the formidable analytical power of data, how it can be used to affect our behavior, and the potential for abuse. Now consider how many of us are more and more reliant on the Gamemakers' digital personal assistants—Google's Assistant, Apple's Siri, and Amazon's Alexa—on our mobile phones, computers, and increasingly our smart appliances and cars.[158] Think how much we share with these digital assistants and how much they will learn about us and our kids. Many are confiding intimate details to these devices, asking for "information about a sensitive health condition or a controversial political figure."[159]

We might perceive these digital assistants as wonderful additions, designed to serve us. Or is it the other way around? As we enjoy these digital assistants, are we serving them, by providing the Gamemakers even more data? Allowing them to reconstruct, as Amazon told one state court judge, "[t]he sum of an individual's private life"?[160]

The Gamemaker with the dominant digital personal assistant can not only control what choices we see (or don't see); it can also affect how we feel and think. The Gamemaker can increasingly influence the news we receive, the shows we watch, and the things we buy. The more we communicate primarily with our digital assistant, the less likely we will search the web for information, read independent customer reviews, use multiple price-comparison websites, and rely on other tools for our understanding of our world. Amazon, for example, patented in 2017 technology that can help its digital assistant Alexa recognize our emotions, discerning among "joy, anger, sorrow, sadness, fear, disgust, boredom, stress, or other emotional states."[161] As *Bloomberg* reported, Amazon could use our emotional state to recommend products or advise us "how to interact more effectively with others."

The Gamemakers' plans are clear: They "envision a future where humans do less thinking when it comes to the small decisions that make up daily life."[162] Eventually, as Google's then CEO Eric Schmidt wrote shareholders in 2016, "[t]he next big step will be for the very concept of the 'device' to fade away. Over time, the computer itself—whatever its form factor—will be an intelligent assistant helping you through your day."[163] Without ever crossing the creepy line—Schmidt once famously remarked that on issues involving "invasiveness" Google's policy "is to get right up to the creepy line but not cross it"—and always preserving our sense of independence and autonomy, the Gamemakers will nonetheless be able to collect even more data from even more devices that continually watch, listen, and track us.

Of course, Google and Facebook aren't the only Gamemakers. We can expect this toxic competition whenever a powerful company is able to design an opaque environment in which it gleans most of the profits. Amazon, for example, controls multiple levers to ramp up the competition among sellers (including the book publishers who were its original base), while collecting massive amounts of data about us, the consumer-producer.

In many ways, particularly with regard to addictiveness, the Gamemakers' business models resemble those of Big Tobacco or Big Sugar: (1) consumers derive some emotional benefit from the engineered product, (2) the business is designed so that companies profit (or survive) by making their products as addictive as possible, and (3) there is the illusion of choice and control, but (4) many will have difficulties in limiting their own or their children's consumption, even as their mental and physical health deteriorate from overconsumption.[164]

To give you an idea of the magnitude of data collected, IDC (which bills itself as the "premier global market intelligence firm") estimates that by 2025, "every connected person in the world on average will have a digital data engagement over 4,900 times per day—that's about 1 digital interaction every 18 seconds."[165]

Moreover, the concept of data-driven, personally targeted advertising is spreading into what we may think of as the unlikeliest—and lowest tech—places. Soon when you reach for a drink or a carton of ice cream in the cooler at your local Walgreens, you may be greeted with a personalized ad, based on your age, gender, and the weather.[166] The drugstore is currently testing a technology that embeds cameras, sensors, and digital screens in the refrigerator and freezer doors of some of its stores.

No doubt the Gamemakers, their lobbyists, and the academics whom they bankroll will point to the benefits from their technology. Facebook's stated mission, after all, is giving "people the power to build community and bring the world closer together,"[167] while Google seeks to "organize the world's information and make it universally accessible and useful."[168] Unlike *The Hunger Games* where almost every tribute is killed, here everyone can benefit from certain aspects of the Gamemakers' ecosystem: Local businesses can affordably target interested customers (with Google offering small businesses a $150 ad credit when they spend $150). Publishers, using the ad revenue, can offer free content, which we clearly enjoy and derive benefits from, and which might be out of reach if we had to directly pay for it.

That's all to the good. But one cannot seriously argue that these benefits should depend on our accepting the inevitability of a toxic competition in which the Gamemakers are always the winners and we have to agree to be the product. Just as US President Dwight D. Eisenhower warned against the creeping powers of the military industrial complex in his farewell address to the nation in 1961, Tim Cook, Apple's CEO, in 2018, warned against the dangers of the "data industrial complex" where "[o]ur own information, from the everyday to the deeply personal, is being weaponized against us with military efficiency. . . . We shouldn't sugarcoat the consequences. This is surveillance. And these stockpiles of personal data serve only to enrich the companies that collect them."[169] Cook also firmly endorsed the creation of "a comprehensive federal privacy law in the United States" and went into some detail about what it should cover.

When Germany's antitrust authority deemed that Facebook's sucking up of our data was "exploitative" and an abuse of the company's dominance,[170] it told the company to stop. Unless a German user expressly and voluntarily consents, Facebook could not track and extract its users' personal data as they surf online, or combine the data it internally collects from multiple platforms. And consent there is not the meaningless exercise it is in the United States, where users click "I accept" because they must—in order to text their friend, or access Instagram and Facebook. The German competition authority ordered that if users do not consent to tracking, then Facebook cannot exclude them from its services. Whether or not the agency ultimately wins on appeal remains unclear. But if Facebook is ordered to offer the benefits of its services in Germany, without its creepy exploitation, then why can't it do so elsewhere?

The answer is simple: It can. However, because privacy legislation would represent a threat to their ecosystem—and their profits—we can expect the Gamemakers and their lobbyists to continue kudzu-ing the US legislators and enforcers with the competition ideology: The market is robustly competitive, with competitors only a click away. Thus, the European-type regulations will chill the innovation that has propelled the United States to the forefront of the digital economy.

And we shouldn't be surprised about this. If you were in the Gamemaker's position, you might do the very same—work hard to ensure that the legal and political environment remains supportive of your efforts, and try to quash arguments in favor of any form of restraint. What should surprise you, however, is the ease with which your elected representatives follow this narrative.

Reflections

After inquiries from the *New York Times* and New Mexico's lawsuit, Google terminated Tiny Lab's account and removed its apps from its Play store.[171] If the allegations against it are true, Tiny Lab did indeed break the law.[172] But is this small Lithuanian start-up the real villain?

Might it be the Gamemaker that pushes the toxic competition to degrade privacy so that it can profit from the personal data it harvests and hoards? Of course it is to blame.

Beyond that, however, does the Gamemaker bear the sole responsibility here? Or does it share responsibility with our legislators and enforcers? After all, the Gamemakers operate in a legal environment that our elected representatives designed. An environment that enables corporations to maximize value and profit for their shareholders, with little regard for consumers. An environment that is anti-regulation and pro-competition, even when the competition is toxic.

Ultimately, the villain is neither Tiny Lab nor the Gamemakers, but the game itself. It is our duty as a society to create an environment in which the game is played differently. In which capital works to serve our interests, rather than us serving its interests. An environment in which the motivation of businesses is aligned with our interests. Where we are not ultimately reduced to data serfs. A legal and social environment in which today's Gamemakers and future ones are limited in their ability to distort and exploit.

So what can we do? What kind of world do we want to live in? Let's consider some solutions—starting with how we define competition.

PART III

What Can We Do about It?

CHAPTER 9

How Greedy Are We?

*Redefining the Competition Ideal
to Reflect Our Values*

When returning to Harvard in 2017 to attend his fifteenth business school reunion, the Pulitzer Prize–winning journalist Charles Duhigg observed that most of his classmates, although doing very well financially, seemed miserable and unfulfilled.[1] They were weary of their work, which was insanely stressful; distrustful and wary of coworkers who were so eager for their next promotion that they were constantly undermining each other; and feeling a sense of emptiness when they questioned the meaning of what they were doing in their professional lives. And they were not alone. Though one survey found that job satisfaction levels across the United States had increased very slightly in the last ten years or so, to 51 percent in 2016, in a disturbing conclusion it also noted that they remain well below what they were in 1987, when 61.1 percent of workers reported being satisfied with their jobs—and moreover that it was unlikely that satisfaction would return to that level in the future.[2]

Duhigg's classmates are unhappy despite well-paying jobs, but many of us don't have the luxury of such well-cushioned unhappiness. We are working too hard for not enough pay, no benefits or lousy ones, and no job security. For us the promise of prosperity never arrived, even though we work in a competitive economy, which we've been told is the pathway to prosperity. That is the rationale policy makers have offered for their efforts to increase competition, fortify the laws to protect it, and eliminate many of the regulatory restraints that they deem harmful and unnecessary.

You would be right to ask: What went wrong? How have we found ourselves at this unfortunate juncture? And what path should we have followed?

Not the mostly abandoned paths of communism and totalitarianism, which are certainly no better and indeed much worse than the one we're on. Few among us would want to work or live in a centrally planned economy. Competition often does promote efficiency, economic growth, innovation, and material well-being, just as the competition ideologues insist. And regulations that restrict the freedom of companies can indeed be counterproductive. But we must acknowledge that the oversimplified version of the competition ideology that is being sold to us today, with its assumption that unfettered competition is always and in every circumstance superior to any other path, has not delivered as promised. Increasingly, we see its darker sides.

If looked at objectively, it becomes apparent how reductive the ideology really is, and how much potential there is for abuse. Rather than competition serving us by improving our material living standards (income, consumption, and wealth), this economic tool has become the master that we must serve, the magic elixir we must swallow whole. The economists' warning labels have been peeled off; the possibility of overdosing from toxic competition has been dismissed outright.

The ever-ascending arrow in the chart on the left depicts the promise of competition; the downward curve of the arrow on the right is a more realistic depiction of where it has led us.

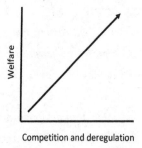

Competition and deregulation

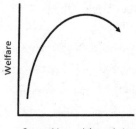

Competition and deregulation

It doesn't have to be that way, however. From the late-1940s until the mid-1970s, competition really did foster innovation, increase quality, and improve our material living standards. But it was competition that operated in an environment with regulatory protections.

Beginning in the late 1970s, such protections were gradually stripped away as the competition ideology, like kudzu, took over and smothered everything in its path—including the social, moral, and ethical values that might have mitigated its pernicious effects.

Over the past forty years lobbyists, powerful firms, and ideologues have pushed for free market solutions, unmonitored and unregulated, even for services—like prisons—that are particularly ill-suited to an ideology that puts profits and "shareholder value" ahead of all other values. Politicians and policy makers promoted competition as the panacea for nearly every societal ill, while striving both to dismantle existing regulations and to resist any new ones, all in the name of avoiding "regulatory creep"—that supposedly lethal blow to the free market. The result: The regulatory framework and safety nets that are crucial to an inclusive and stable economy are gone. With few incentives to invest in infrastructure or the more general needs of society, the competitive companies that our policy makers promised us would maximize our earning potential have delivered their benefits instead to only a tiny percentage (less than 1 percent) of our population. We, the citizens, are often left to pay the bill (recall the financial meltdown) or the side effects (from your pay slip to your social rights). With most of the benefits pocketed by these fortunate few, income inequality around the globe reached its highest level for the past half century by 2018.[3] Wealth inequality (a measure of how much we have rather than how much we earn) was even worse—twice the level of income inequality.[4] The $1.5 trillion in tax cuts by the Trump administration, as the United Nations noted, overwhelmingly benefited the wealthy and worsened inequality: "The consequences of neglecting poverty and promoting inequality are clear. The United States has one of the highest poverty and inequality levels among the OECD countries," and also ranks near the bottom among wealthy countries in terms of labor markets, safety nets, and economic mobility.[5]

The middle class, in the United States and in much of Europe, is shrinking—down to just over 50 percent in the United States and 60 percent in the European Union.[6] Once-thriving manufacturing centers where workers could earn a decent living have been reduced to a state of rusting decay brought about by declines in labor's share of profits, low-skilled workers' wages, labor force participation, and the start-up rate of new firms (due to barriers erected by powerful incumbents).[7] Yet, our elected officials continue to defend the competition ideology, to insist that it will pay off, even as our pocketbooks, health care, and social rights tell us otherwise.

What has happened is that the idealized perfect competition portrayed in the economic textbooks has been squeezed out by the bad forms of competition—monopolistic or toxic or both. Crony capitalism, in which big business and big government cozy up to each other to stifle the *good* forms of competition, is the order of the day. Economists who have studied the data reveal that under this system many markets have actually become *more* concentrated and *less* competitive. And while the profit margins of the most powerful companies increased, innovation may have actually declined.[8]

Yet the consolidation in the marketplace continues to be defended as necessary. "Unless you have scale and power in the marketplace and with the consumer, you're just out there scrambling on your own," an executive at AT&T Inc. said after the federal court allowed it to acquire media conglomerate Time Warner.[9]

The alignment between big government and big business will continue as long as money and corporate help with reelection remain top-of-mind concerns for so many government officials. This means that we can expect many governmental policies to remain skewed toward helping the wealthy and powerful under the façade of competition, and against regulation in the name of freedom. Writers and thinkers as diverse as

Martin Luther King, Jr., Senator Bernie Sanders, former Secretary of Labor Robert Reich, and Robert F. Kennedy, Jr., have inveighed against this state of affairs, which they describe as socialism for the rich (meaning government policy that sees to it that most resources go to the rich, their powerful corporations, and our financial institutions) and capitalism—or as King put it, "rugged individualism"—for the poor (meaning that they are left to struggle on their own). Nobel prize–winning economist Joseph Stiglitz describes the result this way:

> *We haven't achieved the minimalist state that libertarians advocate. What we've achieved is a state too constrained to provide the public goods—investments in infrastructure, technology, and education—that would make for a vibrant economy and too weak to engage in the redistribution that is needed to create a fair society. But we have a state that is still large enough and distorted enough that it can provide a bounty of gifts to the wealthy.*[10]

If we continue along the current path, our infrastructure will continue to crumble. Public education at the primary and secondary school level will deteriorate even further for those in poor or low-income areas. Rising college tuition will plunge even more students and their families into serious debt.[11] And in order to mount a legal defense of their merger strategies, behemoths like AT&T will continue to bleat piteously about having to scramble on their own.

For young Europeans and Americans, unlike the Gamemakers who will determine the future for so many of them, that future looks bleak. One defining feature of our recent history was that children could look forward to enjoying a better life than their parents had. This is the so-called American Dream. If you were born in 1945, you most likely did. Ninety-five percent of Americans born that year went on to earn more than their parents. For Americans born ten years later, 70 percent earned more than their parents. By the 1960s, that had dropped to about

60 percent. And the downward trend is continuing with the millennial generation (those born between 1981 and 1996). Only half of Americans born in 1985, for example, are likely to earn more than their parents.[12] They have on average more debt and less wealth than earlier generations at their age.[13]

This is true despite the fact that many are better educated than their parents and grandparents. As for Generation Z (defined as those born in the mid-1990s to the early or mid-2000s) 17 percent of young adults ages eighteen to twenty-four are out of work in mid to large cities in the United States, totaling 2.3 million young people.[14] They and future generations will likely join the swelling ranks of "precariats"—those clinging precariously to their current economic rung, while bearing ever greater risks in the digital economy.[15]

Should they try to organize to secure fairer wages, as many Uber and Lyft drivers attempted to do in Seattle in 2015, they can expect the government to intervene—and not on their behalf. Competition is inherently good, the FTC and DOJ will tell the court: Antitrust law "forbids independent contractors from collectively negotiating the terms of their engagement."[16] That's price-fixing, which "is at the very core of the harms the antitrust laws seek to address."[17] Unionizing, which may be the only remedy left to the powerless, has also come under attack, in part for being anticompetitive—the very same rationale we saw that sent union leaders (and socialists) to jail under the Sherman Antitrust Act of 1890. With so few protections in place to prevent them from ruin should they become sick or disabled, those on the lower rungs of society will bear even greater risk, operating without a safety net, while some Gamemaker profits from their efforts.

Staring at the prospects for the economy, many of us see anxiety rather than happiness and risk rather than prosperity in our future. When the Federal Reserve Board reports that 40 percent of Americans would have to borrow, sell something, or not be able to pay if confronted with a $400 emergency expense, that tells us something alarming about the extreme precariousness of the financial lives of a very large number of people.[18]

So how can we change the present course? The first thing to do is to return to first principles, and inquire . . .

What Is Competition?

Whenever policy makers peddle competition as the elixir, ask them this question. They might grimace and dismiss the question as idiotic. But there is no commonly accepted definition of competition today. As one legal treatise states, "Today it seems clear that the general goal of the antitrust laws is to promote 'competition' *as the economist understands that term* [our italics]."[19] In other words, as the treatise acknowledges, economists often have a concept of competition that differs from that of lawyers, policy makers, and laypersons. Not that the economists themselves have reached a consensus in defining competition—far from it. Economist Sir John Vickers, who was one of the principal architects of the United Kingdom's post–financial crisis regulatory framework, has said that competition "has taken on a number of interpretations and meanings, many of them vague."[20] Numerous other economists, from all across the political spectrum, agree.[21] This is surprising, considering how central the concept of competition is to our economy and to economic thinking in general.

One reason why defining competition is so difficult is that the concept of competition is like a sponge, which absorbs and reflects the moral, ethical, economic, political, and societal values of its time and place. The competition ideologues have made it seem as though we must choose between competition and communism, or, as the choice is ever more frequently being described today, between competition and socialism. But the concept of competition they've been peddling for the past forty years—one drained of any ethical or moral content—isn't the *only* or even the *best* form of competition for purposes of creating a healthy, prosperous, and just society. Indeed, as we'll see, it is often the worst.

Greed Is Good. Greed Is Right. Greed Works.

President Ronald Reagan told the nation in his first inaugural address, "government is not the solution to our problem; government is the problem." Competition and markets were his answer, and the concept of competition he was espousing was the narrow one espoused by Milton Friedman and his cohorts at the University of Chicago. In touting the power of markets to self-correct, the Chicago School theorists characterized economic competition as relentless zero-sum warfare, where some must lose in order for others to win.

The Reagan administration began appointing judges who were indoctrinated with these Chicago School beliefs for important positions on appellate courts—like the US Court of Appeals for the Seventh Circuit and DC Circuit—where they could influence government policy for life. While our focus is often on the US Supreme Court, these appellate judges can have a far greater impact on our economic and legal policies. They decide many more cases on many more topics than the Supreme Court. These appellate decisions bind not only the parties in the case, but also all the trial courts within their districts. The opinions, which set precedents, also affect the enforcement agencies and other litigants, who rely on these judicial opinions.

And so the Chicago School–ed jurists went to work. "Warfare," wrote Seventh Circuit Judge Frank H. Easterbrook (who got his law degree from the University of Chicago) in one legal opinion, "is competition."[22] Operating on this assumption, competition may involve unfair, even despicable, acts of hatred and greed among competitors. As Judge Easterbrook summarized in another opinion, "Much competition is unfair, or at least ungentlemanly; it is designed to take sales away from one's rivals."[23] Or as he opined in another decision, "a desire to extinguish one's rivals is entirely consistent with, often is the motive behind, competition."[24] And in yet another decision: "[t]he deeper the injury to rivals, the greater the potential benefit."[25]

Needless to say, even *good competition* can be fierce. And in any competition, there will be winners and losers. The latter may indeed be injured or unhappy. As antitrust professors, we do not take issue with this. But we do want to challenge the embedded assumption that greed, as the sole driver of competition, must override all other societal, moral, and ethical values. The Chicago School justification for this is that if we are motivated by greed, we'll compete hard to steal business from our rivals to make even more money, and the end result will be that society as a whole will be wealthier, healthier, and perhaps happier.

Under this concept of competition, greed and selfishness are repackaged as virtues. As Easterbrook opined in another decision, which affirmed a lower court ruling:

> *Greed is the foundation of much economic activity, and Adam Smith told us [in* The Wealth of Nations*] that each person's pursuit of his own interests drives the economic system to produce more and better goods and services for all. "It is not from the benevolence of the butcher, the brewer, or the baker, that we expect our dinner, but from their regard to their own interest. We address ourselves, not to their humanity but to their self-love, and never talk to them of our own necessities but of their advantages."*[26]

In conclusion, Easterbrook agreed that the judge in the lower court had "properly declined to allow the jury to convert moral and ethical claims into legal duties."

Pause for a moment to appreciate the implications of this concept of competition. It tells us that rather than discouraging greed, we, as a society, should encourage it, because greed-inspired competition will drive markets toward the most efficient outcome and also the one best for society. Rather than viewing ourselves as a community striving toward joint goals, we should act only in our self-interest. The government need not intervene because rational market participants primed to pursue their self-interest will prevent or quickly cure most market failures.[27] The Chicago School's economic theory assures us that the "natural laws of the market are in essence good . . . and necessarily work for the good, whatever may be true of the morality of individuals."[28]

Until recently, most economic models of competition assumed that we're purely selfish creatures—and moreover, that this is fine.[29] Companies and consumers exclusively pursue their material self-interest and do "not care about 'social' goals per se."[30] As the Chicago School economist George Stigler wrote, when "self-interest and ethical values with wide verbal allegiance are in conflict, much of the time, most of the time in fact, self-interest theory . . . will win."[31] Karl Marx and Friedrich Engels would have agreed that "naked self-interest" would indeed prevail in a capitalist society.[32] At the moment, that seems to be what's happening.

But is that good? Is selfishness the essential foundation for economic activity in a capitalistic society? Will countries with greedier citizens deliver greater prosperity? And should we, as a society, elevate greed and use it to define ourselves? In answer to all of the above: Absolutely not.

Competition, Collaboration, and Fairness Can Coexist

While many people, not just the Chicago School jurists, quote Adam Smith to justify their belief that "greed is good," far fewer consider the Scottish economist's other important book, *The Theory of Moral Sentiments*.

In this book, Smith praised the virtue of prudence—"The care of the health, the fortune, and the rank and reputation of the individual"—but *only* when it "is combined with many greater and more splendid virtues—valour, extensive and strong benevolence, a sacred regard for the rules of justice." For Smith, benevolence, which causes individuals to act, at times, out of goodness, even when they derive nothing financially from it, was not simply one of mankind's "splendid virtues," but an expression of basic "principles in his nature."[33] And fairness and altruism weren't just qualities without any practical value, but virtues that "played an essential role in market interactions, allowing trust, repeated transactions and material gains to occur."[34] Fairness he viewed as the "main pillar that upholds the whole edifice. If it is removed, the great, the immense fabric of human society . . . must in a moment crumble to atoms."[35] These sentiments are as much a part of classical economic theory as those expressed in *The Wealth of Nations*.

Thus, Smith has become the patron saint of a new wave of economists—known as the behavioral economists—like recent Nobel Prize laureates Daniel Kahneman and Richard Thaler. Looking at the empirical evidence, they conclude that most people are not as purely "self-interested" as the Chicago School's theorists suppose. On the micro level, we actually care about treating others—and being treated—fairly. And on a macro level, the empirical evidence does not support the idea that greed is a prerequisite for a successful market economy.[36] Societies with greedier citizens do not necessarily have stronger economies. Instead, greed can hinder a market economy by eroding trust. Indeed, some evidence suggests that shared values like trust and fairness actually enhance the workings of the marketplace.

Let us consider the results of one popular experiment, the Ultimatum Game, to illustrate the point. Imagine that you are paired with another player, who remains anonymous. You and the other player are both told the rules: You are given one day's wages, which you must divide, as you see fit, with the other player. The only catch is that if the other player rejects your offer, then neither of you gets to keep anything. How much would you offer the other player?

Ask a traditional Chicago School economist, and he'll advise you to offer the smallest amount—one penny—which the other player will accept, because one penny is better than nothing. A study of chimpanzees, who (along with bonobos) are our closest living relatives, shows that they behave just as Chicago School economists describe.[37] But do we?

It turns out, very few of us do. In experiments around the world, most people offer significantly more than the nominal amount (usually 40 to 50 percent of the total amount). Moreover, about half the time recipients will reject low offers (generally less than 20 percent of the total amount available), even if it means they will get nothing at all.[38] So if you offer $20 and try to keep $80 for yourself, the perception of unfairness and the desire to retaliate against that unfairness are likely to cause the other person to say no.[39]

The willingness of players to make a fair offer cannot be explained as the result of wanting to maintain their reputation or goodwill, since the Ultimatum Game and other iterations of it are often exercises in which you play anonymously (or only once so you don't have to worry about playing again with the same person).[40] Knowing this, even a savvy Chicago School economist would ditch the assumption of "cold" self-interest, and offer far more than the nominal, profit-maximizing amount of one penny.

Now, let us turn to another recent experiment, in which the researchers used the Ultimatum Game (along with two other games, Public Goods and Dictator) to study fifteen small-scale economies in twelve countries on five continents.[41] The groups studied were diverse—three foraging groups (East Africa's Hadza, Papua New Guinea's Au and Gnau, and Indonesia's Lamalera), six slash-and-burn horticulturists (the Aché, Machiguenga, Quichua, and Achuar of South America and East Africa's Tsimané and Orma), four nomadic herding groups (the Torguud, Mongols, and Kazakhs of Central Asia, and East Africa's Sangu), and two sedentary, small-scale agricultural societies (South America's Mapuche and Africa's Zimbabwe farmers). The researchers wanted to see whether the behavior observed in the earlier studies, whose subjects were mainly university students, would also be seen in these societies, which exhibit a wide variety of economic and cultural conditions.

The players who shared and cooperated the most in the experimental games were those whose societies had higher levels of market integration (that is, they were more dependent on market exchange in daily life) and offered higher payoffs for such cooperation. Among the whale-hunting Lamalera, for example, more than half (63 percent of the proposers in the Ultimatum Game) divided the pie equally or even more generously (the mean offer was 58 percent). In real life, a large catch, always the product of cooperation among many individual whalers, is meticulously divided into predesignated parts and carefully distributed among the community members. In contrast, the Hadza made low offers and had high rejection rates in the Ultimatum Game. Although these small-scale foragers do share meat, the result reflects the everyday tendency of the Hadza hunters to try to hide their catch from the group.

In general, the study reveals that, contrary to the Chicago School, most people are not inherently selfish. The Chicago concept of optimal competition does not reflect how most societies behave, nor does it consider the legal, social, ethical, and moral norms that are operative in everyday life.

In another study, which included five of the groups that were part of the study described above plus ten others, researchers used three behavioral experiments to address the long-standing puzzle of why people who are strangers to one another decide to engage in transactions that are dependent on a shared sense of trust, fairness, and cooperation.[42] The advantages of such exchanges are numerous, allowing economies to become larger, more complex, and more prosperous. But what the researchers wanted to understand was how humans evolved to share such expectations with people outside their kinship and local groups. What norms and institutions might have been responsible for facilitating trust-based exchanges between strangers, even when they were unlikely to encounter one another again? Among the factors they considered were the degree of market integration and the percentage of individuals reporting adherence to Islam or Christianity—both of which they speculated might be involved in cultivating these shared moral values. They tested 2,148 people in fifteen populations with varying degrees of market integration and adherence to these two religions (which, like all world religions, view greed not as a virtue but as a vice). To measure the individuals' propensities to fairness and their willingness to punish unfairness, they again used the Ultimatum Game (along with two other games). The stakes were again one day's local wages.

The study found a positive correlation between fairness and degree of market integration as well as a positive correlation between participation in Christianity and Islam and the amounts offered in the behavioral experiments. Taken together, the data indicate that in going from a fully subsistence-based society with a local religion to a fully market-incorporated society with many Christians or Muslims, one would see a significant jump in the amount offered in the Ultimatum Game (about 20 percentage points) and other two games. As the authors conclude, "These findings indicate that people living in small communities lacking market integration or world religions—absences that likely characterized all societies until the Holocene—display relatively little concern with fairness or punishing unfairness in transactions involving strangers or anonymous others." So the Chicago School theorists' assumption that *greed is the foundation of economic activity* may well describe transactions in foraging, primitive, subsistence-based societies with little market integration and no adherence to a world religion. But it does not provide an accurate description of the behavior of people in the integrated economies of today.

In reality, as various behavioral experiments have shown, few of us are either purely selfish or purely altruistic. We are what the behavioral scientists have termed "conditional cooperators"—we'll cooperate if we think that others are cooperating. But once we feel that others are simply free-riding off of our efforts, we'll either punish the free-riders or, if that is not possible, stop cooperating ourselves.

And yet, despite the above, the reductive competition ideal that assumes primitive selfishness is being championed and used to design much of the economy that surrounds us. Surely, this is the wrong tool for the job.

Yet to be convinced? Consider the following study.

To assess whether individuals are self-interested, conditional cooperators, or altruists, researchers often use a Public Goods game. As discussed earlier, the concept of public goods can apply to everything from fireworks shows to national defense. Public goods are often crucial for the successful working of the economy and of society, and their availability depends on the willingness of everyone to contribute to them. But if too many people selfishly decide to free-ride on others by contributing nothing while enjoying the benefit, the public goods may deteriorate or disappear. Public Goods games are a way of assessing people's propensity for conditional cooperation, and what factors might either encourage or discourage it.

In one version of a Public Goods game, you and another player are both given the equivalent of one day's wages, say $200 each. According to the rules, you can each put a portion of your $200—anywhere from all of it to none of it—into a pot, without knowing what the other person puts in. Whatever the two of you put into the pot will be multiplied by 1.5, and then divided equally between you. How much would you contribute?

Well, if you and the other player each put in the full amount, then the $400 would increase to $600, and you and the other player will each end up with $300—a lucrative 50 percent return on your original $200 investment. But what if you put in $200, and the other player contributes only $100? The $300 multiplied by 1.5 will become $450, with the result that you'll end up with $225 but the other player will get $225 plus the $100 he held back from the pot—$325. Even worse, what if you put in

$200 and the other player puts in nothing? You'll end up losing money (getting back only $150), while the other player gets $350.

One likely factor in your decision about how much to contribute is your perception of the other person as sharing or selfish. Can you trust the other person? Another factor is the social and ethical norms under which you operate. Cooperation can also vary depending on your perception of the game—for instance, as one study revealed, when the game was called "Community Game," cooperation was much higher than when the same game was called "Wall Street Game."[43] Also important are the rules of the game—do we want to encourage zero-sum competition and greed in which each player is encouraged to get as much of the pie as they can at the expense of the other, or do we want to encourage a positive-sum competition (cooperation), in which the pie will be expanded for both? If we want to deter greed, we might allow one player to be able to punish the other player if that person contributes nothing and yet profits.[44]

In a real-life study, several researchers went to Ethiopia to examine the conditions that encourage cooperation in the management of public goods—in this case, forests that were under a program designed both to save the forests and to preserve the livelihoods of those who depend on them.[45] When forests are owned as common property, each group member faces a dilemma about cooperation: Everyone is better off when all the group members cooperate rather than look out only for themselves; but individual members are even better off if others adhere to the rules while they themselves violate the rules—by, for instance, cutting down more trees than their allotted share and selling the lumber as firewood. But if everyone thinks that, no one will cooperate. Instead, the cooperation will quickly devolve into a zero-sum race to see who can chop down the most trees the fastest. The result: The forest will soon be depleted, and they will all be collectively worse off. Sound familiar? It's our First Overdose, where individual and collective interests diverge. This "tragedy of the commons" applies to overharvesting of fish, cattle overgrazing on public lands, etc.[46] It's why many companies, absent environmental safeguards, will pollute, or why our public roads are congested. But the First Overdose can be averted if communities effectively govern themselves and their shared resources.

In studying forty-nine different forest user groups in Ethiopia, the researchers found that if there are enough conditional cooperators in the group, the First Overdose can be averted. Here, the collective agreement to look beyond self-interest, combined with willingness to trust and norms of cooperation, plus the ability to enforce these norms by punishing free-riders, led to better economic outcomes for everyone involved. Contrary to the belief that our economy prospers only when we are focused on our narrow self-interest, forest user groups with larger shares of conditional cooperators did far better, on average, than the groups dominated by greedy members.[47]

Why was this?

First, the conditional cooperators not only cooperated, but they enacted (and complied with) rules to prevent cheating by harvesting and selling extra firewood.

Second, these rules were enforced by monitoring of the forests, both to deter cheaters and to punish them if discovered. Conditional cooperators each spent an average of thirty-two hours a month monitoring their forest, which was 1.5 times as much as the free-riders spent. This was unpaid labor and personally costly, but each member's voluntary cooperation had a positive effect on the other members, making them more likely to abide by the rules and to enforce them.

We see the same principles in action in neighborhood community organizations, when neighbors agree to abide by local norms (maintaining their lawns, picking up litter, cleaning up after their dogs, etc.) and to monitor infractions among those who do not—admonishing them, fining them if there is a mechanism in place to do so as there is in certain communities, perhaps even trying to shame them. But this cooperation can be fragile. If the group members feel that others are shirking (or even worse, breaking the rules), then it can become an everyone-for-themselves mentality that leaves them collectively worse off.

Most of us are not greedy. We treat others fairly and expect to be treated fairly in turn. Most of us are trusting, too, though our willingness to trust and to cooperate is conditional, depending on the actual or expected cooperation of others. Trust and fairness are the foundation of our market economy, not greed and zero-sum warfare. And this is as it should be, though developments in the last forty years are eroding our sense of the basic fairness of the society we live in, which is an ominous development. Who, after all, would want to live in a society that promotes greed above all other values? A society consumed by suspicion, envy, and distrust, in which we will always be wondering how our fellow citizens—and beyond that, the institutions and laws underpinning our society—are trying to screw us.

But competition doesn't have to be zero-sum. Harvard Business School professor Michael Porter and others have studied how competition can result not in a winner-take-all outcome but in mutual gains for all the competitors. One example is the German printing industry, with its heavy concentration of competitors within a 150-mile radius.[48] Concentration of resources allows the manufacturers to improve the quality of their labor pool and strengthen their network of suppliers. And the localized competition spurs competitors to try to differentiate their products from those of their rivals, resulting in innovation in the products themselves and also in the techniques and strategies used to produce them. Such competition may also have informational benefits as firms learn from their rivals' mistakes and mimic and improve upon their rivals' successes.[49]

So competition need not be simply about stealing business from one's rivals. Rather it can often be positive-sum—expanding the pie by developing new products, designs, and technologies that will satisfy needs currently unmet by those rivals. When firms move beyond "competition as warfare" to "competition in creating value," they benefit, and so does society.

The Costs of Zero-Sum Competition

There is no denying that zero-sum competition may sometimes be the only way to efficiently allocate scarce resources in particular markets. After all, if you and someone else both covet the same house, then competition—how much you offer, on what terms—will probably determine who ultimately gets to live there. But we, as a society, need to be mindful that zero-sum competition has significant risks and costs, in addition to those we already discussed. We'll conclude this chapter with a discussion of four significant costs that policy makers should consider when they draft laws and regulations protecting competition.

Cost of zero-sum competition in crowding out other ethical, moral, and social norms

If competition increases overall welfare, as the competition ideologues insist, should anything be off-limits to competition? Under the logic of competition ideology, the answer is no. But what about such offerings as death bonds—what *Newsweek* called "Wall Street's most macabre investment scheme yet"? Death bonds, as described by Rachel Heng in an essay about the commoditization of life and death, are "financial products that allow investors to bet on people's life spans through speculating when their life insurance policies will pay out."[50] The faster people die, the more money the investors make. Is this the kind of profiteering we want to encourage in our society? Or what about things that have thus far been considered taboo—and illegal—to sell, such as organs?

Although there is a general consensus that there should be some line drawn, some limits set on market competition and market valuations for certain "products," the line is uncertain, the consensus wavering. In 2015, for example, an opinion piece ran in *Forbes* magazine advocating the sale of organs.[51] What about infants? Shall we allow them to be put up for sale? Should we offer drug-addicted women financial incentives to be sterilized?

Philosopher Michael Sandel, whose Justice class at Harvard University is a huge hit on campus and, thanks to being broadcast on PBS, an online hit as well, tackles these issues in his book *What Money Can't Buy: The Moral Limits of Markets*.[52] Positing a world where everything and everyone is potentially for sale—a world, he argues, that we are dangerously close to becoming—he shows how market values can erode or corrode nonmarket ethical, social, and moral values. Ultimately, as Sandel notes, there is an important distinction between a society that *has* a market economy and a society that is *defined* by its market economy.

Cost of zero-sum competition in increasing unethical behavior

Companies may think they benefit when they encourage their employees to compete against each other. One company that famously set up a free-market competition among its employees evaluated its workers every six months, retaining the high-performing ones with higher bonuses, while weeding out the bottom 15 percent.[53] According to standard economic theory, the internal competition should result in a highly efficient organization, with little deadweight. Although this would not seem to result in a company whose employees liked working there, in 2000, the company was #22 on *Fortune* magazine's chart of the "100 Best Companies to Work for in America."[54] Its chairman and CEO said, "We are proud to receive recognition as a top workplace; it's a reflection of our commitment to our employees and to their key role in our company's success."[55]

Six years later that same CEO died of a heart attack, shortly before he was to be sentenced to prison on ten counts of securities fraud. His company, Enron, went bankrupt—the then largest bankruptcy filing in history (in terms of assets). The ferocity of the internal competition, several business professors noted, had created a toxic work environment that promoted and rewarded unethical behavior. Employees had no respect for peers who had received a poor evaluation.[56] To avoid being fired, the "losers" began adopting the unethical behavior of the winners. While Enron emblazoned its corporate slogan—RICE (Respect,

Integrity, Communication, Excellence)—on its letterhead, in its corporate elevators, and elsewhere, its smart, talented employees, under such cutthroat competitive pressure, were racing away from those qualities in a desperate attempt to survive. And what about *Fortune* magazine's best-place-to-work designation, which is supposed to be based mainly on feedback from employees randomly selected to fill out a fifty-seven-question survey? Enron's human resources executives allegedly filled out the surveys—rather than the employees.

Several experiments confirm that encouraging fierce internal zero-sum competition among employees, like Enron's stacking system and other rank-and-yank systems, can promote fear, distrust, anxiety, and unethical behavior.[57] In one study, some participants were evaluated on their relative performance (e.g., how much profit did they generate as compared to their coworkers?), while others were evaluated on absolute terms (how much profit did they generate?).[58] Those evaluated on their performance relative to others were more likely to engage in unethical behavior and to expect their coworkers to use unethical means.

In another similar study, what type of goals employees were expected to meet—interpersonal performance goals (i.e., pitting oneself against others) versus intrapersonal mastery goals (i.e., striving to do better, and avoid doing worse, than one has done before)—affected the participants' intentions to cheat. When the employees were pitted against each other, they cheated significantly more than those employees with self-mastery goals.[59] In short, if a company pits its employees against one another, it increases their temptation to cheat, and a race to the bottom will likely ensue.[60]

Cost of zero-sum competition in our general satisfaction with life

How do we determine the winner in a zero-sum competition that rewards greed? One way would be our wealth per se. But if that were the case, personal savings, investments, and frugality would be a lot higher and consumption much lower than they currently are around the world.

Instead, what counts is *evidence* of our wealth *relative* to our peers. To win this game, we must not only outearn our peers, but outspend them as well through conspicuous leisure and consumption. As the economist Thorstein Veblen observed in his classic book *The Theory of the Leisure Class*, "wealth or power must be put in evidence, for esteem is awarded only on evidence."[61]

In recent years, social networks have upped the stakes in our status competition. We no longer try to keep up with the Joneses next door. Thanks to Facebook, Instagram, and other ubiquitous forms of social media, we're now engaged in a competition with smiling acquaintances around the globe who seem to make more money, work at dream jobs, own fancier cars, go on better vacations, live in nicer homes, and have kids who seem to attend more prestigious schools than our own.

This competition keeps the hedonic treadmill humming, and the consumerist economy, too; but like the desire for power or fame, it results in a hunger that can never be satiated. Under this zero-sum competition, every time others acquire more, we seem to have less, so we feel the need to catch up. Even if we manage to ascend to ever higher rungs, there will always be someone better off and we'll always be striving for the next rung. The dynamic is comparable to the habituation that occurs in drug and alcohol abuse, where once we adapt to a certain level of consumption, our satisfaction diminishes and we want more. Such a competition ultimately has no finish line or satisfactory resting place.[62] To paraphrase T. S. Eliot, the "End of the endless / Journey to no end" competition can be found only in death.[63]

Rather than liberate us, this zero-sum competition commoditizes us.[64] The more we are primed to believe in its importance, the less we understand about what will really bring us greater well-being. Numerous studies of life satisfaction tell us that beyond a certain minimum required to provide for the basics of food, shelter, and health, there is not much correlation between income and happiness. Research on China's rising per capita income, which increased by a factor of 2.5 between 1994 and

2005, showed no increase in reported life satisfaction—and in fact an increase in the percentage of those who were dissatisfied. And while Japan's per capita income increased sixfold between 1958 and 1991, average life satisfaction remained unchanged.[65] Studies of well-being in the United States reveal similar findings.

In promoting selfishness and materialism, the competition ideology ultimately marginalizes those quality-of-life factors that actually *are* correlated with greater well-being, like work-life balance; relationships with family, friends, and members of their community; health; a sense of autonomy; and the quality of the environment.[66]

What can happen when competition causes people to lose sight of the qualities that make for a meaningful life is what we see in a California community synonymous with overachievement, where an epidemic of suicides among its teenagers prompted some heartbroken soul searching. As one high school student put it, talking about the stress that has made her and so many of her peers so miserable: "We are the product of a generation of Palo Altans that so desperately wants us to succeed but does not understand our needs. We are not teenagers," she added. "We are lifeless bodies in a system that breeds competition, hatred, and discourages teamwork and genuine learning. We lack sincere passion. We are sick."[67]

Cost of zero-sum competition in our society

The competition ideology runs the risk not just of promoting personally destructive behavior and increasing misery, but eroding the social capital necessary for a market economy.[68] If we are encouraged to believe that self-interest should trump all other values, if we are consumed with envy of those on the economic rungs above us and with fear of falling to the rungs of those below us, we should not be surprised when more people actually start behaving selfishly.[69] A consumerism utopia does not concern itself with caring for others, wrote sociologist Zygmunt Bauman; the "privatized utopias of the cowboys and cowgirls of the consumerist era show instead vastly expanded 'free space' (free for *my* self, of course)—a kind of empty space of which the . . . consumer, bent on solo performances and solo performances only, never has enough." The space that we the consumers "are advised from all sides to fight for can be conquered only by evicting other humans—and particularly the kind of humans who care for others or may need care themselves."[70]

Among the risks of an ideology that idealizes materialism and competition are less concern for the environment, lower levels of political engagement, and less involvement in family, community, and social issues.[71] Interestingly enough, the competition ideology may even result in less frequent churchgoing and a decrease in the social goods that accrue to churchgoing. Once upon a time, many states in the United States had blue laws, which put restrictions on certain secular activities, including work and many commercial transactions, on Sundays. But in the interest of allowing competition to occur 24/7, these blue laws have fallen to the wayside in most states. Now Sundays (and nearly all major religious holidays) have become ordinary days to work and consume.

The result: States where these blue laws were repealed, according to one study, experienced a 15 percent decline in attendance among weekly churchgoers and a nearly 25 percent drop in donations.[72] "I'm surprised [religious conservatives] haven't picked up on this," said one of the study's authors.[73] "Just like people switch cars when gas goes up, this is a change in the price of going to church; you've got an opportunity cost, you can do something else instead, and that has changed behavior."[74]

Reducing participation in religious and spiritual activities marginalizes our investment in what political scientist Robert Putnam sees as "arguably the single most important repository of social capital in America."[75] As he notes, weekly churchgoers are two to three times more likely to volunteer to help the poor and young people than non-churchgoers, and are much more likely to contribute to those causes.[76] Compared to their non-churchgoing peers, "youth who are involved in a religious organization take tougher courses, get higher grades and test scores, and are less likely to drop out of high school."[77] They're also significantly more likely to go to college.[78] Church attendance is also correlated with (i) lower levels of criminal activity, (ii) lower rates of substance abuse, (iii) better health status and outcomes, (iv) improved self-reported measures of well-being, and (v) greater marital stability.[79]

Non-churchgoing individuals are also affected. Having to spend what was formerly a day of rest in the never-ending rat race of competition gets in the way of their ability to participate in the kinds of social and community interactions that strengthen social bonds. This results in the individual feeling detached from the social group, which has implications for a "wide variety of pro-social behaviors." In a 2016 paper, several economists found a 1 percent drop in overall voter turnout after the state repealed its Sunday blue law, which is significant when you consider that in three of the last five presidential elections the candidates were separated by about 2.5 percentage points or less.[80]

Reflections

While competition is necessary for a market economy, it does not come prepackaged in the form of zero-sum warfare and need not position selfishness as a supreme virtue. The zero-sum competition that has been peddled as part of the value-free competition ideology is not the only kind of competition. Different types of competition exist, which reflect different social, moral, and ethical values. So, one key takeaway is that if we want to navigate toward an inclusive economy that serves us, the citizens, we must distinguish between the zero-sum and positive-sum forms of competition.

A second key takeaway is that if policy makers promote greed and zero-sum competition, then that is exactly what we'll get. Not because this type of competition is the natural and inevitable outcome of our humanity, but rather because we designed the competitive process this way. Yet, we have seen, and we know in our hearts, that the notion of competition as zero-sum warfare conflicts with our natural instincts as humans. Few of us want to compete this way. Rather we long to belong—to feel connected to other people, to something larger than the self. Our well-being, as the economic literature reveals, is not derived from experiencing stuff, but experiencing life in all its richness and fullness.

A third takeaway is that if we elevate zero-sum competition as the only (or ideal) form of competition, then that choice has significant costs and risks. Promoting a distorted and reductive view of competition can marginalize important ethical and moral norms.

A fourth takeaway is that ethics and morals can complement, and inform, the competitive process. There simply is no empirical support that competition requires its participants to disregard important ethical and moral norms. It makes no sense that we are socialized from an early age to treat others fairly and are then expected to throw out those lessons when entering the marketplace. The state can play an important role in reconciling these values to ensure the well-being of all citizens. In Europe, for example, the value of fairness—fair competition—is often championed alongside the values of efficiency and consumer welfare. Referred to as the social side of competition,[81] fairness is viewed as essential to cultivating trust in markets and crystallizing legitimate expectations of market participants.[82] Fairness does not undermine the goals of competition. Rather it advances them.

As a society, we can do better. We can envisage a form of competition that serves as a tool, rather than the ultimate goal. As the economic historian R. H. Tawney wrote, economic activity's proper place should always remain "the servant, not the master, of society."[83] Our concept of competition can promote, not hinder, important ethical and moral values, which actually foster an inclusive market economy and economic prosperity. As Tawney added, while "no change of system or machinery can avert those causes of social *malaise* which consist in the egotism, greed, or quarrelsomeness of human nature, [w]hat it can do is to create an environment in which those are not the qualities which are encouraged."[84]

Or, in the words of His Holiness the Dalai Lama, we need to become aware "of what type of competition we need, which is a sort of friendly competition that would not seek the destruction or the downfall of rivals or other people, but rather would act as a stimulating factor for growth and progress."[85]

Ultimately it is up to us, as a society, to shape the concept of competition and to enact laws to promote that vision. So, how do we do that?

CHAPTER 10

Competition: From Toxic to Noble

As the examples included in the four overdoses have made clear, competition can often be toxic—to consumers, to workers, ultimately to society at large, and sometimes even to the competitors themselves. But if conceived of as a mutual striving for excellence, it can also be beneficial, to some or, at its best, all of the above.

That competition has the potential to bring us together in this common endeavor rather than driving us apart can be seen in the very derivation of the word *compete*—

> *late Latin* competere, *"strive in common, strive after something in company with or together"; classical Latin "to meet or come together, agree or coincide . . ."; from com "with, together" + petere "to strive, seek, fall upon, rush at, attack . . ."*

And one of the oldest and most sanctified forms of competition—the ancient Greek Olympic Games—reminds us of that sense of the word, because the games were not conceived of as a form of warfare; rather they were about peacemaking. Participants came from throughout the city-states and colonies of Greece, and during the games themselves, there was a universal truce, which all observed, regardless of any hostilities that may have existed in the world beyond the games.

Today, there are many different kinds of competition, some clearly healthier than others. Even a fiercely waged competition can yield results somewhere between what is minimally acceptable and—hard as it may be to believe—downright ennobling of those who are participating in it. To assess where a given form of competition falls on this continuum, we suggest asking two basic questions.

First, to what extent does the competition actually serve us collectively, rather than force us to serve it? If we believe that the primary end of government is to enhance the well-being of its citizens, then we should also expect competition to promote—or at least not hinder—our collective well-being.

Second, to what extent can we compete without sacrificing our values and our integrity? The race to the top may be fierce, but should not override our humanity. Ideally, it should bring out the best in us, not the worst. This means that any form of competition should be informed by our moral, ethical, and societal values.

In applying these criteria, we can rank four kinds of competition on a continuum:

Toxic Competition   *Zero-Sum Competition*   *Positive-Sum,*   *Noble Competition*
                            Motivated by Self-Interest   *Ethical Competition*

At one end is the toxic competition described in our four overdoses. This clearly violates the criteria that require competition to both promote overall well-being and abide by ethical standards of behavior.

Along the lower to mid-range of the continuum is zero-sum competition—in which one group's gains must mean another's loss. Zero-sum competition may not always serve us or society (especially when it's a Gamemaker who is profiting), and it often requires us to disregard or outright violate our standards of fairness and morality. Sometimes, however, there is no other choice, and this is the only feasible competition to allocate limited resources.

At other times, however, when we have a choice, we should opt for positive-sum, ethical competition, which we have described earlier as a way of expanding the pie, so that most, if not everyone, benefit.

And finally, at the opposite end of the continuum is the ideal form of competition, *noble competition*, which while not completely attainable, points the way to what we, as a society, should aspire.

Noble Competition

So, what is it? *Noble competition is helping your rivals reach their full potential.* Players compete fiercely, but do so with deep societal and moral awareness. Each player, while seeking to prevail, is aware of her wider community and recognizes how her competitiveness can help her rivals be their best selves.

Sounds counterintuitive? Absolutely—we want rivals to beat each other, not sing "Kum ba yah, my Lord, Kum ba yah" around the campfire. Competition, after all, is about slashing prices, improving service and quality, and innovating in order to gain market share.

As we noted in the preface, both of us have devoted our professional lives to teaching and preaching the virtues of competition. You won't see any reference to noble competition in our books, articles, speeches, and work for antitrust agencies over the past twenty-five years. Thus, however anomalous the concept of noble competition might seem to you, it was far odder to us when we first began thinking about it.

So how did we come to position it as the lodestar toward which competition should be oriented?

The inspiration came from the 2017 Tanner Lecture at Oxford University. The title of the talk was "On the Origin and Nature of Values."[2] Not a surprising topic coming from a philosopher or theologian. But from an applied mathematics professor of complex systems? To be specific: from George Ellis, coauthor with Stephen Hawking of one of the seminal works on general relativity theory, "The Large Scale Structure of Space-Time." How could Professor Ellis enlighten us on morality? A professor at the University of Cape Town, South Africa, Ellis was an outspoken opponent of apartheid in the 1970s and '80s, and has perhaps had more occasion to think about questions of morality than people who grew up in less troubled times and places.

We had no expectations about the lecture, other than intellectual curiosity. In any case, his speech was an eloquent but quiet, unassuming inquiry into the nature of morality. Ellis first explained why moral relativism was wrong. Next, he addressed why science cannot provide moral answers, and why we must go to the source—to the Platonic ideal of morality, which exists just as surely as basic mathematical concepts do. Pythagoras did not invent his theorem, Ellis explained. Instead, he discovered something that preexisted. The theorem would exist, even if Pythagoras hadn't. It would simply have awaited being discovered by someone else. There is an abstract ideal of perfect morality that also awaits discovery—by each of us.

Just as we envisage a continuum of different kinds of competition, Ellis envisions something similar in the realm of morality. First there is morality that operates through force—as when the Church strove to drive people into doing what was right by burning witches. Then there's morality through self-interest—I'll do what is good for me, and you do what is good for you—which seems similar to the point of view of the competition ideologues, who hold that that this will ultimately work out to everyone's benefit. Further along is cooperation (something like positive-sum competition) followed by the Golden Rule and forgiveness. At the far end of the continuum is *kenosis*—the willingness to suffer on behalf of another even if that person is my enemy. This, according to Ellis, is the Platonic ideal of morality.

For Christians, this ideal of morality manifested itself in Jesus's willingness to sacrifice Himself in order to save us. But kenosis underlies every well-established religion, not just Christianity. It is, Ellis argued, the theme of life: the foundation of humanity, learning, and true artistic endeavor. We flourish and attain true happiness through using our gifts and talents for the betterment of others, not through a headlong pursuit of hedonistic pleasures.

For the weeks after Ellis's talk, we struggled with this kenotic view of existence. It was paradoxical to standard economic theory, and seemingly led us to the wrong conclusion about competition. After all, collaboration among competitors often undermines healthy competition, which is why it is often illegal. We kept turning over in our minds a grainy, black-and-white videotape, taken from a hidden FBI camera. Captured on film was Archer Daniels Midland's president telling a senior executive from his largest competitor of ADM's corporate slogan that "penetrated the whole company": "Our competitors are our friends. Our customers are the enemy."[3] If you've seen the biographical movie *The Informant!* by Steven Soderbergh, with Matt Damon playing the role of the real-life informant, Mark Whitacre, you know the ending. These executives were prosecuted for illegally fixing the prices of lysine, an additive used to spur the growth of pigs and chickens. Their cartel ultimately caused purchasers and us to overpay tens of millions of dollars. So won't a kenotic view of competition simply justify price-fixing cartels? Our discussions returned to the same conclusion: *Competition is about beating your opponents, not helping them.*

There seemingly was no way around this conclusion. But the Gamemakers chapter provided a way out of this paradox—a way to look at competition from a different perspective: Imagine a benevolent Gamemaker that seeks to incorporate kenosis into competition. How would it design the game?

Probably along the lines of the way we teach our children. We encourage them to work hard and compete—whether it's on the playing field, in the classroom, or in any other area of endeavor, from spelling bee to theater audition. But if we're thoughtful, we emphasize that values such as friendship, honesty, fairness, and responsibility should shape the way they compete. Ultimately, we try to communicate that any kind of rivalry should serve some greater end and that whatever the outcome, the rivalry should build character and dignify and ennoble the participants.

To illustrate, suppose you have twins who compete in the same sport—let's say tennis. You would not wish one child to thrash or humiliate the other. Nor would you encourage a "win-at-all-costs" attitude. Instead, the athletic competition, if properly designed and overseen, would help build both children's character and make both of them feel good about themselves—and each other. As described by Craig Clifford and Randolph Feezell, two philosophy professors who also played and coached on the college level, competition can be understood as a "mutual striving for excellence," where each competitor helps the others elevate their performance.[4] So, no matter which child prevails in the tennis match, the rivalry will have catalyzed levels of effort and execution that neither child would have been capable of without that spur. The reward, then, isn't just in being acclaimed the winner; the reward also comes from the self-improvement and the camaraderie that result from the rivalry. Seen in this light, noble competition, in encompassing both self-mastery and cooperation, reduces the incentive to behave unethically.

Of course, even in the most public-spirited, ethically informed competition, the goal is to win. Our children will still be intent on beating their opponents. We'll still cheer for our team. And wherever we work, we'll still be competing with other companies, and perhaps with our own colleagues. As individuals, we're in it to win it. But as a societal ideal, noble competition provides us with a valuable compass. That compass should inform policy makers and guide them as they design laws that govern the competitive process.

While unachievable in its purest form on a day-to-day basis, noble competition can point us in the right direction and help us provide safeguards against the dangers of unfettered competition. When we reorient competition toward this ideal, then many of the dark sides of competition disappear.

Let us conclude with a discussion of a path forward: how our policy makers, our companies, and we ourselves—as voters, workers, and consumers—can redesign the competition game to bring out our best, rather than our worst, traits.

The State's Role in Promoting Healthy Competition

As we've seen, many policy makers and government officials operate under the delusion of self-correcting markets, in which the collective self-interest of all the competitors is supposed to eliminate the need for regulation.

However, few markets, if any, match this simplistic vision of perfect competition, where fully informed, self-interested buyers and sellers interact, with few, if any, transaction costs. As a result, nearly every market is regulated—either by the market participants themselves, a few powerful firms, or the government. For example, the closest thing we have to perfect competition—the stock market—is also one of the most heavily regulated, precisely because regulations are needed to provide guardrails to prevent competition from turning toxic. Without the safeguards imposed by the US Securities and Exchange Commission, Commodity Futures Trading Commission (CFTC), and self-regulatory organizations like the New York Stock Exchange, investors would be exploited by all kinds of unethical strategies, like insider trading, Ponzi schemes, and accounting fraud.

The state should play at least two key roles in protecting its citizens from the damage done by toxic competition—first, by using a variety of legal strategies to promote healthy competition; and second, by stepping in to provide what competition itself cannot deliver.

Using our legislative process to protect and promote a competition ideal embedded within a vision of a just society

In the 1990s, well before the financial crisis, the CFTC became alarmed by the lack of oversight of the secretive, multitrillion-dollar, over-the-counter derivatives market, which included the credit derivatives that spawned the mortgage and housing boom (and later bust). The chair of the independent federal agency Brooksley Born attempted to regulate these derivatives, only to be rebuffed by the then Fed Chairman Alan Greenspan, then–Treasury Secretary Robert Rubin, and then–Deputy Treasury Secretary Lawrence Summers.[5] Born left in 1999, after her agency was marginalized, while Greenspan and the other policy makers pushed to deregulate further. Greenspan, as we saw in chapter 5, believed that competition minimized the need for regulatory oversight: "Those of us who support market capitalism in its more competitive forms might argue that unfettered markets create a degree of wealth that fosters a more civilized existence. I have always found that insight compelling."[6]

On April 7, 2010, Born and Greenspan sparred again. Only this time, Born was a commissioner of the Financial Crisis Inquiry Commission, while Greenspan, the once-heralded "maestro" and symbol of American economic preeminence, was called to explain the Fed's failures under his nineteen-year watch. Commissioner Born recounted,

> *You appropriately argue that the role of regulation is preventative but the Fed utterly failed to prevent the financial crisis.*
>
> *The Fed and the banking regulators failed to prevent the housing bubble; they failed to prevent the predatory lending scandal; they failed to prevent our biggest banks and bank holding companies from engaging in activities that would bring them to the verge of collapse without massive taxpayer bailouts; they failed to recognize the systemic risk posed by an unregulated over-the-counter derivatives market; and they permitted the financial system and the economy to reach the brink of disaster.*

You also failed to prevent many of our banks from consolidating and growing into gigantic institutions that are now too big and/or too inter-connected to fail.

Didn't the Federal Reserve system fail to meet its responsibilities, fail to carry its mandates?[7]

Rather than accept responsibility, Greenspan retorted, "I really funda-mentally disagree with your point of view." The chairman of the Federal Reserve was simply following the rules: "I ran my office as required by law. And there's an awful lot of laws that I would not have constructed in the way that they were constructed. But I enforced them, nevertheless, because that was my job."

The Financial Crisis Inquiry Commission ultimately rebuffed Green-span's disavowal of responsibility. He and the other regulators had the power to protect the financial system, as the Commission's final report noted, but they chose not to use it:

The sentries were not at their posts, in no small part due to the widely accepted faith in the self-correcting nature of the markets and the ability of financial institutions to effectively police themselves. More than 30 years of deregulation and reliance on self-regulation by financial institutions, championed by former Federal Reserve chairman Alan Greenspan and others, supported by successive ad-ministrations and Congresses, and actively pushed by the powerful financial industry at every turn, had stripped away key safeguards, which could have helped avoid catastrophe.

This approach had opened up gaps in oversight of critical areas with trillions of dollars at risk, such as the shadow banking system and over-the-counter derivatives markets. In addition, the government permitted financial firms to pick their preferred regulators in what became a race to the weakest supervisor. . . .

Too often, they lacked the political will—in a political and ideo-

logical environment that constrained it—as well as the fortitude to
critically challenge the institutions and the entire system they were
entrusted to oversee.[8]

Although the Commission's report is less than nine years old, its warnings have been already discounted by the Trump administration. Thus, our primary proposal is that policy makers remove their ideological blinders and recognize that competition is not some magical elixir, a sure, simple, and complete remedy to whatever ailment we face. They must guard against toxic competition, while safeguarding healthy competition. That requires regulatory oversight.

It is important to stress that while some marketplaces require oversight and regulation, regulation itself can sometimes result in outcomes that are not in the interest of either the competitors themselves, consumers, or society at large. Government failure may, at times, make regulation costly and ineffective. Such instances require that we not blindly regulate areas where it will be counterproductive, but rather make exceptions when necessary. Thus, a balanced approach is necessary.

So, for example, in our First Overdose, where the competitors' collective and individual interests diverge, policy makers could draft antitrust exemptions that would allow competitors to agree to certain restrictions on their competition, without risking millions of dollars in antitrust fines or even prison sentences, in order to prevent the race to the bottom. Under such exemptions, the government could (and did) allow hockey players to agree among themselves to wear helmets. It could allow colleges to agree to eliminate Restrictive Early Action policies and design a more humane college admissions process. It could, and most emphatically did not, permit college football and basketball programs to agree to cap expenses. Instead, it slapped huge fines on them and made such collaborative agreements completely impossible. None of these collective decisions are the kinds of abuses that antitrust legislation was designed to curb, and an intelligent interpretation of such legislation would allow for such exceptions.

It's true, of course, that competitors might abuse these exemptions and use them to try to eliminate healthy competition (or their rivals). Long before ADM, rivals sought to justify their price-fixing schemes as a way to escape "ruinous" competition. Rather than giving competitors a blanket exemption from competition, policy makers need to be able to define those select areas where an agreement to avoid competition would be warranted, and other areas where it wouldn't and where the rivals should be free to compete.

The exemptions we've been discussing are relevant to instances in which the competition harms the competitors, workers, and customers. But then there are other forms of competition in which the competitors benefit but workers and the consumers are hurt. What's to be done about those? Other than in a boxing match, no parent, seeing their child intentionally hit in the face, would accept the excuse, *Well, that's competition*. No, that's a foul and should not be tolerated. Then why should we accept fouls in the marketplace, especially when they are not inevitable or necessary for economic prosperity? Referees—and regulations—have an important role to play in many markets where competition is far from perfect.

For our Second Overdose, in order to prevent another horsemeat scandal, food poisoning and safety fiascos, or mistreatment of workers, the government must provide regulatory guardrails. While regulation comes at a cost and must not be excessive, the lack of regulatory oversight, when it is desperately needed, can impose an even greater toll.

This goes beyond food safety. Take the case of Boeing, where a design failure and lax regulatory and Congressional oversight caused the company's best-selling airplane to suddenly become a safety and reputational hazard. A fatal flaw in Boeing's anti-stall system caused two of its 737 MAX fleet to crash within five months of each other, killing 346 people on board. In the months following the crashes, "Boeing has admitted that it knew about a problem with its 737 MAX jets a year before the aircraft was involved in two fatal accidents, but took no action."[9] Why no action?

"It was all triggered by this intense competition,"[10] observed Dominic Gates, who covers Boeing for the *Seattle Times*. As Gates explains, "In July of 2011, Boeing executives learned that American Airlines was about to order 200 [Airbus] A320neos . . . and there was total panic here in Seattle." Boeing was in a competitive dogfight with its archrival Airbus in this key airline segment, the single-aisle aircrafts flown on shorter routes. So, Boeing on the spot told American Airlines, "O.K., we will reengine the 737 if you'll give us half that order." American Airlines replied, "Yes."[11] As part of its sales pitch when upgrading its 737, Boeing assured the airlines that its new airplane should be seen as a continuation of the original version of its popular jet and thus would not require expensive retraining of pilots in flight simulators (which would eat into the airlines' bottom line, and thus Boeing's bottom line). And so, Boeing engineers set to work on the new design, limited by the company's mandate of "no extra training." But the new engines and their new positioning increased the risk of stalling. To fix this problem, Boeing introduced new computer software called MCAS (Maneuvering Characteristics Augmentation System). But it never disclosed the existence of the MCAS program to the pilots and airlines. Why? A Boeing insider who was involved in the design of the new airplane and became an FBI informant in the criminal investigation against the company noted:

We were under pressure to minimize any changes, to cut costs and get it done quickly. In my view, Boeing was making decisions on the basis of share price . . . The main requirement driving the design of the Max was that there could be no changes that would require flight simulator training by pilots. We could have really upgraded that aircraft but the company's mandate about no extra training stopped us.[12]

At the time of sending this book to print, Boeing's website proclaimed how the "737 MAX is the fastest-selling airplane in Boeing history with about 5,000 orders from more than 100 customers worldwide" and touted its reliability advantages over Airbus's A320neo.[13] At its annual share-holder meeting in 2019, Chairman and CEO Dennis Muilenburg rejected the argument that there was anything wrong with the design of the 737 MAX.[14]

In years to come, the ongoing investigations will likely expose the origins of these failures. But this was not only a failure of Boeing management or engineers, but also the regulator and elected officials. For years, the US regulator that oversees the development and certification of all US airplanes, the Federal Aviation Administration (FAA), had been accused of being "too cozy" with America's premier exporter, Boeing.[15] After the two 737 MAX crashes, Senator Ted Cruz, who chairs the subcommittee that oversees the FAA, told the media, "We want to know how Boeing, how private companies, are involved in the FAA certification process."[16] But he and his Senate subcommittee already knew that answer. Congress's watchdog, the US Government Accountability Office, flagged this issue in its 2013 report for the Senate.[17] The watchdog warned Congress about the challenges that the FAA was experiencing in approving the design and airworthiness of new aircrafts and equipment before they were introduced into service. Strapped for resources, it was harder for the agency to keep abreast of industry practices, and harder to understand the aircraft or equipment they were tasked with certificating. Given the prevailing deregulatory climate, and to "better leverage its resources," the FAA increasingly allowed Boeing to handle much of the safety certification process.[18] So, if Senator Cruz read the 2013 report prepared for his committee, he would have known that the FAA delegated many certification activities to Boeing and other FAA designees, who by that time already "perform[ed] more than 90 percent of FAA's certification activities."[19]

Congress not only knew about this outsourcing, but actively promoted it. In its 2018 legislation, Congress sought to "reform" the FAA's safety certification of aircrafts.[20] Congress required the FAA to be evaluated on eleven performance objectives, including speeding up the approval process (by "eliminating certification delays and improving cycle times"), relying more on Boeing to certify its own airplanes ("achieving full utilization of FAA delegation and designation authorities"), while "maintaining and improving safety," and perhaps most important, "maintaining the leadership of the United States in international aviation and aerospace"—basically, reduce the regulatory burden so that Boeing can outcompete Airbus.[21]

"The regulator went to sleep," concluded James Hall, a safety consultant and former chairman of the National Transportation Safety Board. "What we have now is a system that essentially provides Boeing with a system of self-certification."[22]

Rather than placing their faith in the beneficent power of competition or outsourcing their oversight to market participants, the government agencies must regularly inspect the boiler to ensure that the competitive pressure does not weaken the bolts. And in areas where the competitive pressure is intense, the government must actually enforce regulations to protect the quality and safety of the products, the conditions under which laborers perform their work, and the health of consumers, passengers, and users of the product or service. Only the vigilant enforcement of these regulations will reduce the competitors' incentive and ability to skimp on safety, and ensure that we are safely getting what is promised.

Let us move on from the Second Overdose and reflect on our Third and Fourth Overdoses. There as well the state has a responsibility, through legislation and enforcement, to prevent abusive practices. In addition to guardrails, like restrictions or bans on drip pricing, the government can increase the cost of engaging in exploitive behavior by defining more areas where consumers are in need of protection—such as personal privacy, which the Gamemakers have so radically invaded—and guaranteeing those protections with the full force of the law.

To illustrate, we discussed in chapter 3 how credit card companies prey on their users' weaknesses, such as their lack of willpower, their overconfidence in repaying the debt, and other mental mistakes, to get them to borrow more. In response, Congress passed several laws, including the Dodd-Frank Wall Street Reform and Consumer Protection Act, which gave the newly formed Consumer Financial Protection Bureau (CFPB) the power to crack down on unfair, deceptive, and *abusive* acts or practices. We emphasize abusive, because it enables the CFPB to stop financial institutions from preying on our weaknesses when offering financial products or services.[23]

The CFPB used this authority to crack down on payday debt traps that have plagued communities around the country. Unscrupulous lenders compete in offering short-term payday loans to consumers who cannot reasonably repay them. The CFPB spent over five years researching this toxic competition, including reviewing over one million comments on its proposed rule from payday borrowers, consumer advocates, faith leaders and tribal leaders, payday and auto title lenders, state regulators, and attorneys general. What it found was that, faced with unaffordable payments, "cash-strapped consumers must choose between defaulting, re-borrowing, or skipping other financial obligations like rent or basic living expenses such as buying food or obtaining medical care."[24] The result was companies' profiting as the cash-strapped borrowers paid far more in fees than what they received in credit. Often the borrowers lost whatever valuable possessions they still possessed (like their cars or trucks).

The CFPB, during the Obama administration, drafted regulations that required the lender to first reasonably determine that the consumer actually had the ability to repay the loan according to its terms without having to go deeper into debt.[25] Basically the lender would undertake the due diligence that any prudent lender would undertake, like verifying the borrower's monthly income, debt obligations, and housing costs. (The regulations provided exceptions for small personal loans that posed less risk to consumers, like loans made by community banks or credit unions to existing customers.)

Before the Obama-era regulation went into effect in August 2019, however, the Trump administration kudzu-ed in a "classic" fashion. The incoming administration, without any significant due diligence, claimed that the regulation would "reduc[e] competition for these products."[26] So, it is proposing a new set of rules to abandon these safeguards. Consumer advocates saw it for what it was, namely a "direct gift to the industry" that contributed tens of thousands of dollars to the acting head of CFPB, Mick Mulvaney, while he was a congressman.[27]

If the Trump administration succeeds in rolling back these regulations, then the CFPB, under the next administration, should restore them to stop the payday debt traps, and go after other abusive practices and products.

Moreover, Congress should broaden the FTC's power to target abusive acts and practices. Currently, the FTC, which polices many more industries than the CFPB, can only prevent deceptive and unfair acts and practices. While that power would appear broad enough to prevent the toxic competition in our Third and Fourth Overdoses, Congress limited the FTC's power to regulate when competition itself is the problem, rather than the cure.[28]

Thus, to empower the regulatory agencies to deter behavioral exploitation, we must first ensure that the people who head these agencies are not blinded by the competition ideology (or beholden to lobbyists). So, when candidates are seeking our votes, we should ask them about abusive and exploitative practices, like payday debt traps. If they tell us to trust the market, we can tell them to stop kudzu-ing and answer the question. If they can't, we should elect politicians who can.

Expanding the safety net to protect and promote the well-being of those left behind by competition

In chapter 5, we heard the chief economist from one antitrust authority describe the limits of competition. Competition may often lead to the most economically efficient outcome, he noted. But there can be a significant gap between an economically efficient outcome and an outcome that is good, fair, or just for society. And when that is the case, he said, "It is for the state to balance between efficiency, competition, and other social values." In other words, the government must provide some kind of safety net.

But for most of us, the safety net is fraying. Nearly 97 percent of bankruptcy filings in the United States were made by individuals, not by businesses.[29] The most commonly reported causes of bankruptcy are unexpected income or expense shocks, such as job loss (which accounted for over two thirds of bankruptcies), divorce, and medical expenses.[30] Rising health care costs, even for the insured, can be catastrophic, wiping out personal savings, retirement accounts, and home equity.[31]

When watching sporting events, we expect an injured player to receive medical attention immediately. It would be quite odd if the game continued while the injured player was left writhing on the field. But walking the streets in any major city, or checking out the people in line at the local soup kitchen, one will encounter the homeless, sick, and impoverished who are the casualties of a government that has abandoned them. Many competed their hardest, but then, through no fault of their own, came up short. Think of the countless numbers of workers at retail outlets like Toys "R" Us, which shuttered because of poor managerial decisions. Over twenty other retail chains were projected to be on the brink of bankruptcy in 2018–19.[32] Imagine what will happen to their employees, many of whom are already living on the margins thanks to low salaries and minimal (if any) benefits. Think of the hardworking UPS and FedEx drivers who are likely to be displaced by automation. Don't they warrant any kind of protection from our government?

The government's role can't be restricted to simply championing competition or prosecuting illegal antitrust violations. If we encourage people to compete, we can't let them descend into bankruptcy—and worse—if they fail. It is the responsibility of every society and its government to provide for and protect those who have become collateral damage in the competitive rat race. Until recently, this was a foundational view of government, shared by many countries around the world and reflected in their policies.

In his 1941 State of the Union address, President Franklin D. Roosevelt announced his vision for the world, "a world attainable in our own time and generation," founded upon four essential human freedoms: freedom of speech and expression, freedom of worship, freedom from want, and freedom from fear. As to the third freedom—the "freedom from want"—Roosevelt was very clear that it was up to the governments of the world to arrive at "economic understandings which will secure to every nation a healthy peacetime life for its inhabitants—everywhere in the world."[33]

The United Nations Human Rights Commission, under the leadership of Eleanor Roosevelt, proposed something similar. After the Second World War, UN representatives "with different legal and cultural backgrounds from all regions of the world" drafted the Universal Declaration of Human Rights, which was to serve as a "common standard . . . for all peoples and all nations."[34] Among the fundamental human rights to be universally protected is "the right [of everyone] to a standard of living adequate for the health and well-being of himself and his family, including food, clothing, housing and medical care and necessary social services, and the right to security in the event of unemployment, sickness, disability, widowhood, old age or other lack of livelihood in circumstances beyond his control."[35]

These are the principles that are protected in some countries, yet abandoned in others. One thing should be clear: The competition ideology cannot serve as an excuse for the lack of humanity and social values. The two, as we saw in chapter 9, can be mutually supportive. So, if any policy maker tells us that competition displaces, or overrides, the freedom of want, then we know that he is probably using the competition ideology to mask an exploitative vision of society.

If we want to encourage entrepreneurship, which requires people to undertake risks to provide us with the goods and services that we actually need, then we cannot allow failure to send them spiraling to their doom, dragging their companies, and indeed their families, along with them. According to the Kauffman Foundation, which was created by a businessman who believed strongly in both entrepreneurialism and the need to provide opportunity to all, a society that values innovation and risk-taking can fully unlock the energies of the risk-takers only if it offers them some protection.[36] Such protections should include:

- strengthening social insurance programs;
- offering family-friendly policies such as subsidized childcare or preschool to boost the number of women entrepreneurs; and
- reforming unemployment insurance to help nascent entrepreneurs mitigate the downside risks of entrepreneurship.[37]

Ultimately, it must be the government's responsibility to ensure that those who help protect our country, improve our welfare, service our needs, and build our infrastructure are not condemned to years of penury. Our policy makers must ensure that basic economic human rights are provided and protected.

Industry's Role in Promoting Healthy Competition

While we place special responsibility on the public leaders charged with protecting our markets and economy, corporate executives also have a key role to play. The role of the state in sustaining and promoting healthy competition can be supplemented by industry-wide efforts to keep it fair and honest—through self-regulation, and through lobbying for rules that will bring everyone into compliance with those efforts.

The UK food industry provides a good illustration of self-regulation.

After the horsemeat scandal, leading supermarkets established the Food Industry Intelligence Network. The network, which now boasts over 2,400 member companies in 75 different countries, shares data, research, and innovation with all its members, and provides microbiological, chemical, physical, and sensory testing of products. Through these and other means, it aims to ensure the integrity of food supply chains in the face of increased competitive pressure, to prevent fraud, and to protect the interests of the consumer.

We can see how the industry identified, in this case, the risk of quality degradation, and brought companies together to create effective safeguards. By mobilizing the resources of its large network of companies, it created a marketplace environment where quality is rewarded, dishonesty and free-riding are limited, and consumers get what they paid for. That's the form of healthy competition we should all aspire to.

Individual companies that are part of the network may reinforce such efforts with programs that uphold their own high standards. To understand how this works in practice, we spoke to Paul Willgoss, one of the founders of the Food Industry Intelligence Network and also the technical director at the upscale UK retailer Marks & Spencer Group. Here is what he had to say about his company's Integrity Program:

> *Our aim is, and has always been, to deliver on our quality promise. When we say a pack includes 100 percent beef, we make sure that it does. To achieve this, we operate a close control over raw materials. In recent years we have also introduced an audit system by which auditors arrive unannounced to suppliers, inspect the premises and take samples to be analyzed in our laboratories. These controls ensure the integrity of our supply chain and create a more resilient structure that eliminates any benefit from fraud or deception. These quality controls enable us to demand competitive prices from our suppliers, with the knowledge that compliance keeps everyone honest.[38]*

In addition to taking these kinds of practical steps, companies can change the way they do business by changing the corporate culture in which their employees operate. As the Financial Crisis Inquiry Commission observed of the chief executives of companies whose failures drove us to the economic crisis: "These individuals sought and accepted positions of significant responsibility and obligation. Tone at the top does matter and, in this instance, we were let down. No one said 'no.'"[39] If the goal is to encourage competition that is ethical, fair, and ultimately designed for the benefit of not just shareholders, but of workers, customers, and society at large, that has to be made explicit, and the message has to go deeper than a company logo.

This process begins by asking: What is your company's *why*? What is its social purpose? What values does your company promote? What values and traits of your company's corporate culture will help it in achieving its social purpose? What values and traits will get in the way of its social purpose?

One common complaint is that companies have lost any sense of purpose beyond maximizing profits and, where applicable, shareholder value. Neither their executives nor their employees can identify any other kind of purpose—and many are not interested in doing so.

One extreme example is an investment bank that once took pride in its ethical organizational culture. Servicing its clients' interests was paramount. But in one of the more famous resignation letters, Greg Smith, a Goldman Sachs executive director, described how toxic competition had eroded the financial institution's once-prized culture:

> *How did we get here? The firm changed the way it thought about leadership. Leadership used to be about ideas, setting an example and doing the right thing. Today, if you make enough money for the firm (and are not currently an ax murderer) you will be promoted into a position of influence.*

What are three quick ways to become a leader? a) Execute on the firm's "axes," which is Goldman-speak for persuading your clients to invest in the stocks or other products that we are trying to get rid of because they are not seen as having a lot of potential profit. b) "Hunt Elephants." In English: get your clients—some of whom are sophisticated, and some of whom aren't—to trade whatever will bring the biggest profit to Goldman. Call me old-fashioned, but I don't like selling my clients a product that is wrong for them. c) Find yourself sitting in a seat where your job is to trade any illiquid, opaque product with a three-letter acronym.

Today, many of these leaders display a Goldman Sachs culture quotient of exactly zero percent. I attend derivatives sales meetings where not one single minute is spent asking questions about how we can help clients. It's purely about how we can make the most possible money off of them. If you were an alien from Mars and sat in on one of these meetings, you would believe that a client's success or progress was not part of the thought process at all.

It makes me ill how callously people talk about ripping their clients off. Over the last 12 months I have seen five different managing directors refer to their own clients as "muppets," sometimes over internal e-mail. Even after the S.E.C., Fabulous Fab, Abacus, God's work, Carl Levin, Vampire Squids? No humility? I mean, come on. Integrity? It is eroding. I don't know of any illegal behavior, but will people push the envelope and pitch lucrative and complicated products to clients even if they are not the simplest investments or the ones most directly aligned with the client's goals? Absolutely. Every day, in fact.[40]

Of course, we see how unrestrained competition does not protect investors—whether the sophisticated client of Goldman Sachs or workers buying mutual funds, whose brokers recommended "high commission, low-yielding investments that resulted in Americans achieving returns that were about 1% lower than they should have been, costing investors about $17 billion annually."[41]

Regulation alone will not change corporate culture. We also need internal corporate guardrails, like management requiring brokers and other financial advisers to act as fiduciaries for their clients, acting in their clients' best interests. Otherwise, as Smith noted, "You don't have to be a rocket scientist to figure out that the junior analyst sitting quietly in the corner of the room hearing about 'muppets,' 'ripping eyeballs out' and 'getting paid' doesn't exactly turn into a model citizen." Ethical concerns have continued to overshadow Goldman Sachs and other financial institutions.[42]

Such a corporate culture is toxic not only to the "muppets," but ultimately to the company itself. Compare, for example, Goldman Sachs and Vanguard Group Inc., whose business culture the business professor Thomas Davenport found from his research represents the "anti-Goldman Sachs." Whereas Goldman's managing directors refer to their clients as "muppets," Vanguard does the opposite: "People there are constantly reminding themselves that the idea is to help clients make better investment decisions at the lowest possible cost."[43] Whereas Goldman people "care only about making money," Vanguard people "don't seem hung up on the fact that people in other firms are more highly compensated on average; they seem to find it rewarding to know they've done the right thing for their customers. [P]eople there are constantly reminding themselves that the idea is to help clients make better investment decisions at the lowest possible cost." Not surprisingly, in the decade after the financial crisis, a lot of the profits, assets, and influence have moved from Goldman Sachs and the other scandal-ridden investment banks to Vanguard and other money-management giants.[44]

Let us move now beyond anecdotal examples and consider the numbers. Empirical observations suggest that having an ethical, social purpose that informs strategic decision-making helps companies unlock opportunities and increase profits.[45] A win-win situation.

In 2015, the *Harvard Business Review* surveyed 474 executives around the globe who were nearly unanimous in their assessment of the importance of a company's having a purpose beyond profit—purpose being defined as "an aspirational reason for being which inspires and provides a call to action for an organization and its partners and stakeholders and provides benefit to local and global society."[46]

- 90 percent of the executives said their company understood the importance of a social purpose;
- 89 percent said a strong sense of collective purpose drives employee satisfaction;
- 84 percent said their business transformation efforts will have greater success if integrated with a purpose;
- 81 percent agreed that purpose-driven firms deliver higher-quality products/services; and
- 80 percent agreed that an organization with shared purpose will have greater customer loyalty.

Similarly, a 2014 Deloitte survey of 300 executives and 753 employees found that those who worked for an organization with a strong sense of purpose were more engaged and upbeat about the company's future prospects.[47] The top two reasons for their confidence were closely aligned with the ideals of noble competition: delivering top quality products/services and focusing on long-term sustainable growth.

Many employees care deeply about their firm's moral, ethical, and social purpose. It can increase internal engagement and well-being, as well as external engagement. Having a strong purpose thus can benefit the firm. A 2019 study by Bates College and Gallup found that 80 percent of college graduates affirm the importance of finding purpose in their work, but less than half report having it.[48] Consequently, Bates College, through its Center for Purposeful Work, is preparing its students "for lives of meaningful work [which] lies at the heart of the liberal arts mission."[49]

But don't we want companies to maximize shareholder value, as opposed to prioritizing these other social purposes? It wasn't on the top of either the Deloitte or Harvard surveys. Instead the top social purposes were having a meaningful impact on clients/customers, and providing business services and/or products that benefit society.

The fact that generating financial returns is relatively low on the priority list doesn't mean that purpose-driven companies aren't successful. Quite the opposite. The *Harvard Business Review* survey showed that 58 percent of the companies with a clearly articulated purpose had experienced 10 percent or more growth in revenues over the past three years, with only 15 percent of them experiencing flat or declining revenues. By comparison, only 42 percent of the companies without a clear sense of purpose could claim 10 percent or more growth in revenues, and another 42 percent had flat or declining revenues.

As we saw with the behavioral experiments, greedy self-interested citizens do not make stronger economies. Likewise, companies bent solely on maximizing profits will not necessarily achieve their goal. But having a sense of purpose seems to unlock the kinds of energies that help them do so.

The Chicago School economist Milton Friedman famously argued that a company's only social responsibility is to maximize profits "within the rules of the game."[50] However, the empirical evidence suggests that just as most of us hold ourselves to standards higher than "the rules of the game"—and we become collectively better off for behaving this way—the companies we work for should do likewise.

Of course, every company has a choice to make about its internal culture. But we see that employees want more from their employer than a paycheck; they want a social purpose. Noble competition unlocks that social purpose, directly benefiting society, while indirectly improving the company's bottom line. Not a bad deal for the corporations, individuals, and society.

Consumers' Role in Promoting
Healthy Competition

And finally, there's us—the workers, consumers, and citizens. We also have a role to play in this story. To illustrate our role, consider the following experiment—something you have probably read about in other contexts, which we find surprisingly relevant to the question of the personal choices we make about our economic lives.

Imagine you are asked to participate in a scientific experiment at Yale University. Upon entering Linsly-Chittenden Hall, you pass Chittenden's main reading room, which features *Education*, a stained glass window by Louis Comfort Tiffany, with angelic figures representing Art, Science, Religion, and Music. A scientist in a white lab coat greets you and another participant. The experiment, you are told, will test the effects of punishment on memory. To determine your assigned roles—teacher and learner—you and the other person draw lots. You receive the teacher role, which requires you to administer a test to the participant who has drawn the learner role, in which he has to memorize word pairs. You're in one room in control of an electric shock generator, and the learner is in another room, strapped into a chair that delivers the electric shocks. Each time the learner answers incorrectly, you must administer an electric shock as punishment. The shock generator has thirty clearly marked voltage levels ranging from 15 to 450 volts, with designations from Slight Shock to Danger: Severe Shock. Two switches after the last designation are simply marked XXX.

Would you administer any electrical shock? If so, when would you stop?

Would you stop when the learner gives a slight grunt from the 75-, 90-, and 105-volt shocks? At 120 volts, when the learner shouts that the shocks are becoming painful? After 150 volts, when the learner cries out that he wants to be released from the experiment, complaining of a heart disturbance? After 180 volts, when the learner cries out, "I can't stand the pain"? After 285 volts, when you hear the learner's agonized scream? At 300 volts, when the victim shouts in desperation that he will no longer provide answers to the memory test? Would you continue administering the shocks after the 300-volt level, when the learner no longer responds to the word tests and there is only silence coming from the other room? Would you defy the scientist in the white lab coat who instructs you to treat the absence of a response as a wrong answer and to keep delivering shocks as punishment? Would you administer increasingly more intense shocks to the nonresponsive learner, even up to 450 volts?

Before conducting his famous set of experiments, Stanley Milgram asked college students, psychiatrists, and middle-class adults for their predictions about the outcome. They predicted that nearly all the subjects would disobey the experimenter, with only 4 percent of the subjects being willing to administer shocks as high as 300 volts, almost no one going over 300 volts, and only a pathological fringe (about one in one thousand) administering the highest shock of 450 volts.

They were all wrong.

In his primary experiment, all forty subjects administered shocks up to 300 volts (when the learner-confederate pounded on the wall), and twenty-six subjects complied until the end and administered 450 volts. In subsequent versions of the experiment (there were nineteen in all) Milgram varied the external situational factors to determine the extent to which they altered the degree of obedience.[51]

Milgram wasn't really using these experiments to test learners' memory, but subjects' compliance. Unbeknownst to the teachers, the learner was actually working with Milgram and was not in fact receiving any shocks. Like the social psychologist Philip Zimbardo, the pioneer of the famous Stanford prison experiment, Milgram was trying to identify the situational factors that enable ordinary people to commit evil acts.

Why do we mention Milgram's and Zimbardo's experiments? Because six of the ten situational factors they identified that led their subjects to commit such horrendous acts could have led us down the path to the dark side of competition (and did).[52]

One situational factor is to present basic rules that seem to make sense before they are actually put into practice, and then to use them "arbitrarily and impersonally to justify mindless compliance."[53] The way Milgram's experiment was explained to participants made sense initially (using the effect of a slight penalty—a mild shock—as an incentive to remember). The danger arose when compliance continued past the point when it could possibly be considered reasonable or helpful.

Likewise, unfettered competition as a market force can appear to be a rational way of achieving the greatest good for the greatest number of people. But the ideology can be used to justify leaving competition unregulated even when it clearly isn't working out that way, as was evident with our financial regulators ignoring multiple red flags and permitting the financial system and economy to reach the brink of disaster.

A second situational factor is when the issue is reframed by "replacing unpleasant reality with desirable rhetoric, gilding the frame so that the real picture is disguised."[54] In a nutshell, to kudzu. In Milgram's experiment, the participants delivering the electric shock were "teachers," who thought they were "helping" the "learners." Likewise, we saw how lobbyists and policy makers use the competition ideology to reframe the toxic effects of competition, in the name of freedom from government restraints, kudzu-ing any efforts to regulate or monitor industry. We saw how self-interest, greed, and zero-sum warfare were re-characterized as virtues when in reality they erode empathy.[55]

A third situational factor is to create a situation that diffuses or abdicates responsibility for negative outcomes. In Milgram's initial study, the authority figure (who was actually a thirty-one-year-old high school biology teacher), speaking in a firm but polite voice, used a series of prods to instruct the teacher-participant to continue. And when questioned by any of the teacher-participants, he said he would take responsibility for anything that happened to the learner. Indeed, the further removed we are from immediate responsibility, the fewer qualms we might have about zapping someone. In one variation of Milgram's experiment, for example, the teacher-participant only administered the test, while one of the lab technicians delivered the shock for every wrong answer. In this situation, the degree of compliance was even higher: thirty-seven of the forty participants proceeded to the highest voltage level of XXX.

Likewise, the competition ideology can be used to diffuse responsibility. Since there will always be winners and losers, the government and industry monoliths are not to blame, even when the primary beneficiary is the Gamemaker and everyone else is victimized. Or, at a more personal level, we justify using every material advantage to get our child into a highly selective university, because if we don't, there will be thousands of other parents who are sending their kids to "educational" internships, SAT prep camps, and elite private and public schools who would exploit that advantage.

A fourth situational factor on the path to the dark side is to keep moving there in steps that are so small and incremental that one barely registers the difference between one step and the next.[56] In Milgram's experiment, the intensity of the electric shocks increased in 15-volt increments. Each increase seemed small, because the increases were relative and on a continuum rather than in isolation, so if the teacher-participant could administer 300 volts, then 15 additional volts would seem relatively minor, and so on.

Likewise, we are easily blinded to the incremental steps on the way to toxic competition. The Gamemakers Google and Facebook probably did not start their game of addiction, surveillance, data extraction, and behavioral advertising with a master plan guiding them each step of the way. Instead the design likely developed incrementally. Indeed, Google's founders, while PhD candidates at Stanford, warned in an academic paper about the risks that we saw in the Gamemakers chapter.[57] Unlike their prototype search engine Google, which in 1998 was not dependent on advertising revenues, Sergey Brin and Lawrence Page predicted that "advertising funded search engines will be inherently biased towards the advertisers and away from the needs of the consumers." They laid out how advertising can distort a search engine's incentives and warned of the "insidiousness" of the resulting search bias. Given these risks, the young entrepreneurs believed "that it is crucial to have a competitive search engine that is transparent and in the academic realm." A series of incremental steps led Google to become the dominant opaque search engine, whose growth was fueled primarily in the commercial realm on advertising revenues. As for the search bias that its founders warned about, the European Commission slapped the monopoly with a €2.42 billion fine for biasing its search results, which it did to squelch competitors and expand its dominance into other markets.

Moving from corporate executives to a more personal level: For years wealthy parents trying to gain admission to US colleges for their children enticed universities indirectly, with large donations. Bribing entrance exam administrators and soccer, rowing, and tennis coaches directly must have seemed like a natural, incremental next step.

A fifth situational factor is to make exit costs high. This would not seem the case in Milgram's experiments, where the actual exit costs for the teacher-participants were nominal. They had no social bonds with the lab workers, had committed themselves to only an hour for the study, and were paid at the beginning of the survey $4.50 (including 50 cents for carfare). This payment, they were told, "was simply for coming to the laboratory, and that the money was theirs no matter what happened after they arrived." To extricate themselves from this experiment, they need only walk out of Linsly-Chittenden Hall. Yet, few did. Why is that? The experimenters made the "process of exiting difficult by allowing verbal dissent (which makes people feel better about themselves) while insisting on behavioral compliance."[58]

For us, however, the exit costs usually are higher. If you feel that toxic competition is rampant in your company or your industry, it can be very hard to find a new job or move into an entirely different industry. If you

are an athletics director at a university in one of the big athletic conferences like the SEC or ACC, you can't avoid the arms race—you can't
just drop out of the competition to pay more money to attract the best
athletes and coaches and build the most state-of-the-art stadiums. And
if you're an admissions officer at a prestigious college, it can be very hard
to de-escalate the toxic competition to attract (and reject) candidates,
even if you work for a university as powerful and desirable as Harvard
or Princeton. So it's easy to see how we can become resigned to toxic
competition as inevitable and inescapable. Sure we can complain about
the rat race, but we are expected to continue competing.

A sixth situational factor is offering "an ideology, or a big lie, to justify
the use of any means to achieve the seemingly desirable, essential goal."[59]
In Milgram's experiment, the "cover story" was assuring the participants
"that science wants to help people improve their memory by judicious
use of reward and punishment."[60]

As Zimbardo notes, the real-world equivalent is ideology. We have
been sold the myth that competition is always good, a miracle elixir. So,
while we may not be administering electrical shocks to the people we
perceive as our rivals in day-to-day life—whether they are competing
with us in business or simply angling to merge into our toll booth lane
ahead of us—if we think that life is always supposed to be about disad-
vantaging our rivals in order to stay on top, we may be delivering other
kinds of punishments that fuel the toxicity of competition.

While multiple situational factors can desensitize us to the toll taken
by this toxic competition, if we remain alert to it, there is one particularly powerful factor within our control that can put a stop to the shocks:
dissent. Our own.

For those of us with managerial or leadership positions, dissent can
be very powerful, even if other leaders disagree. In one variation of Milgram's experiment, for example, two lab scientists of equal status, both
seated at the command desk, gave incompatible demands. The result:
None of the teacher-participants continued to administer any more shocks

past the point of disagreement. The message is clear: Ethical and moral leadership can be profound in shaping the behavior of citizens and employees. And it's not just ethical and moral tone from the top.

Even in situations where we don't have a leadership position, each of us has the potential to stop the experiment or, in our daily lives, to protest the inequities of the system we live in. The teacher-participants in Milgram's experiments, for example, could dissent, and many did. Despite their protestations, however, most of them continued with the study after voicing their reservations. Dissent is only effective if it translates into noncompliance. That's what became clear in one variation of Milgram's experiment when three teachers (two of whom were actors, working with Milgram) were administering the shocks.[61] What was the effect when the two actors playing the role of teacher disobeyed and refused to go beyond a shock level? Thirty-six of the forty of the third teacher-participants likewise refused to continue—a very different outcome from what Milgram found in most of the other versions he did of the experiment, where there were no refusers.

So, while we think we are powerless to stop the toxic competition, that's not true. We can take a stand. Granted, it may be hard at times, and, as happened in the case of Harvard and Princeton, dissent can sometimes fail. But if we don't risk dissent, how can we expect change? If we don't tell our elected officials that we are sick of the crony capitalism and toxic competition and vote for those who want to enact change, we cannot expect policy makers to reorient the path toward noble competition. Speaking up as individuals to call out the injustice and unfairness can be a lot more powerful than we think. It took only one or two people in Milgram's experiment to dissent in order to stop the harmful experiment. Your voice, too, can embolden others to call for change.

Take, for example, the 2016 and 2018 US elections, where we saw progressive ballot initiatives being overwhelmingly approved in both conservative and liberal states. Even if we can't do much under the Trump administration to demand that the CFPB crack down on exploitative abuses by payday lenders, we can act on a local level, like the voters in South Dakota who, in the same election cycle that brought us Trump, overwhelmingly approved a ballot measure that effectively banned payday loans (by capping the permissible interest rate to 36 percent).[62]

We can follow the voters in nineteen states, who through ballot initiatives or political pressure, in 2019 increased their state's minimum wage. This includes Arkansas, whose voters overwhelmingly rebuffed the efforts of the elected Republican officials and chamber of commerce, and raised the minimum wage to $11 per hour, which is significant in a state where one of every 5.5 residents lives in poverty.[63]

We can follow the voters in Idaho, Nebraska, and Utah, who strengthened their safety net by expanding the Medicaid health care programs to adults with incomes of up to 138 percent of the federal poverty line.[64]

Or we can consider a simple conversation Alastair Mactaggart had among friends at a social outing. The San Francisco real estate developer asked an engineer working for Google whether we should be worried about privacy. "Wasn't 'privacy' just a bunch of hype?" Mactaggart asked.[65] The Google engineer's reply was chilling: "If people just understood how much we knew about them, they'd be really worried."

Just as one dissenting voice in the Milgram experiment could stop the downward trajectory, so Mactaggart decided to act. Getting Congress to enact privacy protections seemed hopeless. So, too, did legislation in his state, California, home to Google and Facebook. While Mactaggart made millions in real estate, he was nowhere near as wealthy as the Silicon Valley firms who made trillions of dollars off our personal data. Nonetheless, Mactaggart and his friend Rick Arney drafted a ballot initiative for the 2018 California elections based on three privacy principles: first, greater transparency over what data are collected about us and how the companies use the data; second, greater control in telling companies not to sell our personal information, without fear of retaliation; and third, greater accountability when the company fails to take reasonable precautions in safeguarding our personal data.

In December 2017, they began collecting signatures for their petition. Six months later, their petition had attracted 629,000 signatures, almost double the number needed to qualify for the statewide ballot. In mid-May 2018, two California legislators contacted them to see if they would withdraw the initiative from the November ballot, if the California legislature passed a law addressing their proposed ballot's privacy concerns. Yes, they said. But the privacy statute must replicate all of their ballot's critical components and be enacted before 5 p.m. on Thursday, June 28, 2018, the last day they could withdraw their ballot proposal. The Gamemakers Google and Facebook quietly lobbied to defeat the privacy initiative.[66] But on June 28th, before the 5 p.m. deadline, California passed the most sweeping privacy protection to date, the California Consumer Privacy Act, which other states are now using as a template for protecting their residents' privacy.

Granted, more needs to be done. California's privacy statute has some major shortcomings compared to Europe's privacy regulation, the General Data Protection Regulation (which imposes stricter limits on the collection and use of our personal data), and Europe's privacy regulation remains ineffective in deterring some of the Gamemakers' practices that we saw in chapter 8. Nonetheless, the debate over privacy protection in the United States is evolving far quicker, thanks to the actions of one real estate developer and the many others who volunteered their time and efforts to his petition.

We can also effect change with our wallets. To see how, let us consider the tomato. Industrialized food has been stripped of any identity. We might know our favorite brand of beef lasagna, but we don't know who prepared the meal, what parts of the cattle (if indeed it's cattle) are in the meat, the location of the ranches where those cattle were raised, how they were fed, who grew the tomatoes for the tomato sauce, and from what countries the tomatoes came. "But that is what commerce does; it erases the maker of things, asking us to believe in the idea of a product that appears out of nowhere, connected to no one in particular," noted one food safety lawyer.[67]

And the tomatoes in the sauce (and for that matter the tomatoes in the produce section of the supermarket) are not bred for taste but for their size, their appearance, and their ability to withstand damage during shipping, all qualities that are typical of what the competition machine rewards. The result is that, according to one study (and anyone with taste buds), modern commercial varieties of tomatoes have far fewer flavor-associated chemicals than older varieties.[68] Which is to say: They don't have much flavor. As one scientist who is working on breeding a better-tasting tomato commented, "Have we trained a whole generation that doesn't know what a good tomato is?"[69]

Most of us have forgotten what food can actually taste like. We have become so acclimated to hard peaches and green pears picked before they ripen, apples treated chemically so they can be stored for months, and strawberries bred to be big and red and gorgeous but lacking any smell or taste, that we no longer think to demand anything else.

If you want a tastier tomato or humanely raised (and also better-tasting) grass-fed beef, then you should demand it. One way to do so is to put a face back on your food. A good place to start is your local farmers market, which can offer this combination of price, quality, and service. If you never have, you may be amazed by the taste of the juices dripping down your chin from a peach, the sweetness of a strawberry, the depth of flavors in tomatoes, the vivid tastes of the many varieties of apples that you probably know nothing about. In changing our shopping habits to reward our local farmers—the people who can explain the differences among the heirloom tomatoes, and which variety works better for salads, which for sandwiches, which for sauces—we can mutually benefit.

This is already happening around us as many are seeking better quality, better tasting produce at nearby farmers markets, which have tripled in number over the past decade.[70] The overall demand for locally sourced food has skyrocketed, growing four times faster than industrial agriculture in the past decade, and is projected to double in size over the next five years.[71] But this is not about wealthy, college-educated hipsters feeling good about themselves in helping farmers.[72] It's about deciding what type of market competition we want to promote. By taking a stand, by demanding quality, accountability, and honesty, we can affect the market.

Of course, there's no denying that the fruits, vegetables, and meat you buy in the farmers market can be, at times, more expensive than what you buy in the supermarket.[73] Under a zero-sum approach to competition, price is often paramount, as the more I save (by buying tomatoes at the lowest price), the better off I presumably am. In the Western world, the competition machine has mostly delivered on the most obvious variable—namely price. Thus, much of the food we buy in supermarkets and in fast food restaurants is remarkably cheap. At the same time, much of what we consume is also not very good—in either taste or nutritional quality. If we view the marketplace as simply a way to advance our pecuniary interest, then competition will remain finding the lowest price for the tomato. Ultimately, all that this form of competition can deliver is a great-*looking* tomato at a great price, but not necessarily a great-tasting one. Nor can government regulators provide a great-tasting tomato.

Moving further along our competition continuum, we can view the farmers market as positive-sum competition. The local farmers still compete for your business by offering different varieties of tomatoes at different prices.[74] You get a tastier tomato. But the competition expands the pie: Whichever local farmer you support, it is more likely that the money you spend remains in your local community, which positively impacts you and your local economy.[75] Economists call this the "multiplier effect." On average, 48 percent of each purchase at local independent businesses is recirculated locally, compared to less than 14 percent of purchases at chain stores.[76] As two economic studies found, the farmers markets also have a positive multiplier effect on jobs elsewhere in the local economy. In supporting the local farmers markets, the vendors hire more people, who in turn spend more money in the local economy, which adds other jobs in your community. When people come to Knoxville's farmers market, for example, many also support the other local businesses in the downtown square, like the local bookstore, coffee shop, and restaurants. In a nutshell, when the farmers market adds two jobs, another job is created elsewhere in the local economy.[77] These workers will also pay local taxes, which can potentially reduce the overall tax burden for the rest of us.

And once we view competition as positive sum, we can support markets in which ethical trading and social awareness are celebrated alongside the profit motive. Consider, for example, one study of small to mid-sized farms in Pennsylvania. They are part of the fastest-growing demographic in agriculture, namely women-owned farms that have "redefined successful farming in terms of providing services to their community, as well as in terms of profit and productivity."[78] The study explored how some of these women turn their farms into "a resource for the community." One farmer, for example, brings children with behavioral or academic problems to the farm. As she describes:

> They come from families who either are lacking in the way of resources or life skills and most of them are low income. Some of their situations are pretty bad. You know like abuse, situations of abuse . . . neglect, and poverty . . . I was worried about what was going to happen to them over the summer months because they go back to their families full time. So I suggested that we start a program on the farm over the summer months to support them and incorporate hands on organic farming and nutrition.[79]

These farmers do not view their farms simply as a resource for securing their own livelihood. Instead, their competition is enriched with a social purpose—whether helping at-risk youth or providing both children and adults a way to reconnect spiritually and emotionally through nature—in ways that promote "both the financial well-being of the farm operation and the production of a particular public good (nutrition, education, emotional health, spiritual health)."[80]

In the end, we all have an important role to play in determining the path forward—by exercising our power as citizens and consumers through our behavior in the marketplace. In other words, by choosing what to buy, based on what we value and the type of competition we want to promote. We can help return the marketplace to its etymological roots of bringing us together in a common endeavor. In the end, by helping our farmers cultivate the tasty heirloom tomato, which we enjoy eating at home and in the salads and lasagna prepared at our local restaurant, we'll all be the better for it. Healthier, too.

Reflections

Thank you for taking this journey with us. The odds against our having this time together were actually incredibly high—thanks to the intrusion of social media, which, under the Gamemakers' ecosystem, has us addicted and reduced our time to read.

We are now witnessing, as Andrew Tyrie, head of the UK's competition authority, observed, "a crisis of confidence in the institutions charged with harnessing the forces of capitalism for the public good."[81] The challenge ahead is to not only reorient competition and capitalism, but for the government to provide us what competition cannot. Society can benefit immensely from a lively competitive environment. But we need to make sure we foster the right kind of competition. With greater awareness of the risk of overdosing, we can all work together, as a society, toward a healthier competitive culture. The time is ripe.

No doubt the ideologues, lobbyists, Gamemakers, and policy makers will continue to peddle their competition ideology. Focusing on

short-term profits, they will discount or ignore the long-term implications of the competition overdose on our wallets and well-being.
While they will invariably kudzu the government to roll back any progressive measures, the power of bottom-up democracy can ultimately
make competition and the government work for us, rather than our
serving them. So why not take that path?

Acknowledgments

This book was published with the help of many.

First and foremost, we are grateful to the many scholars, competition officials, policy makers, lawyers, and business leaders who took the time to discuss our ideas and help develop them. We were fortunate to be able to present parts of this book in various venues and universities, and benefit from the audience's feedback and curiosity.

The ideas in this book also benefitted from the exchanges we had at conferences and events, including the Bundeskartellamt's 19th International Conference on Competition in Berlin; Georgetown Tech Law and Policy Colloquium; the conference organized by BEUC, the European Consumer Organization, titled "Bridge Over Troubled Water—Digital Competition in a Trans-Atlantic Dialogue"; the Georgetown Law–Cornell Tech Roundtable on the Political Economy of Data; and The University of Oxford Antitrust Symposium.

For their help, support, and feedback at various stages of this project, special thanks are due to Adi Ayal, Alec Burnside, Julie E. Cohen, Michal Gal, Wolfgang Kerber, Barry Lynn, Rob Nichols, and Spencer Weber Waller. We are also indebted to competition agency officials and industry participants who off-the-record gave us numerous examples and insights. The views in this book do not necessarily reflect those of the individuals noted above. All errors and omissions are ours.

Bringing this book to print was a team effort. We would like to thank Matthew LaPlante for his helpful suggestions. We are grateful to our editor Beth Rashbaum for her thoughtful edits and suggestions, which helped transform our work. We are very much indebted to Sibyl Marshall for her tireless and selfless effort in editing the endnotes of our book.

Thanks are due to our agent Trena Keating for her guidance and outstanding support.

We are grateful to Hollis Heimbouch at HarperCollins for her unflagging enthusiasm and insights, and Rebecca Raskin for shepherding this book through the publication process.

Maurice would also like to thank the University of Tennessee for its summer research grants.

Finally, we thank our families for all of their support—both before, during, and after completing the work on this book. And special thanks to Genevieve for joining us to visit open days at various universities and for being so accommodating.

APPENDIX A:
College Admission Decision Plans

Decision Plan	Application Due Date	Binding?	Restrictions	Examples
Early Decision I	Generally November 1–15	Yes. Student must attend college if accepted (and offered a financial aid package that is considered adequate by the family)	May apply to only one early decision school	Penn, Columbia, Dartmouth, Brown, Cornell, and many of the Little Ivy liberal arts colleges
Early Decision II	Generally January 1–15	Yes	May apply to only one early decision school	Many of the top liberal arts colleges and some of the top-ranked national universities
Single-Choice Early Action	Generally November 1–15	Nonbinding	Limitations on where else you can apply. Generally cannot apply to other private US universities under their Early Action programs	Harvard, Yale, Princeton, Stanford
Early Action	Generally November 1–15	Nonbinding. Student is notified of decision early	No limitation on applying to other schools (unless applying early to colleges with restrictions)	Selective state and some private universities
Regular Decision	Generally January 1	Nonbinding	None	Nearly every college (besides those with rolling decision)
Rolling Decision	Typically late summer until seats are filled	Nonbinding	Can apply and receive decision on a rolling basis	Many of the large state universities

APPENDIX B:
Matriculation of Students from
Fifteen Elite Private Schools

Ivy League	2018 *U.S. News* Ranking	Overall Average % of Students Matriculating
Brown	14	3.17%
Columbia	5	3.23%
Cornell	14	3.0%
Dartmouth	11	2.2%
Harvard	2	4.48%
Penn	8	3.16%
Princeton	1	2.28%
Yale	3	3.28%
Ivy League Subtotal		**24.8%**

Other Top 30	2018 *U.S. News* Ranking	Overall Average % of Students Matriculating
Cal Tech	10	0.25%
Carnegie Mellon	25	1.1%
Chicago	3	3.47%
Duke	9	1.37%
Emory	21	1.06%
Georgetown	20	2.18%
Johns Hopkins	11	0.93%
MIT	5	1.04%
NYU	30	3.02%
Northwestern	11	1.96%
Notre Dame	18	0.42%
Rice	14	0.19%
Stanford	5	2.26%
USC	21	1.97%
Vanderbilt	14	0.84%
Wake Forest	27	0.42%
Washington University in St Louis	18	2.31%
Other Top 30 Subtotal		**24.79%**

Little Ivies	2018 *U.S. News* Ranking	Overall Average % of Students Matriculating
Amherst	2	1.14%
Bates	23	0.62%
Bowdoin	3	1.13%
Colby	12	0.75%
Connecticut College	46	0.38%
Hamilton	18	1.03%
Middlebury	6	1.08%
Trinity	44	0.53%
Tufts	28 (National)	1.89%
Wesleyan	21	1.18%
Williams	1	1.21%
Little Ivies Subtotal		**10.94%**

Other Top 30 Liberal Arts	2018 *U.S. News* Ranking	Overall Average % of Students Matriculating
Barnard	26	0.91%
Carleton College	8	0.58%
Claremont McKenna	8	0.46%
Colgate University	12	0.71%
Colorado College	23	0.38%
Davidson College	10	0.36%
Grinnell College	18	0.21%
Harvey Mudd	12	0.33%
Haverford College	18	0.61%
Kenyon College	26	0.42%
Macalester College	26	0.32%
Oberlin College	26	0.74%
Pomona	6	0.76%
Scripps	26	0.51%
Smith College	12	0.22%
Swarthmore	3	0.56%
United States Air Force Academy	26	0.02%
United States Military Academy	12	0.1%
United States Naval Academy	21	0.19%

Other Top 30 Liberal Arts	2018 *U.S. News* Ranking	Overall Average % of Students Matriculating
University of Richmond	23	0.27%
Vassar College	12	0.41%
Washington and Lee University	10	0.1%
Wellesley	3	0.6%
Other Top 30 Liberal Arts Subtotal		**9.77%**

Public Ivies	2018 *U.S. News* Ranking	Overall Average % of Students Matriculating
Michigan	28	2.01%
UC Berkeley	21	1.09%
UCLA	21	0.65%
UNC Chapel Hill	30	0.41%
UVA	25	0.93%
Public Ivies Subtotal		**5.09%**

Source: Matriculation data for Brearley School (2014–18); Chapin School (2015–19); Collegiate School (2014–2018); Dalton School (2014–18); Georgetown Day School (2015–18); Harvard-Westlake School (2013–18); Hotchkiss School (2015–18); Lakeside School (2014–18); Menlo School (2015–18); Phillips Academy Andover (2015–18); Phillips Exeter Academy (2016–18); St. Paul's School (2015–18); Spence School (2015–19); University of Chicago Laboratory Schools (2014–18): Winsor School (2014–18). As the schools tabulated the matriculation data for different periods, we do not have data for the same time period for all the schools. But the matriculation data generally show for each school that 63 percent or more of the students have opted for one of these sixty colleges in recent years.

APPENDIX C:
Median Earnings of Students
Ten Years after Initial Enrollment

1	MIT	$94,200
2	Babson College	$91,400
3	Harvard University	$90,900
4	Georgetown University	$90,100
5	Stevens Institute of Technology	$87,300
6	Stanford University	$85,700
7	Maine Maritime Academy	$84,000
8	Yale University	$83,200
9	Worcester Polytechnic Institute	$82,600
10	University of Pennsylvania	$82,400
11	Colorado School of Mines	$82,100
12	Carnegie Mellon University	$81,800
13	Bentley University	$80,600
14	Princeton University	$80,500
15	Massachusetts Maritime Academy	$79,300
16	Rose-Hulman Institute of Technology	$79,200
17	California State University Maritime Academy	$79,000
18	US Merchant Marine Academy	$78,900
19	Kettering University	$78,600
20	Columbia University	$78,200
21	Rensselaer Polytechnic Institute	$77,900
22	Duke University	$77,900
23	Lehigh University	$77,200
24	SUNY Maritime	$76,700
25	Georgia Institute of Technology	$75,800
26	Claremont McKenna College	$75,000
27	Villanova University	$74,500
28	Harvey Mudd College	$74,200
29	California Institute of Technology	$74,200
30	Cornell University	$73,600

Source: 2018 Data from the US Department of Education, College Scorecard, https://collegescorecard.ed.gov. The data reflect the median earnings of students who received financial aid ten years after entering the school. Thus, the data do not include the earnings of students from wealthier families who did not opt (or qualify) for financial aid.

APPENDIX D:
Universities' Value-Added Score

Ivy League	2018 *U.S. News* Ranking	Value-Added Score (100 = Most Value Added)
Harvard	2	100
Columbia	5	99
Princeton	1	98
Penn	8	97
Cornell	14	96
Dartmouth	11	90
Yale	3	88
Brown	14	74

Other Top 30 National Universities	2018 *U.S. News* Ranking	Value-Added Score (100 = Most Value Added)
Duke	9	99
Georgetown	20	99
MIT	5	98
Carnegie Mellon	25	97
Cal Tech	10	96
Notre Dame	18	96
Stanford	5	96
Johns Hopkins	11	93
Vanderbilt	14	93
Wake Forest	27	92
USC	21	90
Chicago	3	89
Northwestern	11	82
Emory	21	76
NYU	30	66
Rice	14	54

Little Ivies	2018 *U.S. News* Ranking	Value-Added Score (100 = Most Value Added)
Tufts	28 (National)	96
Hamilton	18	88
Bates	23	77
Connecticut College	46	71
Trinity	44	69
Williams	1	68
Bowdoin	3	67
Middlebury	6	67
Amherst	2	61
Colby	12	54
Wesleyan	21	47

Other Top 30 Liberal Arts Colleges	2018 *U.S. News* Ranking	Value-Added Score (100 = Most Value Added)
Washington and Lee University	10	99
Harvey Mudd College	12	95
Colgate University	12	93
Davidson College	10	91
University of Richmond	23	83
Wellesley	3	81
Barnard	26	74
Haverford College	18	63
Macalester	26	44
Grinnell College	18	43
Scripps	26	37
Smith College	12	37
Carleton College	8	35
Kenyon College	26	24
Swarthmore	3	19
Pomona	6	15
Vassar College	12	15

Other Top 30 Liberal Arts Colleges	2018 *U.S. News* Ranking	Value-Added Score (100 = Most Value Added)
Colorado College	23	14
Oberlin College	26	8
United States Air Force Academy	26	No Score
United States Military Academy	12	No Score
United States Naval Academy	21	No Score
Claremont McKenna	8	No Score

Public Ivies	2018 *U.S. News* Ranking	Value-Added Score (100 = Most Value Added)
UVA	25	91
Michigan	28	82
UNC	30	79
UC Berkeley	21	77
UCLA	21	76

Source: Jonathan Rothwell, "Using Earnings Data to Rank Colleges: A Value-Added Approach Updated with College Scorecard Data," October 29, 2015, https://www .brookings.edu/research/using-earnings-data-to-rank-colleges-a-value-added-approach -updated-with-college-scorecard-data/. The Brookings Institution identified how much the university's alumni actually made approximately six years after graduation. It then estimated how much one would expect these students to earn given, among other things, the students' characteristics (such as family income and SAT scores) and the type of institution (such as curriculum value, STEM orientation, graduation rates, and faculty salaries). Using a scale from 1 to 100, with 100 indicating the highest centile, or top 1 percent of four-year colleges, the study assigned a score for each four-year college. (Basically, the higher the score, the more value the university adds.)

APPENDIX E:
Four-Year Universities with the
Highest Value-Added Score

Albany College of Pharmacy and Health Sciences	Albany	N.Y.	100
MCPHS University	Boston	Mass.	100
The University of Texas Health Science Center at San Antonio	San Antonio	Tex.	100
Maine Maritime Academy	Castine	Maine	100
Massachusetts Maritime Academy	Buzzards Bay	Mass.	100
LIU Brooklyn	Brooklyn	N.Y.	100
University of the Sciences	Philadelphia	Pa.	100
SUNY Maritime College	Bronx	N.Y.	100
California Maritime Academy	Vallejo	Calif.	100
University of Colorado Denver	Denver	Colo.	100
Babson College	Wellesley	Mass.	100
United States Merchant Marine Academy	Kings Point	N.Y.	100
Palmer College of Chiropractic-Davenport	Davenport	Iowa	100
Rose-Hulman Institute of Technology	Terre Haute	Ind.	100
Harvard University	Cambridge	Mass.	100
Kettering College	Kettering	Ohio	99
Worcester Polytechnic Institute	Worcester	Mass.	99
Brigham Young University-Provo	Provo	Utah	99
Rensselaer Polytechnic Institute	Troy	N.Y.	99
Clarkson University	Potsdam	N.Y.	99
Duke University	Durham	N.C.	99
Stevens Institute of Technology	Hoboken	N.J.	99
Lehigh University	Bethlehem	Pa.	99
Alliant International University	San Diego	Calif.	99
Bentley University	Waltham	Mass.	99
Kettering University	Flint	Mich.	99
Georgetown University	Washington	D.C.	99
Washington and Lee University	Lexington	Va.	99
Columbia University in the City of New York	New York	N.Y.	99
Colorado School of Mines	Golden	Colo.	99

Source: Rothwell, "Using Earnings Data to Rank Colleges." Using a scale from 1 to 100, with 100 indicating the highest centile, or top 1 percent of four-year colleges, the study assigned a score for each four-year college. (Basically, the higher the score, the more value the university adds.)

APPENDIX F:
Participation in Varsity Sports 2016

Institution Name	Male Under-graduates	Female Under-graduates	Total Under-graduates	Unduplicated Count Men's Participation	Unduplicated Count Women's Participation	% Men Participate in Varsity Sport	% Women Participate in Varsity Sport	Total % in Varsity Sport
Little Ivies								
Amherst College	921	925	1846	334	253	36%	27%	32%
Bates College	881	899	1780	394	283	45%	31%	38%
Bowdoin College	901	897	1798	358	277	40%	31%	35%
Colby College	894	985	1879	364	296	41%	30%	35%
Connecticut College	673	1145	1818	215	306	32%	27%	29%
Hamilton College	906	960	1866	327	252	36%	26%	31%
Middlebury College	1204	1292	2496	384	314	32%	24%	28%
Trinity College	1104	1028	2132	403	261	37%	25%	31%
Tufts University	2694	2720	5414	415	326	15%	12%	14%
Wesleyan University	1340	1572	2912	363	241	27%	15%	21%
Williams College	1052	992	2044	427	317	41%	32%	36%
Average	*1143*	*1220*	*2362*	*362*	*284*	*35%*	*26%*	*30%*

Ivy League

Brown University	3133	3423	6556	462	429	15%	13%	14%
Columbia University in the City of New York	4044	3508	7552	472	333	12%	9%	11%
Cornell University	6949	7512	14461	646	486	9%	6%	8%
Dartmouth College	2117	2113	4230	485	428	23%	20%	22%
Harvard University	3681	3250	6931	649	483	18%	15%	16%
Princeton University	2707	2529	5236	610	428	23%	17%	20%
University of Pennsylvania	4933	5298	10231	517	373	10%	7%	9%
Yale University	2782	2686	5468	490	354	18%	13%	15%
Average	*3793*	*3790*	*7583*	*541*	*414*	*16%*	*13%*	*14%*

SEC

Auburn University	10026	10234	20260	263	241	3%	2%	2%
Louisiana State University and Agricultural and Mechanical College	10896	12140	23036	251	214	2%	2%	2%

Mississippi State University	7985	8149	16134	230	138	3%	2%	2%
Texas A&M University-College Station	22973	22002	44975	311	277	1%	1%	1%
University of Alabama	13038	16033	29071	295	336	2%	2%	2%
University of Tennessee-Knoxville	10476	10243	20719	269	253	3%	2%	3%
University of Arkansas	9277	10497	19774	251	221	3%	2%	2%
University of Florida	13390	17193	30583	285	240	2%	1%	2%
University of Georgia	11219	15033	26252	232	216	2%	1%	2%
University of Kentucky	9420	11352	20772	308	188	3%	2%	2%
University of Mississippi	7716	9933	17649	218	159	3%	2%	2%
University of Missouri-Columbia	11470	12590	24060	305	197	3%	2%	2%
University of South Carolina-Columbia	11018	12929	23947	283	284	3%	2%	2%
Vanderbilt University	3366	3442	6808	178	165	5%	5%	5%
Average	*10876*	*12269*	*23146*	*263*	*224*	*3%*	*2%*	*2%*

Source: Equity in Athletics Data Analysis, https://ope.ed.gov/athletics

Notes

Chapter 1: First Overdose: The Race to the Bottom

1. "Helmetless Hockey Players," *Hockey History Blog*, August 7, 2010, http://www.greatesthockeylegends.com/2010/08/helmetless-hockey-players.html. The economist Thomas C. Schelling raised this hockey player example in his book, *Micromotives and Macrobehavior* (New York: Norton, 1978).
2. As one hockey player remarked in 1969, "It's foolish not to wear a helmet." Thomas C. Schelling, "Hockey Helmets, Concealed Weapons, and Daylight Saving: A Study of Binary Choices with Externalities," Discussion Paper No. 9, Public Policy Program, John F. Kennedy School of Government, Harvard University, July 1972. http://simson.net/ref/1972/Schelling_Hockey_Helmets.pdf.
3. Caroline M. Hoxby, interview on *Frontline*, PBS, May 23, 2000, https://www.pbs.org/wgbh/pages/frontline/shows/vouchers/choice/choice.html.
4. Graeme Paton, "Teachers 'Falsifying Pupils' Marks' to Inflate School Results," *Daily Telegraph* (London), September 7, 2011, http://www.telegraph.co.uk/education/educationnews/8744510/Teachers-falsifying-pupils-marks-to-inflate-school-results.html.
5. Fran Abrams, "Sats Tests: Why Cheating and Cramming Mean the Numbers Don't Add Up," *Guardian* (US edition), June 6, 2017, https://www.theguardian.com/education/2017/jun/06/sats-tests-cheating-cramming-primary-school-exam.
6. Channel 4, "Dispatches Investigation Reveals Extent of Student Plagiarism," news release, June 15, 2015, https://www.channel4.com/press/news/dispatches-investigation-reveals-extent-student-plagiarism.
7. Channel 4, "Dispatches Investigation."
8. Eleanor Harding, "Schools Caught Cheating in Exams to Boost Rankings with Teachers Altering Answers and Pupils Copying from Text Books," *Daily Mail* (London), June 1, 2015, http://www.dailymail.co.uk/news/article-3123992/How-schools-cheating-exams-boost-league-table-position-claims-teachers-altered-exam-answers.html; Olivia Goldhill, "An Academy School Faked Their Exam Results—by Cheating My Daughter Out of an Education," *Daily Telegraph* (London), June 15, 2015, http://www.telegraph.co.uk/education/secondaryeducation/11675594/An-Academy-school-faked-their-exam-results-by-cheating-my-daughter-out-of-an-education.html.
9. Sean Coughlin, "School Exam Rules to Be Reviewed after Cheat Row," BBC News, August 31, 2017, http://www.bbc.co.uk/news/education-41114798; Carri-Ann Taylor, "Exam Cheat Row: Three of Britain's Top Schools Accused of

Helping Pupils Cheat in Exams with One Professor Suspended Over Scandal," *Sun* (London), September 2, 2017, https://www.thesun.co.uk/news/4337205 /three-of-britains-top-schools-accused-of-helping-pupils-cheat-in-exams-with -one-professor-suspended-over-scandal/.

10. For example, in 2017, Ethiopia shut down its Internet to beat exam leakage and cheating. Abdi Latif Dahir, "Ethiopia Shut Down the Country's Internet to Beat Exam Cheats," Quartz Africa, May 31, 2017, https://qz.com/994990 /ethiopia-shut-down-the-internet-ahead-of-a-scheduled-countrywide-national -exams/.

11. Alan Blinder, "Atlanta Educators Convicted in School Cheating Scandal," *New York Times*, April 1, 2015, https://www.nytimes.com/2015/04/02/us/verdict -reached-in-atlanta-school-testing-trial.html.

12. FairTest, "Atlanta Is the Tip of an Iceberg—New Count Shows Widespread Test Score Corruption in 39 States and D.C.," news release, September 29, 2014, https://fairtest.org/"atlanta-tip-iceberg"-new-count-shows-widespread-t.

13. FairTest, "Standardized Exam Cheating Confirmed in 37 States and D.C.; New Report Shows Widespread Test Score Corruption," news release, March 28, 2013, https://fairtest.org/2013-Cheating-Report-PressRelease.

14. Mike Coldwell and Ben Willis, "Tests as Boundary Signifiers: Level 6 Tests and the Primary Secondary Divide," *Curriculum Journal* 28, no. 4 (2017): 578–97, https://doi.org/10.1080/09585176.2017.1330220.

15. Anonymous, "'I'm Teaching—and I'm Cheating': Confessions of a Primary Sats Teacher," *Guardian* (Manchester), June 6, 2017, https://www.theguardian.com /education/2017/jun/06/teaching-cheating-primary-school-sats-teacher-tests.

16. The White House, Office of the Press Secretary, "Remarks by the President in Town Hall at Binghamton University," August 23, 2013, https://obama whitehouse.archives.gov/the-press-office/2013/08/23/remarks-president-town -hall-binghamton-university.

17. "Issues: Education," Congressman Randy Hultgren, archived December 8, 2016, https://perma.cc/E6MX-XV79.

18. "College Costs Even More than You Think," *American Interest*, March 8, 2016, https://www.the-american-interest.com/2016/03/08/college-costs-even-more -than-you-think/.

19. US Department of Education, National Center for Education Statistics, "Fast Facts: Educational Institutions," accessed April 8, 2019, citing *Digest of Education Statistics*, 2016 (NCES 2017–094), chapter 2, https://nces.ed.gov /fastfacts/display.asp?id=84.

20. About 18 percent of college freshmen in one 2016 survey identified "rankings in national magazines" as "very important" in deciding to go to "this particular college." Kevin Eagan et al., *The American Freshman: National Norms Fall 2016* (Los Angeles: Higher Education Research Institute, UCLA, 2017), https://www .heri.ucla.edu/monographs/TheAmericanFreshman2016.pdf. This may not seem like a lot, but it was a greater factor than college counselors, teachers, or parents.

Moreover, the leading factor, which 65 percent of students identified as very important—"This college has a very good academic reputation"—likely comes from some university ranking. Students and parents, as research has found, may view the rankings as "'expert opinion' that helps to define institutional quality." So parents and students likely internalize—perhaps unknowingly—the university rankings.

21. Suppose ABC University improves its ranking one spot. One study, using university admissions data for top-tier institutions between 1998 and 2005, found that the next year it likely will attract even more applications from students with even higher average SAT scores. Nicholas A. Bowman and Michael N. Bastedo, "Getting on the Front Page: Organizational Reputation, Status Signals, and the Impact of *U.S. News & World Report* on Student Decisions," *Research in Higher Education* 50, no. 5 (August 2009): 415, https://doi.org/10.1007/s11162-009-9129-8. Interestingly, when a college went from the second to first page of the *U.S. News* rankings, it attracted even more applications (on average a 3.9 percent increase), and even more students who graduated in the top 10 percent of their class (on average a 2.3 percent increase). The college, as a result, could be more selective and reject on average 3.6 percent more students (even when controlling for other factors that influence admissions outcomes). Even after the university made the first page in the *U.S. News* national rankings, moving up or down on the first page affected admissions indicators for the following year, namely more applicants with higher SAT scores. For universities in the top 25, moving up one place in the national university rankings yields an additional 2.0 points on average SAT scores, a 0.4 percent decrease in acceptance rates, and a 1.5 percent increase in the number of applications the following year. (For *U.S. News* liberal arts college rankings, moving up one spot only affected changes in yield.)

22. Bowman and Bastedo, "Getting on the Front Page," 415.

23. Bowman and Bastedo, "Getting on the Front Page," 415.

24. Daphne C. Thompson, "Harvard Acceptance Rate Will Continue to Drop, Experts Say," *Harvard Crimson* (Cambridge, MA), April 16, 2015, https://www.thecrimson.com/article/2015/4/16/admissions-downward-trend-experts/.

25. The Common Application, https://www.commonapp.org/.

26. Robert Morse and Eric Brooks, "Best Colleges Ranking Criteria and Weights," *U.S. News & World Report*, September 9, 2018, https://www.usnews.com/education/best-colleges/articles/ranking-criteria-and-weights.

27. "Harvard College Admissions," Harvard University Office of Institutional Research, accessed April 8, 2019, https://oir.harvard.edu/harvard-college-admissions (data for class of 2003 and 2021).

28. "Undergraduate Applicant, Admit, and Matriculant Trends (Fall 1950–Fall 2017)," Stanford University Institutional Research & Decision Support, September 6, 2017, https://irds.stanford.edu/sites/g/files/sbiybj10071/f/multi-term_freshman_app_admt_matr_1950-present_3.pdf.

29. "Undergraduate Admissions," Cornell University Institutional Research & Planning, accessed April 8, 2019, https://irp.dpb.cornell.edu/university-factbook/undergraduate-admissions.

30. Richard Pérez-Peña, "Best, Brightest and Rejected: Elite Colleges Turn Away Up to 95%," *New York Times,* April 8, 2014, https://www.nytimes.com/2014/04/09/us/led-by-stanfords-5-top-colleges-acceptance-rates-hit-new-lows.html.

31. Paul Fain, "Enrollment Slide Continues, at Slower Rate," *Inside Higher Ed,* December 20, 2017, https://www.insidehighered.com/news/2017/12/20/national-enrollments-decline-sixth-straight-year-slower-rate.

32. Pérez-Peña, "Best, Brightest and Rejected." Northeastern University, as *Boston Magazine* outlined, dramatically improved its ranking by heavily investing in increasing the number of applicants to lower its acceptance rate. To facilitate the strategy, Northeastern stopped requiring SAT scores from foreign students, who typically score lower. The strategy boosted its application numbers without jeopardizing its overall SAT average. Max Kutner, "How to Game the College Rankings," *Boston Magazine,* August 26, 2014, http://www.bostonmagazine.com/news/article/2014/08/26/how-northeastern-gamed-the-college-rankings/3/. Selective liberal arts colleges have adopted a similar optional-testing policy. Students with mediocre SAT and ACT scores need not report them, while those with good scores do. This skews the average scores of accepted students upward.

33. We discuss in chapter 8 in the context of behavioral advertising.

34. Janet Lorin, "Ivy League Solicits Students Rejected for Stake of Selectivity," *Bloomberg News,* May 13, 2011, https://www.bloomberg.com/news/articles/2011-05-13/ivy-league-solicits-students-to-boost-selectivity.

35. Quoted in Caitlin Flanagan, "Confessions of a Prep School College Counselor," *Atlantic Monthly,* September 2001, https://www.theatlantic.com/magazine/archive/2001/09/confessions-of-a-prep-school-college-counselor/302281/.

36. William S. Flanagan and Michael E. Xie, "Record 39,494 Apply to Harvard College Class of 2021," *Harvard Crimson* (Cambridge, MA), February 14, 2017, http://www.thecrimson.com/article/2017/2/14/college-application-numbers-2017/.

37. Delano R. Franklin and Samuel W. Zwickel, "Record-Low 4.59 Percent of Applicants Accepted to Harvard Class of 2022," *Harvard Crimson* (Cambridge, MA), March 29, 2018, http://www.thecrimson.com/article/2018/3/29/harvard-regular-admissions-2022/.

38. Janet Lorin, "College Marketing Scrutinized," *Bloomberg News,* May 15, 2011, https://web.archive.org/web/20181221224956/http://www.sfgate.com/news/article/College-marketing-scrutinized-2371559.php (quoting Jon Reider, director of college counseling at San Francisco University High School).

39. Lorin, "College Marketing Scrutinized."

40. "What We Look For," Harvard College Admissions & Financial Aid, accessed April 8, 2019, https://college.harvard.edu/admissions/application-process/what-we-look.

41. If you are a Single-Choice Early Action applicant to Yale, you may apply to another institution's early admission program as follows:
    You may apply to any college's non-binding rolling admission program.
    You may apply to any public institution at any time provided that admission is non-binding.
    You may apply to another college's Early Decision II program, but only if the notification of admission occurs after January 1. If you are admitted through another college's Early Decision II binding program, you must withdraw your application from Yale.
    You may apply to any institution outside of the United States at any time.
    "Single-Choice Early Action," Yale College Undergraduate Admissions, accessed April 8, 2019, https://admissions.yale.edu/faq/single-choice-early-action.

42. Julia Bell, "Penn Made a Major Change to Its Early Decision Policy over the Summer," *Daily Pennsylvanian*, September 7, 2016, https://www.thedp.com /article/2016/09/early-decision-policy-change.

43. "Ivy League Admission Statistics for Class of 2022," Top Tier Admissions, accessed April 8, 2019, https://www.toptieradmissions.com/resources/college -admissions-statistics/ivy-league-admission-statistics-for-class-of-2022/.

44. Given the binding nature of early decision, the average yield rate is 87 percent, which is much higher than these universities' overall average yield rate (26 percent). Melissa Clinedinst, Anna-Maria Koranteng, and Tara Nicola, *2015 State of College Admission* (National Association for College Admission Counseling, 2015), https://www.nacacnet.org/globalassets/documents /publications/research/2015soca.pdf. Suppose a college seeks to admit one thousand freshmen. With a yield of 25 percent, the college must admit four students for every seat (four thousand offers). In filling half the class through binding early decision, however, the university now has to offer only two thousand applicants admission through regular decision for its remaining five hundred seats. Its yield improves significantly to 40 percent (1,000/2,500).

45. One example is the University of Pennsylvania. In 1980, the Ivy League school admitted slightly over 40 percent of its applicants. "Images in Flux: The 20th Century Development of the Undergraduate Experience at Penn," Penn University Archives & Records Center, September 1999, https://archives .upenn.edu/exhibits/penn-history/images-in-flux/part-1. Penn wasn't even mentioned in the *U.S. News* initial 1983 ranking of national universities. James Fallows, "The Early-Decision Racket," *Atlantic Monthly*, September 2001, https://www.theatlantic.com/magazine/archive/2001/09/the-early -decision-racket/302280/. Penn's associate admissions director at the time gave the student newspaper "an excellent summary of the objectives of the 'new' admissions campaign, 'You can't enroll who[m] you haven't admitted, and you can't admit who hasn't applied.'" "Images in Flux: The 20th Century Development of the Undergraduate Experience at Penn." So Penn accordingly

attempted to "attract more academically distinguished applicants, but also to admit fewer of them, while at the same time encouraging more of those admitted to matriculate." Fast forward to Penn's 2021 entering class of 2,457 students. Its overall acceptance rate dropped to 9 percent (3,757 acceptances out of 40,413 applications). "Incoming Class Profile: Statistics for the Class of 2021," University of Pennsylvania, September 18, 2017, https://web.archive .org/web/20180718232900/https://admissions.upenn.edu/admissions-and -financial-aid/what-penn-looks-for/incoming-class-profile. But over half of the incoming class came from these binding early decision students (1,354). Thus 34,266 regular decision applicants competed for the dwindling remaining spots. Are prospective applicants told this? No. Penn's website instead promises a "holistic review of each application." "Holistic Review," University of Pennsylvania, accessed April 8, 2019, http://www.admissions.upenn.edu/apply /whatpennlooksfor/holistic. The committee then summarily rejects over 90 percent of them with a form letter.

46. Eric Hoover, "Application Inflation," *Chronicle of Higher Education*, November 5, 2010, https://www.chronicle.com/article/Application-Inflation/125277.
47. Mary Cross, "The Class of 2022 Makes Its Mark," Tulane University News, May 4, 2018, http://news.tulane.edu/news/class-2022-makes-its-mark.
48. Alicia Jasmin, "Class of 2021 Reflects Tulane's Most Qualified Applicants," *Tulane University News*, April 5, 2017, https://news.tulane.edu/news/class-2021 -reflects-tulane's-most-qualified-applicants.
49. Jasmin, "Class of 2021."
50. Alia Wong, "The Absurdity of College Admissions," *Atlantic Monthly*, March 28, 2016, https://www.theatlantic.com/education/archive/2016/03/where -admissions-went-wrong/475575/; Anemona Hartocollis, "Greater Competition for College Places Means Higher Anxiety, Too," *New York Times*, April 20, 2016, https://www.nytimes.com/2016/04/21/us/greater-competition-for-college -places-means-higher-anxiety-too.html.
51. One critic is Kyle McEntee, the executive director of a nonprofit whose mission is to make entry to the legal profession more transparent. He complains, for example, that the *U.S. News* law school rankings "produce a host of incentives that do not align with the goal of providing an accessible, affordable legal education." As McEntee observed, "Perhaps the most troubling aspect of the *U.S. News* rankings methodology is the expenditures per student component, which actually includes two related metrics. The first, worth 9.75 percent of total rank, is the amount spent on faculty, staff, and services divided by total JD students. The second, worth 1.5 percent of total rank, adds the amount spent on financial aid to the equation. If you burn money (literally), you improve your standing on the rankings as long as there's an educational purpose. The latter metric appears to value schools that help people afford high tuition prices. If law school scholarships came from endowments rather than tuition discounting, it would do a good job of rewarding generosity. However,

based on how law schools do scholarships, this metric simply incentivizes schools to increase sticker tuition and offer price cuts. Schools are rewarded for the aggregate price cut." Kyle McEntee, "How to Fix the *U.S. News* Law School Rankings," Above the Law, January 12, 2016, https://abovethelaw.com/2016/01/how-to-fix-the-u-s-news-law-school-rankings/.

52. Hoover, "Application Inflation."

53. According to one 2015 survey, the average number of applications for each admissions officer was 914 at public universities and 411 at private universities. Selective universities (those accepting fewer than 50 percent of applicants) had on average 923 applications per admissions officer. Melissa Clinedinst, Anna-Maria Koranteng, and Tara Nicola, *2015 State of College Admission*.

54. Melissa Korn, "Some Elite Colleges Review an Application in 8 Minutes (or Less)," *Wall Street Journal*, January 31, 2018, https://www.wsj.com/articles/some-elite-colleges-review-an-application-in-8-minutes-or-less-1517400001.

55. Hoover, "Application Inflation."

56. On the one hand, white students have declined as a percentage of first-time, full-time freshmen from 90.1 percent in 1971 to 57.6 percent in 2015. Between 1971 and 2015, the percentage of Asian students increased from 0.5 percent to 10 percent. Kevin Eagan et al., *The American Freshman: Fifty-Year Trends*, 1966–2015 (Los Angeles: Higher Education Research Institute, UCLA, 2016), 6, http://www.heri.ucla.edu/monographs/50YearTrendsMonograph2016.pdf. While overall enrollment of African-American and Hispanic students has increased since 1971, they are, as the *New York Times* found in 2017, "more underrepresented at the nation's top [100] colleges and universities than they were 35 years ago." Jeremy Ashkenas, Haeyoun Park, and Adam Pearce, "Even with Affirmative Action, Blacks and Hispanics Are More Underrepresented at Top Colleges than 35 Years Ago," *New York Times*, August 24, 2017, https://www.nytimes.com/interactive/2017/08/24/us/affirmative-action.html; see also Andrew McGill, "The Missing Black Students at Elite American Universities," *Atlantic Monthly*, November 23, 2015, https://www.theatlantic.com/politics/archive/2015/11/black-college-student-body/417189/.

57. Gregor Aisch et al., "Some Colleges Have More Students from the Top 1 Percent than the Bottom 60. Find Yours," *New York Times*, January 18, 2017, https://www.nytimes.com/interactive/2017/01/18/upshot/some-colleges-have-more-students-from-the-top-1-percent-than-the-bottom-60.html. The percentage of students whose family comes from the top 1 percent income bracket has been increasing, while the share of students from the bottom 40 percent income bracket has declined. "Nationally, 40 percent of undergraduates receive a Pell Grant, federal aid for students who come from lower-income families," the *Boston Globe* reported. "But at the eight Ivy League institutions, Pell recipients accounted on average for just 16 percent of undergraduates, according to 2014 data published this summer. (At Harvard, that figure is 19.3 percent)." Deirdre Fernandes, "Low-Income Students Remain

Rare at Elite Universities," *Boston Globe*, August 12, 2017, https://www
.bostonglobe.com/metro/2017/08/12/elite-universities-struggle-for-economic
-diversity/ep1Z2oyzAAV8iF9Kk0srWO/story.html.

58. Hoover, "Application Inflation."
59. Hoover, "Application Inflation."
60. Benjamin Wermund, "How *U.S. News* College Rankings Promote Economic Inequality on Campus," *Politico*, September 13, 2017, https://www.politico.com /interactives/2017/top-college-rankings-list-2017-us-news-investigation/.

     And the reply: Robert Morse, "*U.S. News* Responds to *Politico*'s Critiques of Best Colleges," *U.S. News & World Report*, September 13, 2017, https://www.us news.com/education/blogs/college-rankings-blog/articles/2017-09-13/us-news -responds-to-politicos-critiques-of-best-colleges.

61. Adam Clark, "Pricey N.J. College Gets Stung by Credit Agency Junk Rating," *Star-Ledger* (Newark NJ), March 20, 2017, http://www.nj.com /education/2017/03/pricey_nj_college_gets_stung_by_credit_agency_junk _rating.html.

62. Scott Jaschik, "Surrender to Early Admissions," *Inside Higher Ed*, February 25, 2011, https://www.insidehighered.com/news/2011/02/25/surrender-early -admissions.

63. Michele Hernandez, "What Harvard and Princeton Don't Want You to Know," *Huffington Post*, December 6, 2017, https://www.huffingtonpost.com/dr-michele -hernandez/what-harvard-and-princeto_b_828527.html.

64. Jaschik, "Surrender to Early Admissions."
65. Fallows, "The Early-Decision Racket."
66. Amherst's Tom Parker, for example, said, "The places that would have to change are Harvard, Princeton, Columbia, Penn. Those are the four. If they were to drastically reduce the percentage they take early, this would all change in a heartbeat." Fallows, "The Early-Decision Racket."

67. America's Top Fears 2018, Chapman University Survey of American Fears, October 16, 2018, https://blogs.chapman.edu/wilkinson/2018/10/16 /americas-top-fears-2018/; America's Top Fears 2017, Chapman University Survey of American Fears, October 11, 2017, https://blogs.chapman.edu /wilkinson/2017/10/11/americas-top-fears-2017/; America's Top Fears 2016, Chapman University Survey of American Fears, October 11, 2016, https://blogs .chapman.edu/wilkinson/2016/10/11/americas-top-fears-2016/.

68. America's Top Fears 2016.
69. America's Top Fears 2018.
70. "In 1982, young firms [those five years old or younger] accounted for about half of all firms, and one-fifth of total employment," observed Jason Furman, chairman of the Council of Economic Advisers. But by 2013, these figures fell "to about one-third of firms and one-tenth of total employment." See, e.g., Jonathan B. Baker, "Market Power in the U.S. Economy Today," Equitable Growth, March 20, 2017, http://equitablegrowth.org/research-analysis/market

-power-in-the-u-s-economy-today/; Paul Krugman, "Challenging the Oligarchy," review of *Saving Capitalism: For the Many, Not the Few*, by Robert B. Reich. *New York Review of Books*, December 17, 2015, http://www.nybooks.com /articles/2015/12/17/robert-reich-challenging-oligarchy/.

71. Irving Fisher, "Why Has the Doctrine of Laissez Faire Been Abandoned?," *Science* 25, no. 627 (January 4, 1907): 22, DOI: 10.1126/science.25.627.18.

72. Affidavit of Laura Smith in Support of Criminal Complaint, March 11, 2019, https://www.justice.gov/usao-ma/press-release/file/1142951/download; Melissa Korn, Jennifer Levitz, and Jon Kamp, "Parents in College-Admissions Case Discuss Plea Deals with Prosecutors," *Wall Street Journal*, March 29, 2019, https://www.wsj.com/articles/parents-in-college-admissions-case-discuss-plea -deals-with-prosecutors-11553867326.

73. Not every private school posts its matriculation data by year. Some schools identify where their students generally go (without providing numbers).

74. John Allman, Head of School, Trinity School, "Dear Parents," August 30, 2017, https://trinityschoolnyc.myschoolapp.com/podium/push/default.aspx?i=177980.

75. A "significant cross-section of our students, regardless of class or race or privilege, feel disconnected, isolated, alienated from their peers." Allman, "Dear Parents."

76. Eagan et al., *The American Freshman: Fifty-Year Trends, 1966–2015*, 8.

77. Yale College Council, *Report on Mental Health*, September 2013, https://static1 .squarespace.com/static/586d882946c3c40a1c57b1ee/t/5875baf06a49630b1d 28f122/1484110581172/YCC-Mental-Health-Report-1ms1ra1.pdf.

78. Yale News, "Yale to Expand Mental Health Services to Meet Rising Student Need," April 19, 2018, https://news.yale.edu/2018/04/19/yale-expand-mental- health-services-meet-rising-student-need; Bill Murphy Jr., "Yale University's New Course on Happiness Is So Popular That 25 Percent of Its Students Enrolled. Here's What It's About," Inc., January 30, 2018, https://www.inc .com/bill-murphy-jr/yales-super-popular-course-on-happiness-makes-other -professors-sad-so-theyre-not-going-to-teach-it-anymore.html.

79. Yale College Council, *Report on Mental Health*.

80. Susan Svrluga, "Yale Course Is All about Getting an A in Life," *Washington Post*, May 13, 2018, https://www.sfgate.com/news/article/Yale-course-is-all-about -getting-an-A-in-life-12910090.php.

81. Max H. Bazerman and Don A. Moore, *Judgment in Management Decision Making* (Hoboken, NJ: J. Wiley & Sons, 7th ed., 2009), 111. The business literature also discusses the competitive irrationality of firms sacrificing profits and consumer welfare to obtain a relative advantage over a rival. See Lorenz Graf et al., "Debiasing Competitive Irrationality: How Managers Can Be Prevented from Trading Off Absolute for Relative Profit," *European Management Journal* 30, no. 4 (August 2012): 386–403, https://doi.org/10.1016/j.emj.2011.12.001; Dennis B. Arnett and Shelby D. Hunt, "Competitive Irrationality: The Influence of Moral Philosophy," *Business Ethics Quarterly* 12, no. 3 (July 2002): 279–303, https://www.jstor.org/stable/3858018.

82. Bazerman and Moore, *Judgment in Management Decision Making*, 106.

83. Jonathan Rothwell and Siddharth Kulkarni, *Beyond College Rankings: A Value-Added Approach to Assessing Two-and Four-Year Schools*, Metropolitan Policy Program at Brookings, April 2015, https://www.brookings.edu/wp-content/uploads/2015/04/BMPP_CollegeValueAdded.pdf.

84. Stacy Dale and Alan B. Krueger, "Estimating the Return to College Selectivity over the Career Using Administrative Earnings Data," NBER Working Paper No. 17159 (June 2011), http://www.nber.org/papers/w17159. For a summary of one of the studies, see Christopher Farrell, "On the Payoff to Attending an Elite College," National Bureau of Economic Research, accessed April 9, 2019, http://www.nber.org/digest/dec99/w7322.html.

85. The study found that "the average SAT score of the schools students applied to but did not attend is a much stronger predictor of students' subsequent income than the average SAT score of the school students actually attended." Farrell, "On the Payoff to Attending an Elite College."

86. Jonathan Rothwell, *Using Earnings Data to Rank Colleges: A Value-Added Approach Updated with College Scorecard Data*, October 29, 2015, https://www.brookings.edu/research/using-earnings-data-to-rank-colleges-a-value-added-approach-updated-with-college-scorecard-data/; Rothwell and Kulkarni, *Beyond College Rankings: A Value-Added Approach to Assessing Two-and Four-Year Schools*. Using a scale from 1 to 100, with 100 indicating the highest centile, or top 1 percent of four-year colleges, the study assigned a score for each four-year college. (Basically, the higher the score, the more value the university adds.) In their analysis, the authors used the median earnings of the student cohort that enrolled in the 2001–02 academic year and measured their salary ten years following enrollment. They also presented the change in value-added over time by calculating value-added six years following enrollment for the student cohorts that enrolled during the 1997–98 and 2005–06 academic years. They presented the difference between the two as a measure of change in value-added. The study's authors also noted some of the limitations of the government's College Scorecard data (which captures mid-career income from only those students on financial aid).

87. W. Bentley MacLeod and Miguel Urquiola, "Is Education Consumption or Investment? Implications for the Effect of School Competition," NBER Working Paper No. 25117 (October 2018), http://www.nber.org/papers/w25117.

88. Robert Morse, Eric Brooks, and Matt Mason, "How *U.S. News* Calculated the 2019 Best Colleges Rankings," *U.S. News & World Report*, September 9, 2018, https://www.usnews.com/education/best-colleges/articles/how-us-news-calculated-the-rankings.

89. Robert H. Frank, *The Darwin Economy: Liberty, Competition, and the Common Good* (Princeton University Press 2011) 16, 138.

90. Abhijit Vinayak Banerjee, "Inside the Machine: Toward a New Development Economics," *Boston Review* 32, no. 2 (2007), http://bostonreview.net/abhijit-vinayak-banjeree.

91. Andrei Shleifer, "Does Competition Destroy Ethical Behavior?," *American Economic Review* 94, no. 2 (May 2004): 414–16, https://doi.org /10.1257/0002828041301498 (discussing how competition can help spread child labor, corruption and bribery of government officials to reduce the amount companies owe in tariffs and taxes, excessive executive pay, manipulated earnings to lower corporations' cost of capital, and the involvement of universities in commercial activities).

92. Maurice E. Stucke, "Is Competition Always Good?," *Journal of Antitrust Enforcement* 1, no. 1 (April 2013): 1–36, https://doi.org/10.1093/jaenfo/jns008 (collecting studies).

Chapter 2: Second Overdose: "Excuse Me, Sir, I Did Not Order Horsemeat"

1. Ciaran Moran, "How a Horse from Galway Became Part of a European-Wide Food Scam," Independent.ie, July 28, 2017, https://www.independent.ie /business/farming/beef/how-a-horse-from-galway-became-part-of-a -europeanwide-food-scam-35976344.html; Tom Pettifor, "Businessman Who Laced Meat from Pet Ponies with Beef Destined for Burgers, Sausages and Pies Faces Jail," *Daily Mirror* (London), July 26, 2017, https://www.mirror.co.uk /news/uk-news/businessman-who-laced-meat-pet-10878215.

2. Kevin Rawlinson, "Two Men Jailed in UK for Horsemeat Conspiracy," *Guardian* (Manchester), July 31, 2017, https://www.theguardian.com/uk-news /2017/jul/31/two-men-jailed-in-uk-for-horsemeat-conspiracy.

3. Felicity Lawrence, "Horsemeat Scandal: The Essential Guide," *Guardian* (Manchester), February 15, 2013, https://www.theguardian.com/uk/2013 /feb/15/horsemeat-scandal-the-essential-guide#102.

4. Mark King, "Tesco Attempts to Win Back Customers," *Guardian* (Manchester), January 18, 2012, https://www.theguardian.com/money/2012/jan/18/tesco -attempts-win-back-customers.

5. Organisation for Economic Co-operation and Development, "OECD Data: Household Disposable Income," accessed April 10, 2019, https://data.oecd.org /hha/household-disposable-income.htm.

6. Harry Wallop, "Fast Food Becomes the UK's Meal of Choice," *Daily Telegraph* (London), January 15, 2012, https://www.telegraph.co.uk/finance /newsbysector/retailandconsumer/9016251/Fast-food-becomes-the-UKs-meal -of-choice.html.

7. "The Basket Case," *Economist*, June 23, 2012, https://www.economist.com /node/21557377.

8. Ruki Sayid, "Italian Food Soars Pasta British Grub in the Ready Meals Race," *Daily Mirror* (London), February 28, 2012, https://www.mirror.co.uk/news/uk -news/italian-food-soars-pasta-british-745540.

9. Global Price of Beef [PBEEFUSDQ], retrieved from FRED, Federal Reserve Bank of St. Louis, https://fred.stlouisfed.org/series/PBEEFUSDQ, June 4, 2018.

10. Matthew Wall, "Horsemeat Scandal: How Horse Meat Has Kept Ready-Meal Prices Low," BBC News, February 28, 2013, http://www.bbc.com/news/business-21544335.

11. Dan Colombini, "Kerry Foods Blames Competition for Durham Cuts," Food Manufacture, April 5, 2012, https://www.foodmanufacture.co.uk/Article/2012/04/03/Kerry-Foods-blames-competition-for-Durham-cuts.

12. Wall, "Horsemeat Scandal" (global auction price for beef is over $5,300 a ton whereas horsemeat costs only about $1,200 a ton).

13. Derrell S. Peel, "Beef Demand Is the Key to Cattle Prices in 2012," Drovers, January 2, 2012, https://www.drovers.com/article/beef-demand-key-cattle-prices-2012.

14. Lawrence, "Horsemeat Scandal."

15. Lawrence, "Horsemeat Scandal."

16. Felicity Lawrence, "Horsemeat Trial Shines Light on Key Part of International Fraud," Guardian (Manchester), July 26, 2017, https://www.theguardian.com/uk-news/2017/jul/26/horsemeat-trial-shines-light-international-fraud.

17. ABP Food Group, "About Us: Our Process," accessed April 11, 2019, https://abpfoodgroup.com/about-us/our-process/.

18. ABP Food Group, "About Us."

19. Lawrence, "Horsemeat Trial."

20. Chris Elliott, OBE (pro-vice-chancellor, Faculty of Medicine, Health and Life Sciences, Queen's University, Belfast), in discussion with Ariel Ezrachi, June 2018.

21. It is generally accepted that a competitive market environment will "increase quality for a given price or reduce price for a given level of quality." Organisation for Economic Co-operation and Development, The Role and Measurement of Quality in Competition Analysis, (Oct. 28, 2013), 97, http://www.oecd.org/competition/Quality-in-competition-analysis-2013.pdf; US Department of Justice, Antitrust Division, Antitrust Enforcement and the Consumer (2005), http://www.justice.gov/atr/public/div_stats/antitrust-enfor-consumer.pdf.

22. Sandeep Heda, Stephen Mewborn, and Stephen Caine, "How Customers Perceive a Price Is as Important as the Price Itself," Harvard Business Review, January 3, 2017, https://hbr.org/2017/01/how-customers-perceive-a-price-is-as-important-as-the-price-itself.

23. "Eastern Europeans Think Western Food Brands Are Selling Them Dross," Economist, June 29, 2017, https://www.economist.com/news/europe/21724408-dual-foods-furore-hints-eastern-mistrust-west-eastern-europeans-think-western-food; Emmet Livingstone and Simon Marks, "Central Europe Resents Double EU Food Standard," Politico, November 3, 2016, https://www.politico.eu/article/a-snack-by-any-other-name-varying-food-standards-irk-new-eu-countries/.

24. Georgi Gotiv, "Lower Quality of Same Food Brands in Eastern Europe Raises Eyebrows," Euractiv, February 20, 2017, https://www.euractiv.com/section

/health-consumers/news/lower-quality-of-same-food-brands-in-eastern-europe
-raises-eyebrows/.

25. Aidan Mac Guill, "'In Eastern Europe, We Don't Prefer to Eat Garbage':
Readers on Food Inequality," *Guardian* (Manchester), September 21, 2017,
https://www.theguardian.com/inequality/2017/sep/21/in-eastern-europe
-we-dont-prefer-to-eat-garbage-readers-on-food-inequality; Niamh Michail,
"Multinational Firms Sell Poorer Quality (but More Expensive) Food to Eastern
Europeans," Food Navigator, September 26, 2017, https://www.foodnavigator
.com/Article/2016/05/26/Multinational-firms-sell-poorer-quality-but-more
-expensive-food-to-Eastern-Europeans; Daniel Boffey, "Multinationals Fobbing
Us Off with Inferior Food, Says Bulgarian Minister," *Guardian*, May 29, 2017,
https://www.theguardian.com/world/2017/may/29/bulgaria-accuses-food
-companies-cold-war-on-flavour-quality; Rebecca Flood and Monika
Pallenberg, "'It's Food Racism!' New Scandal Erupts in the EU over Nutella,"
Daily Express (UK), March 9, 2017, https://www.express.co.uk/news/uk/775791
/food-racism-EU-European-Union-Nutella-supermarket-eastern-quality.

26. Daniel Boffey, "Food Brands 'Cheat' Eastern European Shoppers with
Inferior Products," *Guardian* (Manchester), September 15, 2017, https://www
.theguardian.com/inequality/2017/sep/15/food-brands-accused-of-selling
-inferior-versions-in-eastern-europe.

27. Daniel Boffey, "Europe's 'Food Apartheid': Are Brands in the East Lower
Quality Than in the West?," *Guardian* (Manchester), September 15, 2017,
https://www.theguardian.com/inequality/2017/sep/15/europes-food-apartheid
-are-brands-in-the-east-lower-quality-than-in-the-west.

28. Lawrence, "Horsemeat Scandal."

29. Lynn Petrak, "Jumpin' Beans," National Provisioner, July 1, 2005, https://www
.provisioneronline.com/articles/94647-jumpin-beans-1.

30. Anthony Fletcher, "Water-Injected Meat: The UK's Latest Food Scandal?," Food
Navigator, July 19, 2008, http://www.foodproductiondaily.com/Supply-Chain
/Water-injected-meat-the-UK-s-latest-food-scandal; "News Aus Der Fischbranche,"
Fischmagazin, March 18, 2013, https://www.fischmagazin.de/newsartikel
-seriennummer-2618.htm, "'Gepanschte' Fische," News Austria, March 20, 2013,
http://www.news.at/a/lebensmittelskandal-gepanschter-fisch-supermarkt.

31. Felicity Lawrence, "Scandal of Beef Waste in Chicken," *Guardian* (Manchester),
May 21, 2003, http://www.theguardian.com/society/2003/may/21/food
.foodanddrink.

32. Koen de Jong, "Too Lidl Too Late," *FoodPersonality* 29, no. 5 (May 2013),
https://www.iplc-europe.com/work/foodpersonality/; see also Sander Grégoire,
"Waarom U Nooit Meer Euro Shopper in De Schappen Van Albert Heijn Zult
Vinden," *de Volkskrant* (Netherlands), April 10, 2013, https://www.volkskrant
.nl/es-b811186f.

33. See Wikipedia, s.v. "ICA meat repackaging controversy," accessed July 28, 2019,
http://en.wikipedia.org/wiki/ICA_meat_repackaging_controversy.

34. Julie Jargon, "McDonald's Growth Suffers in U.S., China," *Wall Street Journal*, August 8, 2014, https://www.wsj.com/articles/mcdonalds-july-sales-slip-on-china-u-s-pressures-1407500403; Liza Lin, "McDonald's Pulls Meat from China Restaurants," Bloomberg News, July 28, 2014, http://www.bloomberg.com/news/2014-07-28/mcdonald-s-supplier-recalls-meat-in-expired-food-scandal.html.

35. Nick Squires, "Italian Olive Oil Scandal: Seven Top Brands 'Sold Fake Extra-Virgin,'" *Daily Telegraph* (London), November 11, 2015, https://www.telegraph.co.uk/news/worldnews/europe/italy/11988947/Italian-companies-investigated-for-passing-off-ordinary-olive-oil-as-extra-virgin.html.

36. Melanie Pinola, "The Most (and Least) Fake Extra Virgin Olive Oil Brands," Lifehacker, November 8, 2013, https://www.coconutbreeze.com/2013/11/the-most-and-least-fake-extra-virgin-olive-oil-brands/.

37. Andrew Don, "Food Fraud Tests Reveal 25% of Dried Oregano Is Adulterated," The Grocer, July 23, 2015, https://www.thegrocer.co.uk/buying-and-supplying/food-safety/food-fraud-tests-reveal-25-of-dried-oregano-is-adulterated/522104.article.

38. "Fake Oregano Being Sold in Australia," News.com.au, April 6, 2016, https://www.news.com.au/lifestyle/food/eat/fake-oregano-being-sold-in-australia/news-story/a141559a3dd96013c8c7096320711ab4d.

39. Julia Calderone, "The Way Some Meat Producers Fatten Up Cattle Is More Bizarre than You Might Think," Business Insider, April 6, 2016, http://www.businessinsider.com/farmers-fatten-cattle-hormone-implants-2016-4.

40. European Commission, "Hormones in Meat," accessed April 11, 2019, https://ec.europa.eu/food/safety/chemical_safety/meat_hormones_en; European Commission Health & Consumer Protection Directorate-General, Opinion of the Scientific Committee on Veterinary Measures Relating to Public Health on the Potential Risks to Human Health from Hormone Residues in Bovine Meat and Meat Products, April 10, 2002, https://ec.europa.eu/food/sites/food/files/safety/docs/cs_meat_hormone-out50_en.pdf.

41. "Carrefour Ceases Pangasius Sales over Environmental Concerns," Undercurrent News, January 25, 2017, https://www.undercurrentnews.com/2017/01/25/carrefour-ceases-pangasius-sales-over-environmental-concerns/. The Vietnamese trade association denied this. "Tra Fish Exports Could Be Hurt by False News: VASEP," Viet Nam News, January 23, 2017, https://vietnamnews.vn/economy/350120/tra-fish-exports-could-be-hurt-by-false-news-vasep.html#74WVgXjtvA4ZcLuP.97.

42. Paul R. Gerber, Caroline Opio, and Henning Steinfeld, *Poultry Production and the Environment—a Review* (Rome, Italy: Animal Production and Health Division, Food and Agriculture Organization of the United Nations, 2008), http://www.fao.org/ag/againfo/home/events/bangkok2007/docs/part2/2_2.pdf.

43. US Food & Drug Administration, "FDA Announces Pending Withdrawal

of Approval of Nitarsone," April 1, 2015, https://wayback.archive-it.org
/7993/20170406075820/https://www.fda.gov/AnimalVeterinary/NewsEvents
/CVMUpdates/ucm440668.htm.

44. Yuanan Hu et al., "Public Health Risk of Arsenic Species in Chicken Tissues
    from Live Poultry Markets of Guangdong Province, China," *Environmental
    Science & Technology*, 51 (February, 2017): 3508, https://pubs.acs.org/doi
    /pdf/10.1021/acs.est.6b06258.

45. Richard Bilton, "Apple 'Failing to Protect Chinese Factory Workers,'" BBC
    News, December 18, 2014, https://www.bbc.com/news/business-30532463;
    Marcus Wohlsen, "Apple Isn't the Only One to Blame for Smartphone Labor
    Abuses," *Wired*, December 19, 2014, https://www.wired.com/2014/12/apple
    -isnt-one-blame-smartphone-supply-chain-abuses/; Charles Arthur, "Samsung
    Accused of Exploiting Younger Workers in China," *Guardian* (Manchester),
    September 5, 2012, https://www.theguardian.com/technology/2012/sep/05
    /samsung-accused-exploiting-workers-china; Charles Arthur, "Samsung Finds
    Labour Violations at Dozens of Its Chinese Suppliers," *Guardian* (Manchester),
    July 1, 2014, https://www.theguardian.com/technology/2014/jul/01/samsung
    -working-practice-breaches-chinese-suppliers.

46. Michelle Chen, "Was Your Smartphone Built in a Sweatshop?," *Nation*,
    January 2, 2018, https://www.thenation.com/article/was-your-smartphone
    -built-in-a-sweatshop/; Jamie Fullerton, "Suicide at Chinese iPhone Factory
    Reignites Concern over Working Conditions," *Daily Telegraph* (London),
    January 7, 2018, https://www.telegraph.co.uk/news/2018/01/07/suicide-chinese
    -iphone-factory-reignites-concern-working-conditions/.

47. Kristi Davis and Khanh T. L. Tran, "Sweatshops Persist in U.S. Garment
    Industry," *Women's Wear Daily*, December 5, 2016, https://wwd.com/business
    -news/government-trade/sweatshops-persist-in-u-s-garment-industry-10716742/;
    Josephine Moulds, "Child Labour in the Fashion Supply Chain," UNICEF and
    Guardian Labs, accessed April 12, 2019, https://labs.theguardian.com/unicef
    -child-labour/; War on Want, "Fashion Victims—The Facts," accessed April 12,
    2019, https://waronwant.org/fashion-victims-facts.

48. Plaintiffs/Appellants' Opening Brief, Doe I v. Nestlé USA, Inc., Docket No.
    10–56739 (9th Cir. June 24, 2011), 2011 WL 2617616.

49. Doe I v. Nestlé USA, Inc., 766 F.3d 1013, 1016–17 (9th Cir. 2014).

50. Doe I, 766 F.3d at 1017 (they "acquired this knowledge first-hand through their
    numerous visits to Ivorian farms" and from the many reports issued by domestic
    and international organizations).

51. McCoy v. Nestlé USA, Inc., 173 F. Supp. 3d 954, 956–57 (N.D. Cal. 2016),
    aff'd sub nom; McCoy v. Nestlé USA, Inc., 730 F. App'x 462 (9th Cir., 2018).

52. McCoy, 173 F. Supp. 3d at 968.

53. Brian O'Keefe, "Bitter Sweets," *Fortune*, March 1, 2016, http://fortune.com
    /big-chocolate-child-labor/.

54. See, e.g., Doe I, 766 F.3d at 1017 (the companies, according to the plaintiffs,

sought the Ivory Coast "with the unilateral goal of finding the cheapest sources of cocoa").

55. Kate Hodal, "Nestlé Admits Slave Labour Risk on Brazil Coffee Plantations," *Guardian* (Manchester), March 2, 2016, https://www.theguardian.com/global-dev elopment/2016/mar/02/nestle-admits-slave-labour-risk-on-brazil-coffee-plantations.

56. Annie Kelly, "Nestlé Admits Slavery in Thailand While Fighting Child Labour Lawsuit in Ivory Coast," *Guardian* (Manchester), February 1, 2016, https:// www.theguardian.com/sustainable-business/2016/feb/01/nestle-slavery -thailand-fighting-child-labour-lawsuit-ivory-coast.

57. Keith Perry, "Airline Pilots Reveal Commercial Pressure to Carry Less Fuel," Exaro News, August 20, 2012, http://www.exaronews.com/articles/4562/airline -pilots-reveal-commercial-pressure-to-carry-less-fuel.

58. David Millward, "Airlines Declare More than 200 Low Fuel Emergency Landings in Four Years," *Daily Telegraph* (London), March 11, 2013, http:// www.telegraph.co.uk/news/aviation/9922161/Airlines-declare-more-than-200 -low-fuel-emergency-landings-in-four-years.html.

59. Roger Wilsher et al., "How Virgin Flight from Florida Ran Low on Fuel after Diversion," Exaro News, August 18, 2012, http://www.exaronews .com/articles/4546/how-virgin-flight-from-florida-ran-low-on-fuel-after -diversion; Keith Perry, "Spain Probes Ryanair over Three Flights in Low-Fuel 'Maydays,'" Exaro News, August 18, 2012, http://www.exaronews.com /articles/4560/spain-probes-ryanair-over-three-flights-in-low-fuel-maydays; Ray Massey, "Ryanair Ordered to 'Review' Fuel Policy after Making Three Emergency Landings Because Planes Almost Ran Out," *Daily Mail*, September 20, 2012, http://www.dailymail.co.uk/news/article-2206322/; Perry, "Airline Pilots Reveal"; Oliver Smith, "The Confessions of an Airline Pilot," *Daily Telegraph* (London), June 24, 2017, https://www.telegraph.co.uk /travel/travel-truths/confessions-of-an-airline-pilot/; Millward, "Pilots Forced to Make Emergency Landings."

60. "Fear of Flying Justified: Airlines, Like Judicious Parents, Keep Secrets for a Reason: What You Don't Know Can't Scare You," Metro, November 11, 2010, https://www.metro.us/news/fear-of-flying-justified/tmWjkj-7fetFPjRZjwWY.

61. Wilsher et al., "How Virgin Flight from Florida Ran Low"; Perry, "Spain Probes Ryanair"; Massey, "Ryanair Ordered to 'Review' Fuel Policy"; Perry, "Airline Pilots Reveal"; Smith, "Confessions."

62. Emma Glanfield, "Eleven Planes Forced to Make Mayday Landings at British Airports Last Year Because They Were Running Out of Fuel," *Daily Mail* (London), February 24, 2015, http://www.dailymail.co.uk/news/article -2947077/.

63. Glanfield, "Eleven Planes."

64. The UK's competition authority observed that:
    Buyers may not know, for example, how quality varies across brands. Markets where customers may be unsure about quality include those for

professional services, used goods and complex mechanical or electronic products. When, as a result of information asymmetries, customers are unable to form an accurate assessment of product quality (e.g. if they consistently underestimate the probability of product failure), a market may operate inefficiently. Imperfect information about quality can be a particularly severe problem for infrequently purchased goods or goods the quality of which cannot be verified even after purchase—so-called credence goods.

OECD, *The Role and Measurement of Quality in Competition Analysis*, 113 (United Kingdom). The question of how to judge quality is so complex that economists and marketers apply what is known as the Search, Experience, and Credence classification to the goods, experiences, and services we purchase with the distinctions between them based on the ease or difficulty with which consumers can assess their quality and obtain information about them. "Search" goods—things like clothing and furniture—are relatively easy to evaluate before buying, based on research we do, direct examination, prior experience, etc. "Experience" goods—like restaurants, travel, theater performances, a bottle of wine, etc.—can be evaluated only after we have actually bought and experienced them, and then, of course, only subjectively. "Credence" goods— like medical care, health products, and many kinds of professional services including those of doctors, lawyers, accountants, and financial advisors—can be hard to evaluate even after we've used them. Think of vitamin pills or dietary supplements. Did they work? Or doctors—would we have been better off with a different doctor, another surgery, the treatment our next-door neighbor received from her doctor for the same condition? Because of the difficulty of evaluating and comparing, economists have observed that competition has the potential to turn particularly toxic in markets with experience goods, and even more so with credence goods. See Denis W. Stearns, "On (Cr)edibility: Why Food in the United States May Never Be Safe," *Stanford Law & Policy Review* 21 (2010): 248–49.

65. OECD, *The Role and Measurement of Quality in Competition Analysis*, 121 (United States), 60 (Canada) (noting how "the components of product quality may be difficult to observe or measure in certain cases"); Kurt R. Brekke, Luigi Siciliani, and Odd Rune Straune, "Price and Quality in Spatial Competition," *Regional Science & Urban Economics* 40, no. 6 (November 2010): 471. The European Commission's decision in Intel is illustrative in this respect. The commission noted the challenge and subjectivity involved in assessing the quality of high-tech products. Indeed, the commission acknowledged the lack of a single parameter that defines the quality of a product, in particular when the product in question is complex. COMP/37.990 Intel Corporation OJ (2009) C 227/07 at [909] 1691.

66. OECD, *The Role and Measurement of Quality in Competition Analysis*, 79 (European Union) and 60 (Canada) (noting that "even when a component of

product quality is quantifiable, consumers may have varied tastes, and may not
agree as to what features of a product constitute better or worse quality").

67. Stanford University, "Price Tag Can Change the Way People Experience Wine,
Study Shows," news release, January 15, 2008, https://news.stanford.edu/pr
/2008/pr-wine-011608.html. As the study found:

> Because perceptions of quality are known to be positively correlated with
> price, the individual is likely to believe that a more expensive wine will
> probably taste better. Our hypothesis goes beyond this by stipulating
> that higher taste expectations would lead to higher activity in the medial
> orbitofrontal cortex (mOFC), an area of the brain that is widely thought
> to encode for actual experienced pleasantness.

Hilke Plassmann et al., "Marketing Actions Can Modulate Neural
Representations of Experienced Pleasantness," *PNAS* 105, no. 3 (January 22,
2008): 1050–54, https://doi.org/10.1073/pnas.0706929105; see also Jonathan D.
Glater and Alan Finder, "In Tuition Game, Popularity Rises with Price," *New
York Times*, December 12, 2006, https://www.nytimes.com/2006/12/12
/education/12tuition.html (discussing how Ursinus College, believing it was
losing applicants because of its low tuition, raised its tuition and fees
17.6 percent in 2000 [but offered more financial aid] and received nearly two
hundred more applications the following year).

68. Dan Ariely, *Predictably Irrational: The Hidden Forces That Shape Our Decisions*
(New York: Harper, 2008), 181–86.

69. Ariely, *Predictably Irrational*, 182–83.

70. Ariely, *Predictably Irrational*, 184–86.

71. $3.97 for a 121-ounce bottle of Clorox bleach versus $2.94 for Walmart's private
label.

72. FTC v. Procter & Gamble Co., 386 U.S. 568 (1967).

73. FTC v. Procter & Gamble. For the intersection of brands and competition
policy, see Deven R. Desai and Spencer Weber Waller, "Brands, Competition
and the Law," *Brigham Young University Law Review* 2010: 1425, https://ssrn
.com/abstract=1545893.

74. PBS Frontline, "Flying Cheap: How Safe Are Regionals?," February 9, 2010,
https://www.pbs.org/wgbh/pages/frontline/flyingcheap/safety/howsafe.html.

75. See Michael Ollinger, Danna Moore, and Ram Chandran, "Meat and Poultry
Plants' Food Safety Investments: Survey Findings," US Department of
Agriculture Economic Research Service, Technical Bulletin no. 1911, May
2004; see also European Commission, "Horse Meat: One Year after—Actions
Announced and Delivered!," accessed April 12, 2019, https://ec.europa.eu/food
/safety/official_controls/food_fraud/horse_meat/q-ans_en.

76. Jim Reed and Adam Eley, "How Safe Is Air Quality on Commercial Planes?,"
BBC News, June 8, 2015, https://www.bbc.co.uk/news/health-32786537; "Air
Quality on Planes: Aerotoxic Syndrome," *Economist*, February 7, 2013, https://
www.economist.com/gulliver/2013/02/07/aerotoxic-syndrome; Association of

Flight Attendants-CWA, "Issues: Aircraft Air Quality—Protecting Against Contaminants," accessed April 12, 2019, http://www.afacwa.org/aircraft_air_quality.

77. George A. Akerlof, "The Market for 'Lemons': Quality Uncertainty and the Market Mechanism," *Quarterly Journal of Economics* 84, no. 3 (August 1970): 488–500, https://doi.org/10.2307/1879431.

78. Healthline, "Experts Agree: Sugar Might Be as Addictive as Cocaine," accessed April 12, 2018, https://www.healthline.com/health/food-nutrition/experts-is -sugar-addictive-drug#1.

79. Nell Boeschenstein, "How the Food Industry Manipulates Taste Buds with 'Salt Sugar Fat,'" NPR, February 26, 2013, https://www.npr.org/sections /thesalt/2013/02/26/172969363/how-the-food-industry-manipulates-taste-buds -with-salt-sugar-fat.

80. Boeschenstein, "How the Food Industry Manipulates Taste Buds."

Chapter 3: Third Overdose: Exploiting Human Weakness

1. As the *Wall Street Journal* reported, if a pound of coffee costs $9, a 33 percent discount drops the price to $6, or $2 for each third of a pound. With 33 percent more coffee at no additional cost, each third (four in all) costs $2.25. Jo Craven McGinty, "50% Off: Why That Deal Isn't as Good as You Think," *Wall Street Journal*, August 3, 2018, https://www.wsj.com/articles/50-off-why-that-deal -isnt-as-good-as-you-think-1533294000.

2. Leonard Green, Astrid F. Fry, and Joel Myerson, "Discounting of Delayed Rewards: A Life-Span Comparison," *Psychological Science* 5, no. 1 (January 1994): 33–36, https://doi.org/10.1111/j.1467-9280.1994.tb00610.x.

3. Samuel M. McClure et al., "Separate Neural Systems Value Immediate and Delayed Monetary Rewards," *Science* 306 (October 15, 2004): 503–7, https:// doi.org/10.1126/science.1100907.

4. For consumers' overconfidence in avoiding fees, see Stefano DellaVigna, "Psychology and Economics: Evidence from the Field," *Journal of Economic Literature* 47, no. 2 (June 2009): 315, 342, http://www.aeaweb.org/articles ?id=10.1257/jel.47.2.315; Oren Bar-Gill and Elizabeth Warren, "Making Credit Safer," *University of Pennsylvania Law Review* 157, no. 1 (November 2008): 1, 49, 47–52, https://ssrn.com/abstract=1137981; Samuel Issacharoff and Erin F. Delaney, "Credit Card Accountability," *University of Chicago Law Review* 73, no. 1 (Winter 2006): 157, 162–63, https://www.jstor.org/stable/4495548; Sha Yang, Livia Markoczy, and Min Qi, "Unrealistic Optimism in Consumer Credit Card Adoption," *Journal of Economic Psychology* 28, no. 2 (April 2007): 170, https://doi.org/10.1016/j.joep.2006.05.006.

5. "The most striking result of the literature so far is that increasing competition through fostering entry of more firms may not on its own always improve outcomes for consumers. Indeed competition may not help when there are at least some consumers who do not search properly or have difficulties judging

quality and prices. . . . In the presence of such consumers it is no longer clear that firms necessarily have an incentive to compete by offering better deals. Rather, they can focus on exploiting biased consumers who are very likely to purchase from them regardless of price and quality." Steffen Huck, Jidong Zhou, and Charlotte Duke, *Consumer Behavioural Biases in Competition: A Survey* (London, Office of Fair Trading, May 2011), ¶ 6.2, https://ssrn.com /abstract=1944446.

6. George A. Akerlof and Robert J. Shiller, *Phishing for Phools: The Economics of Manipulation and Deception* (Princeton, NJ: Princeton University Press, 2015), xii.

7. Huck et al., "Consumer Behavioural Biases in Competition," ¶¶ 3.31, 3.37, 3.43; Matthew Bennett et al., "What Does Behavioral Economics Mean for Competition Policy?," *Competition Policy International* 6, no. 1 (Spring 2010): 111, 118, https://www.competitionpolicyinternational.com/what-does -behavioral-economics-mean-for-competition-policy/; Eliana Garcés, "The Impact of Behavioral Economics on Consumer and Competition Policies," *Competition Policy International* 6, no. 1 (Spring 2010): 145, 150, https://www .competitionpolicyinternational.com/the-impact-of-behavioral-economics-on -consumer-and-competition-policies/; Max Huffman, "Marrying Neo-Chicago with Behavioral Antitrust," *Antitrust Law Journal* 78, no. 1 (Spring 2012): 105, 134, https://ssrn.com/abstract=2079329 ("consciously parallel behavioral exploitation is the nearly industry-wide policy of unbundling charges for checked bags in airline travel").

8. Anthony Giorgianni, "Earn More on Your Savings Account at an Online Bank," Consumer Reports, February 16, 2018, https://www.consumerreports.org /banking/earn-more-on-savings-account-at-online-bank/ (noting how online banks in 2018, for example, were in an "arms race" to get us to save more).

9. "Use Automatic Savings Programs to Reach Your Financial Goals," Woodforest National Bank, accessed April 15, 2019, https://www.woodforest.com /WoodforestCares/Woodforest-U/Articles/Automatic-Savings-Programs.

10. Hui-Yi Lo and Nigel Harvey, "Shopping without Pain: Compulsive Buying and the Effects of Credit Card Availability in Europe and the Far East," *Journal of Economic Psychology*, 32, no. 1 (2011): 79–92, https://doi.org/10.1016/j.joep .2010.12.002.

11. Gail McGovern and Youngme Moon, "Companies and the Customers Who Hate Them," *Harvard Business Review* 85, no. 6 (June 2007): 78–84, https://hbr .org/2007/06/companies-and-the-customers-who-hate-them.

12. The Credit Card Accountability Responsibility and Disclosure Act of 2009, Pub. L. No. 111–24 123 Stat. 1734 (2009).

13. Ronald J. Mann, "Bankruptcy Reform and the 'Sweat Box' of Credit Card Debt," *University of Illinois Law Review* 2007, no. 1: 375–403, https://ssrn.com /abstract=895408.

14. Interview with Shailesh Mehta, CEO, Providian Financial Corp., "*Frontline: The*

Card Game," November 24, 2009, https://www.pbs.org/wgbh/pages/frontline
/creditcards/interviews/mehta.html.

15. Board of Governors of the Federal Reserve System, *Report to the Congress on the Profitability of Credit Card Operations of Depository Institutions* (June 2017) (Table 2), https://www.federalreserve.gov/publications/2017-report-to-congress -profitability-credit-card-operations-depository-institutions.htm ("Although profitability for the large credit card banks has risen and fallen over the years, credit card earnings have almost always been higher than returns on all commercial bank activities").

16. Consumer Financial Protection Bureau, *Monthly Complaint Report*, June 2017, https://s3.amazonaws.com/files.consumerfinance.gov/f/documents/201705 _cfpb_Monthly_Complaint_Report.pdf; Consumer Financial Protection Bureau, *Consumer Response Annual Report*, January 1–December 30, 2017, 25, https://www.consumerfinance.gov/data-research/research-reports/2017 -consumer-response-annual-report/.

17. Consumer Financial Protection Bureau, *Monthly Complaint Report*.

18. Competition and Markets Authority, *Retail Banking Market Investigation: Final Report* (London: August 9, 2016), ¶ 54, https://assets.publishing.service.gov.uk /media/57ac9667e5274a0f6c00007a/retail-banking-market-investigation-full -final-report.pdf.

19. Federal Trade Commission, Warning Letters on Hotel Pricing and Resort Fee Disclosures, April 11, 2013–June 3, 2013, https://www.ftc.gov/system/files /attachments/frequently-requested-records/2016-01006_warning_letters_49 _pgs.pdf.

20. Australian Competition & Consumer Commission, "Drip Pricing," accessed April 15, 2019, https://www.accc.gov.au/consumers/online-shopping/drip-pricing.

21. Splitty Travel, "Booking Info: Circus Circus Hotel, Casino & Theme Park," accessed April 15, 2019, https://www.splittytravel.com/checkout/cbe9c8bc -a2c2–42f4-aa2c-9146dd88f8f.

22. Amelia Fletcher, "Drip Pricing: UK Experience" conference presentation at The Economics of Drip Pricing, Federal Trade Commission Washington, D.C., May 21, 2012, https://www.ftc.gov/sites/default/files/documents/public_events /economics-drip-pricing/afletcher.pdf. 75 percent objected to the use of drip pricing—increasing further for products bought infrequently; 70 percent thought all compulsory charges should be in the headline price; 39 percent thought the cost of extras was much higher than expected; 44 percent would have bought elsewhere if they'd known the total price upfront; 74 percent thought the headline price was unclear on what was included; and 51 percent believed they could have gotten the product cheaper elsewhere.

23. Liz Benston, "Harrah's Sees $$ in Resort-Fee Anger," *Las Vegas Sun*, August 12, 2010, https://lasvegassun.com/news/2010/aug/12/harrahs-sees -resort-fee-anger/.

24. Anthony J. Cordato, "There'll Be No More Drip Pricing by Airbnb and

eDreams in Australia," Lexology, November 2, 2015, https://www.lexology.com
/r.ashx?l=8CEB4ZL.

25. See Lucy Cormack, "Jetstar and Virgin Handed Penalties for 'Drip Pricing'
Techniques," *Sydney Morning Herald*, March 7, 2017, http://www.smh.com.au
/business/consumer-affairs/jetstar-and-virgin-handed-penalties-for-drip-pricing
-techniques-20170306-gurqjs.html; Alex Altman and Kate Pickert, "New Airline
Surcharge: A Bag Too Far?," *Time*, May 22, 2008, http://www.time.com/time
/business/article/0,8599,1808804,00.html; Jad Mouawad and Claire Cain
Miller, "Search for Low Airfares Gets More Competitive," *New York Times*,
February 10, 2011, http://www.nytimes.com/2011/02/11/business/11air.html.

26. In re Dollar Rent-A-Car Systems., Inc., 116 FTC 255 (1993) (requiring Dollar
to disclose to consumers in its ads the existence of any mandatory fuel charges,
airport surcharges, or other charges not reasonably avoidable by consumers); In
re Dollar Rent-A-Car Systems., Inc., 116 FTC 245 (1993) (same); In re Dollar
Rent-A-Car Systems., Inc., 111 FTC 694 (1989) (requiring national car rental
company to disclose charges that are mandatory or are not reasonably avoidable
to every consumer that enquires about prices); In re Alamo Rent-A-Car, Inc.,
111 FTC 644 (1989) (settling charges that its operators failed to disclose to
consumers the existence and amount of airport surcharges and mandatory fuel
charges when consumers inquire about possible rental of Alamo's vehicles).

27. Bennett et al., "What Does Behavioral Economics Mean," 117.

28. Mary W. Sullivan, *Economic Issues: Economic Analysis of Hotel Resort Fees*
(Federal Trade Commission: January 2017), https://www.ftc.gov/system/files
/documents/reports/economic-analysis-hotel-resort-fees/p115503_hotel_resort
_fees_economic_issues_paper.pdf ("Consumers with rational expectations
would recognize when firms are likely to charge undisclosed additional fees, and
would refuse to purchase the product unless the firms offered sufficiently large
discounts to the advertised component of the price").

29. Ariely, *Predictably Irrational*, 26–29; see also Daniel Kahneman, *Thinking, Fast
and Slow* (New York: Farrar, Straus and Giroux, 2011), 119–28 (discussing
anchoring effects generally).

30. Birte Englich, Thomas Mussweiler, and Fritz Strack, "Playing Dice with
Criminal Sentences: The Influence of Irrelevant Anchors on Experts' Judicial
Decision Making," *Personality and Social Psychology Bulletin*, 32, no. 2
(February 2006): 188–200, https://doi.org/10.1177/0146167205282152.

31. Kahneman, *Thinking, Fast and Slow*, 124.

32. Fletcher, "Drip Pricing."

33. Fletcher, "Drip Pricing."

34. Fletcher, "Drip Pricing" (where "consumers have a desire to be consistent with
their previous actions so once they've started the process they are less likely to
walk away").

35. Sullivan, *Economic Issues*.

36. Office of Fair Trading (UK), *The Impact of Price Frames on Consumer Decision Making* (London: May 2010), https://londoneconomics.co.uk/blog/publication /the-impact-of-price-frames-on-consumer-decision-making-2/.

37. Sullivan, *Economic Issues*; A Conference on the Economics of Drip Pricing, Federal Trade Commission, May 21, 2012, https://www.ftc.gov/sites/default /files/documents/public_events/economics-drip-pricing/transcript.pdf ("when you divide a price up into two or more partitions, consumers tend to systematically underestimate the total price").

38. Remarks of Mary W. Sullivan, A Conference on the Economics of Drip Pricing Federal Trade Commission, Washington, D.C., May 21, 2012, https://www .ftc.gov/system/files/documents/reports/economic-analysis-hotel-resort-fees /p115503_hotel_resort_fees_economic_issues_paper.pdf, 120.

39. Harikesh S. Nair et al., "Big Data and Marketing Analytics in Gaming: Combining Empirical Models and Field Experimentation," Faculty Working Paper No. 3088, Stanford University Graduate School of Business, Palo Alto, CA, February 22, 2017, https://www.gsb.stanford.edu/faculty-research/working -papers/big-data-marketing-analytics-gaming-combining-empirical-models- field.

40. Howard A. Shelanski et al., "Economics at the FTC: Drug and Pbm Mergers and Drip Pricing," *Review of Industrial Organization* 41, no. 4 (2012): 303–319, https://doi.org/10.1007/s11151-012-9360-x (discussing Laibson's testimony); see also Xavier Gabaix and David Laibson, "Shrouded Attributes, Consumer Myopia, and Information Suppression in Competitive Markets," *Quarterly Journal of Economics* 121, no. 2 (2006): 505, 506, http://nrs.harvard.edu/urn -3:HUL.InstRepos:4554333.

41. Sullivan, *Economic Issues*.

42. Federal Trade Commission Warning Letters.

43. Bjorn Hanson, "U.S. Lodging Industry Fees and Surcharges Continue Upward Trend in 2011 to New Record—$1.8 Billion," NYU School of Professional Studies: Trend Analysis Report, September 20, 2011, http://lb1.scps.nyu.edu /content/scps/about/newsroom/news/2011/u_s_lodging_industry.html.

44. "Showgirls Take to Las Vegas Boulevard for Rally," *Las Vegas Blog*, July 21, 2011, http://blog.caesars.com/las-vegas/las-vegas-hotels/ballys-las-vegas/showgirls -take-to-las-vegas-boulevard-for-rally/.

45. Ron Sylvester, "Caesars to Start Charging Resort Fees, Says Guests Demanding Them," *Las Vegas Sun*, February 21, 2013, https://lasvegassun.com/news/2013 /feb/21/caesars-hotels-will-start-charging-resort-fees/.

46. Benston, "Harrah's Sees $$."

47. Sylvester, "Caesars to Start Charging Resort Fees."

48. Hanson, "U.S. Lodging Industry Fees and Surcharges."

49. Hanson, "U.S. Lodging Industry Fees and Surcharges."

50. Caesars Entertainment Corporation Annual Report (Form 10-K), filed

February 29, 2016, for the period ending December 31, 2015, https://investor
.caesars.com/node/19266/html.

51. Caesars Entertainment Corporation Annual Report (Form 10-K), filed
February 15, 2017, for the period ending December 31, 2016, https://investor
.caesars.com/node/20031/html.

52. Sullivan, *Economic Issues.*

53. Sullivan, *Economic Issues* ("firms cannot quit using drip pricing when other firms
use drip pricing or their prices would look higher than their competitors' prices
and consumers would not buy their product").

54. Nair et al., "Big Data and Marketing Analytics."

55. Nair et al., "Big Data and Marketing Analytics," 9 n. 4.

56. Nair et al., "Big Data and Marketing Analytics," 9 n. 4.

57. Moreover, the model metrics were "both history-dependent (retrospective)
and forward-looking (prospective)." One example is the customer who visited
the casino once, but spent little. If considering solely this past purchase,
the computer might deem the customer "low value." To avoid this error,
the computer analyzed not only the historical first-visit information on the
consumer but also "the observed long-run spending of other similar consumers."
Even if the customer spent little on the first visit, the model, using data from
other similar gamblers, estimated if she, like these other consumers, would likely
spend a lot in future visits.

Chapter 4: Fourth Overdose: Choice Overload

1. *Borat: Cultural Learnings of America for Make Benefit Glorious Nation of
Kazakhstan,* directed by Larry Charles (20th Century Fox, 2006).

2. Cheese.com, accessed April 16, 2019, https://cheese.com/.

3. Douglas Zucker and Hervé Remaud, "Does Choice Overload Exist in Wine
Retail?," Academy of Wine Business Research, 8th International Conference,
Geisenheim, Germany: June 2014, http://academyofwinebusiness.com/wp
-content/uploads/2014/07/RET02_Remaud_Herve.pdf.

4. John Stuart Mill, *On Liberty,* 109 (1859), https://www.gutenberg.org/ebooks
/34901.

5. Stuart Mill, *On Liberty,* 23 ("The only freedom which deserves the name, is
that of pursuing our own good in our own way, so long as we do not attempt
to deprive others of theirs, or impede their efforts to obtain it."); Ellen Peters
et al., "More Is Not Always Better: Intuitions about Public Policy Can Lead
to Unintended Health Consequences," *Social Issues and Policy Review* 7, no. 1
(January 2013): 116, 133, http://dx.doi.org/10.1111/j.1751-2409.2012.01045.x;
Arne Roets, Barry Schwartz, and Yanjun Guan, "The Tyranny of Choice: A
Cross-Cultural Investigation of Maximizing-Satisficing Effects on Well-Being,"
Judgment and Decision Making 7, no. 6 (November 2012): 689, http://journal
.sjdm.org/12/12815/jdm12815.html.

6. Note, for instance, consumers willing to pay more for the increasing number of fair trade products. M. Todd Henderson and Anup Malani, "Corporate Philanthropy and the Market for Altruism," *Columbia Law Review* 109, no. 4 (May 2009): 571, 617, https://ssrn.com/abstract=1116797 or http://dx.doi.org /10.2139/ssrn.1116797.

7. Steve French and Gwynne Rogers, "Understanding the Lohas Consumer: The Rise of Ethical Consumerism," accessed April 16, 2019, http://www.fusbp.com /wp-content/uploads/2010/10/UNDERSTANDING-THE-LOHAS -CONSUMER.pdf; see also FTC v. Whole Foods Market, Inc., 548 F.3d 1028, 1039 (D.C. Cir. 2008) (FTC's evidence delineating a submarket "catering to a core group of customers who 'have decided that natural and organic is important, lifestyle of health and ecological sustainability is important'").

8. Neil D. Hamilton, "America's New Agrarians: Policy Opportunities and Legal Innovations to Support New Farmers," *Fordham Environmental Law Review* 22, no. 3 (Fall 2011): 523, 526, https://ssrn.com/abstract=2025197.

9. Maurice E. Stucke, "Looking at the Monopsony in the Mirror," *Emory Law Journal* 62, no. 6 (2013) (collecting studies), https://ssrn.com/abstract=2094553.

10. Simona Botti and Sheena S. Iyengar, "The Dark Side of Choice: When Choice Impairs Social Welfare," *Journal of Public Policy & Marketing* 25, no. 1 (April 2006): 24, 25, https://doi.org/10.1509/jppm.25.1.24; (noting how having choices "enhances perceptions of self-determination and intrinsic motivation, which in turn have been associated with desirable consequences, such as greater satisfaction with the task and the decision outcome and more positive affect"; "choice causes decision makers to bolster subjective evaluations of decision outcomes, resulting in greater consistency between attitudes and behaviors and increased psychological well-being"); Richard M. Ryan and Edward L. Deci, "On Happiness and Human Potentials: A Review of Research on Hedonic and Eudaimonic Well-Being," *Annual Review of Psychology* 52, no. 1 (February 2001): 141–66, https://doi.org/10.1146/annurev.psych.52.1.141; Peters et al., "More Is Not Always Better," 26, 33.

11. "Best Shampoos Products Reviewed & Rated," GoodGuide, accessed April 16, 2019, http://www.goodguide.com/categories/152758-shampoo##btr.

12. Sheena S. Iyengar and Mark R. Lepper, "When Choice Is Demotivating: Can One Desire Too Much of a Good Thing?," *Journal of Personality and Social Psychology* 79, no. 6 (December 2000): 995–1006, http://dx.doi.org /10.1037/0022-3514.79.6.995.

13. Kahneman, *Thinking, Fast and Slow*, 39–49; Peters et al., "More Is Not Always Better," 117–18.

14. Barry Schwartz, *The Paradox of Choice: Why More Is Less* (New York: Ecco, 2004), 128.

15. Roets et al., "The Tyranny of Choice," 689; Iyengar and Lepper, "When Choice Is Demotivating"; Peters et al., "More Is Not Always Better"; Gerri Spassova and Alice M. Isen, "Positive Affect Moderates the Impact of Assortment Size

on Choice Satisfaction," *Journal of Retailing* 89, no. 4 (2013): 398, https://doi.org/10.1016/j.jretai.2013.05.003; Marianne Bertrand et al., "What's Advertising Content Worth? Evidence from a Consumer Credit Marketing Field Experiment," *Quarterly Journal of Economics* 125, no. 1 (February 2010): 263, 268, https://doi.org/10.1162/qjec.2010.125.1.263; Botti and Iyengar, "The Dark Side of Choice," 28.

16. Spassova and Isen, "Positive Affect Moderates," 398; Bertrand et al., "What's Advertising Content Worth?," 268; Botti and Iyengar, "The Dark Side of Choice," 28; Chris M. Wilson and Catherine Waddams Price, "Do Consumers Switch to the Best Supplier?," *Oxford Economic Papers* 62, no. 4 (2010): 98–131, https://doi.org/10.1093/oep/gpq006 ("A fascinating study examining the relationship between the number of funds from which employees could choose and their actual choice showed a clear tendency to avoid choosing altogether (and thus implicitly choose none) as the number of alternatives increased").

17. Spassova and Isen, "Positive Affect Moderates," 397, 398; Bertrand et al., "What's Advertising Content Worth?," 268. See also Lisbet Berg and Åse Gornitzka, "The Consumer Attention Deficit Syndrome: Consumer Choices in Complex Markets," *Acta Sociologica* 55, no. 2 (2012): 159, 171–72, https://doi.org/10.1177/0001699312440711.

18. Botti and Iyengar, "The Dark Side of Choice," 30. A study of the Swedish premium pension system also revealed how overabundance of choice possibilities led to adverse consumption decisions in the available choice architecture. Sławomir Czech, "Choice Overload Paradox and Public Policy Design. The Case of Swedish Pension System," *Equilibrium* 11, no. 3 (September 2016): 559, https://www.researchgate.net/publication/313037400_Choice_Overload_Paradox_and_Public_Policy_Design_The_Case_of_Swedish_Pension_System.

19. Peters et al., "More Is Not Always Better," 118; Rebecca J. Hafner, Mathew P. White, and Simon J. Handley, "Spoilt for Choice: The Role of Counterfactual Thinking in the Excess Choice and Reversibility Paradoxes," *Journal of Experimental Social Psychology* 48, no. 1 (January 2012): 28, 34–35, https://doi.org/10.1016/j.jesp.2011.06.022.

20. Roets et al., "The Tyranny of Choice," 689.

21. Arun Sharma and Shreekumar K. Nair, "Switching Behaviour as a Function of Number of Options: How Much Is Too Much for Consumer Choice Decisions?," *Journal of Consumer Behaviour* 16, no. 6 (November 2017): e153–e160 (collecting studies), https://doi.org/10.1002/cb.1670.

22. Jeong-Yeol Park and SooCheong (Shawn) Jang, "Confused by Too Many Choices? Choice Overload in Tourism," *Tourism Management* 35 (April 2013): 1–12, https://doi.org/10.1016/j.tourman.2012.05.004; Nguyen T. Thai and Ulku Yuksel, "Choice Overload in Holiday Destination Choices," *International Journal of Culture, Tourism and Hospitality Research* 11, no. 1 (March 2017): 53–66, https://doi.org/10.1108/IJCTHR-09-2015-0117.

23. Benjamin Scheibehenne, Rainer Greifeneder, and Peter M. Todd, "Can There

Ever Be Too Many Options? A Meta-Analytic Review of Choice Overload," *Journal of Consumer Research* 37, no. 3 (October 2010): 409, 412, https://doi .org/10.1086/651235.

24. Scheibehenne et al., "Can There Ever Be Too Many Options?," 416, 421. In examining the data, the authors "could not reliably identify sufficient conditions that explain when and why an increase in assortment size will decrease satisfaction, preference strength, or the motivation to choose." The authors identified twenty-four experiments with different degrees of choice overload and thirty-one experiments where to different degrees more-was-better, and the overall mean effect size across studies was virtually zero. See also Spassova and Isen, "Positive Affect Moderates," 398; Andrea Morales et al., "Perceptions of Assortment Variety: The Effects of Congruency between Consumers' Internal and Retailers' External Organization," *Journal of Retailing* 81, no. 2 (2005): 159, https://doi.org/10.1016/j.jretai.2005.03.007. One response is that some experiments are designed to identify choice overload and then test factors that may mitigate it. Consequently, counting the number of experiments and combining their results is not informative. Alexander Chernev, Ulf Böckenholt, and Joseph Goodman, "Commentary on Scheibehenne, Greifeneder, and Todd, Choice Overload: Is There Anything to It?," *Journal of Consumer Research* 37, no. 3 (October 2010): 426, 427, https://doi.org/10.1086/655200.

25. Sachin Waikar, "When Are Consumers Most Likely to Feel Overwhelmed by Their Options?," KelloggInsight, October 3, 2017, https://insight.kellogg .northwestern.edu/article/what-predicts-consumer-choice-overload.

26. Ian Clarke, Malcolm Kirkup, and Harmen Oppewal, "Consumer Satisfaction with Local Retail Diversity in the UK: Effects of Supermarket Access, Brand Variety, and Social Deprivation," *Environment & Planning A* 44, no. 8 (2012): 1896, 1897, 1899, https://doi.org/10.1068/a44310 (finding that a supermarket's product assortment "positively relates to consumers' perceptions of the value of the store as a whole" and store satisfaction).

27. Claudia Townsend and Barbara E. Kahn, "The 'Visual Preference Heuristic': The Influence of Visual versus Verbal Depiction on Assortment Processing, Perceived Variety, and Choice Overload," *Journal of Consumer Research* 40, no. 5 (February 2014): 993, https://doi.org/10.1086/673521.

28. Spassova and Isen, "Positive Affect Moderates," 397 (noting that "managers often find that the better part of their sales is accounted for only a small fraction of the offerings in their portfolio," but many firms pursue a strategy of product proliferation to satisfy a wide range of consumer tastes, deter entry, be perceived as being higher quality, and keep customers from switching to competitors).

29. They would exercise market power in significantly changing the mix of variety that would otherwise arise from competition. Accordingly, if one key policy objective "is to ensure that the freedom of choice of consumers of goods and services is not restricted by conduct that is anticompetitive," then the retailers would be liable under the Sherman Act. Blue Cross of Washington & Alaska

v. Kitsap Physicians Service, C81–918V, 1981 WL 2198 (W.D. Wash. Oct. 28, 1981).

30. Aaron Cheris, Darrell Rigby, and Suzanne Tager, "Dreaming of an Amazon Christmas?," Bain & Company, November 9, 2017, https://www.bain.com /insights/retail-holiday-newsletter-2017-issue-2.

31. Scheibehenne et al., "Can There Ever Be Too Many Options?"

32. Swirl Networks, "New Study Reveals That Traditional Retailers Are Failing to Meet Consumer Desires for 'Amazon-Like' Personalization," news release, December 10, 2015, https://www.prnewswire.com/news-releases/new-study -reveals-that-traditional-retailers-are-failing-to-meet-consumer-desires-for -amazon-like-personalization-300191107.html.

33. Julia Angwin and Surya Mattu, "Amazon Says It Puts Customers First. But Its Pricing Algorithm Doesn't," ProPublica, September 20, 2016, https://www .propublica.org/article/amazon-says-it-puts-customers-first-but-its-pricing -algorithm-doesnt.

34. Julie Creswell, "How Amazon Steers Shoppers to Its Own Products," *New York Times*, June 23, 2018, https://nyti.ms/2KcIF2C.

35. Cheris et al., "Dreaming of an Amazon Christmas?" (finding that Alexa "recommends the private-label products 17% of the time. Given that these products represent only about 2% of total first-party unit volume sold, the online retailer clearly positions its own private labels favorably in voice shopping").

36. Cheris et al., "Dreaming of an Amazon Christmas?"

37. "What is Amazon Vine?," Amazon, accessed April 17, 2019, https://www .amazon.com/gp/vine/help.

38. Creswell, "How Amazon Steers."

39. See, e.g., Xavier Gabaix and David Laibson, "Shrouded Attributes, Consumer Myopia, and Information Suppression in Competitive Markets," *Quarterly Journal of Economics* 121, no. 2 (2006): 505–540, https://doi.org/10.1162/ qjec.2006.121.2.505; Bar-Gill and Warren, "Making Credit Safer," 27–28; Simon Johnson and James Kwak, *13 Bankers: The Wall Street Takeover and the Next Financial Meltdown* (New York: Pantheon Books, 2010), 81, 108.

40. Adi Ayal, "Harmful Freedom of Choice: Lessons from the Cellphone Market," *Law and Contemporary Problems* 74, no. 2 (Spring 2011): 91, 94, 118, https:// scholarship.law.duke.edu/lcp/vol74/iss2/6 ("Contractual complexity thus acts to raise switching costs, which allows for raising prices to existing customers while hiding the existence of discrimination among customers paying different prices for similar consumption").

41. See Eugenio J. Miravete, "The Doubtful Profitability of Foggy Pricing," NET Institute Working Paper No. 04–07, October 2004, 2–3, https://ssrn.com /abstract=618465.

42. Peters et al., "More Is Not Always Better," 122:

Too much and too complex information have made it difficult for all but the most technologically savvy to choose the product best suited to their needs. Customers unable to choose based on attribute preferences appeared to make their choices based on price, only to later find out that the product did not meet their needs. This tendency is further complicated by a lack of comprehension. When provided with multiple options, consumers are only able to choose the least expensive about 65 percent of the time. When faced with the complex options of base service fees, additional features, and cost for usage overages, customers tend to choose plans that greatly exceed their requirements, significantly overpaying each month rather than risking the chance of occasional overage costs. Problems navigating the telecommunications industry are not limited to older adults, although they may be particularly vulnerable.

43. We don't address here how (a) one company, IAC, owns not just all these sites but also HomeAdvisor, Angie's List, Vimeo, Dotdash, Dictionary.com, the Daily Beast, and Investopedia; and (b) the chairman of IAC, Barry Diller, also controls the Expedia group, which includes Expedia.com, Hotels.com, Hotwire .com, CarRentals.com, Trivago, Venere.com, Travelocity, Orbitz, CheapTickets, and HomeAway. IAC/InterActiveCorp Annual Report (Form 10-K), filed March 1, 2018, for the period ending December 31, 2017, https://ir.iac.com /node/22596/html. Expedia and IAC/InterActiveCorp are related parties since they are under common control, given that Diller serves as chairman and senior executive of both Expedia and IAC. Expedia, Inc. Annual Report (Form 10-K), filed February 9, 2018, for the period ending December 31, 2017, http:// ir.expediagroup.com/static-files/efeebda9–9df8–4535-a7c9–6542d37ccb65. While unsettling from a privacy and antitrust perspective, that is for another book.

44. "What Makes OkCupid Different?," OkCupid, April 7, 2019, https://help .okcupid.com/article/94-what-makes-okcupid-different.

45. "Single Has Spoken," Tinder, October 8, 2018, https://blog.gotinder.com /single-has-spoken/.

46. "About Match.com," accessed April 17, 2019, https://www.match.com/help /aboutus.aspx?lid=4.

47. "About Match.com."

48. "Success Stories," POF, accessed April 17, 2019, https://www.pof.com/success _v2.aspx.

49. IAC, "IAC Q1 2018 Shareholder Letter," May 9, 2018, https://ir.iac.com/static -files/165fea50-d0d2-4715-906c-265f782f29c2.

50. IAC Annual Report, 13.

51. "Meet Markets: How the Internet Has Changed Dating," Economist, August 18, 2018, https://www.economist.com/briefing/2018/08/18/how-the-internet-has -changed-dating.

52. By 2015, 15 percent of surveyed Americans used an online dating site or mobile dating app. Monica Anderson, "The Never-Been-Married Are Biggest Users of Online Dating," Pew Research Center, February 18, 2016, http://pewrsr.ch

/1QmScp6. For surveyed adults who never married, the percentage is double (30 percent).

53. In 2016, 27 percent of these young adults reported using an online dating app, up from 10 percent in early 2013. Aaron Smith, "15% of American Adults Have Used Online Dating Sites or Mobile Dating Apps," Pew Research Center, February 11, 2016, https://www.pewinternet.org/2016/02/11/15-percent-of -american-adults-have-used-online-dating-sites-or-mobile-dating-apps/.

54. IAC, Q1 2018 Earnings: Supplemental Financial Information and Operating Metrics, https://ir.iac.com/static-files/be7c6de2-e3be-4afd-a962-e0c869749d67.

55. Best Hookup Apps, accessed April 17, 2019, https://www.besthookupapps.net/.

56. Eli J. Finkel et al., "Online Dating: A Critical Analysis from the Perspective of Psychological Science," *Psychological Science in the Public Interest* 13, no. 1 (January 2012): 1–64, https://doi.org/10.1177/1529100612436522.

57. Finkel et al., "Online Dating."

58. Finkel et al., "Online Dating."

59. Jonathan D. D'Angelo and Catalina L. Toma, "There Are Plenty of Fish in the Sea: The Effects of Choice Overload and Reversibility on Online Daters' Satisfaction with Selected Partners," *Media Psychology* 20, no. 1 (January 2017): 1–27, https://doi.org/10.1080/15213269.2015.1121827.

60. Smith, "15% of American Adults."

61. Evan Marc Katz, "Bounce Back from Rejection," Match, accessed April 17, 2019, https://www.match.com/magazine/article/9069/Bounce-Back-From-Rejection/.

62. Kari Paul, "Tired of Swiping Right, Some Singles Try Slow Dating," *Wall Street Journal*, August 28, 2018, https://www.wsj.com/articles/tired-of-swiping-right -some-singles-try-slow-dating-1535468479.

63. Paul, "Tired of Swiping Right" (quoting Moira Weigel).

64. Kaitlyn Tiffany, "Why Are We Still Debating Whether Dating Apps Work?," The Verge, February 15, 2018, https://www.theverge.com/2018/2/15/17017096 /dating-app-debate-tinder-okcupid-match-science-stats.

65. Gian Gonzaga, the then eharmony relationship psychologist, was quoted in Dan Slater, "A Million First Dates," *Atlantic Monthly*, January/February 2003, https://www.theatlantic.com/magazine/archive/2013/01/a-million-first -dates/309195/.

66. Wendy Wang and Kim Parker, "Record Share of Americans Have Never Married: What Never-Married Adults Are Looking for in a (Potential) Spouse," Pew Research Center, September 24, 2014, http://pewrsr.ch/1wKHjzo.

67. Wang and Parker, "Record Share." Of those not married, fewer in 2014 said they would like to marry, compared to those asked just four years earlier. About half of all never-married adults—53 percent—said in 2014 they would like to marry eventually, down from 61 percent in 2010.

68. According to one study, the surveyed couples who met online (which includes social networks and dating platforms) and were married between 2005 and 2012 had a slightly higher rate of marital satisfaction and slightly lower rate of

marital breakup than the surveyed couples who met off-line. John T. Cacioppo et al., "Marital Satisfaction and Break-Ups Differ across On-Line and Off-Line Meeting Venues," *Proceedings of the National Academy of Sciences (PNAS)* 110, no. 25 (May 1, 2013), https://www.pnas.org/content/110/25/10135.

69. Aaron Smith and Maeve Duggan, "Online Dating and Relationships," Pew Research Center, October 21, 2013, http://pewrsr.ch/1m8eRG2.

70. Paul, "Tired of Swiping Right."

71. IAC Annual Report.

72. IAC Annual Report.

73. IAC Annual Report.

74. Shana Lebowitz, "The Latest Relationship Trend Is 'Slow Dating'—and It's a Recoil from Years of Swiping through Apps," Business Insider, March 22, 2018, https://www.businessinsider.com/dating-apps-fewer-matches-2018-3.

75. Casey Cavanaugh, "The Biggest Turnoffs for Women on Tinder," Ranker, https://www.ranker.com/list/tinder-turnoffs-for-women/casey-cavanagh.

Chapter 5: The Ideologues: The Defenders of Competition Ideology

1. United States ex rel. United States Coast Guard v. Cerio, 831 F. Supp. 530, 534 (E.D. Va. 1993).

2. See Stucke, "Is Competition Always Good?," 162–97 (collecting some of the studies).

3. A. C. Pigou, *The Economics of Welfare*, 4th ed. (New York: St. Martin's Press, 1962), 192; John Black, *A Dictionary of Economics* (Oxford: Oxford University Press, 1997), 168 (the "cost or benefit arising from any activity which does not accrue to the person or organization carrying on the activity").

4. Carl Shapiro, "Competition Policy in Distressed Industries," presentation at ABA Antitrust Symposium: Competition as Public Policy, Jackson Hole, WY, May 13, 2009, http://www.justice.gov/atr/public/speeches/245857.htm ("In terms of the classic categories of market failure from the Fundamental Theorem of Welfare Economics, most regulations—including environmental regulations, health and safety regulations, and consumer protection regulations—primarily address problems of externalities, public goods, and imperfect information. Competition policy primarily addresses the problem of market power").

5. Joseph M. Alioto, "Antitrust on the Rebound," *Santa Clara Law Review* 39, no. 3 (1999): 809, https://digitalcommons.law.scu.edu/lawreview/vol39/iss3/5.

6. Standard Oil Co. v. Federal Trade Commission, 340 U.S. 231, 248 (1951); see also City of Columbia v. Omni Outdoor Advertising, Inc., 499 U.S. 365, 388 n. 3 (1991); National Society of Professional Engineers v. United States, 435 U.S. 679, 695 (1978); Exxon Corp. v. Governor of Maryland, 437 U.S. 117, 133 n. 24 (1978); Robertson v. Sea Pines Real Estate Companies, Inc., 679 F.3d 278, 286 (4th Cir. 2012); United States v. Brown University, 5 F.3d 658, 673 (3d Cir. 1993); Smith v. Pro Football, Inc., 593 F.2d 1173, 1194 (D.C. Cir. 1978);

United States v. Realty Multi-List, Inc., 629 F.2d 1351, 1364 (5th Cir. 1980); Anheuser-Busch, Inc. v. Federal Trade Commission, 289 F.2d 835, 840 (7th Cir. 1961).

7. National Society of Professional Engineers, 435 U.S. at 695.

8. National Society of Professional Engineers.

9. 137 Cong. Rec. E979–02 (March 19, 1991) (remarks of Vice President Dan Quayle, quoting President George H. W. Bush).

10. United States v. Philadelphia National Bank, 374 U.S. 321, 363 (1963).

11. C. Dawn Causey, "The Future of Nonbank Depository Financial Institutions," *North Carolina Banking Institute* 3 (1999): 1, 6, https://scholarship.law.unc.edu /ncbi/vol3/iss1/4.

12. Speech by Robert Kramer, US Department of Justice, before the Antitrust Section of the American Bar Association, "'Mega-Mergers' in the Banking Industry," Washington D.C., April 14, 1999, https://www.justice.gov/atr/public /speeches/214845.pdf.

13. Federal Reserve Board, Travelers Group Inc., and Citicorp, "Order Approving Formation of a Bank Holding Company and Notice to Engage in Nonbanking Activities," *Federal Reserve Bulletin* 84, no. 9 (September 23, 1998): 985, https:// www.federalreserve.gov/boarddocs/press/BHC/1998/19980923/19980923.pdf.

14. Financial Crisis Inquiry Commission, *The Financial Crisis Inquiry Report: Final Report of the National Commission on the Causes of the Financial and Economic Crisis in the United States* (US Government Printing Office, 2011): 210, https://www.govinfo.gov/app/details/GPO-FCIC.

15. Lionel Barber, "Can Banking Clean Up Its Act?" (speech, Cambridge University, Cambridge, England, May 1, 2014), *Vital Speeches of the Day*, 80, no. 7: 243–246.

16. Sheila Bair, *Bull by the Horns: Fighting to Save Main Street from Wall Street and Wall Street from Itself* (New York: Free Press, 2012); Associated Press, "Greenspan Admits 'Mistake' That Helped Crisis," NBC News, October 23, 2008, http://www.nbcnews.com/id/27335454/ns/business-stocks_and _economy/t/greenspan-admits-mistake-helped-crisis/.

17. Paul Krugman, "Hiding behind the Invisible Hand," *The Conscience of a Liberal* (blog), *New York Times*, March 22, 2008, https://krugman.blogs.nytimes.com /2008/03/22/hiding-behind-the-invisible-hand/.

18. Paul Krugman, "Blindly into the Bubble," *New York Times,* December 21, 2007, https://nyti.ms/2N4F1sv.

19. *Financial Crisis Inquiry Report*, xvii.

20. Associated Press, "Greenspan Admits 'Mistake.'"

21. Administration of Barack Obama, Weekly Address: Ensuring Our Free Market Works for Everyone, 2016 Daily Comp. Presidential Documents 1 (April 16, 2016), https://obamawhitehouse.archives.gov/the-press-office/2016/04/16 /weekly-address-ensuring-our-free-market-works-everyone.

22. President George W. Bush, Remarks to the National Cattlemen's Beef

Association, March 28, 2007, Public Papers of the Presidents of the United States: George W. Bush (2007, Book I): 347–56, https://www.govinfo.gov/app /details/PPP-2007-book1/PPP-2007-book1-doc-pg347–2.

23. Associated Press, "Keeping Up with the Clemsons: ACC Schools under Construction," *USA Today*, October 3, 2018, https://www.usatoday.com/story /sports/ncaaf/2018/10/03/keeping-up-with-the-clemsons-acc-schools-under -construction/38031877/.

24. Knight Foundation Commission on Intercollegiate Athletics, *A Call to Action— Reconnecting College Sports and Higher Education*, June 2001, 26, https://www .knightcommission.org/wp-content/uploads/2008/10/2001_knight_report.pdf.

25. Knight Foundation Commission, *A Call to Action*, 24.

26. Law v. NCAA, 134 F.3d 1010, 1012–15 (10th Cir. 1998).

27. Law v. NCAA. A volunteer coach could not receive any compensation from the university's athletic department. A graduate assistant coach had to be enrolled in a graduate studies program and could only receive compensation equal to the value of the cost of the educational experience (Grant-in-Aid) depending on the coach's residential status (i.e., a nonresident graduate assistant coach could receive greater compensation to reflect the higher cost of out-of-state tuition than could an in-state student). The NCAA limited compensation to part-time assistants to the value of full Grant-in-Aid compensation based on the value of out-of-state graduate studies.

28. Universities employed "these part-time coaches in lucrative summer jobs at profitable sports camps run by the school or by hiring them for part-time jobs in the physical education department in addition to the coaching position. Further, many of these positions were filled with seasoned and experienced coaches, not the type of student assistant envisioned by the rule." Law v. NCAA, 134 F.3d at 1012–15.

29. Law v. NCAA, 134 F.3d at 1013.

30. Law v. NCAA, 134 F.3d at 1023 (quoting National Society of Professional Engineers, 435 U.S. at 695). The Tenth Circuit also stated that the NCAA rule did not equalize the overall amount of money Division I schools could spend on their basketball programs. Thus, there was "no reason to think that the money saved by a school on the salary of a restricted-earnings coach will not be put into another aspect of the school's basketball program, such as equipment or even another coach's salary, thereby increasing inequity in that area." Law v. NCAA, 134 F.3d at 1023.

31. Knight Commission on Intercollegiate Athletics, *Restoring the Balance: Dollars, Values, and the Future of College Sports*, June 2010, 1, https://www.knight commission.org/wp-content/uploads/2017/09/restoring-the-balance-0610 -01.pdf.

32. Knight Commission, *Restoring the Balance*, 3.

33. Knight Commission, *Restoring the Balance*, 18.

34. Average salary calculated from the data contained in *USA Today*, "NCAA

Salaries: NCAAF Coaches," accessed April 22, 2019, https://sports.usatoday .com/ncaa/salaries/.

35. "Average Department Chair (College/University) Salary," PayScale, accessed April 22, 2019, https://www.payscale.com/research/US/Job=Department _Chair_(College_%2f_University)/Salary.

36. The SEC's 2016 revenues were $639 million. That equals, *USA Today* reported, "roughly two-thirds of the $952 million that the NCAA reported on its most recently available tax return, which covered a period ending Aug. 31, 2015." Steve Berkowitz, "Some SEC Schools Received $40M-Plus in 2016 Fiscal Year," *USA Today*, February 2, 2017, https://www.usatoday.com/story/sports/ncaaf/sec /2017/02/02/sec-tax-return-639-million-in-revenues-2016-fiscal-year/97400990/.

37. The NESCAC schools offer twenty-seven conference championship sports (thirteen for men and fourteen for women), which far exceeds the ten-sport minimum that Division III institutions have to sponsor. New England Small College Athletic Conference, "About the NESCAC," July 2018, http://www .nescac.com/about/about; NCAA, "Divisional Differences and the History of Multidivision Classification," accessed April 22, 2019, https://www.ncaa.org /about/who-we-are/membership/divisional-differences-and-history-multidivision -classification. In contrast, the SEC schools offer only between six and nine men's varsity sports and eight to twelve women's varsity sports. Wikipedia, s.v. "Southeastern Conference: Men's Sponsored Sports by School," April 20, 2019, https://en.wikipedia.org/wiki/Southeastern_Conference#Men.27s_sponsored _sports_by_school. A few schools participate in some varsity sports outside of the SEC, like women's rowing.

38. Noel-Levitz Inc., *Why Did They Enroll? The Factors Influencing College Choice* (2012), 5 (33.7 percent of freshmen at private universities and 33.2 percent of freshmen at public universities); Ruffalo Noel Levitz, 2017 National Student Satisfaction and Priorities Report (2017) (33 percent of freshmen at private universities and 29 percent of freshmen at public universities).

39. Knight Commission, *Restoring the Balance*.

40. Only twelve schools' athletic programs in 2015, according to the *USA Today* data, were profitable (that is, not being subsidized). Instead, most of these 178 public universities were spending millions of dollars to subsidize their athletic programs. Erik Brady, Steve Berkowitz, and Jodi Upton, "As Colleges Spend, Warnings Grow; Some See Pattern as Unsustainable," *USA Today*, April 18, 2016, https://www.pressreader.com; see also Eben Novy-Williams, "Football Is Forever: The Money-Losing Drug These Schools Can't Quit," *Chicago Tribune*, January 6, 2017, http://www.chicagotribune.com/sports/college/ct-college -football-is-forever-20170106-story.html.

41. Shaun R. Harper, *Black Male Student-Athletes and Racial Inequities in]NCAA Division I College Sports* (Los Angeles: USC Race and Equity Center, 2018), 3, https://race.usc.edu/wp-content/uploads/2018/03/2018_Sports_Report.pdf.

42. NESCAC, "About the NESCAC."

43. US Department of Education, Equity in Athletics Data Analysis, https://ope
.ed.gov/athletics (2016 Men's and Women's Team Average Annual Institutional
Salary per FTE).

44. University of Alabama at Birmingham announced in 2014 it was eliminating
college football. Its outside consultant estimated that if the university were to
continue to compete at a competitive level within its mid-tier conference, expenses
would likely increase from $30.2 million in 2015 to $38.5 million in 2019, while
revenues would grow by less than $1 million. Even if the university subsidized the
athletic department by approximately $14.5 million annually, "along with modest
Student Fee increases of 3 percent per year," expenses would still significantly
surpass revenues; overall, the university would bear $25.3 million in cumulative
losses over five years. If, however, the university dropped football, with the current
level of institutional investment for the other sports, the athletic department over
that same five-year period would likely have a surplus of approximately $2 million.
But the gap in operating financials was even greater than $27.3 million over
five years. Additionally, to continue to compete in football, UAB would have to
invest an additional $22.2 million in football facilities (football practice field,
multisport indoor practice facility, and a football administration building). That
did not include a new football stadium. All told, UAB, according to its outside
consultants, "would be required to make a minimum additional investment of
approximately $47.5 million, over the next five years to operate a competitive . . .
football program." CarrSports Consulting, *UAB Athletics Strategic Planning:
NCAA Division I Considerations* (November 18, 2014), https://www.scribd.com
/document/248979169/CarrSports-Report-on-UAB-Athletics.

45. Cody Estremera, "UAB Coach Bill Clark Ready for Football's Return,"
Tuscaloosa News, June 12, 2017, http://www.tuscaloosanews.com/news
/20170612/uab-coach-bill-clark-ready-for-footballs-return.

46. Novy-Williams, "Football Is Forever."

47. Joseph Heller, *Catch-22* (New York: Simon & Schuster, 1955), 52.

48. CBS News, "NCAA to Pay Coaches $54.5M," March 9, 1999, https://www
.cbsnews.com/news/ncaa-to-pay-coaches-545m/.

49. Need-Based Educational Aid Act of 2015, Pub. L. 114–44, 129 Stat. 472,
https://www.congress.gov/bill/114th-congress/senate-bill/1482.

50. 163 Cong. Rec. S5776–04, S5777 (daily ed. September 18, 2017) (statement of
Senator Lee).

51. 155 Cong. Rec. S1117–01, S1118 (daily ed. January 30, 2009) (statement of
Senator Hatch).

Chapter 6: The Lobbyists: How to Kudzu the Competition Ideology Like a Pro

1. Bill Finch, "The True Story of Kudzu, the Vine That Never Truly Ate the
South," *Smithsonian*, September 2015, https://www.smithsonianmag.com
/science-nature/true-story-kudzu-vine-ate-south-180956325/.

2. Finch, "The True Story of Kudzu." While often proclaimed as the vine that ate the South, kudzu is in fact relatively less noxious than other invasive plants. Kudzu, for example, "rarely penetrates deeply into a forest; it climbs well only in sunny areas on the forest edge and suffers in shade."

3. The Australian competition authority, in 2014, for example, alleged that the airlines Jetstar and Virgin "each made representations on their websites and mobile sites that certain domestic airfares were available for purchase at specific prices, when in fact those prices were only available if payment was made using particular methods." Australian Competition & Consumer Commission, "ACCC Takes Action against Jetstar and Virgin for Drip Pricing Practices," news release no. MR 156/14, June 19, 2014, http://www.accc.gov.au/media -release/accc-takes-action-against-jetstar-and-virgin-for-drip-pricing-practices; Lucy Cormack, "Jetstar and Virgin Handed Penalties for 'Drip Pricing' Techniques," *Sydney Morning Herald*, March 7, 2017, https://www.smh.com.au /business/consumer-affairs/jetstar-and-virgin-handed-penalties-for-drip-pricing -techniques-20170306-gurqjs.html (Virgin was ultimately fined $200,000 and Jetstar $545,000 for their use of drip pricing); Australian Competition & Consumer Commission, "ACCC Joins International Drip Pricing Sweep," news release no. MR 231/15, November 24, 2015, https://www.accc.gov.au/media -release/accc-joins-international-drip-pricing-sweep.

4. Leslie J. Milton, "More Penalties for Digital 'Drip Pricing,'" *Competition Chronicle*, May 2, 2017, https://www.competitionchronicle.com/2017/05/more -penalties-for-digital-drip-pricing/.

5. "ACM Fines Tour Operator Corendon for Displaying Incorrect Prices," Authority for Consumers and Markets, July 13, 2016, https://www.acm.nl /en/publications/publication/16041/ACM-fines-tour-operator-Corendon-for -displaying-incorrect-prices.

6. Jon Chapple, "Dutch Ticketers Comply with Drip Pricing Ban," IQ Magazine: Live Music Intelligence, October 16, 2017, https://www.iq-mag.net/2017/10 /dutch-ticketers-comply-acm-drip-pricing-ban/.

7. Competition and Markets Authority, "Online Hotel Booking: CMA Launches Consumer Law Investigation into Hotel Booking Sites," October 27, 2017, https://www.gov.uk/cma-cases/online-hotel-booking; Competition and Markets Authority, "Hotel Booking Sites to Make Major Changes after CMA Probe," February 6, 2019, https://www.gov.uk/government/news/hotel-booking-sites-to -make-major-changes-after-cma-probe.

8. "Las Vegas Resort Fees 2018 Guide," Las Vegas Jaunt, March 6, 2018, https:// www.lasvegasjaunt.com/las-vegas-resort-fees-2018-guide/.

9. Federal Trade Commission, "FTC Warns Hotel Operators That Price Quotes That Exclude 'Resort Fees' and Other Mandatory Surcharges May Be Deceptive," news release, November 28, 2012, https://www.ftc.gov/news-events /press-releases/2012/11/ftc-warns-hotel-operators-price-quotes-exclude-resort -fees-other.

10. Federal Trade Commission Warning Letters.

11. FTC Warning Letters.

12. FTC Warning Letters.

13. FTC Warning Letters.

14. Federal Trade Commission, Hotel Pricing/Resort Fee: Released Documents, "Consumer Complaints (Nov. 29, 2012 to July 6, 2016)," complaint no. 58486719, https://www.ftc.gov/about-ftc/foia/frequently-requested-records/hotel-pricingresort-fee.

15. S. 2599, 114th Congress (2016), https://www.congress.gov/bill/114th-congress/senate-bill/2599/text. Senators Edward J. Markey (D-MA), Barbara Boxer (D-CA), and Elizabeth Warren (D-MA) cosponsored the legislation.

16. Andrew Sheivachman, "The Political Push to Destroy Hidden Hotel Fees Has Begun," March 1, 2016, https://skift.com/2016/03/01/the-political-push-to-destroy-hidden-hotel-fees-has-begun.

17. American Gaming Association, Board of Directors Meeting: Strategic Priorities and Accomplishments (Las Vegas, NV: November, 2016), 14, https://www.americangaming.org/sites/default/files/AGA_Board-Fall-2016-3.pdf.

18. American Gaming Association, Board of Directors Meeting.

19. American Gaming Association, Board of Directors Meeting.

20. American Gaming Association, Board of Directors Meeting.

21. *Oversight of the Federal Trade Commission: Hearing before the Committee on Commerce, Science, and Transportation*, United States Senate, S. Hearing 114–631, 26, https://www.govinfo.gov/content/pkg/CHRG-114shrg25376/pdf/CHRG-114shrg25376.pdf.

22. S. Hearing 114–631.

23. US Federal Trade Commission, Hotel Pricing/Resort Fee: Released Documents, "Consumer Complaints."

24. Aaron Stanley, "Freeman: Expect Congressional Hearings on Sports Betting in 2017," CDC Gaming Reports, May 25, 2017, http://www.cdcgamingreports.com/freeman-expect-congressional-hearings-on-sports-betting-in-2017/.

25. John Brennan, "2016 Was 'Most Monumental Year' Ever for Gaming Industry, Says AGA President," *Bergen Record*, June 1, 2017, https://njersy.co/2sjcsy2.

26. Brennan, "2016 Was 'Most Monumental Year' Ever."

27. Byron Tau and Alexandra Berzon, "Justice Department's Reversal on Online Gambling Tracked Memo from Adelson Lobbyists," *Wall Street Journal*, January 18, 2019, https://www.wsj.com/articles/justice-departments-reversal-on-online-gambling-tracked-memo-from-adelson-lobbyists-11547854137.

28. Todd Prince, "MGM Resorts to Increase Resort Fees on Thursday," *Las Vegas Review-Journal*, February 28, 2018, https://www.reviewjournal.com/post/1321962.

29. "Las Vegas Resort Fees 2017 Guide," Las Vegas Jaunt, January 16, 2017, https://www.lasvegasjaunt.com/las-vegas-resort-fees-2017-guide/.

30. "Las Vegas Resort Fees Go Up Again for 2018," 99.5 QYK, February 6, 2018, https://995qyk.com/2018/02/06/las-vegas-resort-fees-go-2018/.

31. For hotels with cheaper rooms, fees exceed the price of the room. "Oasis and Circus Circus are $20 and $28 respectively, exceeding the price of the room and bringing the total cost with taxes to $44.07 for the downtown hotel and $54.20 for the Strip casino." Prince, "MGM Resorts to Increase Resort Fees on Thursday."

32. Prince, "MGM Resorts to Increase Resort Fees on Thursday."

33. Citizens United v. Federal Election Commission, 558 U.S. 310 (2010).

34. "Longtime Las Vegas casino executive Dan Lee said in a recent interview that Strip consolidation has also enabled companies to push through various fees. MGM, Caesars, Wynn and Las Vegas Sands account for more than 80 percent of rooms on the Strip. 'If the Strip were more diverse, that would never have happened 20 years ago,' Lee said referring to the parking fees. 'If one guy said we are going to charge for parking, somebody else would say "OK, fine, come and park at my place for free. My business will go up." You now have an oligopoly there.'" Prince, "MGM Resorts to Increase Resort Fees on Thursday."

35. "FTC 'Has Gone Dark' on Fighting Hidden Resort Fees, D.C. Attorney General Says," CBS News, December 27, 2017, https://www.cbsnews.com/news/resort-fee-investigation-ftc-allegedly-backing-off-trump-administration/.

36. 155 Cong. Rec. H4003–02, H4004 (daily ed. March 25, 2009) (statement of Rep. Kaptur).

37. David Lazarus, "2017 Marked a Year of Tearing Down Consumer Protections 'Brick by Brick,'" *Los Angeles Times*, December 31, 2017, http://www.latimes.com/business/lazarus/la-fi-lazarus-trump-deregulation-cfpb-20171231-story.html.

38. Brookings Institution, "Tracking Deregulation in the Trump Era," April 22, 2019, http://brook.gs/2xNYcDV.

39. Renae Merle, "Mulvaney Discloses 'Hierarchy' for Meeting Lobbyists, Saying Some Would Be Seen Only If They Paid," *Washington Post*, April 25, 2018, https://wapo.st/2qW8f4n.

40. Merle, "Mulvaney Discloses."

41. Kimberly Amadeo, "What Is the Average American Net Worth?," The Balance, April 22, 2019, https://www.thebalance.com/american-net-worth-by-state-metropolitan-4135839.

42. "United States Net Worth Brackets, Percentiles, and Top One Percent in 2017," Don't Quit Your Day Job, April 21, 2019, https://dqydj.com/net-worth-brackets-wealth-brackets-one-percent/ ($10,374,030.10 for the top 1 percent).

43. Matt Egan, "Record Inequality: The Top 1% Controls 38.6% of America's Wealth," CNN Business, September 27, 2017, http://cnnmon.ie/2fSqXnW.

Chapter 7: The Privatizers: When in Doubt, Privatize!

1. Adrian T. Moore, *Private Prisons: Quality Corrections at a Lower Cost* (Los Angeles, CA: Reason Public Policy Institute, Policy Study No. 240, 1999),

https://reason.org/wp-content/uploads/files/d14ffa18290a9aeb969d1a6c
1a9ff935.pdf.

2. Oliver Hart, Andrei Shleifer, and Robert W. Vishny, "The Proper Scope of
   Government: Theory and an Application to Prisons," *Quarterly Journal of
   Economics* 112, no. 4 (November 1997): 1127–61, https://doi.org/10.1162
   /003355300555448.

3. Invoking the competition ideology, and money savings, in the context of prisons
   has a long—and dishonorable—history. After the Civil War, many prisons in
   the South contracted out their inmates to provide cheap labor to manufacturers,
   mining firms, railroads, and local and state governments. The prisons that did
   this were viewed as "an instrument of Southern industrialization, allowing it to
   push against the 'overgrown monopolies' of the North." Shane Bauer, *American
   Prison: A Reporter's Undercover Journey into the Business of Punishment* (New
   York: Penguin Press, 2018), 82.

4. The Sentencing Project, "Private Prisons in the United States," August 2, 2018,
   https://www.sentencingproject.org/publications/private-prisons-united-states/.

5. CoreCivic Annual Report (Form 10-K), for the period ending December 31,
   2017, 30, http://ir.corecivic.com/static-files/f242d017-6ce3-4bb5-ae33-f68
   88059dc9b.

6. GEO Group, Inc. Annual Report (Form 10-K), for the period ending
   December 31, 2017, 39 ("While a substantial portion of our cost structure is
   generally fixed, most of our revenues are generated under facility management
   contracts which provide for per diem payments based upon daily occupancy.
   Several of these contracts provide fixed-price payments that cover a portion
   or all of our fixed costs. However, many of our contracts have no fixed-
   price payments and simply provide for a per diem payment based on actual
   occupancy."), http://www.snl.com/Interactive/newlookandfeel/4144107/2017
   -GEO-Annual-Report.pdf.

7. Anita Mukherjee, "Impacts of Private Prison Contracting on Inmate Time
   Served and Recidivism," August 20, 2017, https://ssrn.com/abstract=2523238 or
   http://dx.doi.org/10.2139/ssrn.2523238.

8. Bauer, *American Prison*, 68.

9. Christian Henrichson and Ruth Delaney, *The Price of Prisons: What
   Incarceration Costs Taxpayers* (New York: Vera Institute of Justice, 2012), https://
   shnny.org/uploads/Price-of-Prisons.pdf.

10. While the supply of crime can be elastic, and an increase in sentences at the
    margin can deter crime, as one law and economics casebook notes, there is the
    point of diminishing returns:

    Perhaps the most important finding is that people are too short-sighted
    to be deterred by long criminal sentences. If the punishment increases
    from, say, two years in prison to three years, the additional years has
    little [effect] on deterring criminals, especially the young men who
    commit most violent crimes. Lee and McCrary demonstrated this fact

in a remarkable study. The length of the sentence faced by a person who commits a crime increases sharply on the criminal's eighteenth birthday. Consequently, the deterrence hypothesis predicts a sharp decrease in crime when juvenile delinquents turn eighteen. A careful statistical analysis of Florida arrest data shows no discontinuity in the probability of committing a crime at the age of majority. So, the longer punishments when the criminal turns eighteen apparently are not deterring them from committing crime. This fact has a simple, powerful implication for criminal justice policy: Shortening sentences and redirecting expenditures away from prisons and toward police, which would decrease the severity of the punishment and increase its certainty, would deter more crimes at no more expense to taxpayers.

Robert Cooter and Thomas Ulen, *Law and Economics*, 6th ed. (Berkeley, CA: Berkeley Law Books, 2016), 495, http://scholarship.law.berkeley.edu/books/2.

11. CoreCivic, "CoreCivic Reports Third Quarter 2018 Financial Results," November 5, 2018, http://ir.corecivic.com/news-releases/news-release-details /corecivic-reports-third-quarter-2018-financial-results.

12. GEO Group, Inc. Quarterly Report (Form 10-Q), for the quarterly period ending September 30, 2018, 30, http://investors.geogroup.com/Doc/Index ?did=47719964.

13. John Gramlich, "America's Incarceration Rate Is at a Two-Decade Low," Pew Research Center, May 2, 2018, https://pewrsr.ch/2rfSmVL.

14. Morris Hoffman, "A Judge on the Injustice of America's Extreme Prison Sentences," *Wall Street Journal*, February 7, 2019, https://www.wsj.com/articles /a-judge-on-the-injustice-of-americas-extreme-prison-sentences-11549557185.

15. Bauer, *American Prison*, 204.

16. Bauer, *American Prison*, 204.

17. Mukherjee, "Impacts of Private Prison Contracting."

18. Order Approving Settlement, DePriest v. Epps, No. 3:10-cv-00663-CWR-FKB (S.D. Miss. Mar. 26, 2012), https://www.aclu.org/files/assets/order.pdf.

19. Order Approving Settlement, DePriest v. Epps.

20. US Department of Justice, Office of the Inspector General, *Review of the Federal Bureau of Prisons' Monitoring of Contract Prisons* (August 2016), https://oig. justice.gov/reports/2016/e1606.pdf.

21. DOJ, *Review of the Federal Bureau of Prisons' Monitoring*, 15.

22. Justice Policy Institute, *Gaming the System: How the Political Strategies of Private Prison Companies Promote Ineffective Incarceration Policies* (June 2011), http:// www.justicepolicy.org/uploads/justicepolicy/documents/gaming_the_system.pdf.

23. CoreCivic, "Political & Lobbying Activity," accessed April 23, 2019, http:// ir.corecivic.com/corporate-governance/political-lobbying-activity.

24. In 2015, CoreCivic expended approximately $1.48 million in fees and other payments relating to lobbying at the federal, state, and local level. CoreCivic, *Political Activity and Lobbying Report 2015*, http://ir.corecivic.com/static-files

/1b5dc6a7-75ab-4499-b261-30eff23bf08c. In 2016, that amount increased to $1.78 million. CoreCivic, *Political Activity and Lobbying Report 2016,* http:// ir.corecivic.com/static-files/97258613-4822-432c-a985-20a8af253431. In 2017, CoreCivic spent approximately $1.5 million. CoreCivic, *Political Activity and Lobbying Report 2017,* http://ir.corecivic.com/static-files/2fb9e280-b271 -4d3f-a4f7-f0a644364ca4. But this amount excludes the company's "grassroots lobbying" communications ("communications directed to the general public that refer to specific legislation or regulation, reflect a view on such legislation, or regulation or encourage the recipients to take action with respect to such legislation or regulation"). The largest for-profit prison "works with a number of consultant lobbyists to ensure that public officials are made aware of the issues impacting our industry." *Political Activity and Lobbying Report 2017,* 6.

25. Michael Cohen, "How For-Profit Prisons Have Become the Biggest Lobby No One Is Talking About," *Washington Post,* April 28, 2015, http://wapo.st /1HUDy3h.

26. Associated Press, "Pa. Judges Accused of Jailing Kids for Cash," NBC News, February 11, 2009, http://www.nbcnews.com/id/29142654/.

27. Associated Press, "Pa. Judges."

28. US Department of Justice, "Phasing Out Our Use of Private Prisons," August 18, 2016, https://www.justice.gov/archives/opa/blog/phasing-out-our-use-private -prisons.

29. Memorandum by Sally Q. Yates, "Reducing Our Use of Private Prisons," August 18, 2016, https://www.justice.gov/archives/opa/file/886311/download.

30. "Under Mr. Trump, Private Prisons Thrive Again," *New York Times,* February 24, 2017, https://nyti.ms/2lF7TLI.

31. Aviva Shen, "Private Prisons Spend $45 Million on Lobbying, Rake In $5.1 Billion for Immigrant Detention Alone," ThinkProgress, August 3, 2012, https://thinkprogress.org/private-prisons-spend-45-million-on-lobbying-rake-in -5-1-billion-for-immigrant-detention-alone-b9ef073758be/; Fredreka Schouten, "Private Prisons Back Trump and Could See Big Payoffs with New Policies," *USA Today,* February 23, 2017, http://usat.ly/2lzV85h.

32. Matt Stroud, "Private Prisons Get a Boost from Trump," Bloomberg Businessweek, November 18, 2016, https://www.bloomberg.com/news /articles/2016-11-18/private-prisons-get-a-boost-from-trump.

33. "Under Mr. Trump, Private Prisons Thrive Again."

34. Federal Bureau of Prisons, "Memorandum on Use of Private Prisons Rescinded," February 24, 2017, https://www.bop.gov/resources/news/20170224 _doj_memo.jsp.

35. Lauren-Brooke Eisen, "Private Prisons Lock Up Thousands of Americans with Almost No Oversight," *Time,* November 8, 2017, http://ti.me/2zEXvgV.

36. Memorandum by F. Lara, "Increasing Population Levels in Private Contract Facilities," January 24, 2018, https://admin.govexec.com/media/gbc/docs/pdfs _edit/012518privateprisons.pdf.

37. Eric Katz, "Leaked Memo: Trump Admin to Boost Use of Private Prisons While Slashing Federal Staff," Government Executive, January 25, 2018, https://www .govexec.com/management/2018/01/trump-administration-looks-boost-use -private-prisons-while-slashing-federal-staff/145496/.

38. German Lopez, "Senators to Trump Administration: Your Use of Private Prisons Looks Like a Reward to Campaign Donors," Vox, April 3, 2017, https:// www.vox.com/policy-and-politics/2017/4/3/15140576/; Sharita Gruberg, "Trump's Executive Order Rewards Private Prison Campaign Donors," Center for American Progress, June 28, 2018, https://www.americanprogress.org/issues /immigration/news/2018/06/28/452912/.

39. Michael Sainato, "Private Prison Industry Lobbying, Profits Soar under Trump Administration," Observer, October 27, 2017, http://observer.com/2017/10 /geo-group-private-prison-industry-profits-soar-under-trump/; Eli Watkins and Sophie Tatum, "Private Prison Industry Sees Boon under Trump Administration," CNN, August 18, 2017, https://edition.cnn.com/2017/08/18 /politics/private-prison-department-of-justice/index.html.

40. CoreCivic, Inc., Q3 2018 Earnings Conference Call, November 6, 2018, http:// ir.corecivic.com/events/event-details/q3-2018-corecivic-inc-earnings-conference -call.

41. The Sentencing Project, "Fact Sheet: Private Prisons in the United States," August 2018, https://www.sentencingproject.org/wp-content/uploads/2017/08 /Private-Prisons-in-the-United-States.pdf.

42. Victoria Law, "End Forced Labor in Immigrant Detention," New York Times, January 29, 2019, https://nyti.ms/2SfgmrE.

43. Law, "End Forced Labor."

44. Betsy Woodruff, "Is Donald Trump Private Prison Companies' Last Hope?," Daily Beast, September 29, 2016, https://www.thedailybeast.com/is-donald -trump-private-prison-companies-last-hope.

45. Amy Brittain and Drew Harwell, "Private-Prison Giant, Resurgent in Trump Era, Gathers at President's Resort," Washington Post, October 25, 2017, http:// wapo.st/2yQh6t6.

46. Megan Mumford, Diane Whitmore Schanzenbach, and Ryan Nunn, "The Economics of Private Prisons," Brookings Institution, October 20, 2016, http:// brook.gs/2eaWfXi.

47. Mumford et al., "The Economics of Private Prisons."

48. Figures from Timothy Williams and Richard A. Oppel Jr., "Escapes, Riots and Beatings. But States Can't Seem to Ditch Private Prisons," New York Times, April 10, 2018, https://nyti.ms/2HnHpsR.

49. Chris Burn, "Privatisation in the Dock over 'The Biggest Forensic Science Scandal for Decades,'" November 28, 2017, Yorkshire Post (Leeds), https://www .yorkshirepost.co.uk/news/privatisation-in-the-dock-over-the-biggest-forensic -science-scandal-for-decades-1-8882287.

50. Linda Geddes, "Forensic Failure: 'Miscarriages of Justice Will Occur,'" New

Scientist, February 8, 2012, https://www.newscientist.com/article/mg21328514
-600-forensic-failure-miscarriages-of-justice-will-occur/.

51. Paul Rincon, "Forensics 'Safe in Private Hands,'" BBC News, March 2, 2011,
https://www.bbc.co.uk/news/science-environment-12627754; Paul Peachey,
"Privatisation Is a Catastrophe, Warns Godfather of Forensics," *Independent*,
April 2, 2012, https://www.independent.co.uk/news/uk/crime/privatisation-is-a
-catastrophe-warns-godfather-of-forensics-7606789.html; Nick Collins, "Forensic
Science Service Closure 'Will Lead to Miscarriages of Justice,'" *Daily Telegraph*
(London), February 8, 2012, https://www.telegraph.co.uk/news/science/science
-news/9068971/Forensic-Science-Service-closure-will-lead-to-miscarriages-of
-justice.html.

52. One empirical economic study looked at corporate bond and issuer ratings
between the mid-1990s and mid-2000s. Bo Becker and Todd Milbourn, "How
Did Increased Competition Affect Credit Ratings?," *Journal of Financial
Economics* 101, no. 3 (2011): 493, 494–95, https://www.nber.org/papers
/w16404. During this period, Fitch Ratings shook up the S&P/Moody's
duopoly by substantially increasing its share of corporate bond ratings. It
was Moody's and S&P's policy to rate essentially all taxable corporate bonds
publicly issued in the United States. So Moody's and S&P, under their policy,
should have had little incentive to inflate their ratings for corporate bonds:
"Even if an issuer refuses to pay for a rating, the raters publish it anyway as
an unsolicited rating and thereby compromise any potential advantage of
ratings shopping." But even here, as competition intensified, ratings quality
for corporate bonds and issuers deteriorated with more AAA ratings by S&P
and Moody's, and greater inability of the ratings to explain bond yields and
predict defaults.

53. *Financial Crisis Inquiry Report*, 210.

54. Vikas Bajaj, "New York Says Appraiser Inflated Value of Homes," *New York
Times*, November 2, 2007, https://nyti.ms/2IHTAEz; Les Christie, "Taming
Inflated Home Appraisals," CNN Money, January 14, 2009, https://money.
cnn.com/2009/01/14/real_estate/appraisal_reform/index.htm; "Appraisers Say
Pressure on Them to Fudge Values Is Up Sharply," RealtyTimes, February 4,
2007, https://realtytimes.com/headlines/item/7476-20070205_appraisers
(90 percent of 1,200 surveyed real estate appraisers said mortgage brokers, realty
agents, lenders, and individual home sellers pressured them to raise property
valuations, a huge increase over the 2003 survey results, and 75 percent of
appraisers reported "negative ramifications" when they declined requests for
inflated valuations); Julie Haviv, "Home Appraisers Say They Feel Pressured
to Overstate Values," *Wall Street Journal*, February 11, 2004 (citing a 2003
October Research survey of five hundred fee appraisers across the country, with
at least five years of experience in the residential real estate appraisal business, that
55 percent said they have felt pressure to inflate the values of properties, with
25 percent of those respondents saying it happens nearly half the time), https://web

.archive.org/web/20170415153608/http://www.octoberresearch.com/about-news
-releases-details.cfm?ID=4 and https://perma.cc/6BHL-FGAJ (screenshot view).

55. Victor Manuel Bennett et al., "Customer-Driven Misconduct: How
Competition Corrupts Business Practices," *Management Science* 59, no. 8
(2013): 1725, 1726, https://doi.org/10.1287/mnsc.1120.1680.

56. Paul Peachey, "Privatisation of Forensic Services 'Threat to Justice' and Putting
the Work in Police Hands Would Be 'Disastrous,' Warn Experts," *Independent*,
January 21, 2015, https://www.independent.co.uk/news/uk/crime/privatisation
-of-forensic-services-a-threat-to-justice-and-putting-the-work-in-police-hands
-would-be-9991356.html; Geddes, "Forensic Failure."

57. Robert McFarland led an independent review of the FSS for the Home Office.
His comments are quoted in written evidence submitted by LGC Forensics,
"Forensic Science Service," February 14, 2011, https://publications.parliament
.uk/pa/cm201011/cmselect/cmsctech/writev/forensic/m63.htm.

58. Geddes, "Forensic Failure."

59. LGC Forensics, "Forensic Science Service."

60. Hannah Devlin and Vikram Dodd, "Police Review 10,000 Cases in Forensics
Data 'Manipulation' Inquiry," *Guardian* (Manchester), November 21, 2017,
https://www.theguardian.com/uk-news/2017/nov/21/forensics-data
-manipulation-may-have-affected-10000-cases.

61. Steve Thomas, "Dubious Forensic Evidence? That's What Happens When We
Sell Off Public Services," *Guardian* (Manchester), November 27, 2017, https://
www.theguardian.com/public-leaders-network/2017/nov/27/dubious-forensic
-evidence-privatisation-public-services; Lizzie Dearden, "Convictions in
Doubt as More than 10,000 Cases Could Be Affected by Data Manipulation
at Forensics Lab," *Independent*, November 21, 2017, https://www.independent.
co.uk/news/uk/crime/forensic-labs-data-manipulation-criminal-convictions
-doubt-randox-testing-services-investigation-a8066966.html.

62. This includes: "Results from all tests carried out by Trimega between 2010
and 2014 are currently being treated as potentially unreliable although it is
not clear how many tests from Trimega during that period may have been
manipulated. . . . Most drug tests from RTS between 2013 and 2017 are
being treated as potentially unreliable." Nick Hurd, "Toxicology: Written
Statement—HCWS265," November 21, 2017, https://www.parliament.uk
/business/publications/written-questions-answers-statements/written-statement
/Commons/2017-11-21/HCWS265.

63. Fiona Hamilton, "Police Foot the Bill after Collapse of Forensics Firm," *Times*
(UK), January 31, 2018, https://www.thetimes.co.uk/article/police-foot-the-
bill|-after-collapse-of-forensics-firm-key-forensic-services-limited-bg5nbxkxt; J. D.
McGregor, "Police Forced to Waste Millions of Taxpayer's Money Bailing Out
Collapsed Private Forensics Firm," Evolve Politics, February 1, 2018, https://
evolvepolitics.com/police-forced-to-waste-millions-of-taxpayers-money-bailing
-out-collapsed-private-forensics-firm/.

64. Forensic Science Regulator Annual Report for the period November 2017
    –November 2018 (published on March 15, 2019), page 3, https://assets
    .publishing.service.gov.uk/government/uploads/system/uploads/attachment
    _data/file/786137/FSRAnnual_Report_2018_v1.0.pdf.

65. House of Lords Science and Technology Committee, "Forensic Science
    Inquiry," https://www.parliament.uk/business/committees/committees-a-z
    /lords-select/science-and-technology-committee/inquiries/parliament-2017
    /forensic-science; Science and Technology Select Committee, Forensic Science
    and the Criminal Justice System: A Blueprint for Change, 3rd Report of Session
    2017–19, published May 1, 2019, HL Paper 333, https://publications.parliament
    .uk/pa/ld201719/ldselect/ldsctech/333/33302.htm.

66. Tom McTague, "George Osborne on Course to Privatise More Public Assets
    Than Any Chancellor since 1979," Independent, December 26, 2015, https://
    www.independent.co.uk/news/uk/politics/george-osborne-on-course-to-sell-off
    -more-public-assets-than-any-chancellor-for-more-than-30-years-a6786926.html.

67. International Monetary Fund, Fiscal Monitor: Managing Public Wealth (October
    2018), 5, https://www.imf.org/en/Publications/FM/Issues/2018/10/04/fiscal
    -monitor-october-2018.

68. IMF, Fiscal Monitor.

69. Most notable are asymmetric information, uncertainty as to outcome
    of treatment, and the fact that many social services may be viewed as
    "uneconomic" or "unquantifiable."

70. See, for example, "The Mandate: A Mandate from the Government to NHS
    England," https://www.gov.uk/government/publications/nhs-mandate-2017-to-2018.

71. In fact, large sums of money allocated for the NHS have actually been spent
    on private care providers. Katie Forster, "Half of £2Bn NHS Cash Injection
    Spent on Outsourced Private Care Providers Labelled a 'Disgrace,'" Independent,
    March 27, 2017, https://www.independent.co.uk/news/uk/politics/nhs-cash
    -injection-2-billion-spent-outsourcing-private-care-providers-disgrace-healthcare
    -service-a7651531.html.

72. The government reaffirmed its commitment to privatisation and outsourcing.
    Gill Plimmer, "UK's Biggest Health Outsourcer in Groundbreaking NHS
    Deal," Financial Times (London), October 26, 2018, https://www.ft.com
    /content/a698c100-d5df-11e8-ab8e-6be0dcf18713; Gill Plimmer, "Private
    Companies Given More Chances to Win NHS Work," Financial Times
    (London), January 2, 2017, https://www.ft.com/content/2a9315ee-c937-11e6
    -8f29-9445cac8966f; Stephen Adams, "NHS Patients to Be Treated by Virgin
    Care in £500M Deal," Daily Telegraph (London), March 30, 2012, https://www
    .telegraph.co.uk/news/health/news/9176733/NHS-patients-to-be-treated-by-
    Virgin-Care-in-500m-deal.html.

73. Neena Modi, Jonathan Clarke, and Martin McKee, "Health Systems Should Be
    Publicly Funded and Publicly Provided," British Medical Journal 362, no. 8167
    (September 15, 2018): 318–320, https://doi.org/10.1136/bmj.k3580.

74. Margaret Thatcher, "Speech to Conservative Central Council" (Scarborough, UK, March 18, 1989), https://www.margaretthatcher.org/document/107605.

75. Karol Yearwood, "The Privatised Water Industry in the UK. An ATM for Investors," working paper (University of Greenwich, Public Services International Research Unit, September 2018), https://gala.gre.ac.uk/id /eprint/21097/20/21097%20YEARWOOD_The_Privatised_Water_Industry _in_the_UK_2018.pdf. Contrast with official data that indicates an increase in investment post privatisation. See: World Bank, *Water Privatization and Regulation in England and Wales* (Note No. 115, May 1997), http://documents .worldbank.org/curated/en/175641468761418353/Water-privatization-and -regulation-in-England-and-Wales.

76. Rachel Graham, "Water in the UK—Public versus Private," Open Democracy, December 19, 2014, https://www.opendemocracy.net/en/opendemocracyuk /water-in-uk-public-versus-private/.

77. "Reality Check: Has Privatisation Driven Up Water Bills?," BBC News, May 16, 2017, https://www.bbc.co.uk/news/election-2017-39933817.

78. Jonathan Ford and Gill Plimmer, "Pioneering Britain Has a Rethink on Privatisation," *Financial Times* (London), January 22, 2018, https://www .ft.com/content/b7e28a58-f7ba-11e7-88f7-5465a6ce1a00; Toby Helm, "Private Water Payouts Are a Public Scandal, Says Labour," *Guardian* (Manchester), February 10, 2018, https://www.theguardian.com/politics/2018/feb/10/private -water-payouts-public-scandal-labour-john-mcdonnell.

79. Germà Bel, "Retrospectives: The Coining of 'Privatization' and Germany's National Socialist Party," *Journal of Economics Perspectives*, 20, no. 3 (Summer 2006): 191, https://pubs.aeaweb.org/doi/pdf/10.1257/jep.20.3.187.

80. Maxine Yaple Sweezy, *The Structure of the Nazi Economy* (Cambridge, MA: Harvard University Press, 1941), 27.

81. Sweezy, *The Structure of the Nazi Economy,* 28.

82. Sidney Merlin, "Trends in German Economic Control Since 1933," *Quarterly Journal of Economics* 57, no. 2 (February 1943): 169–207, https://doi.org /10.2307/1882751.

83. Bel, "Retrospectives" (quoting Sweezy, *The Structure of the Nazi Economy*).

84. Justice Robert Jackson, "Summation for the Prosecution" (Nuremberg War Crimes Tribunal, July 26, 1946), https://www.famous-trials.com/nuremberg /1933-jacksonsummation.

Chapter 8: The Gamemakers

1. APKPure, "Fun Kid Racing," September 3, 2018, https://apkpure.com/fun-kid -racing/com.TinyLabProductions.FunKidRacing.

2. APKPure, "Fun Kid Racing."

3. "About Tiny Lab," https://www.tinylabkids.com/about (accessed July 28, 2019).

4. Complaint, New Mexico ex rel. Balderas v. Tiny Lab Productions, No.

18-cv-854, 2018 WL 4348044 (D.N.M. Sept. 11, 2018), https://www
.courtlistener.com/docket/7868349/balderas-v-tiny-lab-productions/ ("NM
AG Complaint"); see also "Request to Investigate Google's YouTube Online
Service and Advertising Practices for Violating the Children's Online Privacy
Protection Act," filed with Federal Trade Commission, April 9, 2018, https://
www.commercialfreechildhood.org/sites/default/files/devel-generate/tiw
/youtubecoppa.pdf ("YouTube COPPA Complaint") ("COPPA makes it
unlawful for any operator of a website or online service or a portion thereof that
is directed to children, or that has actual knowledge that it collects information
from children, from collecting, using or disclosing personal information from
a child unless the operator gives parents notice of its data collection practices
and obtains verifiable parental consent before collecting the data"). Alyssa
Newcomb, "Google Hit with FTC Complaint over 'Inappropriate' Kids Apps,"
NBC News, December 19, 2018, https://www.nbcnews.com/tech/tech-news
/google-hit-ftc-complaint-over-inappropriate-kids-apps-n949666; Google Play
Developer Policy Center, "Families," accessed April 30, 2019, https://play
.google.com/about/families/.

5. Tiny Lab, "Tiny Lab Kids," accessed April 30, 2019, https://www.tinylabkids
.com.

6. Scott Goodson, "If You're Not Paying for It, You Become the Product," *Forbes*,
March 5, 2012, https://www.forbes.com/sites/marketshare/2012/03/05/if-youre
-not-paying-for-it-you-become-the-product.

7. NM AG Complaint ¶ 3.

8. Shoshana Zuboff, *The Age of Surveillance Capitalism: The Fight for a Human
Future at the New Frontier of Power* (New York: Public Affairs, 2019), 11.

9. NM AG Complaint.

10. *Unlocking Digital Competition: Report of the Digital Competition Expert Panel*
(London: March 2019), https://assets.publishing.service.gov.uk/government
/uploads/system/uploads/attachment_data/file/785547/unlocking_digital
_competition_furman_review_web.pdf (the "Furman Report").

11. Autorité de la Concurrence, *Opinion no. 18-A-03 of 6 March 2018 on Data
Processing in the Online Advertising Sector*, http://www.autoritedelaconcurrence
.fr/doc/avis18a03_en_.pdf ("Autorité Report").

12. Australian Competition & Consumer Commission (ACCC), *Digital Platforms
Inquiry: Preliminary Report* (December 2018), https://www.accc.gov.au/
focus-areas/inquiries/digital-platforms-inquiry/preliminary-report ("ACCC
Preliminary Report").

13. Bundeskartellamt, "Bundeskartellamt Prohibits Facebook from Combining
User Data from Different Sources," news release, February 7, 2019, https://www
.bundeskartellamt.de/SharedDocs/Meldung/EN/Pressemitteilungen/2019
/07_02_2019_Facebook.html; Bundeskartellamt, "Preliminary Assessment
in Facebook Proceeding: Facebook's Collection and Use of Data from Third-
Party Sources Is Abusive," news release, December 19, 2017, https://www

.bundeskartellamt.de/SharedDocs/Meldung/EN/Pressemitteilungen
/2017/19_12_2017_Facebook.html.

14. James B. Stewart, "Facebook Has 50 Minutes of Your Time Each Day. It Wants More," *New York Times*, May 5, 2016, https://nyti.ms/1TpIVI7.

15. Adam Levy, "People Still Spend an Absurd Amount of Time on Facebook," Motley Fool, February 6, 2018, https://www.fool.com/investing/2018/02/06 /people-still-spend-an-absurd-amount-of-time-on-fac.aspx.

16. Furman Report ¶ 1.53 and Chart 1.D; Autorité Report, 50:

   Google provides a range of over seventy products and services to Internet users, to "get answers" (Google Search, Google Maps, Translate, Chrome), "watch, listen and play" (YouTube, Google Play Musique, Chromecast, Google Play Movies & TV), "stay connected across screens" (Android Phones, Android Wear, Chromebook, Android Auto), "stay in touch" (Gmail, Google Allo, Google Duo, Google+, Google News), "organise your stuff" (Google Photos, Contacts, Google Agenda, Keep), and "work smarter" (Docs, Sheets, Sides, Drive).

17. YouTube Official Blog, "You Know What's Cool? A Billion Hours," February 27, 2017, https://youtube.googleblog.com/2017/02/you-know-whats-cool-billion -hours.html.

18. YouTube Official Blog, "You Know What's Cool?"

19. Alphabet Inc. Annual Report (Form 10-K), for the year ending December 31, 2018, https://abc.xyz/investor/static/pdf/20180204_alphabet_10K.pdf?cache =11336e3, 3.

20. YouTube, "YouTube for Press," accessed April 30, 2019, https://www.youtube .com/yt/about/press/.

21. YouTube COPPA Complaint.

22. Hackernoon, "How Much Time Do People Spend on Their Mobile Phones in 2017?," May 9, 2017, https://hackernoon.com/how-much-time-do-people -spend-on-their-mobile-phones-in-2017-e5f90a0b10a6; see also Xavier Carbonell et al., "Problematic Use of the Internet and Smartphones in University Students: 2006–2017," *International Journal of Environmental Research and Public Health* 15, no. 3 (March 2018): 475, https://doi.org/10.3390/ijerph15030475.

23. The *Diagnostic and Statistical Manual of Mental Disorders* (DSM-5) defines and classifies mental disorders in order to improve diagnoses, treatment, and research. American Psychiatric Association, *Diagnostic and Statistical Manual of Mental Disorders: DSM-5* 5th ed. (Arlington, VA: American Psychiatric Publishing), accessed April 30, 2019, https://www.psychiatry.org/psychiatrists /practice/dsm.

24. Daria J. Kuss and Mark D. Griffiths, "Social Networking Sites and Addiction: Ten Lessons Learned," *International Journal of Environmental Research and Public Health* 14, no. 3 (March 2017): 311; https://doi.org/10.3390/ijerph 14030311.

25. Gustavo Ferreira da Veiga et al., "Emerging Adults and Facebook Use: The

Validation of the Bergen Facebook Addiction Scale (BFAS)," *International Journal of Mental Health and Addiction* 17, no. 2 (November 2018): 279, https://doi.org/10.1007/s11469-018-0018-2; Julia Brailovskaia and Jürgen Margraf, "Facebook Addiction Disorder (FAD) among German Students—a Longitudinal Approach," *PLoS One* 12, no. 12 (December 2017), https://doi.org /10.1371/journal.pone.0189719 (noting how Facebook use is very attractive for narcissists and could make them especially vulnerable to Facebook addiction disorder).

26. Cecilie Schou Andreassen and Stale Pallesen, "Social Network Site Addiction—An Overview," *Current Pharmaceutical Design* 20, no. 25 (2014): 4053–61, https://doi.org/10.2174/13816128113199990616; see also Brailovskaia and Margraf, "Facebook Addiction Disorder" (defining Facebook addiction disorder through six typical characteristics of addiction disorders: "salience (e.g., permanent thinking of Facebook use), tolerance (e.g., requiring increasing time on Facebook to achieve previous positive using effect), mood modification (e.g., mood improvement by Facebook use), relapse (e.g., reverting to earlier use pattern after ineffective attempts to reduce Facebook use), withdrawal symptoms (e.g., becoming nervous without possibility to use Facebook), and conflict (e.g., interpersonal problems caused by intensive Facebook use)".

27. For the impact of smartphones on children, see Jean M. Twenge, *iGen: Why Today's Super-Connected Kids Are Growing Up Less Rebellious, More Tolerant, Less Happy—and Completely Unprepared for Adulthood* (New York: Atria Books, 2017).

28. Eve Smith, "The Techlash against Amazon, Facebook and Google—and What They Can Do," *Economist*, January 20, 2018, https://www.economist.com /briefing/2018/01/20/the-techlash-against-amazon-facebook-and-google-and -what-they-can-do.

29. Haley Sweetland Edwards, "The Masters of Mind Control," *Time*, April 23, 2018, 30–37, https://www.scribd.com/article/376290832/The-Masters-of-Mind-Control.

30. Tristan Harris, "How Technology Hijacks People's Minds—from a Magician and Google's Design Ethicist," May 19, 2016, http://www.tristanharris.com /essays/; Edwards, "The Masters of Mind Control."

31. Edwards, "The Masters of Mind Control."

32. Jonas Abromaitis, interview with Startup Lithuania, October 18, 2016, https:// www.startuplithuania.com/news/tiny-lab-productions-subscription-model -sounds-promising/ (Tiny Lab CEO noting the difficulty to maintain the children's "attention and encourage their loyalty to our games").

33. Google, "Rewarded Ads: A Win for Users, Developers, and Advertisers," accessed April 30, 2019, https://admob.google.com/home/resources/rewarded -ads-win-for-everyone/.

34. ACCC Preliminary Report, 4.

35. Betsy Morris, "The New Tech Avengers," *Wall Street Journal*, June 29, 2018, https://www.wsj.com/articles/the-new-tech-avengers-1530285064; Levi

Sumagaysay, "Former Google, Facebook Employees Step Up Battle against Tech Addiction," *Mercury News* (San Jose), February 5, 2018, http://bayareane .ws/2EIqLTB; Nellie Bowles, "Early Facebook and Google Employees Form Coalition to Fight What They Built," *New York Times*, February 4, 2018, https://nyti.ms/2GJoKHg; Tia Ghose, "What Facebook Addiction Looks Like in the Brain," Live Science, January 27, 2015, https://www.livescience .com/49585-facebook-addiction-viewed-brain.html.

36. NM AG Complaint ¶¶ 150–60 (identifying Google among the software development kit defendants).

37. NM AG Complaint ¶ 153.

38. NM AG Complaint ¶ 151, citing *60 Minutes*, Brain Hacking, April 9, 2017, https://youtu.be/awAMTQZmvPE; Nicholas Kardaras, *Glow Kids: How Screen Addiction Is Hijacking Our Kids—and How to Break the Trance* (New York: St. Martin's Press, 2015), xviii–xix, 22, 32.

39. NM AG Complaint ¶ 152.

40. NM AG Complaint ¶ 232; see also Natasha Singer and Jennifer Valentino-DeVries, "Google's Marketing of Children's Apps Misleads Parents, Consumer Groups Say," *New York Times*, December 19, 2018, https://nyti.ms/2GENEMa. In 2018, security researchers at the University of California, Berkeley, told Google of the privacy-invasive technology and practices in Tiny Lab's gaming apps. Google "ended the dialogue by simply stating that Tiny Lab apps are not directed to children," even though it knew otherwise. NM AG Complaint ¶ 118. But Google did add, "We really appreciate the research that your organization has been looking into, to make the internet a more safe space for everyone."

41. Roger McNamee, "I Mentored Mark Zuckerberg. I Loved Facebook. But I Can't Stay Silent about What's Happening," *Time*, January 17, 2019, https:// time.com/5505441.

42. McNamee, "I Mentored Mark Zuckerberg."

43. McNamee, "I Mentored Mark Zuckerberg" ("Every action a user took gave Facebook a better understanding of that user—and of that user's friends—enabling the company to make tiny 'improvements' in the user experience every day, which is to say it got better at manipulating the attention of users"); Roger McNamee, *Zucked: Waking Up to the Facebook Catastrophe* (New York: Penguin Press, 2019), 9, 62–63, 98–101.

44. McNamee, *Zucked*, 103.

45. Chang Liu and Jianling Ma, "Social Support Through Online Social Networking Sites and Addiction among College Students: The Mediating Roles of Fear of Missing Out and Problematic Smartphone Use," *Current Psychology* (2018), https://doi.org/10.1007/s12144-018-0075-5.

46. Zephoria Digital Marketing, "The Top 20 Valuable Facebook Statistics—Updated April 2019," accessed April 30, 2019, https://zephoria.com/top-15 -valuable-facebook-statistics/.

47. Todd Clarke, "22+ Instagram Stats That Marketers Can't Ignore This Year," Hootsuite Blog, March 5, 2019, https://blog.hootsuite.com/instagram-statistics/.

48. Rani Molla and Kurt Wagner, "People Spend Almost as Much Time on Instagram as They Do on Facebook," Recode, June 25, 2018, https://www.vox.com/2018/6/25/17501224/instagram-facebook-snapchat-time-spent-growth-data (data for Android users).

49. Facebook Inc., Third Quarter 2018 Results Conference Call (October 30, 2018), https://s21.q4cdn.com/399680738/files/doc_financials/2018/Q3/Q318-earnings-call-transcript.pdf.

50. Rayna Sariyska et al., "The Motivation for Facebook Use—Is It a Matter of Bonding or Control over Others?," *Journal of Individual Differences* 40, no. 1 (2019): 26–35, https://doi.org/10.1027/1614-0001/a000273 (finding from its study that European Facebook users are motivated to use Facebook to control others, since power was associated with attitudes and online sociability. "Thus, next to the opportunity to communicate with others and participate in online social activities, Facebook also offers a platform where information is exchanged, which can be used to control or manipulate behavior").

51. Sabine Reich, Frank M. Schneider, and Leonie Heling, "Zero Likes—Symbolic Interactions and Need Satisfaction Online," *Computers in Human Behavior* 80 (March 2018): 97–102, https://doi.org/10.1016/j.chb.2017.10.043.

52. McNamee, *Zucked* 98.

53. Facebook, Inc. Annual Report (Form 10-K), for the year ending December 31, 2017, https://s21.q4cdn.com/399680738/files/doc_financials/annual_reports/FB_AR_2017_FINAL.pdf, 9 (noting how the size of its user base and users' engagement, including the time spent on its products, are critical to its financial success).

54. Deepa Seetharaman, "Facebook Prods Users to Share a Bit More," *Wall Street Journal*, November 2, 2015, https://www.wsj.com/articles/facebook-prods-users-to-share-a-bit-more-1446520723.

55. Jacob Weisberg, "We Are Hopelessly Hooked," *New York Review of Books*, February 25, 2016, https://www.nybooks.com/articles/2016/02/25/we-are-hopelessly-hooked/; McNamee, *Zucked*, 81–110.

56. Seetharaman, "Facebook Prods Users."

57. Seetharaman, "Facebook Prods Users."

58. David Cohen, "Facebook Uses Space atop News Feed to Prompt Users to Discuss Events, Moments; Share Holiday Cards," *Adweek*, December 20, 2016, https://www.adweek.com/digital/atop-news-feed-events-moments-holiday-cards/.

59. NM AG Complaint ¶¶ 155–60.

60. Gaya Dowling, interview by Anderson Cooper, *60 Minutes*, CBS, December 9, 2018, https://www.cbsnews.com/news/groundbreaking-study-examines-effects-of-screen-time-on-kids-60-minutes/.

61. Campaign for a Commercial-Free Childhood, letter to Mark Zuckerberg,

January 30, 2018, http://www.commercialfreechildhood.org/sites/default/files
/devel-generate/gaw/FBMessengerKids.pdf; da Veiga et al., "Emerging Adults
and Facebook Use"; Brailovskaia and Margraf, "Facebook Addiction Disorder"
(finding that Facebook addiction disorder was significantly positively related
to narcissism, depression, anxiety, and stress symptoms); Barbara Caci et al.,
"The Dimensions of Facebook Addiction as Measured by Facebook Addiction
Italian Questionnaire and Their Relationships with Individual Differences,"
Cyberpsychology, Behavior, and Social Networking 20, no. 4 (April 2017): 251
(defining Facebook addiction with (i) interpersonal irritability—negative
influence of Facebook on social relationship quality; (ii) elapsed time—altered
perception of time and time management that is dysfunctional; (iii) social
performance impairment—negative influence of Facebook on work, study
habits, and friendships; and (iv) facebook anxiety—feeling anxious and nervous
when not connected); David Ginsberg and Moira Burke, "Hard Questions: Is
Spending Time on Social Media Bad for Us?," Facebook Newsroom, December 15,
2017, https://newsroom.fb.com/news/2017/12/hard-questions-is-spending-time
-on-social-media-bad-for-us/.

62. Abromaitis interview.

63. Abromaitis interview.

64. "Why do developers choose to monetize their games with mobile ads?" asks
Google in its pitch to gaming app developers. "Users expect free games."
Google, "Mobile Ads: The Key to Monetizing Gaming Apps," accessed
May 1, 2019, https://admob.google.com/home/resources/monetize-mobile
-game-with-ads/.

65. Google, "Google AdMob > Mobile Ads SDK (Android) > Get Started,"
January 17, 2019, https://developers.google.com/admob/android/quick-start
("Integrating the Google Mobile Ads SDK into an app is the first step toward
displaying ads and earning revenue").

66. Abbas Razaghpanah et al., "Apps, Trackers, Privacy, and Regulators: A Global
Study of the Mobile Tracking Ecosystem," paper presented at the 25th Annual
Network and Distributed System Security Symposium, San Diego, CA,
February 2018, http://eprints.networks.imdea.org/1744/1/trackers.pdf; New
Mexico AG Complaint ¶ 34:

> The AdMob SDK is incorporated into over one million apps, facilitating
> two hundred billion ad requests per month, and paying developers over
> $3.5 billion since July 2012. [Google, "AdMob by Google," https://web
> .archive.org/web/20180904214013/https://www.google.com/admob/,
> https://perma.cc/8937-LS99.] The AdMob SDK is "[p]owered by Google's
> ad technology" and enables developers "to segment . . . users, then view
> reports to understand which ones are earning [the developers] the most
> revenue." [Google, "Why AdMob?—Platform Benefits," accessed May 1,
> 2019, https://admob.google.com/home/admob-advantage/.]

See also Autorité Report, 29–31.

67. As Facebook's chief operating officer told the investment community,
    What happens on our platform is often people that will start out doing
    demand generation and use the repeat opportunity to show people
    ads, moving down the funnel to demand fulfillment. If you use our
    targeting tools well, you can actually start out with demand fulfillment.
    So some of these examples I've shared on this call, from Holiday Inn to
    Gymshark, are about people using the targeting tools to find people who
    are interested in the products, and then you can get closer and down the
    funnel to demand fulfillment.
    Facebook Inc., Fourth Quarter and Full Year 2017 Results Conference
    Call (January 31, 2018), https://s21.q4cdn.com/399680738/files/doc
    _financials/2017/Q4/Q4-17-Earnings-call-transcript.pdf; Facebook, "Dynamic
    Ads," accessed May 1, 2019, https://www.facebook.com/business/ads/dynamic
    -ads ("Facebook dynamic ads automatically show the right products to people
    who have expressed interest on your website, in your app or elsewhere on the
    internet"); Autorité Report, 33 (discussing tools developed by Google among
    others, that "allow analysis of the behaviour of users on a given site to various
    degrees. This includes origin, journey, destinations, time spent on a page,
    exposure of the user to the advertising message, the user's interaction with the
    ad, and identification of the pages that facilitate conversions. Conversion is a
    key element in online advertising. A conversion can be defined as the point at
    which an internet user or the recipient of a marketing campaign performs a
    desired action. This action can be a purchase, filling out a form, downloading
    a document or a visit behaviour model. The conversion can also be an action
    performed offline").

68. Michael Reilly, "Is Facebook Targeting Ads at Sad Teens?," *MIT Technology
    Review*, May 1, 2017, https://www.technologyreview.com/s/604307/; McNamee,
    Zucked, 69; Sam Levin, "Facebook Told Advertisers It Can Identify Teens
    Feeling 'Insecure' and 'Worthless,'" *Guardian* (Manchester), May 1, 2017,
    https://www.theguardian.com/technology/2017/may/01/facebook-advertising
    -data-insecure-teens.

69. Sam Machkovech, "Report: Facebook Helped Advertisers Target Teens Who
    Feel 'Worthless,'" Ars Technica, May 1, 2017, https://arstechnica.com/?post
    _type=post&p=1087191; Nick Whigham, "Leaked Document Reveals Facebook
    Conducted Research to Target Emotionally Vulnerable and Insecure Youth,"
    news.com.au, May 1, 2017, http://www.news.com.au/technology/online
    /social/leaked-document-reveals-facebook-conducted-research-to-target
    -emotionally-vulnerable-and-insecure-youth/news-story/d256f850be6b1
    c8a21aec6e32dae16fd.

70. Facebook, "Comments on Research and Ad Targeting," April 30, 2017, https://
    newsroom.fb.com/news/h/comments-on-research-and-ad-targeting/.

71. Sahil Chinoy, "What 7 Creepy Patents Reveal About Facebook," *New York
    Times*, June 21, 2018, https://nyti.ms/2MGqm7T.

72. As an executive of DraftFCB, one of the leaders in thinking about how to incorporate the discipline of behavioral economics with the practice and business of modern advertising and marketing, observed: "You can't understand the success of digital platforms like Amazon, Facebook, Farmville, Nike Plus, and Groupon if you don't understand behavioral economic principles like social proof, the impact of variable intermittent social rewards, feedback loops, and scarcity. Behavioral economics will increasingly be providing the behavioral insight that drives digital strategy." John Kenny, interview with Nudge Blog, "Where Is Behavioral Economics Headed in the World of Marketing?," October 9, 2011, http://nudges.org/2011/10/09/where-is-behavioral-economics -headed-in-the-marketing-worlding/.

73. For elaboration on behavioral discrimination, see Ariel Ezrachi and Maurice E. Stucke, *Virtual Competition: The Promise and Perils of the Algorithm-Driven Economy* (Cambridge, MA: Harvard University Press, 2016).

74. Michal Kosinski, David Stillwell, and Thore Graepel, "Private Traits and Attributes Are Predictable from Digital Records of Human Behavior," *PNAS* 110, no. 15 (April 9, 2013): 5802–5; https://doi.org/10.1073/pnas.1218772110.

75. Damien Geradin and Dimitrios Katsifis, "An EU Competition Law Analysis of Online Display Advertising in the Programmatic Age," *European Competition Journal*, in press 2019, 8–9, https://doi.org/10.1080/17441056.2019.1574440 ("The more (and better) user data advertisers have, the higher they are willing to bid for a user within their target group, leading in principle to higher revenues for the publisher. If, on the other hand, advertisers have limited data about the user, they will take a more cautious approach and bid lower (the bid is 'blind')").

76. Since over 60 percent of people use Google's browser Chrome, Google knows where many people are browsing when not on Google. Autorité Report, 57; ACCC Preliminary Report, 48. George Cox, "Researchers Find Google Collects More Data than Users Think," *The Spectrum*, September 3, 2018, https://www .thespectrum.com/story/news/local/mesquite/2018/09/03/p-c-periodicals -google-collects-more-data-than-users-think/1161460002/; Geoffrey A. Fowler, "Goodbye, Chrome: Google's Web Browser Has Become Spy Software," *Washington Post*, June 21, 2019, https://www.washingtonpost.com/technology /2019/06/21/google-chrome-has-become-surveillance-software-its-time -switch/?utm_term=.25cc4b42cd7b (privacy experiment found Chrome ushered more than 11,000 tracker cookies into the tested browser—in a single week).

77. Autorité Report, 57; ACCC Preliminary Report, 48.

78. ACCC Preliminary Report, 48; Autorité Report, 57: "Google and Facebook also collect massive volumes of data generated on third-party sites that can also be used for advertising campaigns."

79. Autorité Report, 38 (discussing how Google and Facebook can negotiate with ad blocker publishers to receive special treatment and not have their ads blocked [this is the case for Google, which negotiated with Adblock (Eyeo) to be put on a list of authorized ads] and have the technological and human resources to find

ways around ad-blocking technologies [this is the case for Facebook, which has developed techniques for rendering ad blockers ineffective]).

80. Bundeskartellamt, "Bundeskartellamt Prohibits Facebook" (noting how Facebook can collect "an almost unlimited amount of any type of user data from third-party sources, allocate these to the users' Facebook accounts, and use them for numerous data processing processes. Third-party sources are Facebook-owned services such as Instagram or WhatsApp, but also third-party websites that include interfaces such as the Like or Share buttons."); Bundeskartellamt, "Preliminary Assessment in Facebook Proceeding."

81. Bundeskartellamt, "Bundeskartellamt Prohibits Facebook."

82. Autorité Report, 6.

83. Josh Constine, "Facebook Pays Teens to Install VPN That Spies on Them," Tech Crunch, January 29, 2019, https://tcrn.ch/2WolJ4J.

84. Geradin and Katsifis, "An EU Competition Law Analysis of Online Display Advertising" (discussing the *Publisher Ad Servers*, who determine and record how ad inventory is filled each time a user visit the publisher's website; *Advertiser Ad Servers*, who store and deliver the advertisement and help advertisers monitor and optimize their ad campaign by tracking where ads are served and providing detailed reporting on their performance; *Supply Side Platforms,* who once were created to organize demand for ad inventory and help the publisher choose the most profitable ad to display, and have evolved into ad exchanges; *Demand Side Platforms*, who manage the purchasing of ad inventory for advertisers via a single management interface; and *Ad Exchanges*, which are the digital marketplaces for ad inventory where supply and demand meet).

85. While both are more powerful than any other rival, Google is relatively more advanced in designing and controlling this game than Facebook. Google operates the leading Android mobile phone operating system (and controls the app store). Google controls the leading web browser Chrome, which plays a key role in blocking ads, tracking users, and working with the ad network. Net Market Share, "Browser Market Share," accessed May 1, 2019, https://www.netmarketshare.com/browser-market-share.aspx. Google has businesses in all advertising intermediation fields. Autorité Report, 40. It provides several services to advertisers to implement campaigns and deliver ads on its own services and third-party websites and applications, and determine the effectiveness of the campaigns. In addition, Google offers several key services to publishers (including ad network, ad exchange, and ad server). Google also provides several data collection and processing services (including data analytics) and a range of cloud computing tools that can be used conjointly with advertising tools to process extremely large volumes of data. See also Geradin and Katsifis, "An EU Competition Law Analysis of Online Display Advertising," 17–19 (discussing Google's leading position as the ad server for publishers, ad server solutions for advertisers, ad exchange, and demand side platform for advertisers).

86. Alphabet Inc. Annual Report (Form 10-K), for the year ending December 31,

2017, https://abc.xyz/investor/static/pdf/20171231_alphabet_10K.pdf, at 6; Autorité Report, 6 (discussing how Google and, to a lesser degree, Facebook act as intermediaries to sell the advertising inventories of many third-party publishers of websites and mobile applications).

87. See, e.g., ACCC Preliminary Report, 66 ("Google and Facebook are the channels by which most digital advertising is purchased and sold in Australia"); Autorité Report, 9:

> Among the technical intermediaries, many stakeholders do not have proprietary sites where they could sell advertising space directly, and their position appears to be fragile in many ways. They cannot provide advertisers access to inventories that are as extensive as those offered by Google and remain in an uncertain situation regarding their possibilities to collect data on third-party sites and applications, in order to be able to offer personalized advertising.

See also Autorité Report, 4 ("Google can therefore draw on the assets of its general search engine, platforms such as YouTube, and its presence at all levels of the online advertising chain, especially technical intermediation. Facebook, for its part, can take advantage of its capacity to use the data of its subscribers and sell the inventories of its social network and of Instagram, which are particularly sought after"). Google also controls the bidding process for both search advertising and display advertising sectors, which gives it an additional advantage. Autorité Report, 53.

88. Autorité Report, 3, 61, and 23 (real-time bidding is the most widely used programmatic transaction method); ACCC, Summary of Digital Platforms Inquiry Advertiser Forum (Melbourne, May 30, 2018), https://www.accc.gov.au/focus-areas/inquiries/digital-platforms-inquiry/forums-key-meetings, 2 ("Stakeholders noted that the pricing for a significant proportion of advertising on digital platforms (including on Google and Facebook) was determined via an auction system"); Facebook, "Fundamentals Beginner's Guide: Ad Auction," accessed May 1, 2019, https://www.facebook.com/business/help/1630666 63757985.

89. Google Ads, "Display Campaigns: Reach More People in More Places Online," accessed May 1, 2019, https://ads.google.com/intl/en_us/home/campaigns /display-ads/.

90. Google promotes this website as one of its success stories. Google, "Google for Publishers: Success Stories," accessed May 1, 2019, https://www.google.com/ads /publisher/#/success-stories ("Les Kenny built a website to show people how to build things. With AdSense, he turned his woodworking hobby into a full-time job").

91. Autorité Report, 22; Geradin and Katsifis, "An EU Competition Law Analysis of Online Display Advertising," 20–23.

92. See, e.g., "Request to Investigate Google's YouTube Online Service and Advertising Practices" (major advertisers pay Google a premium to guarantee

that their ads will be placed on popular YouTube channels targeted at children).

93. Geradin and Katsifis, "An EU Competition Law Analysis of Online Display Advertising," 8–9.

94. Geradin and Katsifis, "An EU Competition Law Analysis of Online Display Advertising," 9; ACCC Preliminary Report, 1, 5, 85; Furman Report, 1.143–44, 3.190.

95. Autorité Report, 41.

96. Google reports that its traffic acquisition cost (TAC) to its Network Members as a percentage of Google Network Members' properties revenues was 70.8 percent. Alphabet 2018 10-K, 32. TAC represents the amounts paid to Google Network Members primarily for ads displayed on their properties. Alphabet 2018 10-K, 51. But others report the amount that the publishers actually receive is lower. See, e.g., Geradin and Katsifis, "An EU Competition Law Analysis of Online Display Advertising," 4, 34 (noting that intermediaries garner up to 70 percent of advertising revenues); ACCC Preliminary Report, 85.

97. David Pidgeon, "Where Did the Money Go? *Guardian* Buys Its Own Ad Inventory," Mediatel, October 4, 2016, https://mediatel.co.uk/newsline/2016/10/04/where-did-the-money-go-guardian-buys-its-own-ad-inventory; House of Lords Select Committee on Communications, *UK Advertising in a Digital Age*, HL Paper 116 (April 11, 2018), https://publications.parliament.uk/pa/ld201719/ldselect/ldcomuni/116/116.pdf.

98. Autorité Report, 10 ("The market stakeholders are not all benefiting from the global growth in the sector: those that are reaping the most rewards are companies that have access to vast sets of high-quality personal data and have the capacity to process them optimally in terms of technologies, services, and the sale of their inventories. This confirms the fact that holding high volumes of data with high added value, as well as having expertise in the area of technological tools making it possible to use these data and leverage their value, have become decisive competitive advantages"); Furman Report, 1.136, 1.61, 1.143–145; Claire Ballentine, "Google-Facebook Dominance Hurts Ad Tech Firms, Speeding Consolidation," *New York Times*, August 12, 2018, https://nyti.ms/2OX5CKd.

99. Over 86 percent of Google's 2017 revenues and 98 percent of Facebook's 2017 revenues came from advertising. Alphabet 2017 10-K, 6; Facebook 2017 10-K, 9; Autorité Report, 6, 39.

100. Facebook's profits grew from $1.5 billion in 2013 to $15.934 billion in 2017 to $22.112 billion in 2018. Facebook, Inc. Annual Report (Form 10-K), for the fiscal year ending December 31, 2018, https://d18rn0p25nwr6d.cloudfront.net/CIK-0001326801/a109a501-ed16-4962-a3af-9cd16521806a.pdf. Google's profits more than doubled between 2014 and 2018 (from $14.136 billion to $30.736 billion). Alphabet 2018 10-K, 24. Advertising revenue on Google websites and network members' websites have both increased between 2010 and 2018. But ad revenue on Google's own websites increased nearly four times

(from $19.444 billion to $96.336 billion) in comparison to the 127 percent growth in ad revenue on its advertising network (from $8.792 billion to $19.982 billion). This trend favors Google, as it recoups even more revenue from ads on its own platform.

101. Autorité Report, 6; Spencer Soper, "Amazon Increases Ad Market Share at Expense of Google, Facebook," *Bloomberg News*, September 19, 2018, https://www.bloomberg.com/news/articles/2018-09-19/amazon-increases-ad-market-share-at-expense-of-google-facebook.

102. Leonid Bershidsky, "The Digital Ad Market Is Overdue for Antitrust Review," *Bloomberg News*, December 5, 2018, https://www.bloomberg.com/opinion/articles/2018-12-05/amazon-google-facebook-are-ripe-for-a-european-antitrust-review; see also ACCC Preliminary Report, 66 ("Google and Facebook receive the majority of digital advertising revenue in Australia; and have captured more than 80 percent of growth in digital advertising in the past three years").

103. BIA Advisory Services, "Google to Dominate Local Digital Advertising in 2018, according to BIA Advisory Services," news release, May 7, 2018, http://www.biakelsey.com/google-dominate-local-digital-advertising-2018-according-bia-advisory-services/.

104. Tom Wheeler, *The Root of the Matter: Data and Duty* (Harvard Kennedy School: November 2, 2018), 20, https://shorensteincenter.org/wp-content/uploads/2018/11/Root-of-the-Matter-Wheeler.pdf?x78124.

105. See, e.g., ACCC Preliminary Report, 6 ("Both Google and Facebook are important sources of internet traffic (and therefore audience) for news media businesses. Approximately 50 per cent of traffic to Australian news media websites comes from Google or Facebook. The significance of the referral traffic from Google and Facebook to Australian news media businesses has provided these digital platforms with a substantial degree of market power in the market for news media referral services").

106. Elisa Shearer and Jeffrey Gottfried, "News Use Across Social Media Platforms 2017," Pew Research Center, September 7, 2017, http://pewrsr.ch/2xdh8vt; Elisa Shearer and Katerina Eva Matser, "News Use Across Social Media Platforms 2018," Pew Research Center, September 10, 2018, https://pewrsr.ch/2x1umJR.

107. ACCC Preliminary Report, 3.

108. Natasha Tracy, "Types of Addiction: List of Addictions," Healthy Place, April 22, 2019, https://www.healthyplace.com/addictions/addictions-information/types-of-addiction-list-of-addictions.

109. Melissa Kirsch, "Change Your Screen to Grayscale to Combat Phone Addiction," Life Hacker, June 5, 2017, https://lifehacker.com/change-your-screen-to-grayscale-to-combat-phone-addicti-1795821843.

110. Google Safety Center, "Privacy Controls," accessed May 2, 2019, https://safety.google/privacy/privacy-controls/.

111. Facebook, Privacy Basics, accessed May 2, 2019, https://www.facebook.com/about/basics.

112. Wheeler, *The Root of the Matter*, 8.

113. For an early report of the scandal, see Matthew Rosenberg, Nicholas Confessore, and Carole Cadwalladr, "How Trump Consultants Exploited the Facebook Data of Millions," *New York Times*, March 17, 2018, https://nyti .ms/2GB9dK4; Cyrus Farivar and Sean Gallagher, "Facebook: It Wasn't 50M Hit by Cambridge Analytica Breach, but Rather 87M," Ars Technica, April 4, 2018, https://arstechnica.com/?post_type=post&p=1288245.

114. ACCC Preliminary Report, 6.

115. Ryan Nakashima, "Google Tracks Your Movements, Like It or Not," Associated Press, https://apnews.com/828aefab64d4411bac257a07c1af0ecb.

116. Kashmir Hill, "'Do Not Track,' the Privacy Tool Used by Millions of People, Doesn't Do Anything," Gizmodo, October 15, 2018, https://gizmodo. com/do-not-track-the-privacy-tool-used-by-millions-of-peop-1828868324; Bundeskartellamt, "Bundeskartellamt Prohibits Facebook."

117. Hill, "'Do Not Track.'"

118. Privacy International, "How Apps on Android Share Data with Facebook— Report," December 2018, https://privacyinternational.org/report/2647/how -apps-android-share-data-facebook-report.

119. Sam Schechner and Mark Secada, "You Give Apps Sensitive Personal Information. Then They Tell Facebook," *Wall Street Journal*, February 22, 2019, https://www.wsj.com/articles/you-give-apps-sensitive-personal-information -then-they-tell-facebook-11550851636.

120. John M. Newman, "The Myth of Free," *George Washington Law Review* 86, no. 2 (March 2018): 513, 563, https://www.gwlr.org/the-myth-of-free/.

121. Newman, "The Myth of Free," 563.

122. Federal Trade Commission, "FTC Staff Reminds Influencers and Brands to Clearly Disclose Relationship," news release, April 19, 2017, https://www.ftc .gov/news-events/press-releases/2017/04/ftc-staff-reminds-influencers-brands -clearly-disclose.

123. Richard Wong, "Influencer Marketing Is Going Mainstream with Facebook's Upcoming Tool," *Adweek*, June 25, 2018, https://www.adweek.com/digital /influencer-marketing-is-going-mainstream-with-facebooks-upcoming-tool/.

124. Jack Nicas, "They Tried to Boycott Facebook, Apple and Google. They Failed," *New York Times*, April 1, 2018, https://nyti.ms/2GpLrnv.

125. Autorité Report, 54.

126. Facebook, "Reach More People with Facebook Audience Network," accessed May 2, 2019, https://www.facebook.com/audiencenetwork/products/advertisers. Facebook claims on its website that "1 billion+ people see a Facebook Audience Network ad each month." Facebook, "About Audience Network," accessed May 2, 2019, https://www.facebook.com/business/help/788333711222886.

127. Autorité Report, 19 ("Most publishers who sell their inventory (i.e. their ad spaces, corresponding to various spaces on a webpage viewed by internet users: in columns, between paragraphs of text, etc.) through programmatic

technologies use intermediaries, in that their ad space could not be sold through a vertically integrated model due to a lack of audience"), 42.

128. European Commission, Decision AT.39704, *Google Search (Shopping)*, June 27, 2017, http://ec.europa.eu/competition/antitrust/cases/dec_docs/39740/39740 _14996_3.pdf.

129. See, e.g., Bundeskartellamt, *Online Advertising*, February 2018, https://www .bundeskartellamt.de/SharedDocs/Publikation/EN/Schriftenreihe_Digitales _III.pdf, 8 (noting how "[s]ome even claim that the value of advertising is now first and foremost the value of the data and that the big platforms have huge market advantages on account of their combining reach with data depth"); Furman Report, 1.52, 1.73, 1.79, 1.136.

130. ACCC Preliminary Report, 80.

131. House of Commons Digital, Culture, Media and Sport Committee, *Disinformation and 'Fake News,'* Final Report 2019–8, HC 1791 (February 14, 2019), https://publications.parliament.uk/pa/cm201719/cmselect/cmcumeds /1791/1791.pdf, ¶ 116.

132. House of Commons 2019 Report, ¶ 96 ("From the Six4Three case documents, it is clear that spending substantial sums with Facebook, as a condition of maintaining preferential access to personal data, was part and parcel of the company's strategy of platform development as it embraced the mobile advertising world."); Sam Levin, "Facebook Documents Published by UK—the Key Takeaways," *Guardian* (Manchester), December 5, 2018, https://www .theguardian.com/technology/2018/dec/05/facebook-documents-uk-parliament -key-facts.

133. House of Commons 2019 Report, ¶ 106.

134. House of Commons 2019 Report, ¶ 106.

135. Google Ads, "Grow Your Business with Google Ads," accessed May 2, 2019, https://ads.google.com/home/ ("Your digital ads can appear on Google at the very moment someone is looking for products or services like yours").

136. See, e.g., ACCC Preliminary Report, 87 ("Over the past two years, almost half of all complaints received by the ACCC about Google and Facebook from small businesses have been in relation to a lack of transparency in advertising services, including difficulties in disputes."); see also Bundeskartellamt, *Online Advertising*:

> Advertisers often refer to online advertising platforms like those run by Google and Facebook as walled gardens, that is closed platforms or systems on which producers or operators impose user restrictions. It is claimed that walled gardens deny users deeper insights into the platforms. That is why these advertising platforms are less transparent for advertisers, the claim goes, which makes it more difficult to independently measure advertising coverage or impact, for instance. Some claim that data collected during advertising campaigns cannot

be exported from these systems and that it will also be much harder to combat ad fraud. In addition, walled gardens are accused of prioritising their own inventory on their own platforms, although that is hard to make out given that the platforms are closed to third parties.

137. ACCC Preliminary Report, 6.

138. ACCC Preliminary Report, 8.

139. Juniper Research, "Ad Fraud to Cost Advertisers $19 Billion in 2018, Representing 9% of Total Digital Advertising Spend," news release, Business Wire, September 26, 2017, https://www.businesswire.com/news/home /20170926005177/en/Juniper-Research-Ad-Fraud-Cost-Advertisers-19.

140. Paul P. Murphy, Kaya Yurieff, and Gianluca Mezzofiore, "YouTube Ran Ads from Hundreds of Brands on Extremist Channels," CNN, April 20, 2018, https://money.cnn.com/2018/04/19/technology/youtube-ads-extreme-content -investigation/index.html.

141. ACCC Preliminary Report, 2; see also Bundeskartellamt, "Bundeskartellamt Prohibits Facebook from Combining User Data from Different Sources: Background Information on the Bundeskartellamt's Facebook Proceeding," February 7, 2019, https://www.bundeskartellamt.de/SharedDocs/Publikation /EN/Pressemitteilungen/2019/07_02_2019_Facebook_FAQs.pdf?__blob =publicationFile&v=4 (Bundeskartellamt 2019 Background Paper) (noting how "Facebook is becoming more and more indispensable for advertising customers").

142. After the Sherman Act was enacted, the five antitrust lawyers at the Justice Department prosecuted Eugene V. Debs and other socialists, as well as labor unions. Paul E. Hadlick, *Criminal Prosecutions under the Sherman Anti-Trust Act* (Washington, D.C.: Ransdell, 1939), 140 (the first persons to serve jail sentences resulting from Sherman Act violations were Debs and others, growing out of the Pullman strike of 1894). Before the law was amended to immunize trade unions, the United States prosecuted numerous unions and union officials. United States, *Federal Antitrust Laws with Summary of Cases Instituted by the United States, 1890–1951* (Chicago: Commerce Clearing House, 1952), 459–60 (index of cases against unions).

143. Tom Simonite, "If Facebook Can Profit from Your Data, Why Can't You?," *MIT Technology Review*, July 30, 2013, https://www.technologyreview.com/s/517356 /if-facebook-canprofit-from-your-data-why-cant-you/.

144. Eleonora Ocello, Cristina Sjödin, and Anatoly Subočs, "What's Up with Merger Control in the Digital Sector? Lessons from the Facebook/WhatsApp EU Merger Case," *Competition Merger Brief*, February 2015, 2, 6, http://ec.europa .eu/competition/publications/cmb/2015/cmb2015_001_en.pdf.

145. Brave, accessed May 2, 2019, https://brave.com/.

146. United States v. Internet Research Agency, Indictment, Case No. 1:18-cr-00032 -DLF (D.D.C. Feb. 16, 2018), https://www.justice.gov/file/1035477/download, ¶¶ 32, 43.

147. Craig Timberg and Tony Romm, "New Report on Russian Disinformation, Prepared for the Senate, Shows the Operation's Scale and Sweep," *Washington Post*, December 17, 2018, https://www.washingtonpost.com/technology /2018/12/16/new-report-russian-disinformation-prepared-senate-shows -operations-scale-sweep/.

148. See, e.g., Bundeskartellamt 2019 Background Paper.

149. Wheeler, *The Root of the Matter*, 8.

150. Wheeler, *The Root of the Matter*, 8.

151. Romain Dillet, "French Data Protection Watchdog Fines Google $57 Million under the GDPR," Tech Crunch, January 21, 2019, https://tcrn.ch/2R0M8E9.

152. Graeme Burton, "Google Now Pays More in EU Fines Than It Does in Taxes," *The Inquirer*, February 6, 2019, https://www.theinquirer.net/3070503/.

153. Bundeskartellamt 2019 Background Paper.

154. Dissenting Statement of Commissioner Rohit Chopra, In re Facebook, Inc. Commission File No. 1823109, dated, July 24, 2019, https://www.ftc.gov /system/files/documents/public_statements/1536911/chopra_dissenting _statement_on_facebook_7-24-19.pdf.

155. This was the "first experimental evidence for massive-scale emotional contagion via social networks." Adam D. I. Kramer, Jamie E. Guillory, and Jeffrey T. Hancock, "Experimental Evidence of Massive-Scale Emotional Contagion Through Social Networks," *PNAS* 111, no. 24 (June 17, 2014), https://doi.org /10.1073/pnas.1320040111, 8788 (2014).

156. Kramer et al., "Experimental Evidence."

157. Kramer et al., "Experimental Evidence" ("a larger percentage of words in the users' status updates were negative and a smaller percentage were positive").

158. Amazon, "Amazon Customers Made This Holiday Season Record-Breaking with More Items Ordered Worldwide Than Ever Before," news release, December 26, 2018, https://press.aboutamazon.com/news-releases/news -release-details/amazon-customers-made-holiday-season-record-breaking -more-items (noting increase in devices with Alexa); Eli Blumenthal, "Alexa, Google Home and Fitbit Ring In Strong Holidays according to Post-Christmas App Charts," *USA Today*, December 26, 2018, https://www .usatoday.com/story/tech/talkingtech/2018/12/26/alexa-google-home-fitbit -notch-strong-holidays-based-app-charts/2414598002/; Raghuram Gaddam, "Amazon Unveils Plans to Push Forth Its Alexa Services to Cars in CES 2019," Tech Portal, January 9, 2019, https://thetechportal.com/2019/01/09 /amazon-unveils-plans-to-push-forth-its-alexa-services-to-cars-in-ces -2019/.

159. Memorandum of Law in Support of Amazon's Motion to Quash Search Warrant, Arkansas v. Bates, Case No. Cr-2016–370–2 (Circuit Court of Benton County Arkansas filed Feb. 17, 2017), https://regmedia.co.uk/2017/02/23/alexa .pdf, 5.

160. Memorandum of Law in Support of Amazon's Motion to Quash Search Warrant (quoting Riley v. California, 134 S. Ct. 2473, 2489 [2014]), 9.

161. Matt Day, "Amazon Is Working on a Device That Can Read Human Emotions," *Bloomberg*, May 23, 2019, https://www.bloomberg.com/news /articles/2019-05-23/amazon-is-working-on-a-wearable-device-that-reads -human-emotions.

162. Danny Yadron, "Google Assistant Takes on Amazon and Apple to Be the Ultimate Digital Butler," *Guardian* (Manchester), May 18, 2016, https://www.theguardian .com/technology/2016/may/18/google-home-assistant-amazon-echo-apple-siri.

163. Jay Greene, "Microsoft, Other Tech Giants Race to Develop Machine Intelligence," *Wall Street Journal*, June 14, 2016, http://www.wsj.com/articles /tech-giants-race-to-develop-machine-intelligence-1465941959.

164. James Surowiecki, "A Big Tobacco Moment for the Sugar Industry," *New Yorker*, September 15, 2016, https://www.newyorker.com/business/currency/a-big -tobacco-moment-for-the-sugar-industry. The authors thank one of the students from the Georgetown Tech Law and Policy Colloquium for this observation.

165. David Reinsel, John Gantz, and John Rydning, "The Digitization of the World: From Edge to Core," IDC White Paper no. US44413318, November 2018, 13, https://www.seagate.com/files/www-content/our-story/trends/files/idc-seagate -dataage-whitepaper.pdf.

166. Lara O'Reilly, "Walgreens Tests Digital Cooler Doors with Cameras to Target You with Ads," *Wall Street Journal*, January 11, 2019, https://www.wsj.com /articles/walgreens-tests-digital-cooler-doors-with-cameras-to-target-you-with -ads-11547206200.

167. Facebook, "About: Mission," accessed May 2, 2019, https://www.facebook.com /pg/facebook/about/.

168. Google, "About Google," accessed May 2, 2019, https://www.google.com/about/.

169. Tim Cook, "Remarks before the International Conference of Data Protection & Privacy Commissioners" (Brussels, October 24, 2018), https://www.privacy conference2018.org/system/files/2018-10/Tim%20Cook%20speech%20-%20 ICDPPC2018.pdf.

170. Bundeskartellamt, "Bundeskartellamt Prohibits Facebook."

171. Jennifer Valentino-DeVries et al., "How Game Apps That Captivate Kids Have Been Collecting Their Data," *New York Times*, September 12, 2018, https://nyti .ms/2N90yFh.

172. The protection of that privacy law is very narrow: Tiny Lab is liable only if its games were *directed* to children under thirteen years old, or if Tiny Lab had actual knowledge that it was collecting personal information online from children under thirteen years of age. Federal Trade Commission, "Children's Online Privacy Protection Rule ('COPPA')," 16 C.F.R. part 312, https://www .ftc.gov/enforcement/rules/rulemaking-regulatory-reform-proceedings/childrens -online-privacy-protection-rule.

Chapter 9: How Greedy Are We? Redefining the Competition Ideal to Reflect Our Values

1. Charles Duhigg, "Wealthy, Successful, and Miserable," *New York Times Magazine*, February 21, 2019, https://nyti.ms/2NimgU5.
2. Gad Levanon, "Job Satisfaction Keeps Getting Better," Conference Board, September 6, 2017, https://www.conference-board.org/blog/postdetail.cfm ?post=6391; David Z. Morris, "U.S. Job Satisfaction Hits Its Highest Level Since 2005," *Fortune*, September 1, 2017, https://fortune.com/2017/09/01/job -satisfaction-highest-since-2005/.
3. Organisation for Economic Co-operation and Development, "Social and Welfare Issues: Inequality," accessed May 3, 2019, https://www.oecd.org/social /inequality.htm.
4. Carlotta Balestra and Richard Tonkin, "Inequalities in Household Wealth across OECD Countries: Evidence from the OECD Wealth Distribution Database," OECD Statistics Working Papers, January 2018, https://read.oecd -ilibrary.org/economics/inequalities-in-household-wealth-across-oecd-countries _7e1bf673-en#page7.
5. United Nations Human Rights Council, "Report of the Special Rapporteur on Extreme Poverty and Human Rights on His Mission to the United States of America," A/HRC/38/33/Add.1, June–July 2018, https://undocs.org/A/HRC /38/33/ADD.1, 4.
6. Liz Alderman, "Europe's Middle Class Is Shrinking. Spain Bears Much of the Pain," *New York Times*, Feb. 14, 2019, https://nyti.ms/2V3Xkm7:
   Since the recession of the late 2000s, the middle class has shrunk in over two-thirds of the European Union, echoing a similar decline in the United States and reversing two decades of expansion. While middle-class households are more prevalent in Europe than in the United States—around 60 percent, compared with just over 50 percent in America—they face unprecedented levels of vulnerability.
7. Jan De Loecker and Jan Eeckhout, "The Rise of Market Power and the Macroeconomic Implications," NBER Working Paper No. 23687 (2017), 31, http://www.nber.org/papers/w23687.
8. Jan De Loecker and Jan Eeckhout, "Global Market Power," NBER Working Paper No. 24768 (June 2018), http://www.nber.org/papers/w24768. The study, which examines the financial statements of over 70,000 firms in 134 countries, identifies a steady rise in markups (i.e., the ratio of the price to the marginal cost of production): "Globally, since 1980 there has been a steady rise from a markup of around 1.1 to a markup of 1.6 in 2016 . . . steady rise in the first two decades (1980s and 1990s), and the virtually flat evolution in 2000s. In the last few years, there has again been a sharp increase." Likewise, a 2018 IMF working paper provides further context and considers the adverse effects on innovation. The study analyzes data of companies from various sectors in 74 countries,

and considers the link among market concentration, corporate profits, and investment in innovation. Similarly to De Loecker and Eeckhout's 2018 study, the IMF working paper unveils a significant increase of markups between prices and marginal costs of publicly traded firms in developed economies. Federico J. Diez, Daniel Leigh, and Suchanan Tambunlertchai, "Global Market Power and its Macroeconomic Implications," IMF Working Paper No. 18/137 (June 2018), https://www.imf.org/en/Publications/WP/Issues/2018/06/15/Global-Market -Power-and-its-Macroeconomic-Implications-45975.

9. Benjamin Mullin, "WarnerMedia's Greenblatt Preaches Consolidation, Says Rivals 'Are Eating Our Lunch,'" *MarketWatch*, March 6, 2019, https://on.mktw .net/2IXedxl.

10. Joseph E. Stiglitz, *The Price of Inequality: How Today's Divided Society Endangers Our Future* (New York: W.W. Norton, 2012), 155.

11. Josh Mitchell, "The U.S. Makes It Easy for Parents to Get College Loans— Repaying Them Is Another Story," *Wall Street Journal*, April 24, 2017, https:// www.wsj.com/articles/the-u-s-makes-it-easy-for-parents-to-get-college -loansrepaying-them-is-another-story-1493047388.

12. Opportunity Insights, "The Fading American Dream," accessed May 3, 2019, https://opportunityinsights.org.

13. Aimee Picchi, "Millennials Are Much Poorer than Their Parents," CBS News, November 30, 2018, https://www.cbsnews.com/news/millennials-are-much -poorer-than-their-parents-data-show/; Kristen Bialik and Richard Fry, "Millennial Life: How Young Adulthood Today Compares with Prior Generations," Pew Research Center, February 14, 2019, https://pewrsr. ch/2TKzziB ("The median net worth of households headed by Millennials (ages 20 to 35 in 2016) was about $12,500 in 2016, compared with $20,700 for households headed by Boomers the same age in 1983. Median net worth of Gen X households at the same age was about $15,100").

14. Martha Ross and Natalie Holmes, "Meet the Millions of Young Adults Who Are Out of Work," Brookings Institution, April 9, 2019, https://brook.gs /2UveFHI.

15. To illustrate how the digital economy can shift the risk from the powerful tech platforms to the worker, consider Uber and Lyft drivers. When the ride-sharing app enters into a new city, it needs to attract drivers. The first few drivers initially have a lot of power, as Uber and Lyft need to hold onto them (while recruiting even more drivers). They could possibly demand better wages. But as Uber and Lyft keep adding drivers, each driver now becomes slightly more expendable. As their numbers swell from a dozen to a few hundred and then a few thousand, each driver must compete even more fiercely for work, while each driver has even less power to negotiate for better wages and benefits.

16. Brief for the United States and the Federal Trade Commission as Amici Curiae in Support of Appellant and in Favor of Reversal, Chamber of Commerce of

the United States of Am. v. City of Seattle, Case No. 2:17-cv-00370 (9th Cir. Nov. 6, 2017), https://www.ftc.gov/system/files/documents/amicus_briefs /chamber-commerce-united-states-america-rasier-llc-v-city-seattle-et-al /seattle_17-35640_-_ftcdoj_amicus_11317.pdf.

17. Nor can our cities allow the independent drivers to bargain collectively (unless the city, with the help of the legislature, qualifies for a narrow antitrust exception). Chamber of Commerce of the United States of Am. v. City of Seattle, 890 F.3d 769 (9th Cir. 2018) (holding that city ordinance was not entitled to state-action immunity from federal antitrust laws).

18. "Report on the Economic Well-Being of U.S. Households in 2017–May 2018" (Last Update: June 19, 2018), www.federalreserve.gov/publications/2018 -economic-well-being-of-us-households-in-2017-dealing-with-unexpected -expenses.htm.

19. Phillip E. Areeda and Herbert Hovenkamp, *Antitrust Law: An Analysis of Antitrust Principles and Their Application*, 2d ed. (Boston: Little, Brown & Co., 2000).

20. John Vickers, "Concepts of Competition," *Oxford Economic Papers* 47, no. 1 (January 1995): 1, 3, https://doi.org/10.1093/oxfordjournals.oep.a042155.

21. United States v. Kennecott Copper Corp., 231 F. Supp. 95, 103 (S.D.N.Y. 1964) ("There is no one definition of competition. Economists do not agree over the meaning of the term nor do they agree how it can be achieved"); *The Attorney General's National Committee to Study the Antitrust Laws: Report* (Washington D.C.: U.S. G.P.O., 1955), 318 ("The idea of competition itself . . . is not so easy to define"); Michael E. Porter, "Building the Microeconomic Foundations of Prosperity: Findings from the Business Competitive Index 2004," in *Unique Value: Competition Based on Innovation Creating Unique Value for Antitrust, the Economy, Education and Beyond*, ed. Charles D. Weller (Ashland, OH: Innovation Press, 2004), 64 (competitiveness "remains a concept that is not well understood, despite widespread acceptance of its importance"); World Bank, *World Development Report 2002: Building Institutions for Markets* (New York: Oxford University Press, 2002), 140 (finding in its survey of fifty countries' competition laws "that different conceptions of competition exist across countries"); Jay B. Barney, "Types of Competition and the Theory of Strategy: Toward an Integrative Framework," *Academy of Management Review* 11, no. 4 (October 1986): 791, 798, https://doi.org/10.5465/amr.1986.4283938 ("Competition . . . is a concept that can mean different things at different times to different firms"); Michael S. Lewis-Beck, "Maintaining Economic Competition: The Causes and Consequences of Antitrust," *Journal of Politics* 41, no. 1 (February 1979): 169, 171, https://doi.org/10.2307/2129599 (noting "the lack, among economists, of a generally accepted definition of competition"); Paul J. McNulty, "Economic Theory and the Meaning of Competition," *Quarterly Journal of Economics* 82, no. 4 (November 1968): 639, https://doi.org /10.2307/1879604 ("There is probably no concept in all of economics that

is at once more fundamental and pervasive, yet less satisfactorily developed, than the concept of competition"); Donghyun Park, "The Meaning of Competition: A Graphical Exposition," *Journal of Economic Education* 29, no. 4 (1998): 347, 356, DOI:10.1080/00220489809595927 ("[C]ompetition has become one of the most ambiguous concepts in economics"); George J. Stigler, "Perfect Competition, Historically Contemplated," *Journal of Political Economy* 65 (1957): 1, https://doi.org/10.1086/257878 (noting that the concept of competition was long treated with casualness); Neri Salvadori and Rodolfo Signorino, "The Classical Notion of Competition Revisited," *History of Political Economy* 45, no. 1 (Spring 2013): 149, 152, https://doi.org/10.1215/00182702 -1965222 (noting that few would disagree with Vickers's statement).

22. Schachar v. American Academy of Ophthalmology, Inc., 870 F.2d 397, 399 (7th Cir. 1989). General George S. Patton concurred, saying "Battle is the most magnificent competition in which a human being can indulge. It brings out all that is best; it removes all that is base."

23. Sanderson v. Culligan International Co., 415 F.3d 620, 623 (7th Cir. 2005).

24. A.A. Poultry Farms, Inc. v. Rose Acre Farms, Inc., 881 F.2d 1396, 1402 (7th Cir. 1989).

25. Ball Memorial Hospital, Inc. v. Mutual Hospital Insurance, Inc., 784 F.2d 1325, 1338 (7th Cir. 1986).

26. Kumpf v. Steinhaus, 779 F.2d 1323, 1326 (7th Cir. 1985).

27. Justin Fox, *The Myth of the Rational Market: A History of Risk, Reward, and Delusion on Wall Street* (New York: Harper Business, 2009), 192; Andrei Shleifer, *Inefficient Markets: An Introduction to Behavioral Finance* (New York: Oxford University Press, 2000), 2–5.

28. Joseph Ratzinger Benedict XVI, "Church and Economy: Responsibility for the Future of the World Economy," *Communio International Catholic Review* 13, no. 3 (Fall 1986): 199, 200, https://www.communio-icr.com/files/ratzinger13-3.pdf.

29. Robert H. Frank, Thomas Gilovich, and Dennis T. Regan, "Does Studying Economics Inhibit Cooperation?," *Journal of Economic Perspectives* 7, no. 2 (Spring 1993): 159, http://www.aeaweb.org/articles?id=10.1257/jep.7.2.159 (quoting Gordon Tullock, *The Vote Motive* [1976]).

30. Ernst Fehr and Klaus M. Schmidt, "A Theory of Fairness, Competition, and Cooperation," in *Advances in Behavioral Economics*, eds. Colin F. Camerer, George Loewenstein, and Matthew Rabin (New York: Russell Sage Foundation, 2004), 271; see also Richard A. Posner, "The Value of Wealth: A Comment on Dworkin and Kronman," *Journal of Legal Studies* 9, no. 2 (March 1980): 243, 247, https://doi.org/10.1086/467638 ("Partly because there is no common currency in which to compare happiness, sharing, and protection of rights, it is unclear how to make the necessary trade-offs among these things in the design of a social system. Wealth maximization makes the trade-offs automatically"). For criticisms of this theory that wealth maximization does not suffer the same infirmities of measurement as utilitarianism, see Jules L. Coleman, "Efficiency,

Utility and Wealth Maximization," *Hofstra Law Review* 8, no. 3 (Spring 1980): 509, 521, https://scholarlycommons.law.hofstra.edu/hlr/vol8/iss3/3; and Jeanne L. Schroeder, "The Midas Touch: The Lethal Effect of Wealth Maximization," *Wisconsin Law Review* 1999, no. 4 (1999): 687, 754–60.

31. George J. Stigler, "Economics or Ethics?," in *The Tanner Lectures on Human Values*, ed. Sterling M. McMurrin (Salt Lake City, UT: University of Utah Press, 1981), 143, 176; see also Robert H. Bork, *The Antitrust Paradox: A Policy at War with Itself* (New York: Basic Books, 1978), 119 (reasoning profit-maximization assumption is "crucial" to the Chicago School's theories); Richard A. Posner, *Economic Analysis of Law*, 3rd ed. (Boston: Little, Brown 1986), 3 ("The task of economics . . . is to explore the implications of assuming that man is a rational maximizer of his ends in life, his satisfactions—what we shall call his 'self-interest'"); Robert A. Prentice, "Chicago Man, K-T Man, and the Future of Behavioral Law and Economics," *Vanderbilt Law Review* 56, no. 6 (November 2003): 1663, 1665 n.4, https://researchers.dellmed.utexas.edu/en/publications /chicago-man-k-t-man-and-the-future-of-behavioral-law-and-economic.

32. Karl Marx and Friedrich Engels, "Manifesto of the Communist Party," in *Basic Writings on Politics and Philosophy*, ed. Lewis S. Feuer (New York: Doubleday, 1959), 9 (arguing that the bourgeoisie has pitilessly torn asunder the motley feudal ties that bound man to his "natural superiors," and has left no other bond between man and man than naked self-interest, than callous "cash payment").

33. *Theory of Moral Sentiments* at I.I.1 ("How selfish soever man may be supposed, there are evidently some principles in his nature, which interest him in the fortune of others, and render their happiness necessary to him, though he derives nothing from it, except the pleasure of seeing it").

34. Nava Ashraf, Colin F. Camerer, and George Loewenstein, "Adam Smith, Behavioral Economist," *Journal of Economic Perspectives* 19, no. 3 (Summer 2005): 131, 136, http://www.aeaweb.org/articles?id=10.1257/089533005774357897.

35. Ashraf et al., "Adam Smith," 136 (quoting Smith).

36. See Yochai Benkler, "The Unselfish Gene," *Harvard Business Review* 89, no. 7/8 (July–August 2011): 79, https://hbr.org/2011/07/the-unselfish-gene ("In no society examined under controlled conditions have the majority of people consistently behaved selfishly"; "Dozens of field studies have identified cooperative systems, many of which are more stable and effective than incentive-based ones"); Lynn Stout, *Cultivating Conscience: How Good Laws Make Good People* (Princeton, NJ: Princeton University Press, 2011), 91–92 ("Although in some contexts [the assumption that people are selfish actors] may be realistic [e.g., anonymous market transactions], a half-century of experimental gaming research demonstrates that in many other contexts, people simply refuse to behave like the 'rational maximizers' economic theory says they should be").

37. Keith Jensen, Josep Call, and Michael Tomasello, "Chimpanzees Are Rational Maximizers in an Ultimatum Game," *Science* 318, no. 5847 (October 5, 2007): 107, DOI:10.1126/science.1145850.

38. Richard H. Thaler, *The Winner's Curse: Paradoxes and Anomalies of Economic Life* (New York: Free Press, 1992), 21–25; Werner Güth, Rolf Schmittberger, and Bernd Schwarze, "An Experimental Analysis of Ultimatum Bargaining," *Journal of Economic Behavior and Organization* 3, no. 4 (December 1982): 367, 371–74, 375, tables 4–5, https://doi.org/10.1016/0167-2681(82)90011-7; Daniel Kahneman, Jack Knetsch, and Richard Thaler, "Fairness and the Assumptions of Economics," *Journal of Business* 59, no. 4 (November 1986): S285, S291, table 2, Persistent link: https://EconPapers.repec.org/RePEc:ucp:jnlbus:v:59:y:1986 :i:4:p:s285-300.

39. Maurice E. Stucke, "Behavioral Economists at the Gate: Antitrust in the Twenty-First Century," *Loyola University of Chicago Law Journal* 38, no. 3 (Spring 2007): 513, 530 n.79, https://ssrn.com/abstract=981530.

40. Christine Jolls, Cass R. Sunstein, and Richard Thaler, "A Behavioral Approach to Law and Economics," *Stanford Law Review* 50, no. 3 (May 1998): 1471, 1492, https://www.law.harvard.edu/programs/olin_center/papers/pdf/236.pdf. Even when the game is repeated ten times to allow for learning, the results are similar.

41. Joseph Henrich et al., "In Search of *Homo Economicus*: Behavioral Experiments in 15 Small-Scale Societies," *American Economic Review* 91, no. 2 (May 2001): 73, 73–76, https://www.aeaweb.org/articles?id=10.1257/aer.91.2.73.

42. Joseph Henrich et al., "Markets, Religion, Community Size, and the Evolution of Fairness and Punishment," *Science* 327, no. 5972 (March 19, 2010): 1480, 1480–84, https://science.sciencemag.org/content/327/5972/1480.full.

43. Varda Liberman, Steven M. Samuels, and Lee Ross, "The Name of the Game: Predictive Power of Reputations versus Situational Labels in Determining Prisoner's Dilemma Game Moves," *Personality and Social Psychology Bulletin* 30, no. 9 (September 2004): 1175, 1177, https://doi.org/10.1177/0146167204264004 ("When playing the Community Game, 67% of the most likely to cooperate nominees and 75% of the most likely to defect nominees cooperated on the first round. When playing the Wall Street Game, 33% of participants with each nomination status cooperated"). Overall, cooperation was greater in subsequent rounds of the Cooperation Game, contrary to the predictions of people who knew the players very well.

44. Ernst Fehr and Simon Gächter, "Cooperation and Punishment in Public Goods Experiments," *American Economic Review* 90, no. 4 (September 2000): 980–94, http://www.aeaweb.org/articles?id=10.1257/aer.90.4.980.

45. Devesh Rustagi, Stefanie Engel, and Michael Kosfeld, "Conditional Cooperation and Costly Monitoring Explain Success in Forest Commons Management," *Science* 330, no. 6006 (November 12, 2010): 961, http://science .sciencemag.org/content/330/6006/961.full.

46. Garrett Hardin, "The Tragedy of the Commons," *Science* 162, no. 3859 (December 13, 1968): 1243–48, https://science.sciencemag.org/content/162 /3859/1243.full.

47. Forest user groups with a higher percentage of conditional cooperators had more

potential crop trees per hectare. A 10 percent increase in the share of free-riders led to an average drop in the forest management outcome by almost seven potential crop trees per hectare.

48. See Michael E. Porter, *The Competitive Advantage of Nations* (New York: Free Press, 1990), 148–57, 194–95, 662–69; Michael E. Porter, "Competition and Antitrust: A Productivity Approach," in Weller et al., eds., *Unique Value*; Grant Miles, Charles C. Snow, and Mark P. Sharfman, "Industry Variety and Performance," *Strategic Management Journal* 14, no. 3 (March 1993): 163, 164, https://doi.org/10.1002/smj.4250140302 (collecting studies).

49. Everett M. Rogers, *Diffusion of Innovations*, 5th ed. (New York: Free Press, 1993), 15, 146 (discussing how information exchange, trialability, and observability are crucial in the innovation-development process).

50. Rachel Heng, "You Bet Your Life: 'Death Bonds,' the Investments That Want You Dead," *Catapult*, August 2, 2018, https://catapult.co/stories/you-bet-your -life-death-bonds-the-investments-that-want-you-dead.

51. Abigail Hall, "Let People Sell Their Organs," *Forbes*, December 14, 2015, https://www.forbes.com/sites/realspin/2015/12/14/sell-organs/.

52. Michael J. Sandel, *What Money Can't Buy: The Moral Limits of Markets* (New York: Farrar, Straus and Giroux, 2012).

53. Brian W. Kulik, Michael J. O'Fallon, and Manjula S. Salimath, "Do Competitive Environments Lead to the Rise and Spread of Unethical Behavior? Parallels from Enron," *Journal of Business Ethics* 83, no. 4 (December 2008): 703, https://psycnet.apa.org/doi/10.1007/s10551-007-9659-y.

54. Enron Corp., "Enron Named #22 of '100 Best Companies to Work for in America,'" news release, December 17, 2000, http://www.csrwire.com/press _releases/25879.

55. Enron Corp., "Enron Named #22."

56. Kulik et al., "Do Competitive Environments Lead."

57. See, e.g., Kulik et al., "Do Competitive Environments Lead," 712; Konstantina Tzini and Kriti Jain, "Unethical Behavior under Relative Performance Evaluation: Evidence and Remedy," *Human Resource Management* 57, no. 6 (November 2018): 1399–1413, https://doi.org/10.1002/hrm.21913; Anna Steinhage, Dan Cable, and Duncan Wardley, "The Pros and Cons of Competition among Employees," *Harvard Business Review*, March 20, 2017, https://hbr.org/2017/03/the-pros-and-cons-of-competition-among-employees.

58. Tzini and Jain, "Unethical Behavior," 1402–4 (finding that the incidence and magnitude of cheating was significantly higher in the relative performance condition as compared to that in the absolute performance and the control conditions, even though there was no difference in actual performance among the participants across all three conditions).

59. Nico W. Van Yperen, Melvyn R. W. Hamstra, and Marloes van der Klauw, "To Win, or Not to Lose, at Any Cost: The Impact of Achievement Goals on Cheating," *British Journal of Management* 22, supp. (March 2011): S5, S6,

S9-S10, https://doi.org/10.1111/j.1467-8551.2010.00702.x; see also Gavin J. Kilduff et al., "Whatever It Takes to Win: Rivalry Increases Unethical Behavior," *Academy of Management Journal* 59, no. 5 (October 2016): 1508, 1513, http://dx.doi.org/10.5465/amj.2014.0545 (collecting other studies).

60. Niki A. Den Nieuwenboer and Muel Kaptein, "Spiraling Down into Corruption: A Dynamic Analysis of the Social Identity Processes That Cause Corruption in Organizations to Grow," *Journal of Business Ethics* 83, no. 2 (December 2008): 133, 138–39, https://doi.org/10.1007/s10551-007-9617-8 (discussing how "performing well through corruption will automatically increase the threat to identity, starting a self-perpetuating spiral of increasing pressures to commit corruption" and a "cross-level field study among 187 employees from 35 groups in 20 organizations . . . showed that the level of corruption exhibited by an individual was positively related to the level of corruption exhibited by their co-workers").

61. Thorstein Veblen, *The Theory of the Leisure Class* (1899; repr., New York: Penguin Books, 1994), 36. Indeed, Veblen predicted that as communities become larger and have greater turnover as mobility increases, then the utility of conspicuous consumption will increase relative to conspicuous leisure.

62. Veblen, *The Theory of the Leisure Class*, 32 ("[S]ince the struggle is substantially a race for reputability on the basis of an invidious comparison, no approach to a definitive attainment is possible").

63. T. S. Eliot, "Ash-Wednesday," *Collected Poems 1909–1962* (New York: Harcourt Brace Jovanovich, 1991).

64. Zygmunt Bauman, *Does Ethics Have a Chance in a World of Consumers?* (Cambridge, MA: Harvard University Press, 2008), 58.

65. Daniel Kahneman et al., "Would You Be Happier If You Were Richer? A Focusing Illusion," *Science* 312, no. 5782 (June 30, 2006): 1908, 1910, https://doi.org/10.1126/science.1129688; see also Daniel Nettle, *Happiness: The Science Behind Your Smile* (New York: Oxford University Press, 2005), 15, 72–73; Rafael Di Tella and Robert MacCulloch, "Some Uses of Happiness Data in Economics," *Journal of Economic Perspectives* 20, no. 1 (Winter 2006): 25, 26, http://www.aeaweb.org/articles?id=10.1257/089533006776526111; Daniel Kahneman and Alan B. Krueger, "Developments in the Measurement of Subjective Well-Being," *Journal of Economic Perspectives* 20, no. 1 (Winter 2006): 3, 15–16, http://www.aeaweb.org/articles?id=10.1257/089533006776526030 (stating that despite China's real income per capita increasing by a factor of 2.5 between 1994 and 2005, there has been no increase in reported life satisfaction, and an increase in percentage who are dissatisfied); Bruno S. Frey and Alois Stutzer, "What Can Economists Learn from Happiness Research?," *Journal of Economic Literature* 40, no. 2 (June 2002): 402, 413, http://www.aeaweb.org/articles?id=10.1257/002205102320161320 (stating that Japan's income per capita increased sixfold between 1958 and 1991, while average life satisfaction remained unchanged).

66. For a review of the happiness literature, see Maurice E. Stucke, "Should Competition Policy Promote Happiness?," *Fordham Law Review* 81, no. 5 (April 2013): 2575, https://ssrn.com/abstract=2203533.

67. Maggie Gallagher, "Why Are Palo Alto Kids Killing Themselves?," *National Review*, May 22, 2015, https://www.nationalreview.com/2015/05/why-are-palo -alto-kids-killing-themselves-maggie-gallagher/.

68. Robert D. Putnam, *Bowling Alone: The Collapse and Revival of American Community* (New York: Simon & Schuster, 2000), 19–26; Richard Layard, "Now Is the Time for a Less Selfish Capitalism," *Financial Times*, March 11, 2009, https://www.ft.com/content/3f6e2d5c-0e76-11de-b099-0000779fd2ac (noting that a zero-sum mentality is often counterproductive and does not generally produce a happy workplace).

69. Kathleen D. Vohs, Nicole L. Mead, and Miranda R. Goode, "The Psychological Consequences of Money," *Science* 314, no. 5802 (November 17, 2006): 1154, DOI:10.1126/science.1132491.

70. Bauman, *Does Ethics Have a Chance*, 54.

71. James A. Roberts and Aimee Clement, "Materialism and Satisfaction with Over-All Quality of Life and Eight Life Domains," *Social Indicators Research* 82, no. 1 (May 2007): 79, 82, https://doi.org/10.1007/s11205-006-9015-0.

72. Jonathan Gruber and Daniel M. Hungerman, "The Church versus the Mall: What Happens When Religion Faces Increased Secular Competition?," *Quarterly Journal of Economics* 123, no. 2 (May 2008): 831, 844, 848, https:// doi.org/10.1162/qjec.2008.123.2.831.

73. Justin Ewers, "Blue Laws: Easing Up on Sunday Liquor Sales," *U.S. News & World Report*, July 8, 2008, http://www.usnews.com/articles/news/ national /2008/07/08/easing-up-on-sunday-liquor-sales.html.

74. Ewers, "Blue Laws." The article also quotes David Laband, author of *Blue Laws: The History, Economics, and Politics of Sunday-Closing Laws*: "All of these repeal efforts are related to economics now. . . . There's no vestige of a religious component anymore."

75. Putnam, *Bowling Alone*.

76. Robert D. Putnam, *Our Kids: The American Dream in Crisis* (New York: Simon & Schuster, 2015), 223.

77. Putnam, *Our Kids,* 224.

78. Putnam, *Our Kids,* 224.

79. Alan S. Gerber, Jonathan Gruber, and Daniel M. Hungerman, "Does Church Attendance Cause People to Vote? Using Blue Laws' Repeal to Estimate the Effect of Religiosity on Voter Turnout," *British Journal of Political Science* 46, no. 3 (July 2016): 482–83, https://doi.org/10.1017/S0007123414000416.

80. Gerber et al., "Does Church Attendance Cause People to Vote?"

81. Jean-Claude Juncker, State of the Union 2016 (Strasbourg: September 14, 2016), http://ec.europa.eu/priorities/state-union-2016_en, quoted in Directorate-General for Competition (European Commission), *Report on Competition Policy 2016*, 2.

82. See statement made by commissioner Margrethe Vestager stating that she is "convinced that real and fair competition has a vital role to play, in building the trust we need to make the best of our societies." Margrethe Vestager, "The New Age of Corporate Monopolies," New York, September 20, 2017, TED video, 14:54, https://www.ted.com/talks/margrethe_vestager_the_new_age_of _corporate_monopolies; Thomas J. Horton, "The Coming Extinction of Homo Economicus and the Eclipse of the Chicago School of Antitrust: Applying Evolutionary Biology to Structural and Behavioral Antitrust Analyses," *Loyola University of Chicago Law Journal* 42, no. 3 (Spring 2011): 469, 517, https:// ssrn.com/abstract=2494871 ("For our competitive capital system to thrive as an evolutionary economic ecosystem, consumers and businesspersons must be able to trust that suppliers, customers, and competitors will generally behave fairly and morally").

83. R. H. Tawney, *The Acquisitive Society* (1920; repr., Mineola, NY: Dover Publications, 2004), 183.

84. Tawney, *The Acquisitive Society*, 180.

85. Dalai Lama XIV, Thupten Jinpa, and Howard C. Cutler, *The Art of Living: A Guide to Contentment, Joy and Fulfillment* (New York: Gramercy Books, 2005), 24.

Chapter 10: Competition: From Toxic to Noble

1. Online Etymology Dictionary, s.v. "compete," accessed May 10, 2019, www .etymonline.com/word/compete.

2. George Ellis, "On the Origin and Nature of Values," Tanner Lectures on Human Values (Oxford, June 8, 2017), https://podcasts.ox.ac.uk/origin-and -nature-values.

3. Scott D. Hammond, "Caught in the Act: Inside an International Cartel," OECD Competition Committee, Public Prosecutors Program (Paris, October 18, 2005), https://www.justice.gov/atr/speech/caught-act-inside-international -cartel.

4. Craig Clifford and Randolph M. Feezell, *Coaching for Character: Reclaiming the Principles of Sportsmanship* (Champaign IL: Human Kinetics, 1997), 15.

5. Brooksley Born, interview, *Frontline*, PBS, October 20, 2009, https://www.pbs .org/wgbh/pages/frontline/warning/interviews/born.html.

6. *The Financial Crisis Inquiry Report*, 34.

7. Testimony of Alan Greenspan before the Financial Crisis Inquiry Commission, April 7, 2010, https://fcic.law.stanford.edu/hearings/testimony/subprime -lending-and-securitization-and-enterprises, 92–93.

8. *Financial Crisis Inquiry Report*, xviii.

9. Theo Leggett, "Boeing Admits Knowing of 737 Max Problem," BBC News, May 6, 2019, https://www.bbc.co.uk/news/business-48174797.

10. Dominic Gates, interview, "Fatal Flaw," *60 Minutes Australia*, Nine Network, May 5, 2019, https://www.youtube.com/watch?v=QytfYyHmxtc.

11. "Fatal Flaw," *60 Minutes Australia*; Dominic Gates, "Long before First 737 Max Crash, Boeing Knew a Key Sensor Warning Light Wasn't Working, but Told No One," *Seattle Times*, May 5, 2019, https://www.seattletimes.com/business /boeing-aerospace/long-before-first-737-max-crash-boeing-knew-a-key-sensor -warning-light-wasnt-working-but-told-no-one/.

12. "Fatal Flaw," *60 Minutes Australia*.

13. Boeing, "About the Boeing 737 MAX," accessed May 10, 2019, https://www .boeing.com/commercial/737max/index.page; Boeing, "737 MAX: By Design," accessed May 10, 2019, https://www.boeing.com/commercial/737max/by -design/#/max-reliability.

14. Dominic Gates, "Facing Sharp Questions, Boeing CEO Refuses to Admit Flaws in 737 Max Design," *Seattle Times*, April 29, 2019, https://www.seattletimes .com/business/boeing-aerospace/facing-sharp-questions-boeing-ceo-refuses-to -admit-flaws-in-737-max-design/.

15. Laurent Belsie, "'Too Cozy.' Boeing Crashes Raise Doubts over FAA Certification," *Christian Science Monitor*, March 26, 2019, https://www .csmonitor.com/Business/2019/0326/Too-cozy.-Boeing-crashes-raise-doubts -over-FAA-certification.

16. Leslie Josephs, "DOT's Watchdog Says FAA to Improve Air Safety Oversight Procedures by This Summer," CNBC, March 27, 2019, https://www.cnbc.com /2019/03/27/faa-boeings-737-max-to-face-heat-in-congress.html.

17. Government Accountability Office, *Aviation Safety: FAA Efforts Have Improved Safety, but Challenges Remain in Key Areas*, statement of Gerald L. Dillingham before the US Senate Committee on Commerce, Science, and Transportation, April 16, 2013, https://www.gao.gov/assets/660/653801.pdf.

18. GAO, *Aviation Safety*, 3; Susan Webb Yackee and Simon F. Haeder, "Boeing 737 Max: The FAA Wanted a Safe Plane—but Didn't Want to Hurt America's Biggest Exporter Either," The Conversation, March 22, 2019, https://theconversation .com/boeing-737-max-the-faa-wanted-a-safe-plane-but-didnt-want-to-hurt -americas-biggest-exporter-either-113892; Testimony of Daniel K. Elwell before the US Senate Committee on Commerce, Science, and Transportation, March 27, 2019, https://www.faa.gov/news/testimony/news_story.cfm ?newsId=23514 ("As a result of regular meetings between the FAA and Boeing teams, the FAA determined in February 2012 that the project qualified as an amended type certificate project eligible for management by the Boeing ODA").

19. GAO, *Aviation Safety*, 3 n. 7.

20. Title II of the FAA Reauthorization Act of 2018, H.R. 302, 115th Congress, https://www.congress.gov/115/bills/hr302/BILLS-115hr302enr.pdf.

21. FAA Reauthorization Act of 2018 § 211(c).

22. Belsie, "'Too Cozy'"; see also Andy Pasztor, Andrew Tangel, and Alison Sider, "FAA Didn't Treat Suspect 737 MAX Flight-Control System as Critical Safety Risk: Conclusion Is Part of Internal Agency Review of Jetliner Certification

Process," *Wall Street Journal*, May 14, 2019, https://www.wsj.com/articles/faa
-saw-737-max-flight-control-system-as-non-critical-safety-risk-11557831723.

23. 12 U.S.C. § 5531(d) (2012) (defining an abusive act or practice as—"(1)
materially interferes with the ability of a consumer to understand a term or
condition of a consumer financial product or service; or (2) takes unreasonable
advantage of—(A) a lack of understanding on the part of the consumer of the
material risks, costs, or conditions of the product or service; (B) the inability
of the consumer to protect the interests of the consumer in selecting or using
a consumer financial product or service; or (C) the reasonable reliance by the
consumer on a covered person to act in the interests of the consumer").

24. Consumer Financial Protection Bureau, "CFPB Finalizes Rule to Stop Payday
Debt Traps," news release, October 5, 2017, https://www.consumerfinance.gov
/about-us/newsroom/cfpb-finalizes-rule-stop-payday-debt-traps/.

25. Payday, Vehicle Title, and Certain High-Cost Installment Loans, 82 Fed. Reg.
54472 (November 17, 2017), https://www.govinfo.gov/app/details/FR-2017-11
-17/2017-21808.

26. Payday, Vehicle Title, and Certain High-Cost Installment Loans, 84 Fed. Reg.
4252 (proposed February 14, 2019), https://www.federalregister.gov/documents
/2019/02/14/2019-01906/payday-vehicle-title-and-certain-high-cost-installment
-loans.

27. Charles Elmore, "Payday Loan Crackdown on Ice under Trump Pick Who Got
Donations," *Palm Beach Post*, January 17, 2018, https://www.palmbeachpost
.com/business/payday-loan-crackdown-ice-under-trump-pick-who-got
-donations/4cxbrwOnM3YtvLg8Oo4YbJ/.

28. 15 U.S.C. § 45(n) (2012) (defining unfair acts or practices as those that cause
or are "likely to cause substantial injury to consumers which is not reasonably
avoidable by consumers themselves and not outweighed by countervailing
benefits to consumers or to competition").

29. "Top 10 Reasons People Go Bankrupt," Huffington Post, May 24, 2015,
https://www.huffingtonpost.com/simple-thrifty-living/top-10-reasons-people
-go-_b_6887642.html.

30. Will Dobbie, Paul Goldsmith-Pinkham, and Crystal S. Yang, "Consumer
Bankruptcy and Financial Health," NBER Working Paper no. 21032, March
2015, https://www.nber.org/papers/w21032, 2 n. 3.

31. "Top 5 Reasons Why People Go Bankrupt," Investopedia, accessed May 10,
2019, https://www.investopedia.com/slide-show/top-5-reasons-why-people-go
-bankrupt/.

32. Clark Howard, "22 Retailers on Bankruptcy Watch for 2018 and 2019,"
August 6, 2018, https://clark.com/shopping-retail/retailers-on-bankruptcy
-watch-for-2018/.

33. President Franklin D. Roosevelt, Annual Message to Congress: The Four
Freedoms (January 6, 1941), https://voicesofdemocracy.umd.edu/fdr-the-four
-freedoms-speech-text/.

34. Universal Declaration of Human Rights, December 10, 1948, https://www
.un.org/en/universal-declaration-human-rights/.

35. Universal Declaration of Human Rights, article 25.1.

36. "Can Social Insurance Unlock Entrepreneurial Opportunities?," Kauffman
Foundation, July 8, 2016, https://www.kauffman.org/what-we-do/resources
/entrepreneurship-policy-digest/can-social-insurance-unlock-entrepreneurial
-opportunities.

37. Mark Muro and Clara Henderson, "Gouging the Safety Net Is Especially
Untimely Now," Brookings Institution, December 20, 2017, http://brook.gs
/2oPuCKo.

38. Paul Willgoss, technical director, Marks & Spencer, in discussion with the
authors, July 2018. For more information on the company's approach to
product standards, see Marks & Spencer, Product Standards, https://corporate
.marksandspencer.com/sustainability/food-and-household/product-standards
(accessed May 10, 2019).

39. *Financial Crisis Inquiry Report*, xxiii.

40. Greg Smith, "Why I Am Leaving Goldman Sachs," *New York Times*, March 14,
2012, https://nyti.ms/2jADL55.

41. Daniel J. Morrissey, "Reforming Wall Street's Biggest Gravy Train: Making
Mutual Funds Fiduciaries for Retirement Savers," *Securities Regulation Law
Journal* 47, no. 1 (Spring 2019): article 1.

42. Emily Flitter, Kate Kelly, and David Enrich, "A Top Goldman Banker Raised
Ethics Concerns. Then He Was Gone," *New York Times*, September 11, 2018,
https://nyti.ms/2N1pnmm.

43. Thomas H. Davenport, "The Anti-Goldman Culture," *Harvard Business Review*,
March 15, 2012, https://hbr.org/2012/03/the-anti-goldman-culture.

44. Liz Hoffman, "How Banks Lost the Battle for Power on Wall Street," *Wall
Street Journal*, September 7, 2018, https://www.wsj.com/articles/how-banks
-lost-the-battle-for-power-on-wall-street-1536312634; Vanguard in the first
seven months of 2017 attracted over $177.3 billion in investments, which was
about as much as its ten closest competitors—combined. And the biggest losers
were Goldman Sachs and the other scandal-ridden banks that lost their social
purpose, like JPMorgan Chase & Co. and Wells Fargo & Co. Ryan Vlastelica,
"Investors Flock to Vanguard Funds, Dump Goldman, Wells Fargo, and
Others," MarketWatch, July 12, 2017, https://on.mktw.net/2OomPvp.

45. One important foundation of this literature is the shared value initiative, led
by Harvard Business Professor Michael Porter. https://www.sharedvalue.org
/partners/thought-leaders/michael-e-porter.

46. Harvard Business Review Analytic Services, *The Business Case for Purpose*
(2015), 1, https://hbr.org/resources/pdfs/comm/ey/19392HBRReportEY.pdf.
The organizational purpose was defined as "an aspirational reason for being
which inspires and provides a call to action for an organization and its partners
and stakeholders and provides benefit to local and global society."

47. Deloitte, *Culture of Purpose: Building Business Confidence; Driving Growth* (2014), https://www2.deloitte.com/content/dam/Deloitte/us/Documents/about -deloitte/us-leadership-2014-core-beliefs-culture-survey-040414.pdf. Eighty-two percent of the respondents who work for an organization with a strong sense of purpose were confident that their company would grow in 2014.

In contrast, many respondents in companies without a strong sense were far less optimistic about their organization's long-term prospects in five to ten years. They were far less confident (a 42 percent differential) over their organization's ability to maintain (or strengthen) its brand reputation and loyalty; far less confident (a 41 percent differential) about their organization being able to stay ahead of industry disruption; and far less confident (a 32 percent differential) that their organization could remain or become an industry leader and outperform the competition. The Deloitte survey also found that people working at organizations with a strong sense of purpose were more upbeat about the value their companies offered both customers and employees than those at organizations without a strong sense of purpose. They were much more likely to agree to the following statements:

Our clients trust that we will deliver the highest quality products/services (89 percent vs. 66 percent);

Our clients have long lasting relationships with us (92 percent vs. 69 percent);

Our organization has been in good standing with regulators in the past year (86 percent vs. 68 percent);

Our communities believe that we are good and helpful corporate citizens (85 percent vs. 50 percent);

Our employees trust in our culture and beliefs (78 percent vs. 32 percent);

Our stakeholders trust our organization's leadership (81 percent vs. 54 percent);

Our employees are fully engaged with the organization (73 percent vs. 23 percent); and

Our investors are confident in our growth prospects over the next year and beyond (74 percent vs. 52 percent).

48. Jeremy Bauer-Wolf, "Purpose as Well as Paycheck," Inside Higher Ed, April 11, 2019, https://www.insidehighered.com/news/2019/04/11/gallup-bates-report -shows-graduates-want-sense-purpose-careers. About 59 percent of graduates who reported purpose in their jobs said they had a high sense of well-being. Only 6 percent of students who had a low purpose at work said they had great well-being.

49. Bates College, "Purposeful Work: Aligning Who You Are with What You Do," https://www.bates.edu/purposeful-work/.

50. Milton Friedman, "The Social Responsibility of Business Is to Increase Its Profits," *New York Times Magazine*, September 13, 1970, https://nyti.ms

/2J9d0xS (the incentives are to use the company "resources and engage in activities designed to increase its profits so long as it stays within the rules of the game").

51. Stanley Milgram, "Behavioral Study of Obedience," *Journal of Abnormal & Social Psychology* 67, no. 4 (October 1963): 371–378, http://dx.doi.org/10.1037 /h0040525.

52. Philip Zimbardo, *The Lucifer Effect: Understanding How Good People Turn Evil* (New York: Random House, 2008), 273–75.

53. Zimbardo, *The Lucifer Effect*, 273.

54. Zimbardo, *The Lucifer Effect*, 274.

55. Simon Baron-Cohen, *The Science of Evil: On Empathy and the Origins of Cruelty* (New York: Basic Books, 2011), 183 (discussing how empathy is one of the most valuable resources in the world, in effectively anticipating and resolving interpersonal problems).

56. Zimbardo, *The Lucifer Effect*, 274.

57. Sergey Brin and Lawrence Page, "The Anatomy of a Large-Scale Hypertextual Web Search Engine," paper presented at the Seventh International World-Wide Web Conference (Brisbane Australia, April 14–18, 1998), http://ilpubs.stanford .edu:8090/361/.

58. Zimbardo, *The Lucifer Effect*, 274.

59. Zimbardo, *The Lucifer Effect*, 274.

60. Zimbardo, *The Lucifer Effect*, 274.

61. Stanley Milgram, "The Perils of Obedience," *Harper's Magazine*, December 1973, 77, https://harpers.org/archive/1973/12/the-perils-of-obedience/.

62. "South Dakota Payday Lending Initiative, Initiated Measure 21 (2016)," Ballotpedia, accessed May 10, 2019, https://ballotpedia.org/South_Dakota _Payday_Lending_Initiative,_Initiated_Measure_21_(2016); Nicholas Confessore, "Mick Mulvaney's Master Class in Destroying a Bureaucracy from Within," *New York Times Magazine*, April 16, 2019, https://www.nytimes.com /2019/04/16/magazine/consumer-financial-protection-bureau-trump.html.

63. Heather Long, "19 States Are Raising Their Minimum Wage Jan. 1. Progressives Plan Even More for 2020," *Washington Post*, December 31, 2018, https://wapo .st/2EWg5CS.

64. Amy Goldstein, "Three Deep Red States Vote to Expand Medicaid," *Washington Post*, November 7, 2018, https://wapo.st/2qwzwd8.

65. Californians for Consumer Privacy, "About Us," accessed May 13, 2019, https:// www.caprivacy.org/about-us.

66. Lee Fang, "Google and Facebook Are Quietly Fighting California's Privacy Rights Initiative, Emails Reveal," *Intercept*, June 26, 2018, https://interc.pt /2KljM8h.

67. Denis W. Stearns, "A Continuing Plague: Faceless Transactions and the Coincident Rise of Food Adulteration and Legal Regulation of Quality,"

Wisconsin Law Review 2014, no. 2 (March–April 2014): 421, 433–34, https://
digitalcommons.law.seattleu.edu/cgi/viewcontent.cgi?article=1497
&context=faculty.

68. Denise Tieman et al., "A Chemical Genetic Roadmap to Improved Tomato
Flavor," *Science* 355, no. 6323 (January 2017): 391–94, https://dx.doi.org/10.1126
/science.aal1556.

69. Kenneth Chang, "A Genetic Fix to Put the Taste Back in Tomatoes," *New York
Times*, January 27, 2017, https://nyti.ms/2jFOZCu.

70. Hayden Stewart, "Shopping at Farmers' Markets and Roadside Stands Increases
Fruit and Vegetable Demand," US Department of Agriculture Economic
Research Service, March 5, 2018, https://www.ers.usda.gov/amber-waves/2018
/march/shopping-at-farmers-markets-and-roadside-stands-increases-fruit-and
-vegetable-demand/ (from 2,746 farmers markets in 1998 to 8,687 in 2017).

71. Forager, accessed May 13, 2019, https://goforager.com/.

72. Hayden Stewart and Diansheng Dong, "The Relationship between Patronizing
Direct-to-Consumer Outlets and a Household's Demand for Fruits and
Vegetables," US Department of Agriculture Economic Research Report
no. 242 (January 2018): 4, https://www.ers.usda.gov/publications/pub
-details/?pubid=86877.

73. Stewart and Dong, "The Relationship between Patronizing Direct-to-Consumer
Outlets," 5 (observing that surveyed households sometimes paid more money
for fruits and vegetables when shopping at farmer markets and sometimes they
paid less, and that this finding is consistent with a number of studies that find
farmers market prices can be higher or lower than prices at the supermarket
stores).

74. Michael E. Porter, "The Five Competitive Forces That Shape Strategy," *Harvard
Business Review* 86, no. 1 (January 2008): 78–93, https://hbr.org/2008/01/the
-five-competitive-forces-that-shape-strategy.

75. Stephen Martinez et al., "Local Food Systems: Concepts, Impacts, and Issues,"
US Department of Agriculture Economic Research Report no. 97 (May 2010):
43, https://www.ers.usda.gov/publications/pub-details/?pubid=46395.

76. American Independent Business Alliance, "The Multiplier Effect of Local
Independent Businesses," accessed May 13, 2019, https://www.amiba.net
/resources/multiplier-effect/.

77. In Oklahoma and Iowa, for example, the multiplier effects were 1.41 and 1.45,
respectively, which means adding two full-time jobs at a local farmers market
creates nearly one additional job elsewhere in the local economy. Daniel Otto
and Theresa Varner, "Consumers, Vendors, and the Economic Importance of
Iowa Farmers' Markets: An Economic Impact Survey Analysis," Leopold
Center Papers no. 145 (Iowa State University, Ames, IA, 2005), https://lib.dr
.iastate.edu/cgi/viewcontent.cgi?article=1146&context=leopold_pubspapers;
Shida Rastegari Henneberry, Brian Whitacre, and Haerani N. Agustini, "An

Evaluation of the Economic Impacts of Oklahoma Farmers' Markets," *Journal of Food Distribution Research* 40, no. 3 (November 2009): 64–78, https://ideas .repec.org/a/ags/jlofdr/99760.html. While we could not find the multiplier for supermarkets, the retail trade as an overall category generates fewer additional jobs (with a multiplier of 0.8). Content First, "Employment Multipliers," accessed May 13, 2019, http://www.contentfirst.com/multiplier.shtml.

78. Amy Trauger et al., "'Our Market Is Our Community': Women Farmers and Civic Agriculture in Pennsylvania, USA," *Agriculture and Human Values*, 27, no. 1 (March 2010): 43–55, https://doi.org/10.1007/s10460-008-9190-5; Lisa Elaine Held, "How Female Farmers Are Changing the Field," Food Tank, November 2018, https://foodtank.com/news/2018/11/a-womans-place-voices -from-the-field/ (noting that when the National Young Farmers Coalition surveyed more than 3,500 farmers under 40 in 2017, 60 percent of the farmer respondents were women, and in 2012, the US Department of Agriculture Census of Agriculture found that 14 percent of principal farm operators were women, a nearly 300 percent increase since 1978, when it began counting women as farmers). Maine, for example, has seen over 1,000 new farms start since 2008, the majority of which are by farmers younger than 35 and 35 percent of which were started by women. Forager, https://goforager.com/.

79. Trauger et al., "'Our Market Is Our Community,'" 48.

80. Trauger et al., "'Our Market Is Our Community,'" 49.

81. Speech by Lord Andrew Tyrie,"Is Competition Enough? Competition for Consumers, on Behalf of Consumers," before the Social Market Foundation about protecting and promoting the consumer interest in the modern economy (published May 8 2019), https://www.gov.uk/government/speeches/is -competition-enough-competition-for-consumers-on-behalf-of-consumers.

Index

About the Authors

MAURICE E. STUCKE has twenty-five years of experience handling competition issues in private practice, as a prosecutor at the US Department of Justice and as a law professor at the University of Tennessee. He lives in Knoxville, Tennessee, with his wife, Elizabeth, and their four children, Amelia, Thomas, Clara, and Walt.

ARIEL EZRACHI is the Slaughter and May Professor of Competition Law at the University of Oxford, a fellow of Pembroke College, and the director of the Oxford Centre for Competition Law and Policy. He lives in Oxford, England, with his wife, Miriam, and their children, Jonathan and Guy.

Their research, including their book—*Virtual Competition: The Promise and Perils of the Algorithm-Driven Economy* (Harvard University Press, 2016)—has been featured in numerous media outlets, including the *Atlantic*, the BBC, Bloomberg, CNBC, *CNNMoney*, the *Economist*, *Financial Times*, *Forbes*, *Fortune*, Fox News, the *Guardian*, *Harvard Business Review*, *Hong Kong Radio*, *MIT Technology Review*, *New Scientist*, the *New York Times*, the *New Yorker*, *Politico*, *Science*, *Times Higher Education*, *USA Today*, the *Wall Street Journal*, and *Wired*.